DAREDEVIL
VISIONARIES: FRANK MILLER
VOLUME 1

FRANK MILLER
cover art

STEVE BUCCELLATO
cover color

MARIE JAVINS with
COLORGRAPHIX/
VELAZQUEZ/
GIARRUSO/HERRERA
interior color seps

JG ROSHELL
of COMICRAFT
design

JOE QUESADA
editor in chief

DAREDEVIL® VISIONARIES: FRANK MILLER VOL. 1. Contains material originally published in magazine form as DAREDEVIL (Vol. 1) #158-167. Second Printing, March 2002. ISBN 0-7851-0757-6. Published by MARVEL COMICS, a division of MARVEL ENTERTAINMENT GROUP, INC. OFFICE OF PUBLICATION: 10 EAST 40th STREET, NEW YORK, NY 10016. Copyrig © 1979, 1980, 2000 and 2002 Marvel Characters, Inc. All rights reserved. Price $17.95 in the U.S. and $28.75 in Canada (GST #R127032852). No similarity between any of the name characters, persons, and/or institutions in this publication with those of any living or dead person or institutions is intended, and any such similarity which may exist is purely coincid tal. This publication may not be sold except by authorized dealers and is sold subject to the conditions that it shall not be sold or distributed with any part of its cover or markings remov nor in a mutilated condition. DAREDEVIL (including all prominent characters featured in this publication and the distinctive likenesses thereof) is a trademark of MARVEL CHARACTE INC. Printed in Canada. PETER CUNEO, Chief Executive Officer; AVI ARAD, Chief Creative Officer; GUI KARYO, Chief Information Officer; STAN LEE, Chairman Emeritus.

10 9 8 7 6 5 4 3 2

DAREDEVIL

INTRODUCTION: FRANK MILLER

It was a jolly time to be working at Marvel Comics. You couldn't walk through the Bullpen without running into other artists and joining them in a round or three of show-and-tell, pouring over bristol boards to see the latest inks by Joe Rubenstein or Bob Wiacek or Terry Austin, the newest pencils by Herb Trimpe or John Buscema or John Byrne. Just to name a few. It was quite possible to wander into an editor's office and find yourself kibitzing with the writer over the next plot course for Dr. Strange.

There was electricity in the air. Jim Shooter, at the top of his form, had (not gently) used his new authority as editor in chief to increase the sense of competition among talent and bring renewed focus to the sprawling pantheon of Marvel super heroes.

I'd been banging around the offices for months, snapping up the occasional fill-in job, eagerly devouring the advice of Al Milgrom, John Romita Sr., Marie Severin... veteran talents, all generous with their advice to the struggling newcomer from Vermont.

My guardian angel was writer and staffer Jo Duffy. Ever patient, she guided me past many a rocky professional shoal. When Gene Colan decided to end his historic run on DAREDEVIL, it was Jo I sought out.

I wanted the job. Boy, did I want that job. I'd always been intrigued by the notion of a hero whose defining attribute is a disability - a blind protagonist in a purely visual medium - and, most importantly, DAREDEVIL offered up a chance to draw the kind of spooky crime comics I'd always wanted to do.

Jo didn't laugh at my feigned confidence. Sure, I recall her raising a startled eyebrow, but she didn't laugh. She put my name in to Jim Shooter, who agreed to take the chance, and, of course, proceeded to kibitz ferociously.

Things got better yet. Klaus Janson agreed to stay on the book as inker. Klaus had to sand down many a rough edge, and rescue many a panel outright. Across time, we developed a creative rapport that bordered on the psychic. Roger MacKenzie and I babbled our way through countless afternoons, figuring out what new way we'd push things to the edge of what the Comics Code would allow, as well as what editorial could tolerate, and conspiring to steal away as many SPIDER-MAN villains as we could.

Nobody – from Klaus to Roger to wizard colorist Glynis Oliver to editors Milgrom and Duffy to Shooter – held back their best.

We had a blast.

FM

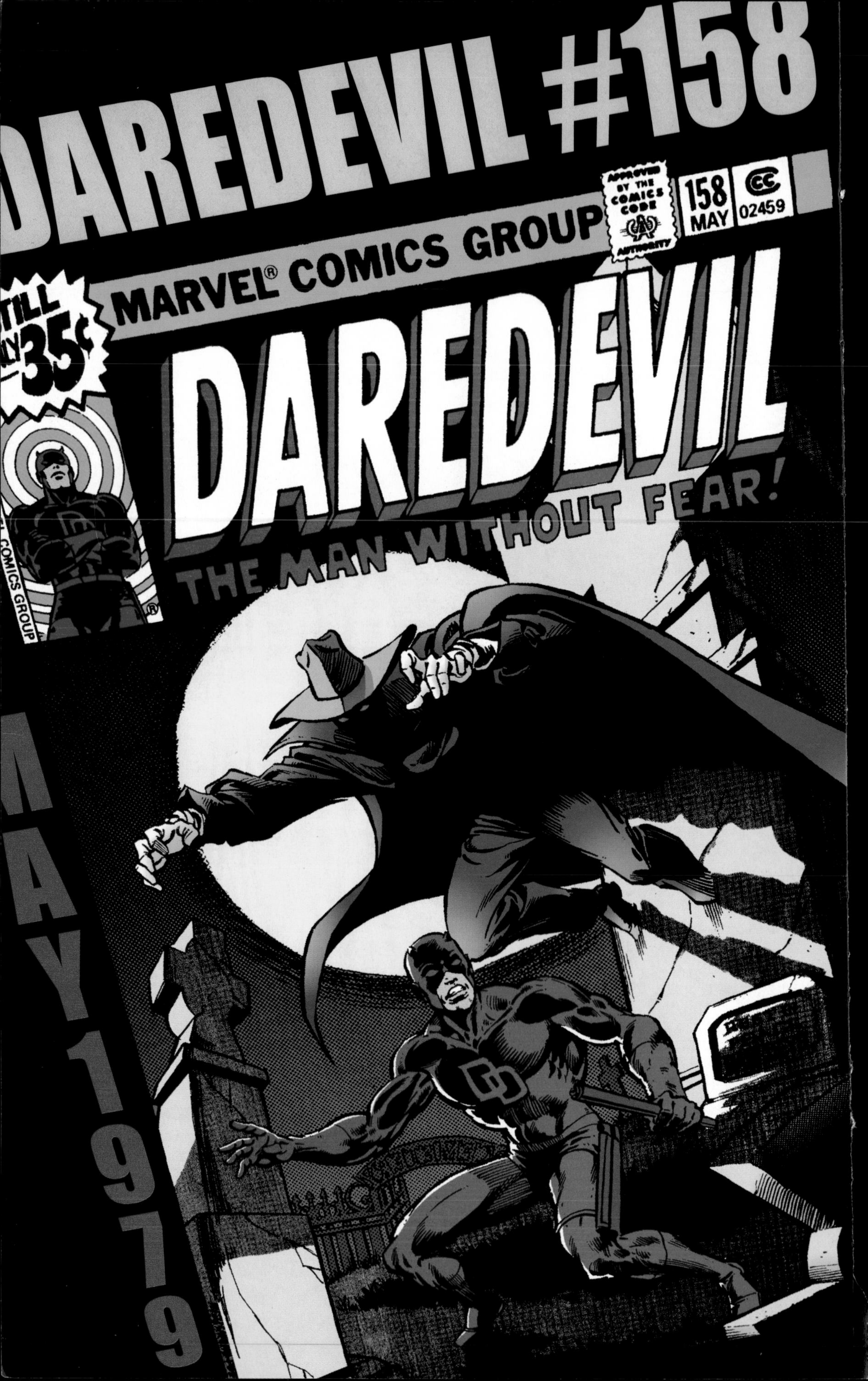
DAREDEVIL #158
MARVEL® COMICS GROUP
APPROVED BY THE COMICS CODE AUTHORITY
158 MAY
CC 02459
35¢
DAREDEVIL
THE MAN WITHOUT FEAR!
MAY 1979

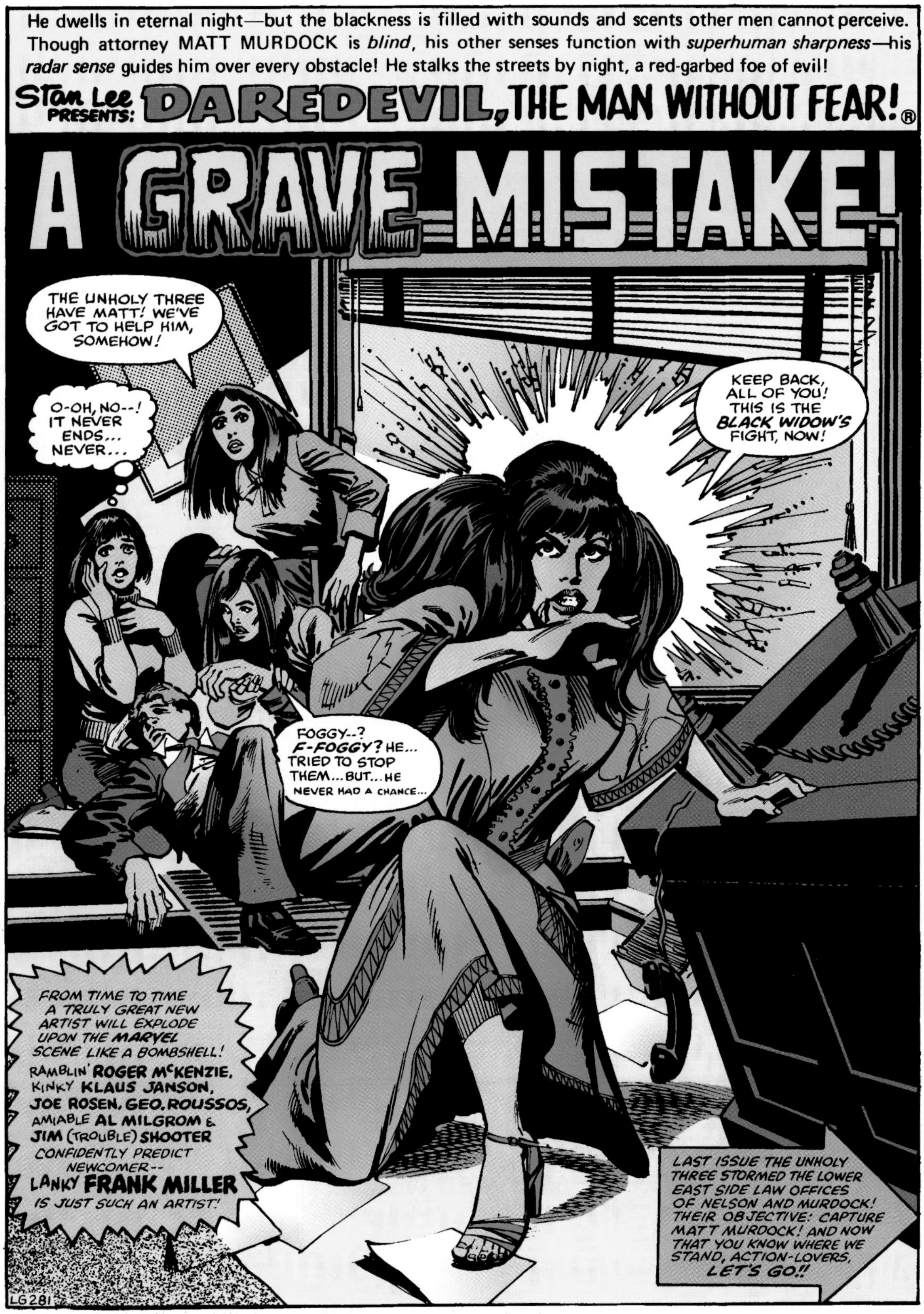
He dwells in eternal night—but the blackness is filled with sounds and scents other men cannot perceive. Though attorney MATT MURDOCK is *blind*, his other senses function with *superhuman sharpness*—his *radar sense* guides him over every obstacle! He stalks the streets by night, a red-garbed foe of evil!
STAN LEE PRESENTS: DAREDEVIL, THE MAN WITHOUT FEAR!®
A GRAVE MISTAKE!
THE UNHOLY THREE HAVE MATT! WE'VE GOT TO HELP HIM, SOMEHOW!
O-OH, NO--! IT NEVER ENDS... NEVER...
KEEP BACK, ALL OF YOU! THIS IS THE BLACK WIDOW'S FIGHT, NOW!
FOGGY--? F-FOGGY? HE... TRIED TO STOP THEM... BUT... HE NEVER HAD A CHANCE...
FROM TIME TO TIME A TRULY GREAT NEW ARTIST WILL EXPLODE UPON THE MARVEL SCENE LIKE A BOMBSHELL! RAMBLIN' ROGER McKENZIE, KINKY KLAUS JANSON, JOE ROSEN, GEO. ROUSSOS, AMIABLE AL MILGROM & JIM (TROUBLE) SHOOTER CONFIDENTLY PREDICT NEWCOMER-- LANKY FRANK MILLER IS JUST SUCH AN ARTIST!
LAST ISSUE THE UNHOLY THREE STORMED THE LOWER EAST SIDE LAW OFFICES OF NELSON AND MURDOCK! THEIR OBJECTIVE: CAPTURE MATT MURDOCK! AND NOW THAT YOU KNOW WHERE WE STAND, ACTION-LOVERS, LET'S GO!!
LG281

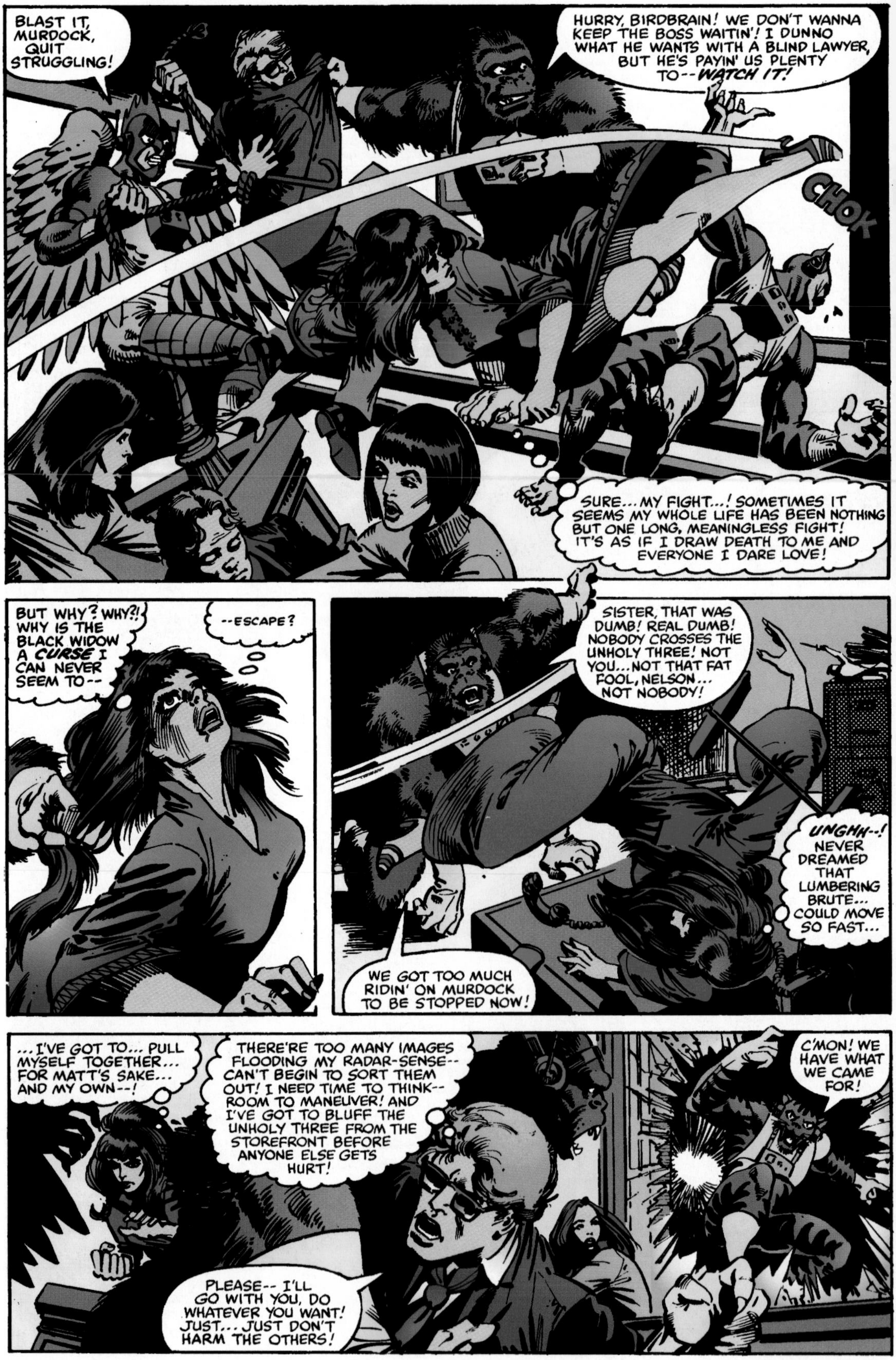

BLAST IT, MURDOCK, QUIT STRUGGLING!
HURRY, BIRDBRAIN! WE DON'T WANNA KEEP THE BOSS WAITIN'! I DUNNO WHAT HE WANTS WITH A BLIND LAWYER, BUT HE'S PAYIN' US PLENTY TO--WATCH IT!
CHOK
SURE... MY FIGHT...! SOMETIMES IT SEEMS MY WHOLE LIFE HAS BEEN NOTHING BUT ONE LONG, MEANINGLESS FIGHT! IT'S AS IF I DRAW DEATH TO ME AND EVERYONE I DARE LOVE!
BUT WHY? WHY?! WHY IS THE BLACK WIDOW A CURSE I CAN NEVER SEEM TO--
--ESCAPE?
SISTER, THAT WAS DUMB! REAL DUMB! NOBODY CROSSES THE UNHOLY THREE! NOT YOU...NOT THAT FAT FOOL, NELSON... NOT NOBODY!
UNGHH--! NEVER DREAMED THAT LUMBERING BRUTE... COULD MOVE SO FAST...
WE GOT TOO MUCH RIDIN' ON MURDOCK TO BE STOPPED NOW!
...I'VE GOT TO... PULL MYSELF TOGETHER... FOR MATT'S SAKE... AND MY OWN--!
THERE'RE TOO MANY IMAGES FLOODING MY RADAR-SENSE-- CAN'T BEGIN TO SORT THEM OUT! I NEED TIME TO THINK-- ROOM TO MANEUVER! AND I'VE GOT TO BLUFF THE UNHOLY THREE FROM THE STOREFRONT BEFORE ANYONE ELSE GETS HURT!
C'MON! WE HAVE WHAT WE CAME FOR!
PLEASE-- I'LL GO WITH YOU, DO WHATEVER YOU WANT! JUST... JUST DON'T HARM THE OTHERS!

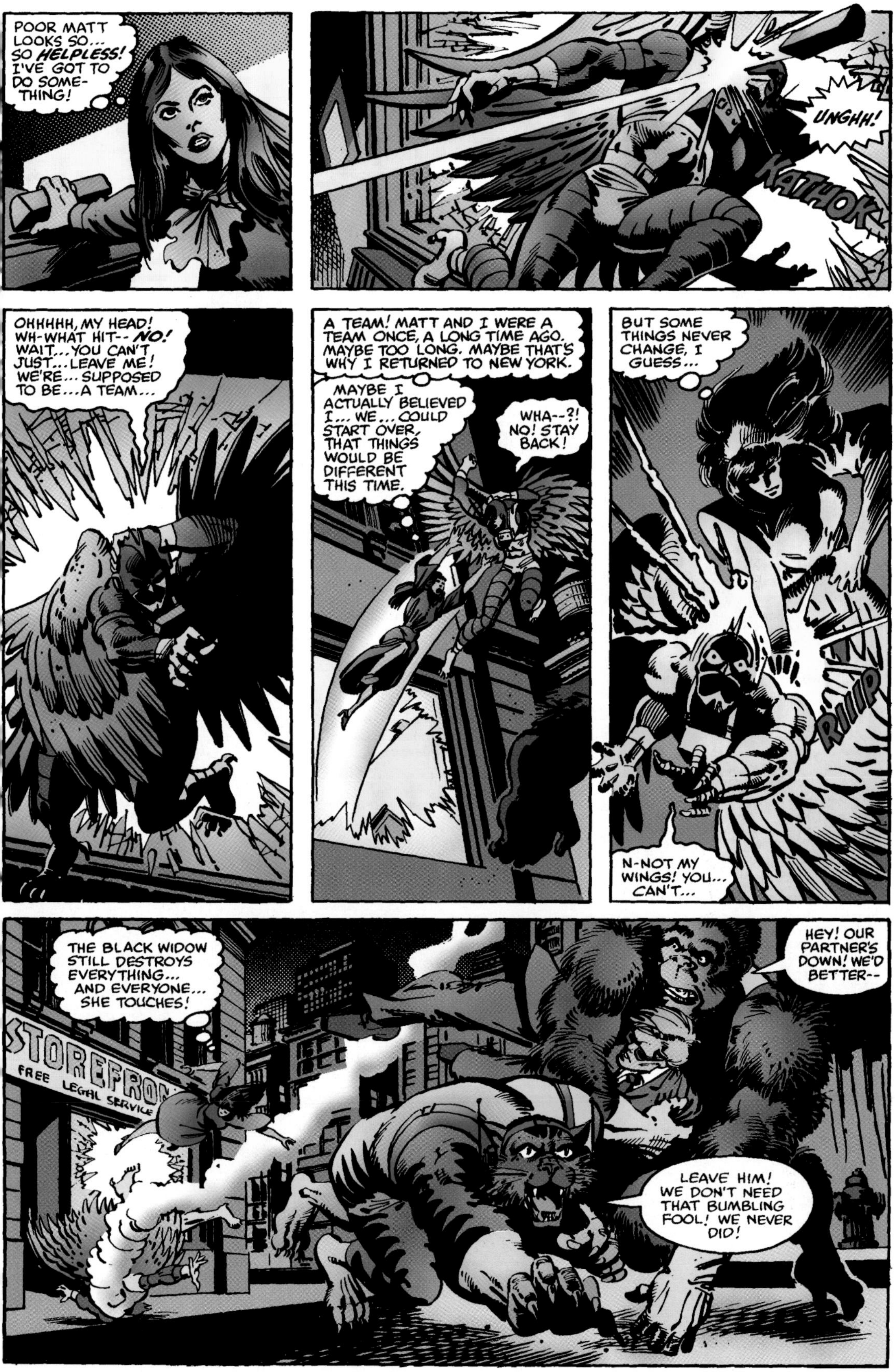
POOR MATT LOOKS SO... SO HELPLESS! I'VE GOT TO DO SOME-THING!
UNGHH!
KATHOK
OHHHHH, MY HEAD! WH-WHAT HIT-- NO! WAIT... YOU CAN'T JUST... LEAVE ME! WE'RE... SUPPOSED TO BE... A TEAM...
A TEAM! MATT AND I WERE A TEAM ONCE, A LONG TIME AGO. MAYBE TOO LONG. MAYBE THAT'S WHY I RETURNED TO NEW YORK.
MAYBE I ACTUALLY BELIEVED I... WE... COULD START OVER, THAT THINGS WOULD BE DIFFERENT THIS TIME.
WHA--?! NO! STAY BACK!
BUT SOME THINGS NEVER CHANGE, I GUESS...
RIIIP
N-NOT MY WINGS! YOU... CAN'T...
THE BLACK WIDOW STILL DESTROYS EVERYTHING... AND EVERYONE... SHE TOUCHES!
STOREFRON
FREE LEGAL SERVICE
HEY! OUR PARTNER'S DOWN! WE'D BETTER--
LEAVE HIM! WE DON'T NEED THAT BUMBLING FOOL! WE NEVER DID!

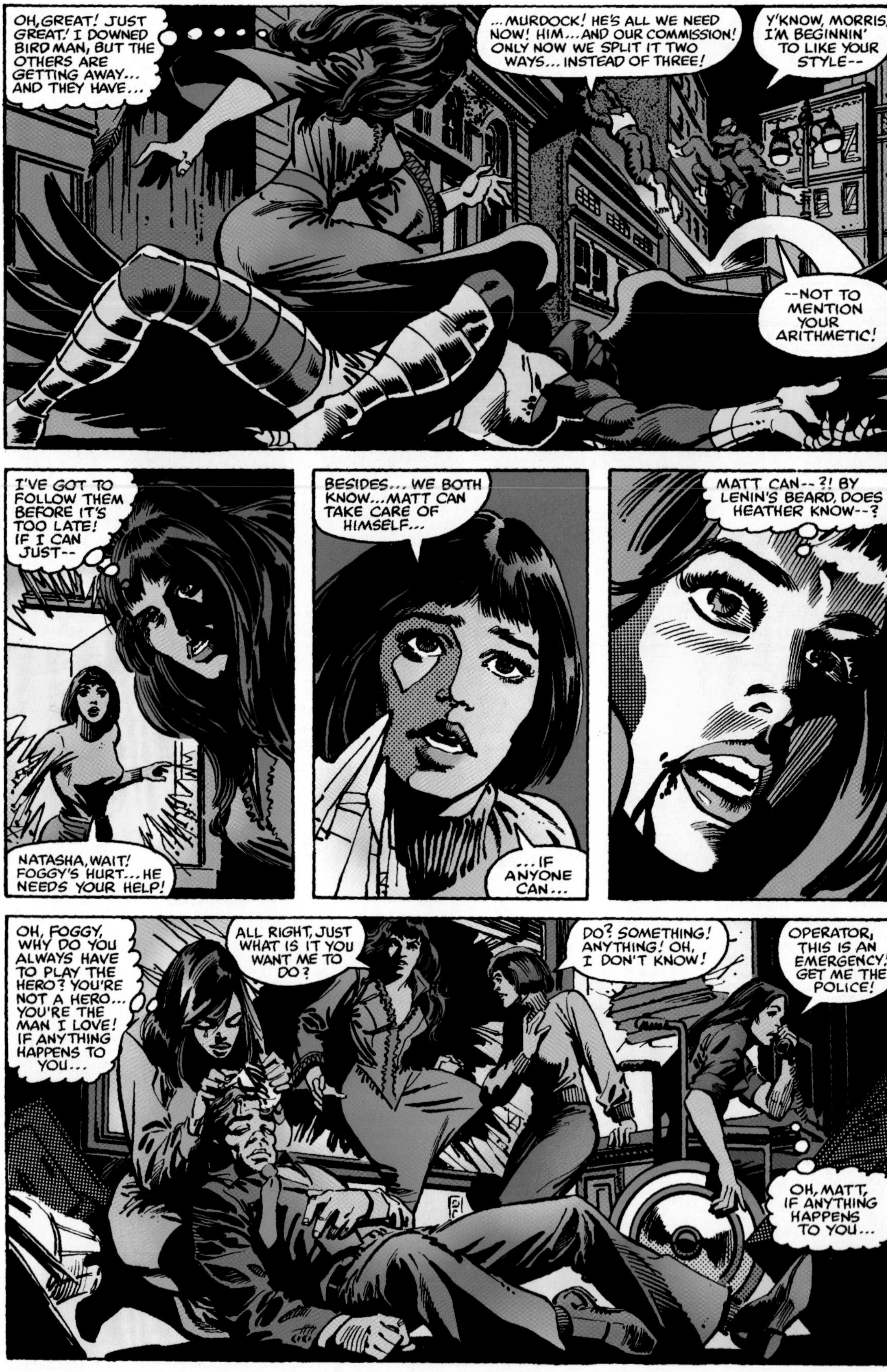
OH, GREAT! JUST GREAT! I DOWNED BIRD MAN, BUT THE OTHERS ARE GETTING AWAY... AND THEY HAVE...
...MURDOCK! HE'S ALL WE NEED NOW! HIM...AND OUR COMMISSION! ONLY NOW WE SPLIT IT TWO WAYS... INSTEAD OF THREE!
Y'KNOW, MORRIS, I'M BEGINNIN' TO LIKE YOUR STYLE--
--NOT TO MENTION YOUR ARITHMETIC!
I'VE GOT TO FOLLOW THEM BEFORE IT'S TOO LATE! IF I CAN JUST--
NATASHA, WAIT! FOGGY'S HURT...HE NEEDS YOUR HELP!
BESIDES... WE BOTH KNOW...MATT CAN TAKE CARE OF HIMSELF...
...IF ANYONE CAN...
MATT CAN--?! BY LENIN'S BEARD, DOES HEATHER KNOW--?
OH, FOGGY, WHY DO YOU ALWAYS HAVE TO PLAY THE HERO? YOU'RE NOT A HERO... YOU'RE THE MAN I LOVE! IF ANYTHING HAPPENS TO YOU...
ALL RIGHT, JUST WHAT IS IT YOU WANT ME TO DO?
DO? SOMETHING! ANYTHING! OH, I DON'T KNOW!
OPERATOR, THIS IS AN EMERGENCY! GET ME THE POLICE!
OH, MATT, IF ANYTHING HAPPENS TO YOU...

MEANWHILE...

MURDOCK, YOU DON'T KNOW IT YET, BUT YOU'RE GONNA MAKE US RICH MEN! VERY RICH MEN! AND THIS'S ONLY THE BEGINNIN'! WITH THESE *SPECIAL OUTFITS* THERE AIN'T NOTHIN' WE CAN'T DO--

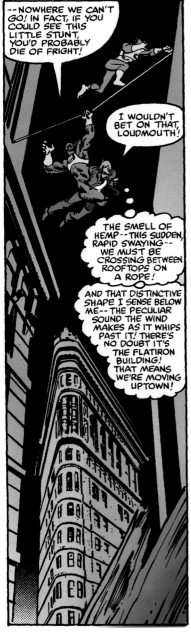

--NOWHERE WE CAN'T GO! IN FACT, IF YOU COULD SEE THIS LITTLE STUNT, YOU'D PROBABLY DIE OF FRIGHT!

I WOULDN'T BET ON THAT, LOUDMOUTH!

THE SMELL OF HEMP--THIS SUDDEN, RAPID SWAYING-- WE MUST BE CROSSING BETWEEN ROOFTOPS ON A ROPE!

AND THAT DISTINCTIVE SHAPE I SENSE BELOW ME-- THE PECULIAR SOUND THE WIND MAKES AS IT WHIPS PAST IT! THERE'S NO DOUBT IT'S THE FLATIRON BUILDING! THAT MEANS WE'RE MOVING UPTOWN!

YEAH, WELL IF YOU DON'T HOLD STILL I'M JUST LIABLE TO DROP YOU! DEATH-STALKER NEVER SAID HE WANTED YOU ALIVE, ANYHOW!

DEATH-STALKER--?!

YOU'VE GOT TO LISTEN TO ME! DEATH-STALKER'S A KILLER! A COLD-BLOODED, INHUMAN KILLER! HE'S JUST USING YOU! AND WHEN YOU'VE SERVED HIS PURPOSE, HE'LL--!

NICE TRY, SHYSTER, BUT IT WON'T WASH! WHAT COULD A STUFFED SHIRT LIKE YOU KNOW ABOUT HIM ANYWAY? BESIDES...

WE'RE HERE!

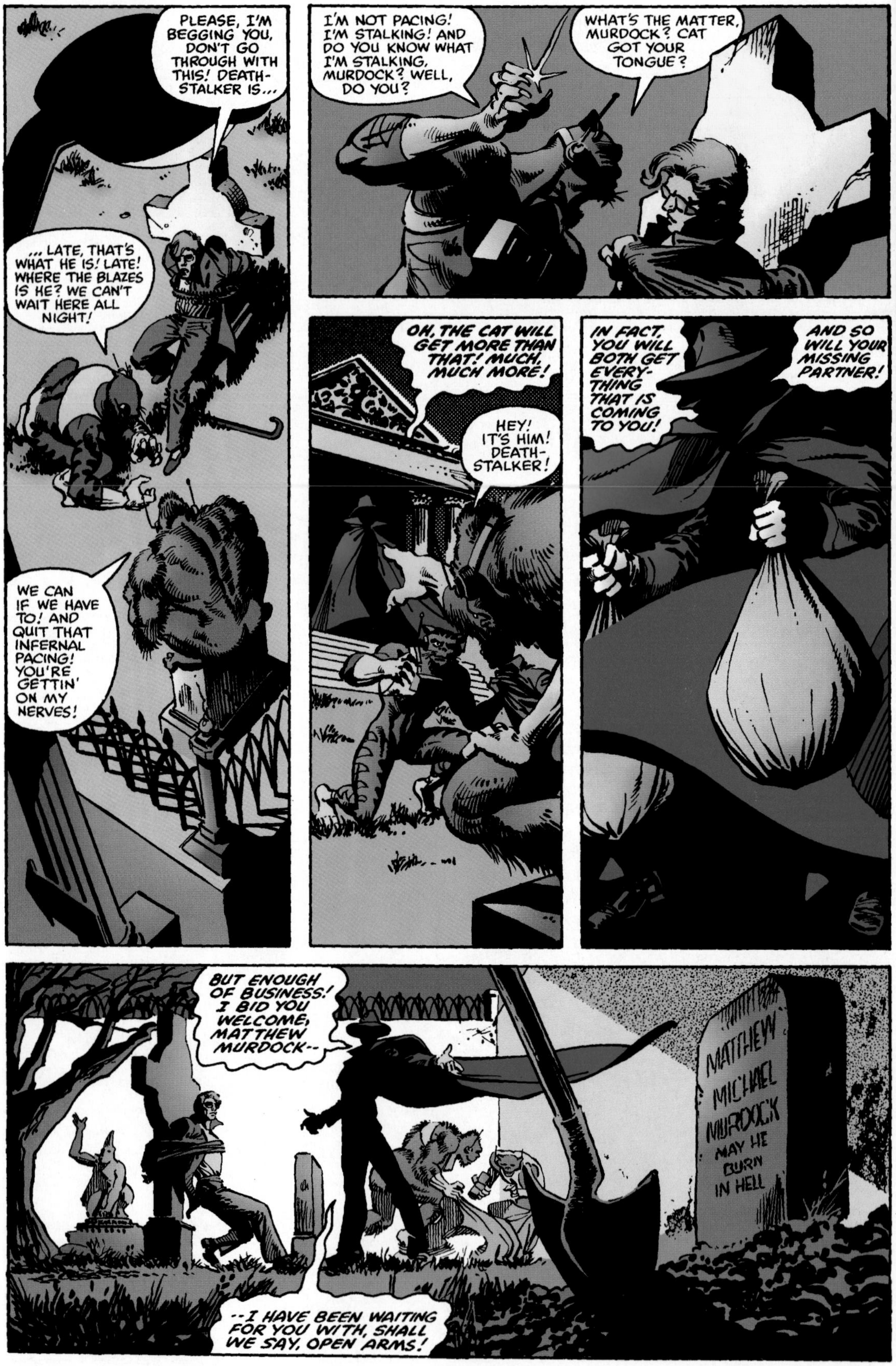
PLEASE, I'M BEGGING YOU, DON'T GO THROUGH WITH THIS! DEATH-STALKER IS...
...LATE, THAT'S WHAT HE IS! LATE! WHERE THE BLAZES IS HE? WE CAN'T WAIT HERE ALL NIGHT!
WE CAN IF WE HAVE TO! AND QUIT THAT INFERNAL PACING! YOU'RE GETTIN' ON MY NERVES!
I'M NOT PACING! I'M STALKING! AND DO YOU KNOW WHAT I'M STALKING, MURDOCK? WELL, DO YOU?
WHAT'S THE MATTER, MURDOCK? CAT GOT YOUR TONGUE?
OH, THE CAT WILL GET MORE THAN THAT! MUCH, MUCH MORE!
HEY! IT'S HIM! DEATH-STALKER!
IN FACT, YOU WILL BOTH GET EVERY-THING THAT IS COMING TO YOU!
AND SO WILL YOUR MISSING PARTNER!
BUT ENOUGH OF BUSINESS! I BID YOU WELCOME, MATTHEW MURDOCK--
MATTHEW MICHAEL MURDOCK MAY HE BURN IN HELL
--I HAVE BEEN WAITING FOR YOU WITH, SHALL WE SAY, OPEN ARMS!

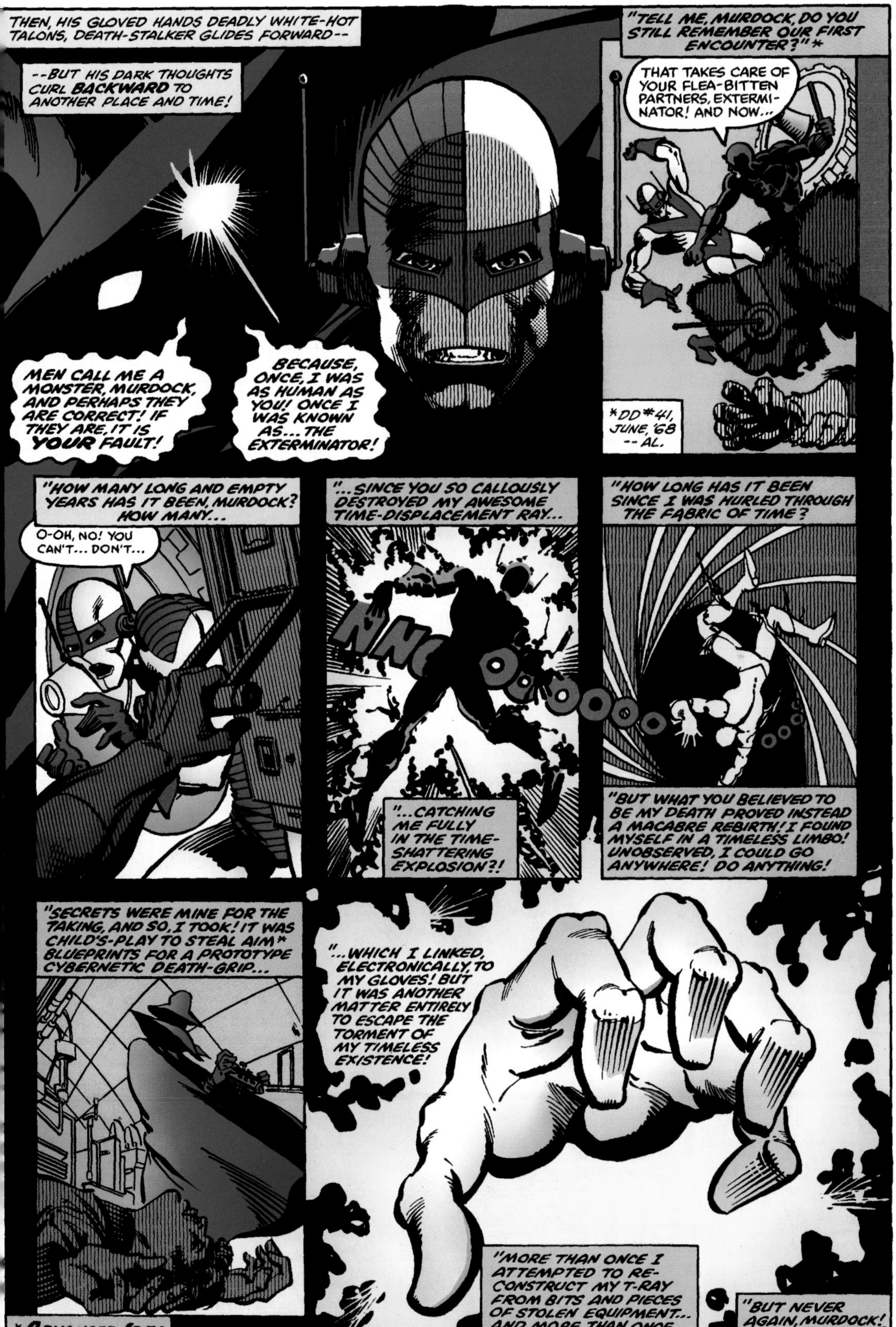
THEN, HIS GLOVED HANDS DEADLY WHITE-HOT TALONS, DEATH-STALKER GLIDES FORWARD--
--BUT HIS DARK THOUGHTS CURL BACKWARD TO ANOTHER PLACE AND TIME!
MEN CALL ME A MONSTER, MURDOCK, AND PERHAPS THEY ARE CORRECT! IF THEY ARE, IT IS YOUR FAULT!
BECAUSE, ONCE, I WAS AS HUMAN AS YOU! ONCE I WAS KNOWN AS... THE EXTERMINATOR!
"TELL ME, MURDOCK, DO YOU STILL REMEMBER OUR FIRST ENCOUNTER?"*
THAT TAKES CARE OF YOUR FLEA-BITTEN PARTNERS, EXTERMINATOR! AND NOW...
*DD #41, JUNE, '68 --AL.
"HOW MANY LONG AND EMPTY YEARS HAS IT BEEN, MURDOCK? HOW MANY...
O-OH, NO! YOU CAN'T... DON'T...
"...SINCE YOU SO CALLOUSLY DESTROYED MY AWESOME TIME-DISPLACEMENT RAY...
NNOOOOOOOOO
"...CATCHING ME FULLY IN THE TIME-SHATTERING EXPLOSION?!
"HOW LONG HAS IT BEEN SINCE I WAS HURLED THROUGH THE FABRIC OF TIME?
"BUT WHAT YOU BELIEVED TO BE MY DEATH PROVED INSTEAD A MACABRE REBIRTH! I FOUND MYSELF IN A TIMELESS LIMBO! UNOBSERVED, I COULD GO ANYWHERE! DO ANYTHING!
"SECRETS WERE MINE FOR THE TAKING, AND SO, I TOOK! IT WAS CHILD'S-PLAY TO STEAL AIM* BLUEPRINTS FOR A PROTOTYPE CYBERNETIC DEATH-GRIP...
*ADVANCED IDEA MECHANICS --AL.
"...WHICH I LINKED, ELECTRONICALLY, TO MY GLOVES! BUT IT WAS ANOTHER MATTER ENTIRELY TO ESCAPE THE TORMENT OF MY TIMELESS EXISTENCE!
"MORE THAN ONCE I ATTEMPTED TO RE-CONSTRUCT MY T-RAY FROM BITS AND PIECES OF STOLEN EQUIPMENT... AND MORE THAN ONCE I WAS THWARTED!
"BUT NEVER AGAIN, MURDOCK! DO YOU HEAR ME? NEVER AGAIN!

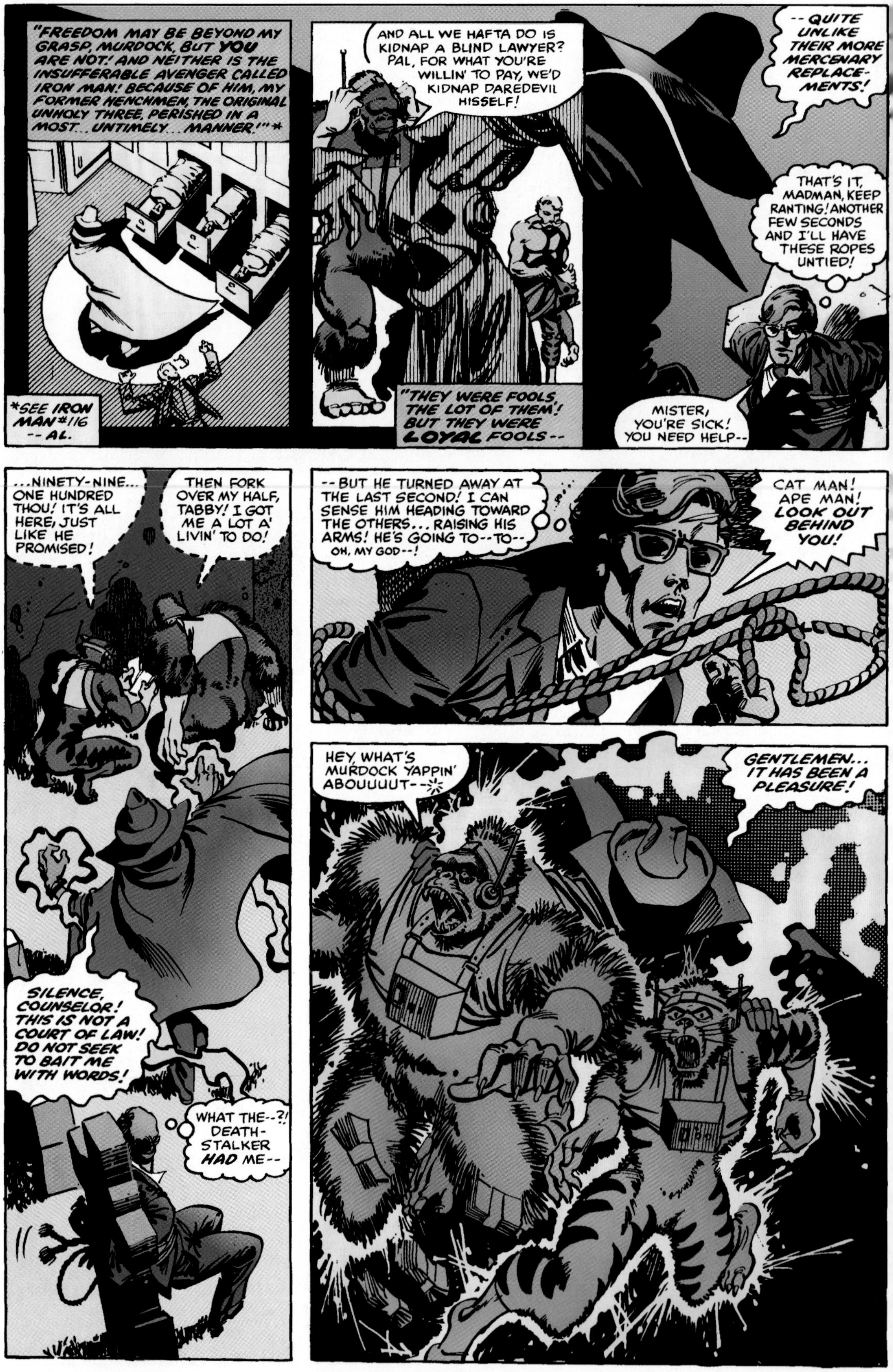
"FREEDOM MAY BE BEYOND MY GRASP, MURDOCK, BUT YOU ARE NOT! AND NEITHER IS THE INSUFFERABLE AVENGER CALLED IRON MAN! BECAUSE OF HIM, MY FORMER HENCHMEN, THE ORIGINAL UNHOLY THREE, PERISHED IN A MOST... UNTIMELY... MANNER."*
*SEE IRON MAN #116 --AL.
AND ALL WE HAFTA DO IS KIDNAP A BLIND LAWYER? PAL, FOR WHAT YOU'RE WILLIN' TO PAY, WE'D KIDNAP DAREDEVIL HISSELF!
"THEY WERE FOOLS, THE LOT OF THEM! BUT THEY WERE LOYAL FOOLS--
--QUITE UNLIKE THEIR MORE MERCENARY REPLACEMENTS!
THAT'S IT, MADMAN, KEEP RANTING! ANOTHER FEW SECONDS AND I'LL HAVE THESE ROPES UNTIED!
MISTER, YOU'RE SICK! YOU NEED HELP--
...NINETY-NINE... ONE HUNDRED THOU! IT'S ALL HERE, JUST LIKE HE PROMISED!
THEN FORK OVER MY HALF, TABBY! I GOT ME A LOT A' LIVIN' TO DO!
SILENCE, COUNSELOR! THIS IS NOT A COURT OF LAW! DO NOT SEEK TO BAIT ME WITH WORDS!
WHAT THE--?! DEATH-STALKER HAD ME--
--BUT HE TURNED AWAY AT THE LAST SECOND! I CAN SENSE HIM HEADING TOWARD THE OTHERS... RAISING HIS ARMS! HE'S GOING TO--TO-- OH, MY GOD--!
CAT MAN! APE MAN! LOOK OUT BEHIND YOU!
HEY, WHAT'S MURDOCK YAPPIN' ABOUUUUT--
GENTLEMEN... IT HAS BEEN A PLEASURE!

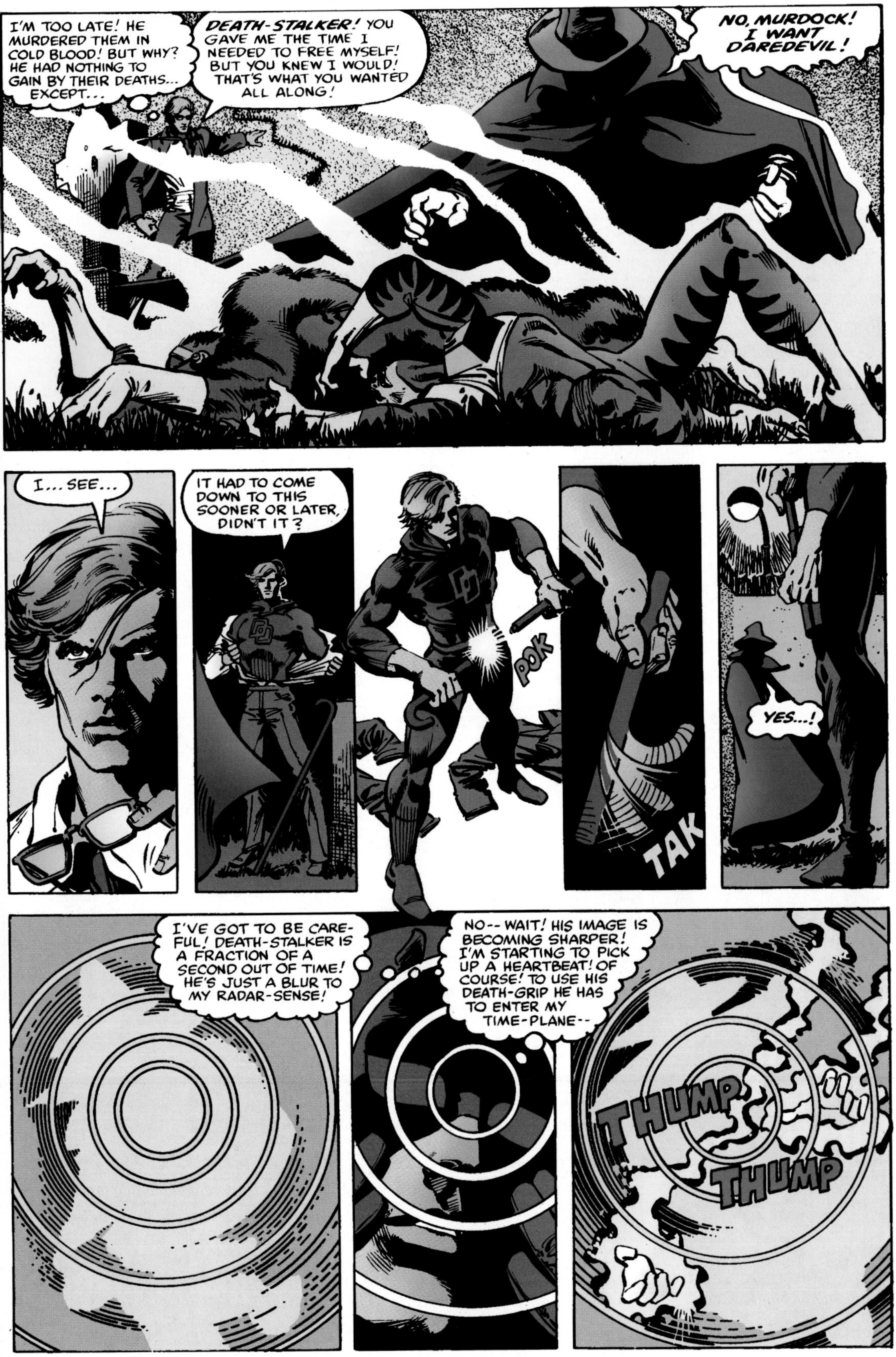
I'M TOO LATE! HE MURDERED THEM IN COLD BLOOD! BUT WHY? HE HAD NOTHING TO GAIN BY THEIR DEATHS... EXCEPT...
DEATH-STALKER! YOU GAVE ME THE TIME I NEEDED TO FREE MYSELF! BUT YOU KNEW I WOULD! THAT'S WHAT YOU WANTED ALL ALONG!
NO, MURDOCK! I WANT DAREDEVIL!
I... SEE...
IT HAD TO COME DOWN TO THIS SOONER OR LATER, DIDN'T IT?
POK
TAK
YES...!
I'VE GOT TO BE CAREFUL! DEATH-STALKER IS A FRACTION OF A SECOND OUT OF TIME! HE'S JUST A BLUR TO MY RADAR-SENSE!
NO-- WAIT! HIS IMAGE IS BECOMING SHARPER! I'M STARTING TO PICK UP A HEARTBEAT! OF COURSE! TO USE HIS DEATH-GRIP HE HAS TO ENTER MY TIME-PLANE--
THUMP
THUMP

--AND, IF HE CAN TOUCH ME, THAT MEANS *I* CAN TOUCH HIM! THAT MAY BE THE EDGE I NEED!

NOW--! HIS PULSE RATE JUST INCREASED! HE'S LUNGING AT ME! BUT IF I CAN GRAB HIS ARMS WELL *ABOVE* THOSE DEADLY GLOVES--

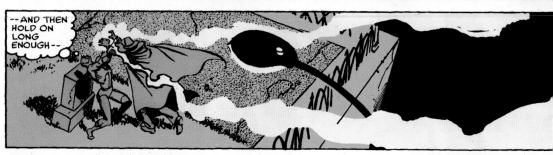

--AND THEN HOLD ON LONG ENOUGH--

-- I SHOULD BE ABLE TO GET IN SOME KICKS OF MY--

--HUH--? HE PULLED ANOTHER FADE-OUT! I'VE LOST HIM! THERE'S NOTHING BUT A STONE WALL IN FRONT OF ME!

AND I DON'T SENSE HIM BEHIND ME! BUT I'VE GOT TO BE READY FOR ANYTHING! HE COULD BE ANYWHERE--

--ANY-WHERE AT ALL!

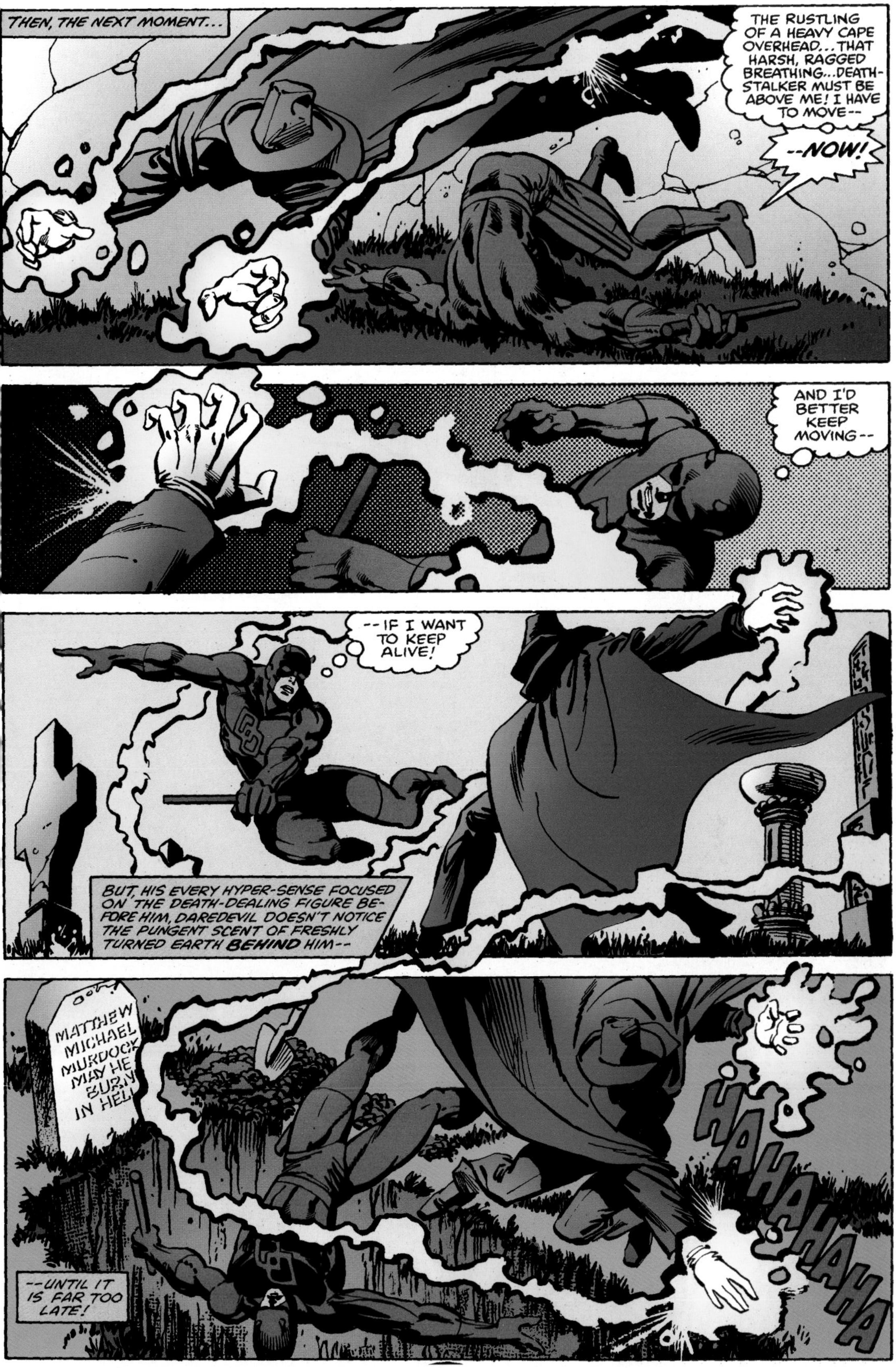
THEN, THE NEXT MOMENT...
THE RUSTLING OF A HEAVY CAPE OVERHEAD... THAT HARSH, RAGGED BREATHING... DEATH-STALKER MUST BE ABOVE ME! I HAVE TO MOVE--
--NOW!
AND I'D BETTER KEEP MOVING--
--IF I WANT TO KEEP ALIVE!
BUT, HIS EVERY HYPER-SENSE FOCUSED ON THE DEATH-DEALING FIGURE BEFORE HIM, DAREDEVIL DOESN'T NOTICE THE PUNGENT SCENT OF FRESHLY TURNED EARTH BEHIND HIM--
MATTHEW MICHAEL MURDOCK MAY HE BURN IN HELL
HAHAHAHAHAHA
--UNTIL IT IS FAR TOO LATE!

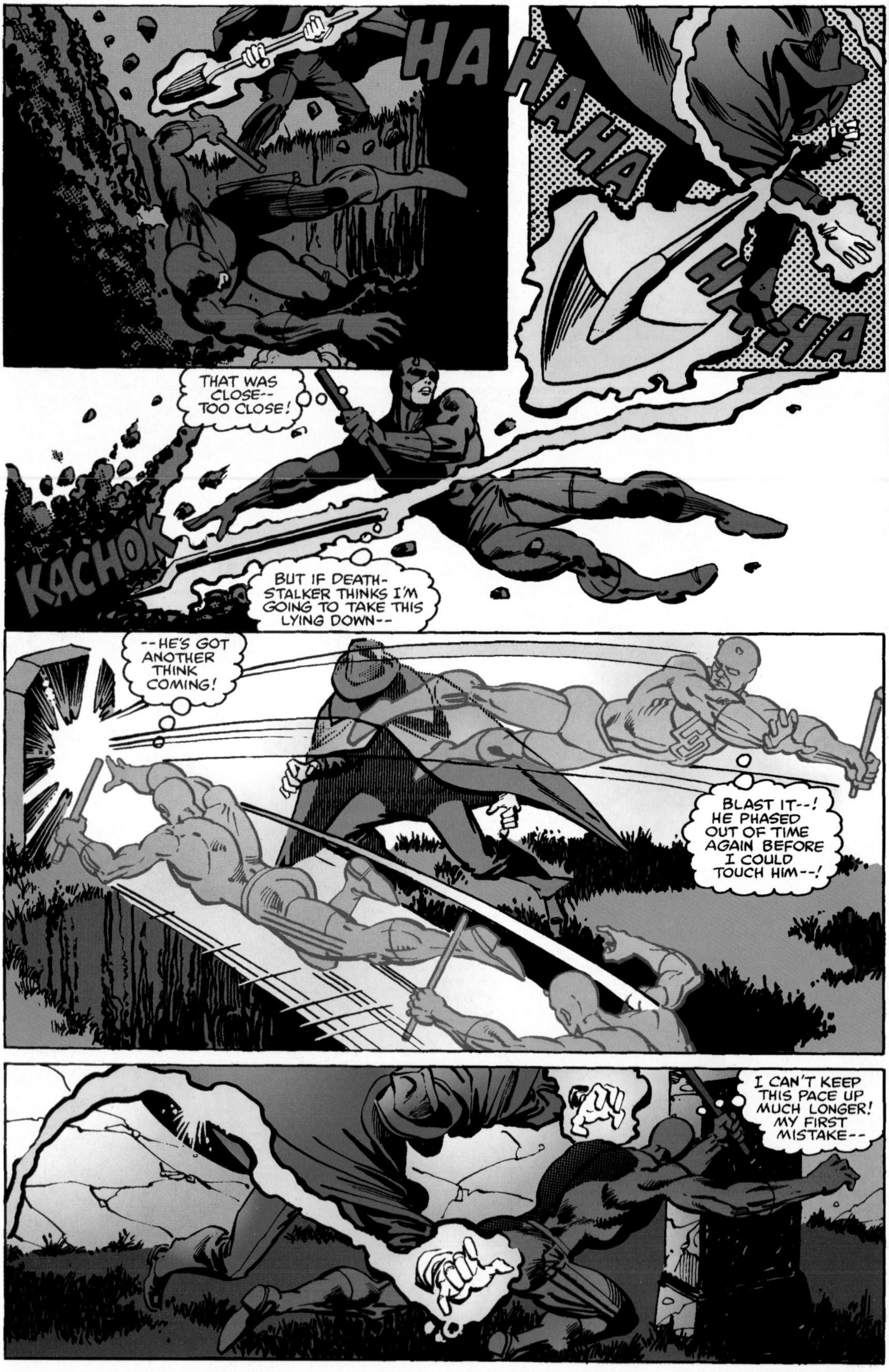

HA HA HA HA
HA HA
THAT WAS CLOSE-- TOO CLOSE!
KACHOK
BUT IF DEATH-STALKER THINKS I'M GOING TO TAKE THIS LYING DOWN--
--HE'S GOT ANOTHER THINK COMING!
BLAST IT--! HE PHASED OUT OF TIME AGAIN BEFORE I COULD TOUCH HIM--!
I CAN'T KEEP THIS PACE UP MUCH LONGER! MY FIRST MISTAKE--

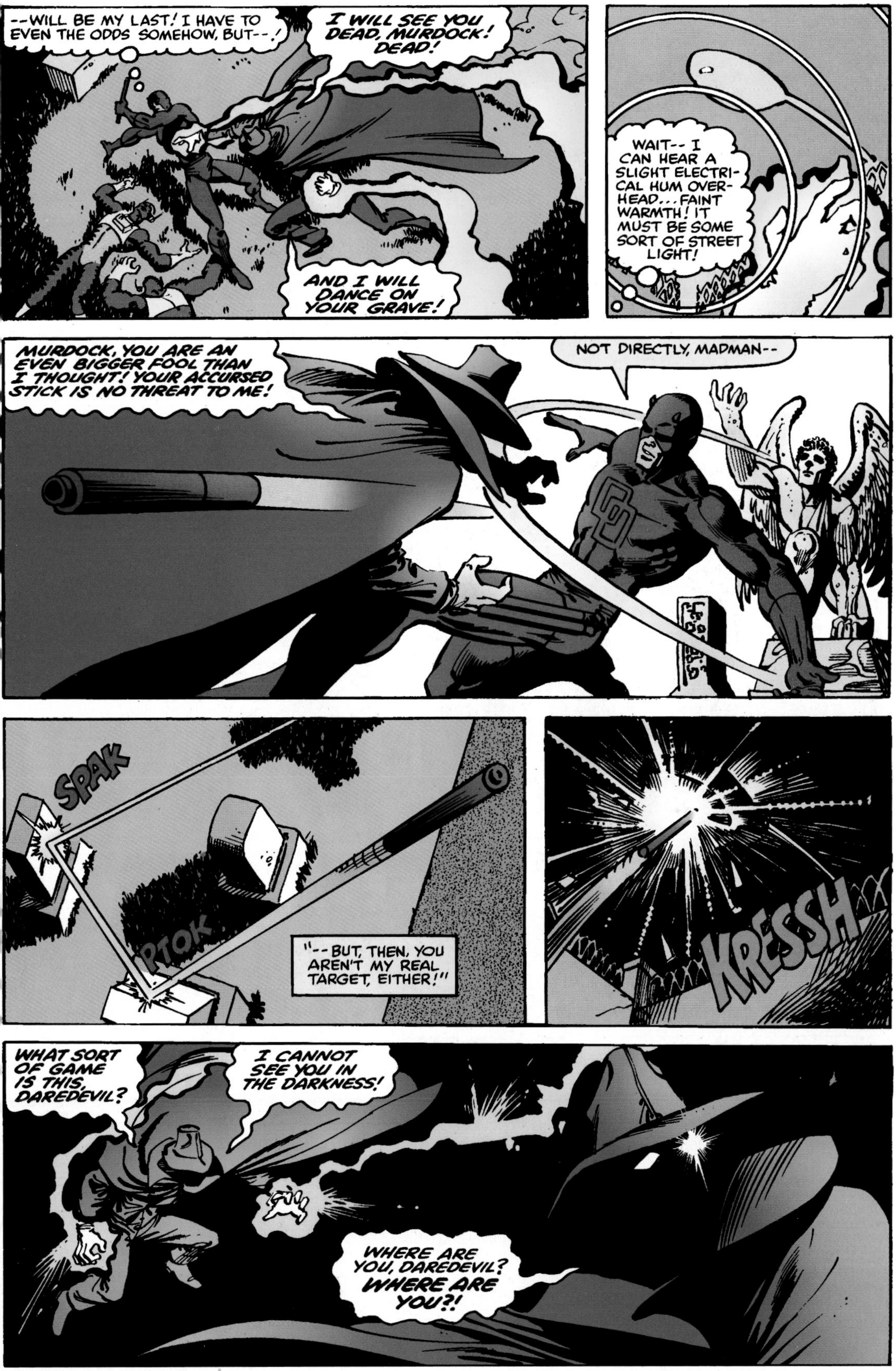
--WILL BE MY LAST! I HAVE TO EVEN THE ODDS SOMEHOW, BUT--!
I WILL SEE YOU DEAD, MURDOCK! DEAD!
AND I WILL DANCE ON YOUR GRAVE!
WAIT-- I CAN HEAR A SLIGHT ELECTRICAL HUM OVERHEAD... FAINT WARMTH! IT MUST BE SOME SORT OF STREET LIGHT!
MURDOCK, YOU ARE AN EVEN BIGGER FOOL THAN I THOUGHT! YOUR ACCURSED STICK IS NO THREAT TO ME!
NOT DIRECTLY, MADMAN--
SPAK
PTOK
"--BUT, THEN, YOU AREN'T MY REAL TARGET, EITHER!"
KRESSH
WHAT SORT OF GAME IS THIS, DAREDEVIL?
I CANNOT SEE YOU IN THE DARKNESS!
WHERE ARE YOU, DAREDEVIL? WHERE ARE YOU?!

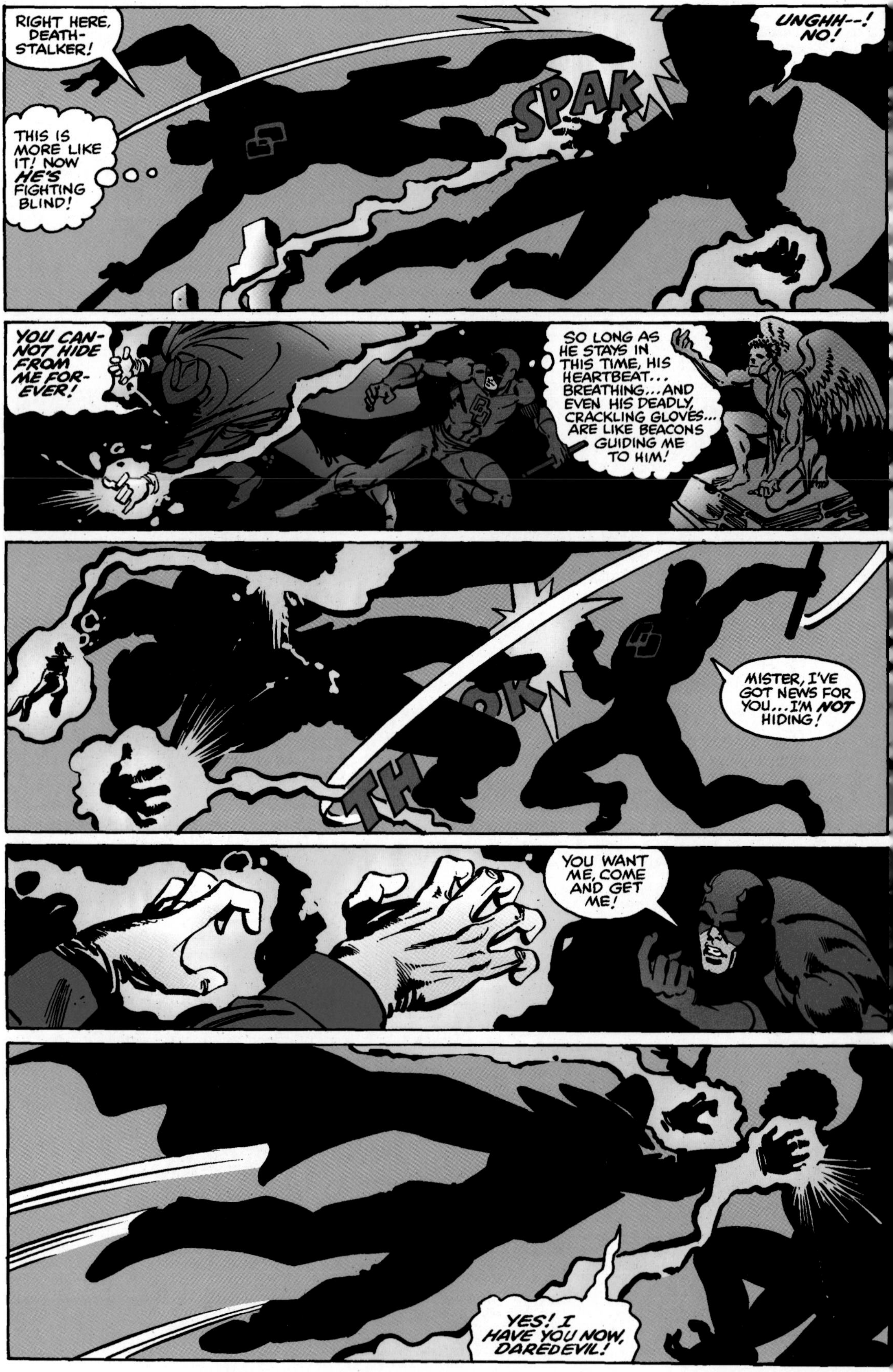

RIGHT HERE, DEATH-STALKER!
THIS IS MORE LIKE IT! NOW HE'S FIGHTING BLIND!
SPAK
UNGHH--! NO!
YOU CAN-NOT HIDE FROM ME FOR-EVER!
SO LONG AS HE STAYS IN THIS TIME, HIS HEARTBEAT... BREATHING... AND EVEN HIS DEADLY, CRACKLING GLOVES... ARE LIKE BEACONS GUIDING ME TO HIM!
MISTER, I'VE GOT NEWS FOR YOU... I'M NOT HIDING!
YOU WANT ME, COME AND GET ME!
YES! I HAVE YOU NOW, DAREDEVIL!

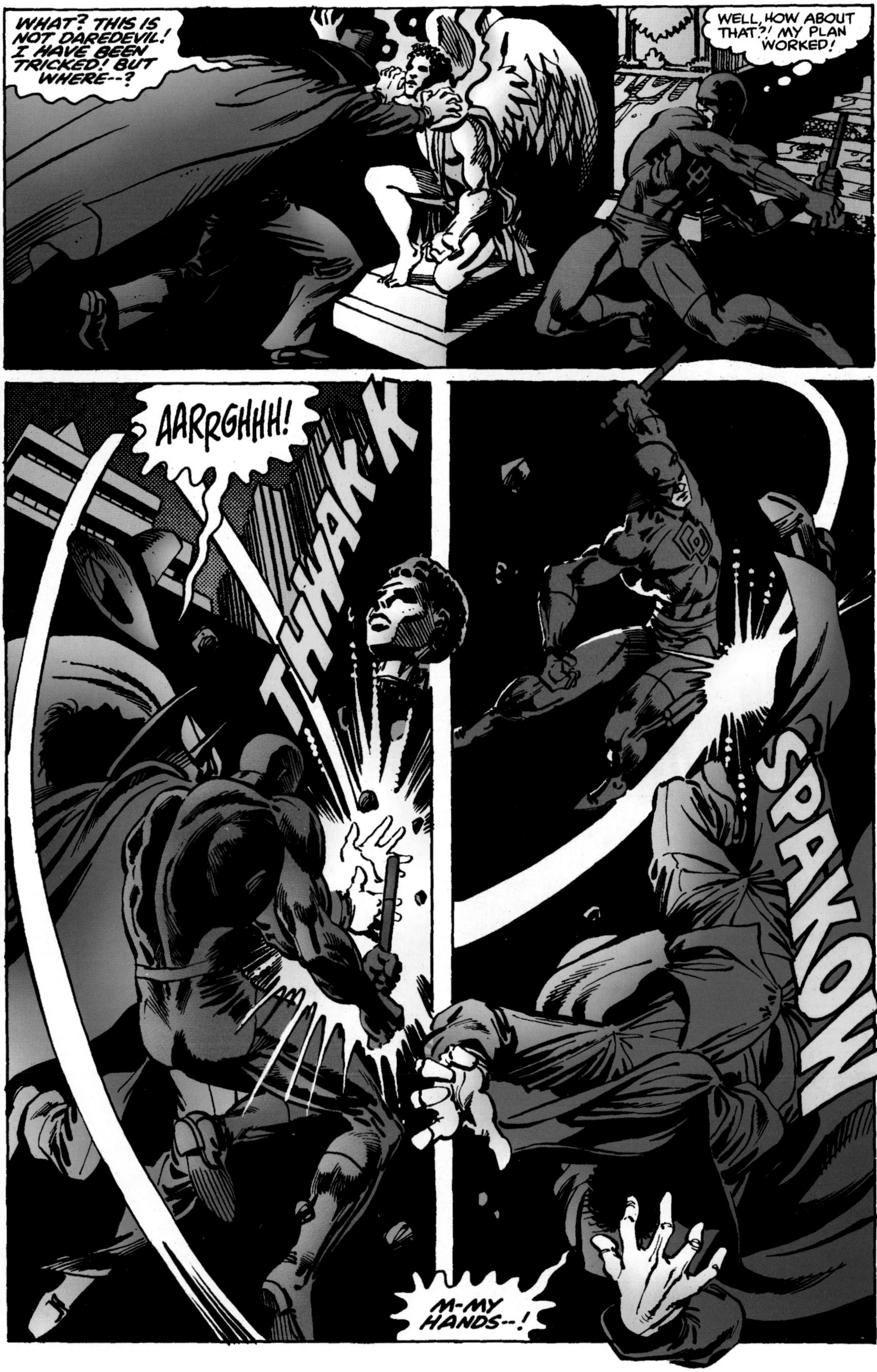
WHAT? THIS IS NOT DAREDEVIL! I HAVE BEEN TRICKED! BUT WHERE--?
WELL, HOW ABOUT THAT?! MY PLAN WORKED!
AARRGHHH!
THHAK-K
SPAKOW
M-MY HANDS--!

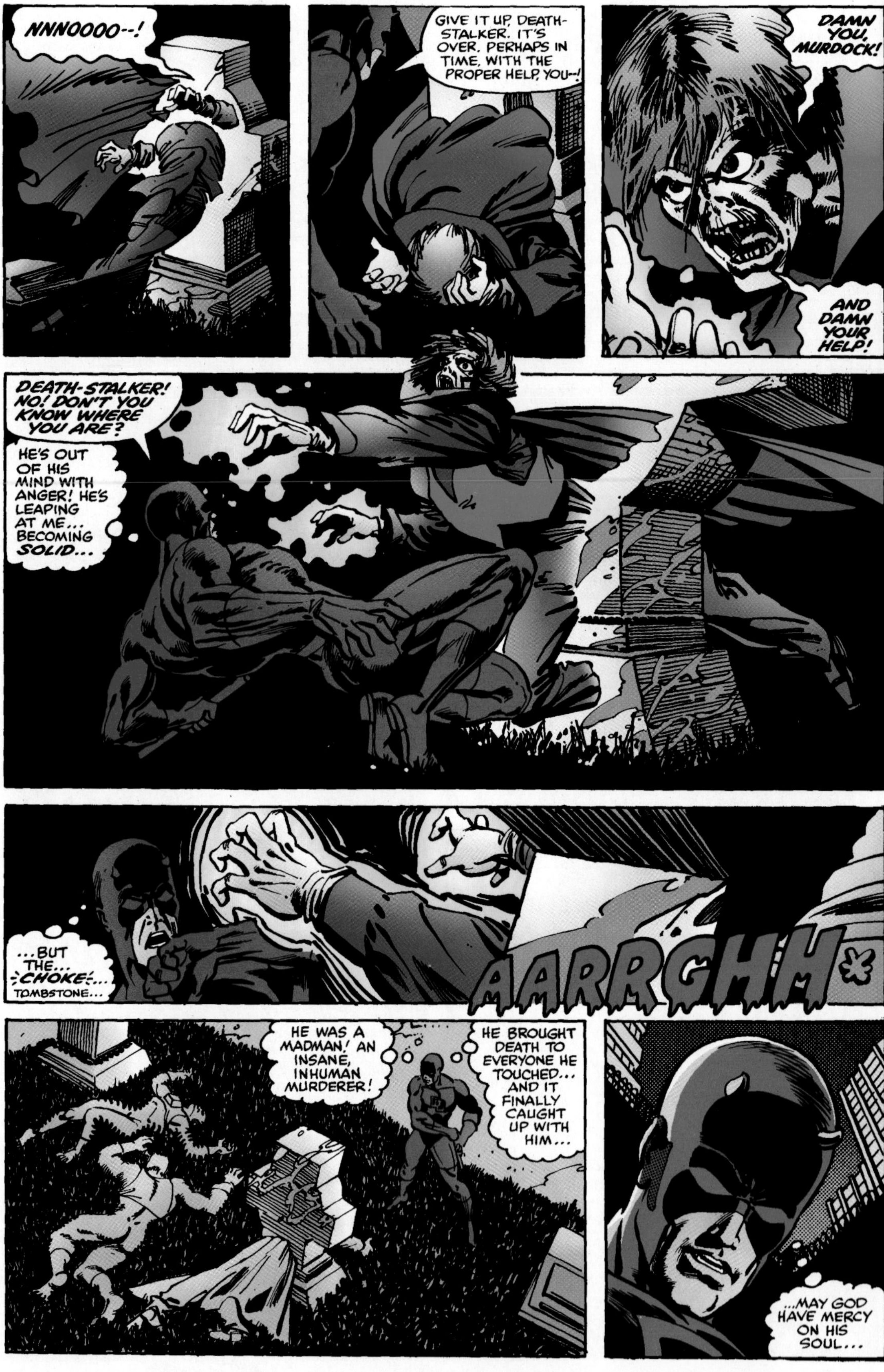
NNNOOOO--!
GIVE IT UP, DEATH-STALKER. IT'S OVER. PERHAPS IN TIME, WITH THE PROPER HELP, YOU--!
DAMN YOU, MURDOCK!
AND DAMN YOUR HELP!
DEATH-STALKER! NO! DON'T YOU KNOW WHERE YOU ARE?
HE'S OUT OF HIS MIND WITH ANGER! HE'S LEAPING AT ME... BECOMING SOLID...
...BUT THE... -CHOKE-... TOMBSTONE...
AARRGHH*
HE WAS A MADMAN! AN INSANE, INHUMAN MURDERER!
HE BROUGHT DEATH TO EVERYONE HE TOUCHED... AND IT FINALLY CAUGHT UP WITH HIM...
...MAY GOD HAVE MERCY ON HIS SOUL...

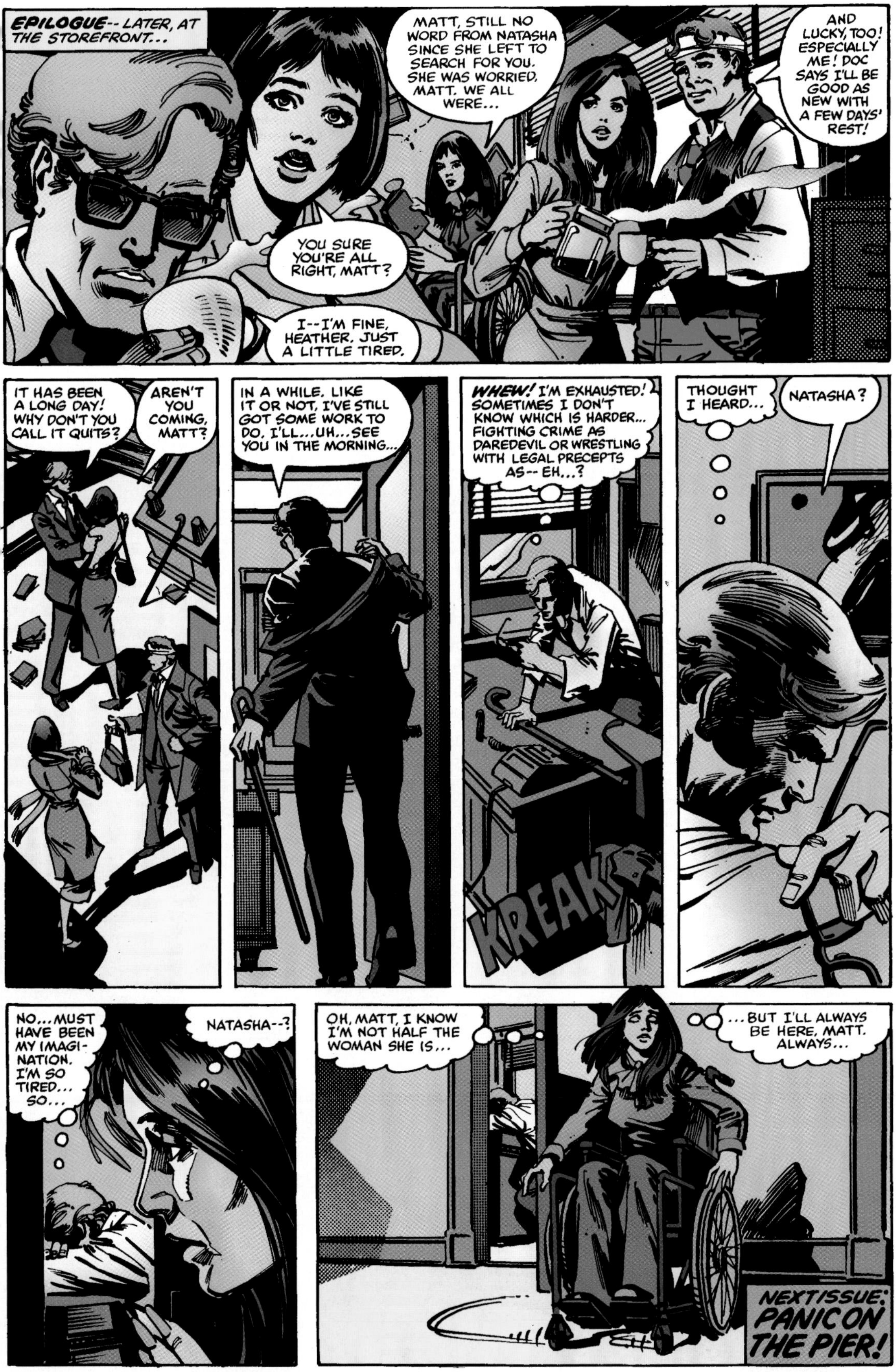
EPILOGUE-- LATER, AT THE STOREFRONT...
MATT, STILL NO WORD FROM NATASHA SINCE SHE LEFT TO SEARCH FOR YOU. SHE WAS WORRIED, MATT. WE ALL WERE...
AND LUCKY, TOO! ESPECIALLY ME! DOC SAYS I'LL BE GOOD AS NEW WITH A FEW DAYS' REST!
YOU SURE YOU'RE ALL RIGHT, MATT?
I--I'M FINE, HEATHER. JUST A LITTLE TIRED.
IT HAS BEEN A LONG DAY! WHY DON'T YOU CALL IT QUITS?
AREN'T YOU COMING, MATT?
IN A WHILE. LIKE IT OR NOT, I'VE STILL GOT SOME WORK TO DO. I'LL...UH...SEE YOU IN THE MORNING...
WHEW! I'M EXHAUSTED! SOMETIMES I DON'T KNOW WHICH IS HARDER... FIGHTING CRIME AS DAREDEVIL OR WRESTLING WITH LEGAL PRECEPTS AS-- EH...?
KREAK
THOUGHT I HEARD...
NATASHA?
NO...MUST HAVE BEEN MY IMAGI-NATION. I'M SO TIRED... SO...
NATASHA--?
OH, MATT, I KNOW I'M NOT HALF THE WOMAN SHE IS...
...BUT I'LL ALWAYS BE HERE, MATT. ALWAYS...
NEXT ISSUE: PANIC ON THE PIER!

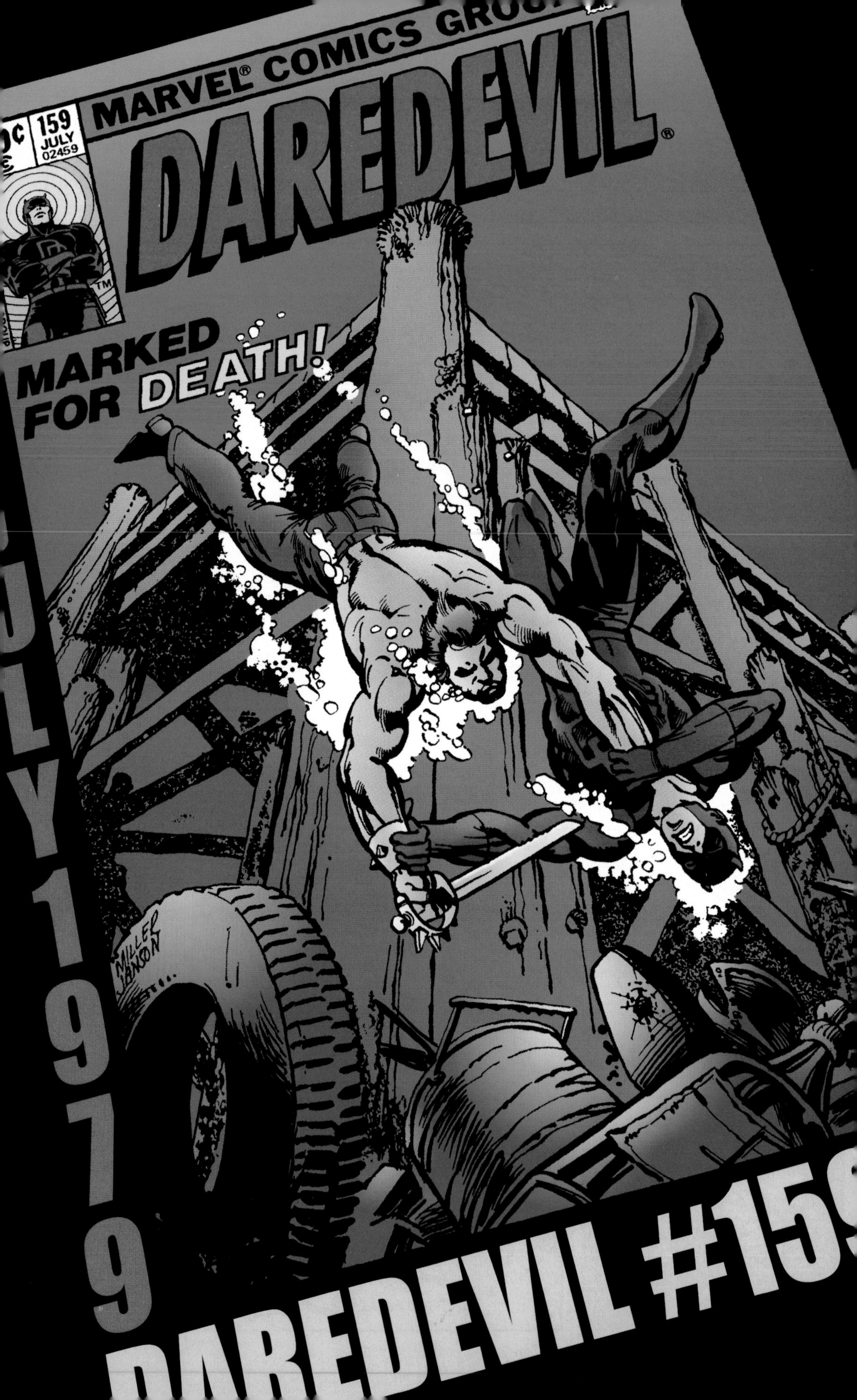

MARVEL® COMICS GROUP
DAREDEVIL®
159
JULY
02459
MARKED FOR DEATH!
MILLER JANSON
JULY 1979
DAREDEVIL #159

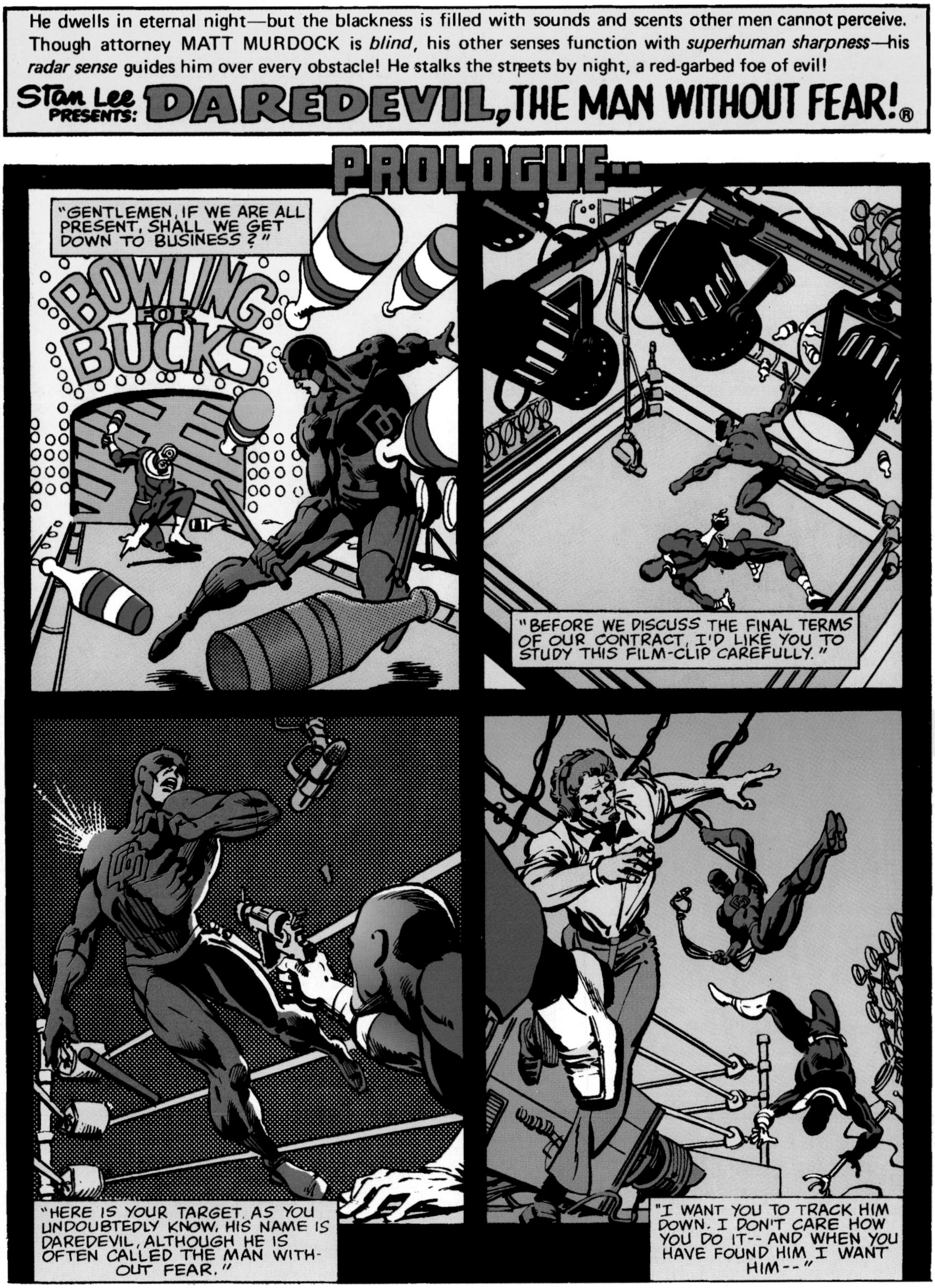
He dwells in eternal night—but the blackness is filled with sounds and scents other men cannot perceive. Though attorney MATT MURDOCK is *blind*, his other senses function with *superhuman sharpness*—his *radar sense* guides him over every obstacle! He stalks the streets by night, a red-garbed foe of evil!
Stan Lee PRESENTS: DAREDEVIL, THE MAN WITHOUT FEAR!®
PROLOGUE..
"GENTLEMEN, IF WE ARE ALL PRESENT, SHALL WE GET DOWN TO BUSINESS?"
BOWLING FOR BUCKS
"BEFORE WE DISCUSS THE FINAL TERMS OF OUR CONTRACT, I'D LIKE YOU TO STUDY THIS FILM-CLIP CAREFULLY."
"HERE IS YOUR TARGET. AS YOU UNDOUBTEDLY KNOW, HIS NAME IS DAREDEVIL, ALTHOUGH HE IS OFTEN CALLED THE MAN WITHOUT FEAR."
"I WANT YOU TO TRACK HIM DOWN. I DON'T CARE HOW YOU DO IT-- AND WHEN YOU HAVE FOUND HIM, I WANT HIM--"

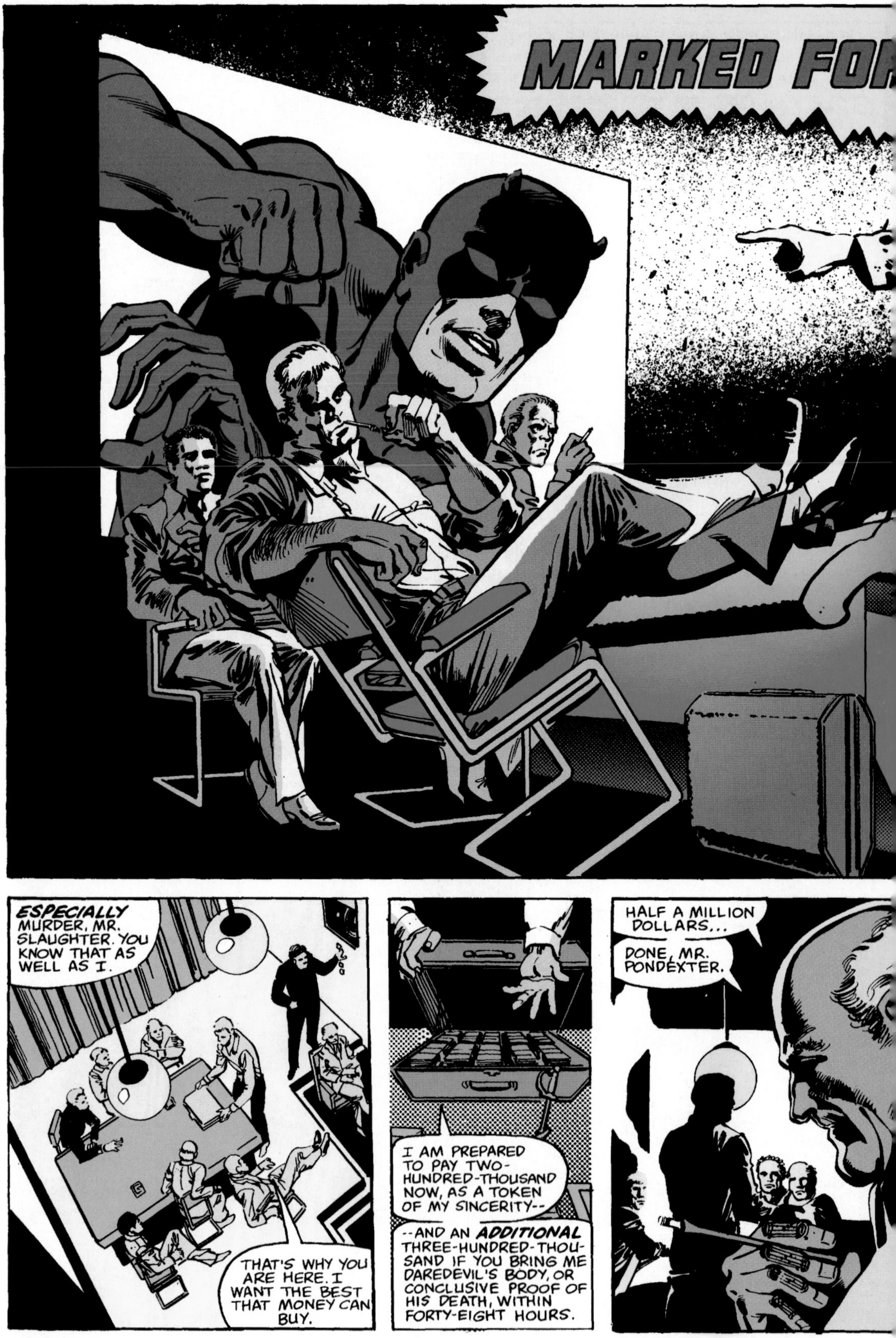

MARKED FO
ESPECIALLY MURDER, MR. SLAUGHTER. YOU KNOW THAT AS WELL AS I.
THAT'S WHY YOU ARE HERE. I WANT THE BEST THAT MONEY CAN BUY.
I AM PREPARED TO PAY TWO-HUNDRED-THOUSAND NOW, AS A TOKEN OF MY SINCERITY--
--AND AN ADDITIONAL THREE-HUNDRED-THOUSAND IF YOU BRING ME DAREDEVIL'S BODY, OR CONCLUSIVE PROOF OF HIS DEATH, WITHIN FORTY-EIGHT HOURS.
HALF A MILLION DOLLARS...
DONE, MR. PONDEXTER.

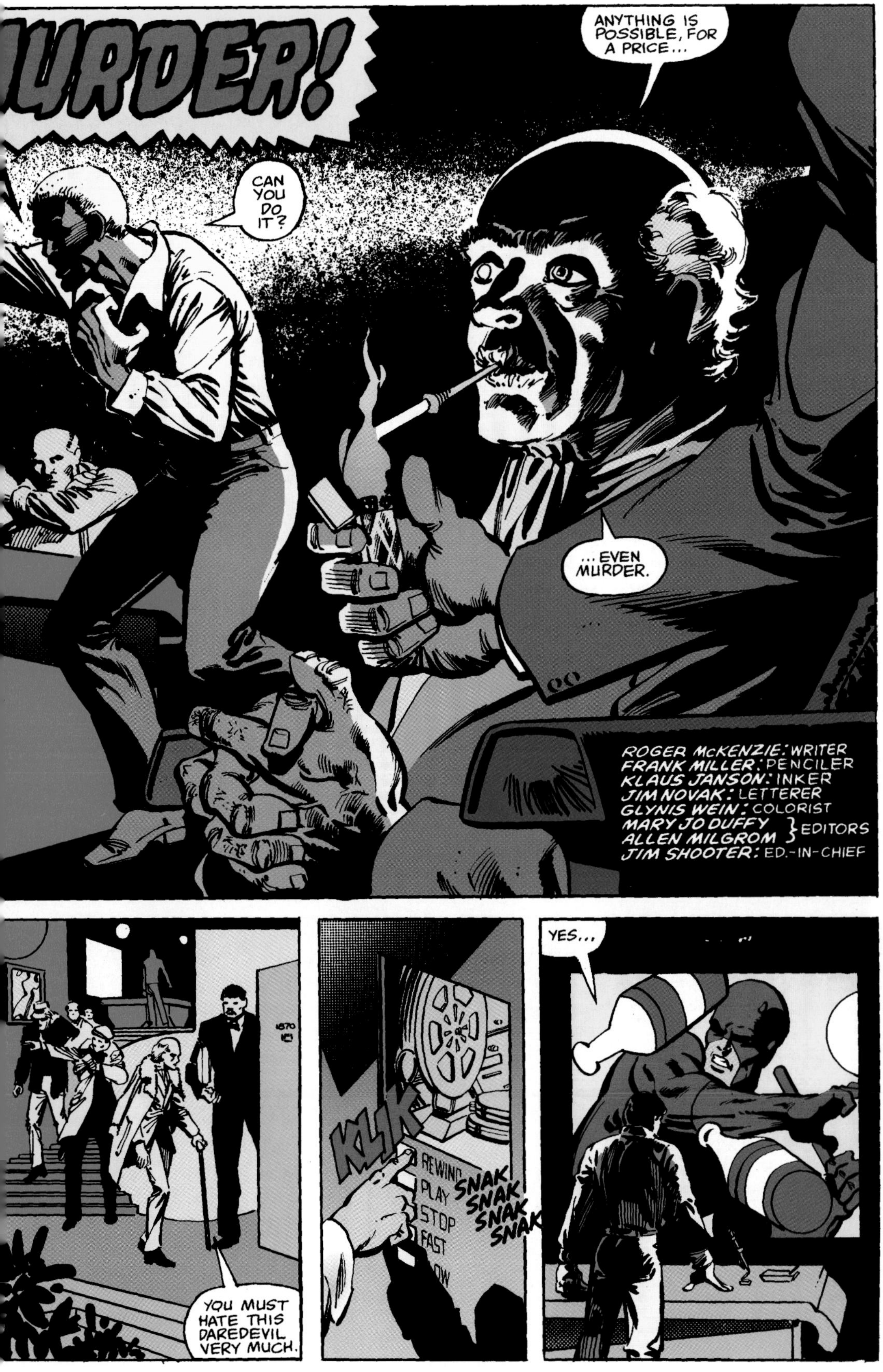

MURDER!
ANYTHING IS POSSIBLE, FOR A PRICE...
CAN YOU DO IT?
...EVEN MURDER.
ROGER McKENZIE: WRITER
FRANK MILLER: PENCILER
KLAUS JANSON: INKER
JIM NOVAK: LETTERER
GLYNIS WEIN: COLORIST
MARY JO DUFFY
ALLEN MILGROM } EDITORS
JIM SHOOTER: ED.-IN-CHIEF
YOU MUST HATE THIS DAREDEVIL VERY MUCH.
KLIK
REWIND
PLAY
STOP
FAST
SNAK SNAK SNAK SNAK
YES...

THE FOLLOWING AFTERNOON...

I'M SORRY, YOU'LL HAVE TO ASK DAREDEVIL ABOUT THAT!

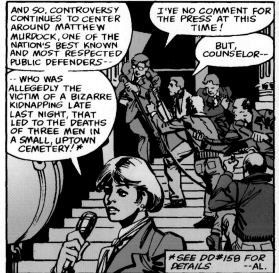

AND SO, CONTROVERSY CONTINUES TO CENTER AROUND MATTHEW MURDOCK, ONE OF THE NATION'S BEST KNOWN AND MOST RESPECTED PUBLIC DEFENDERS--

-- WHO WAS ALLEGEDLY THE VICTIM OF A BIZARRE KIDNAPPING LATE LAST NIGHT, THAT LED TO THE DEATHS OF THREE MEN IN A SMALL, UPTOWN CEMETERY! *

I'VE NO COMMENT FOR THE PRESS AT THIS TIME!

BUT, COUNSELOR--

*SEE DD#158 FOR DETAILS   --AL.

YOU HEARD MY PARTNER-- *NO* COMMENT!

IT'S WHAT WE *DIDN'T* HEAR THAT INTERESTS ME!

THERE'S MORE TO MATT MURDOCK THAN MEETS THE EYE-- I'D BET MY PRESS CARD ON IT!

BEN URICH TAKES A FINAL DRAG ON HIS CIGARETTE. THE VETERAN REPORTER DOESN'T REALIZE IT YET, BUT HE'S JUST EMBARKED ON WHAT WILL PROVE TO BE THE MOST ASTOUNDING STORY OF HIS CAREER...

YOU'RE LATE, COUNSELOR! ENJOYING YOUR SUDDEN NOTORIETY?

THAT'S HIM, LEACH, THE BLIND GUY! TELL MR. SLAUGHTER EVERYTHING'S GOING ACCORDING TO PLAN!

YOUR HONOR, WITH THE COURT'S INDULGENCE--

--AND ON BEHALF OF MY CLIENT, I MOVE FOR A TEMPORARY POSTPONEMENT OF THIS HEARING.

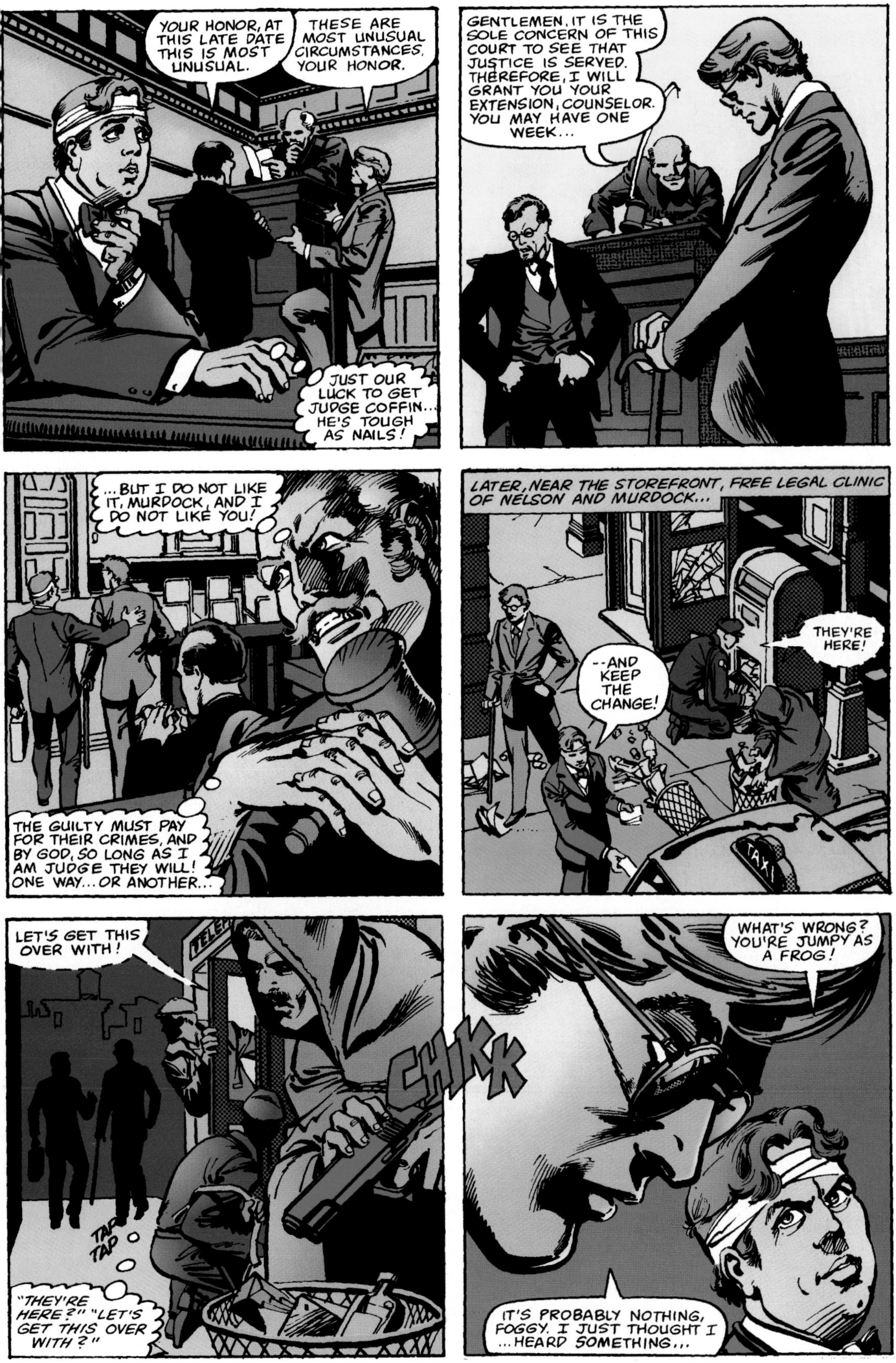
YOUR HONOR, AT THIS LATE DATE THIS IS MOST UNUSUAL.
THESE ARE MOST UNUSUAL CIRCUMSTANCES, YOUR HONOR.
JUST OUR LUCK TO GET JUDGE COFFIN... HE'S TOUGH AS NAILS!
GENTLEMEN, IT IS THE SOLE CONCERN OF THIS COURT TO SEE THAT JUSTICE IS SERVED. THEREFORE, I WILL GRANT YOU YOUR EXTENSION, COUNSELOR. YOU MAY HAVE ONE WEEK...
...BUT I DO NOT LIKE IT, MURDOCK, AND I DO NOT LIKE YOU!
THE GUILTY MUST PAY FOR THEIR CRIMES, AND BY GOD, SO LONG AS I AM JUDGE THEY WILL! ONE WAY... OR ANOTHER...
LATER, NEAR THE STOREFRONT, FREE LEGAL CLINIC OF NELSON AND MURDOCK...
--AND KEEP THE CHANGE!
THEY'RE HERE!
TAXI
LET'S GET THIS OVER WITH!
TAP TAP
"THEY'RE HERE?" "LET'S GET THIS OVER WITH?"
CHIKK
WHAT'S WRONG? YOU'RE JUMPY AS A FROG!
IT'S PROBABLY NOTHING, FOGGY. I JUST THOUGHT I ...HEARD SOMETHING...

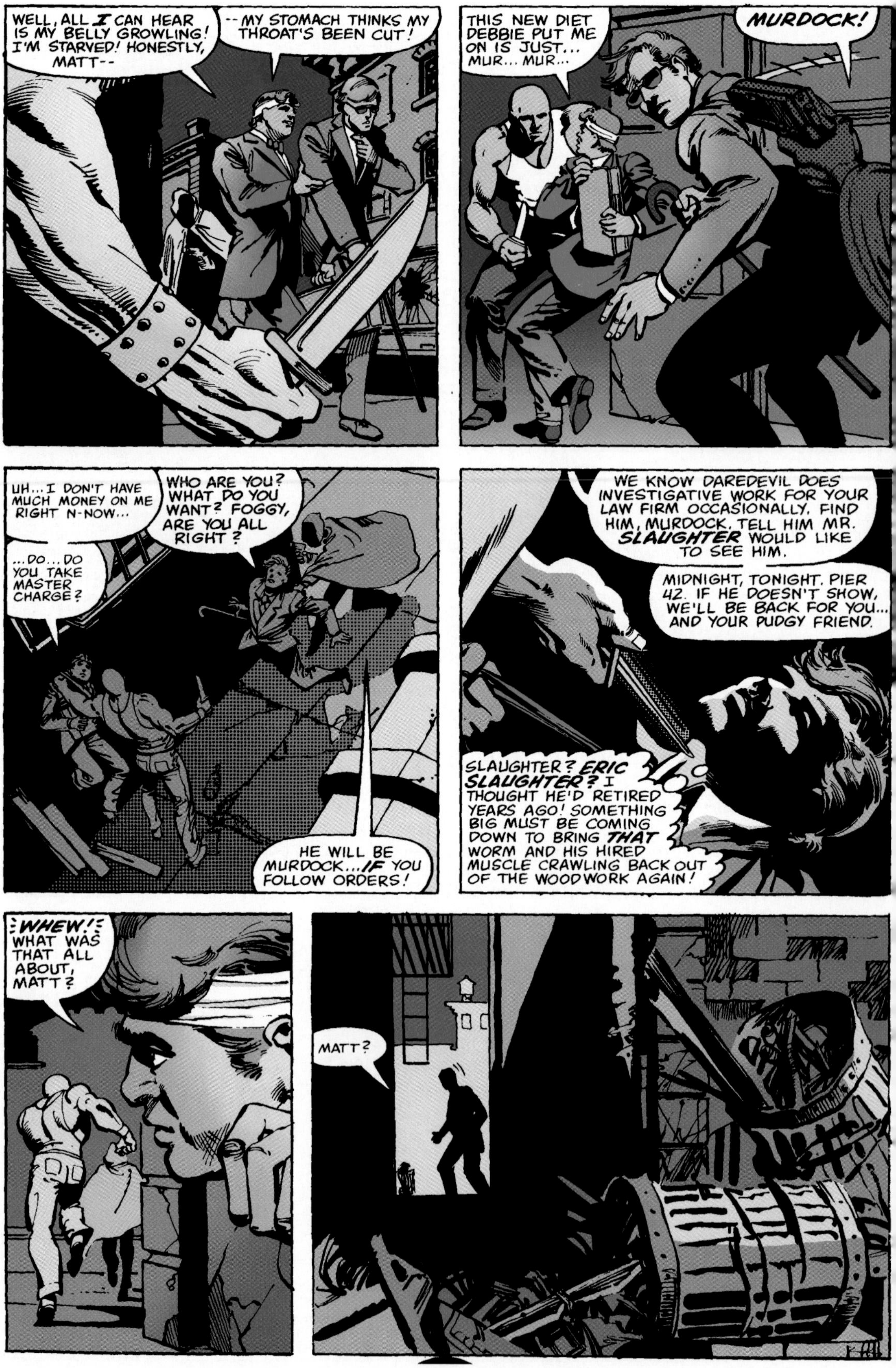
WELL, ALL I CAN HEAR IS MY BELLY GROWLING! I'M STARVED! HONESTLY, MATT--
--MY STOMACH THINKS MY THROAT'S BEEN CUT!
THIS NEW DIET DEBBIE PUT ME ON IS JUST... MUR... MUR...
MURDOCK!
UH... I DON'T HAVE MUCH MONEY ON ME RIGHT N-NOW...
...DO... DO YOU TAKE MASTER CHARGE?
WHO ARE YOU? WHAT DO YOU WANT? FOGGY, ARE YOU ALL RIGHT?
HE WILL BE MURDOCK... IF YOU FOLLOW ORDERS!
WE KNOW DAREDEVIL DOES INVESTIGATIVE WORK FOR YOUR LAW FIRM OCCASIONALLY. FIND HIM, MURDOCK. TELL HIM MR. SLAUGHTER WOULD LIKE TO SEE HIM.
MIDNIGHT, TONIGHT. PIER 42. IF HE DOESN'T SHOW, WE'LL BE BACK FOR YOU... AND YOUR PUDGY FRIEND.
SLAUGHTER? ERIC SLAUGHTER? I THOUGHT HE'D RETIRED YEARS AGO! SOMETHING BIG MUST BE COMING DOWN TO BRING THAT WORM AND HIS HIRED MUSCLE CRAWLING BACK OUT OF THE WOODWORK AGAIN!
WHEW! WHAT WAS THAT ALL ABOUT, MATT?
MATT?

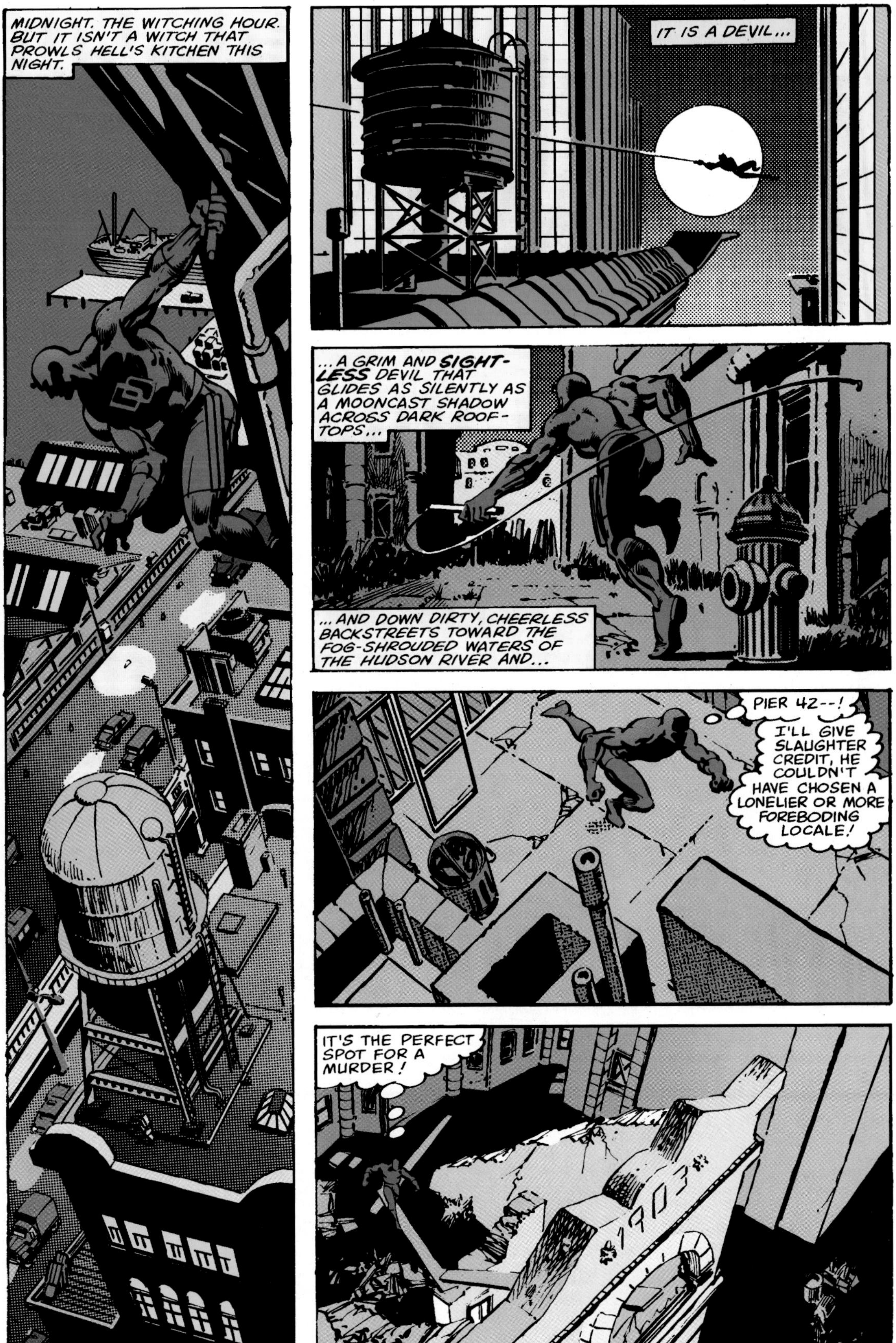
MIDNIGHT. THE WITCHING HOUR. BUT IT ISN'T A WITCH THAT PROWLS HELL'S KITCHEN THIS NIGHT.
IT IS A DEVIL...
...A GRIM AND SIGHT-LESS DEVIL THAT GLIDES AS SILENTLY AS A MOONCAST SHADOW ACROSS DARK ROOF-TOPS...
...AND DOWN DIRTY, CHEERLESS BACKSTREETS TOWARD THE FOG-SHROUDED WATERS OF THE HUDSON RIVER AND...
PIER 42--!
I'LL GIVE SLAUGHTER CREDIT, HE COULDN'T HAVE CHOSEN A LONELIER OR MORE FOREBODING LOCALE!
IT'S THE PERFECT SPOT FOR A MURDER!
1903

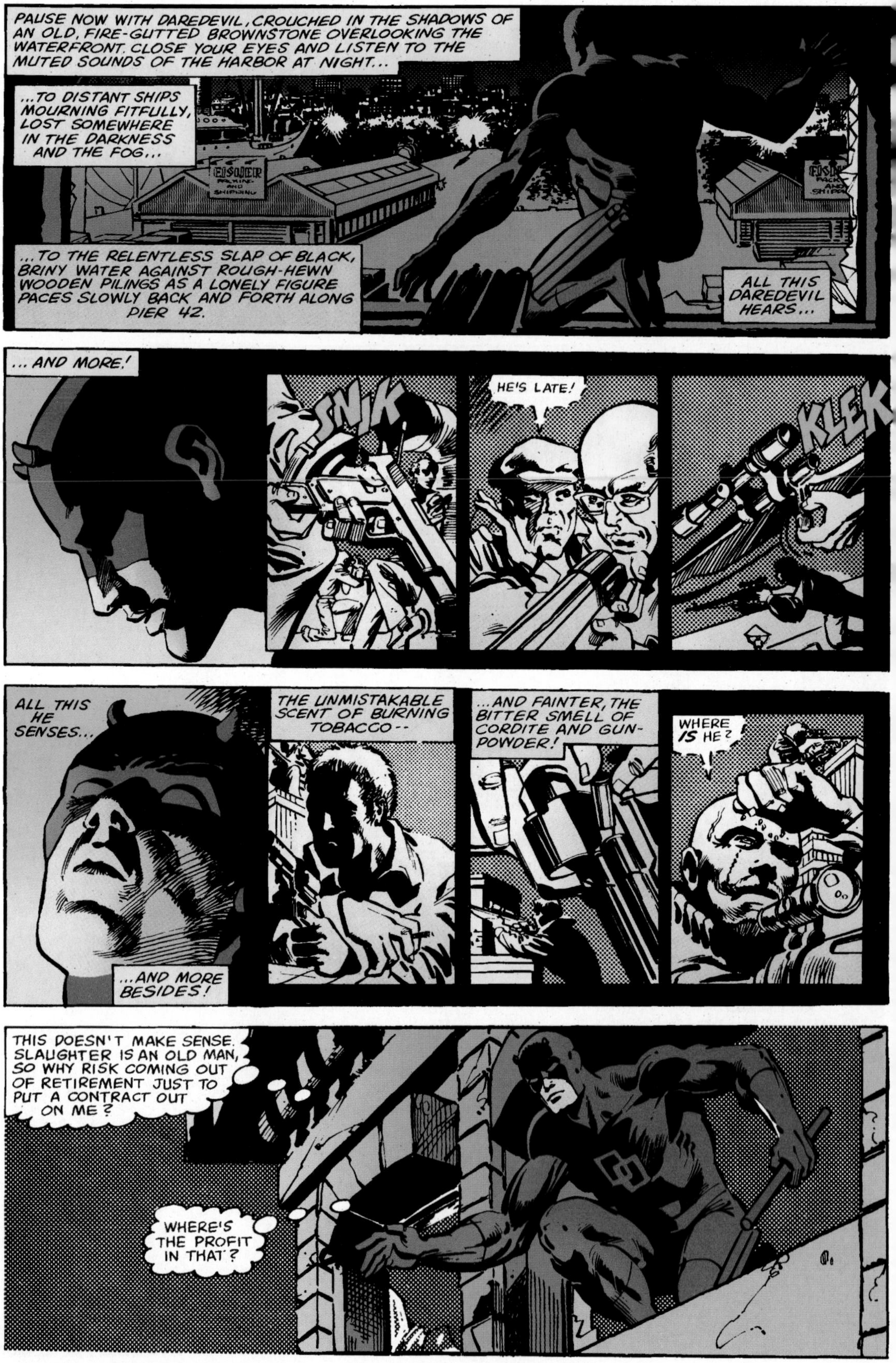
PAUSE NOW WITH DAREDEVIL, CROUCHED IN THE SHADOWS OF AN OLD, FIRE-GUTTED BROWNSTONE OVERLOOKING THE WATERFRONT. CLOSE YOUR EYES AND LISTEN TO THE MUTED SOUNDS OF THE HARBOR AT NIGHT...
...TO DISTANT SHIPS MOURNING FITFULLY, LOST SOMEWHERE IN THE DARKNESS AND THE FOG...
FISHER PACKING AND SHIPPING
...TO THE RELENTLESS SLAP OF BLACK, BRINY WATER AGAINST ROUGH-HEWN WOODEN PILINGS AS A LONELY FIGURE PACES SLOWLY BACK AND FORTH ALONG PIER 42.
ALL THIS DAREDEVIL HEARS...
...AND MORE!
SNIK
HE'S LATE!
KLEK
ALL THIS HE SENSES...
...AND MORE BESIDES!
THE UNMISTAKABLE SCENT OF BURNING TOBACCO--
...AND FAINTER, THE BITTER SMELL OF CORDITE AND GUN-POWDER!
WHERE IS HE?
THIS DOESN'T MAKE SENSE. SLAUGHTER IS AN OLD MAN, SO WHY RISK COMING OUT OF RETIREMENT JUST TO PUT A CONTRACT OUT ON ME?
WHERE'S THE PROFIT IN THAT?

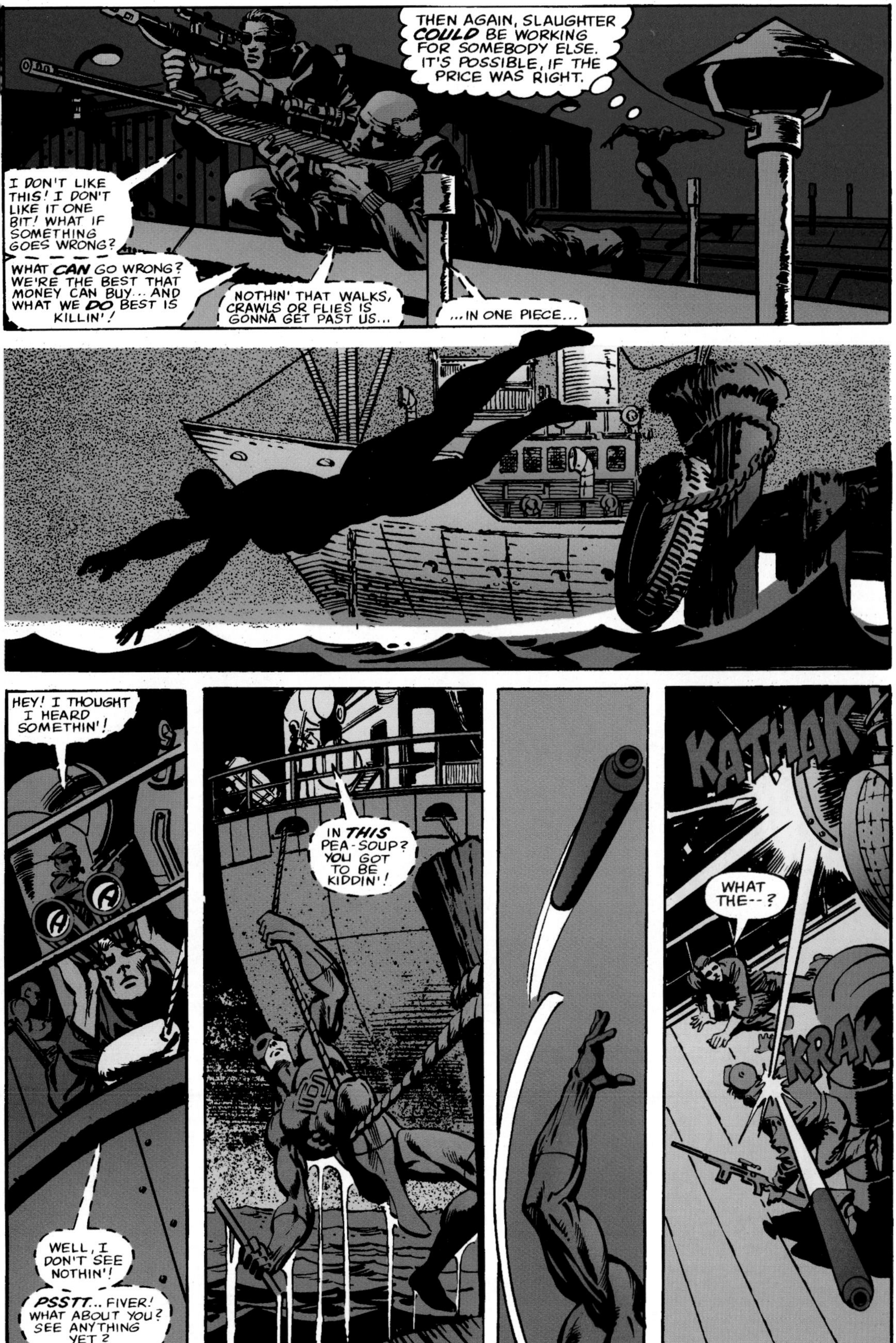
THEN AGAIN, SLAUGHTER COULD BE WORKING FOR SOMEBODY ELSE. IT'S POSSIBLE, IF THE PRICE WAS RIGHT.
I DON'T LIKE THIS! I DON'T LIKE IT ONE BIT! WHAT IF SOMETHING GOES WRONG?
WHAT CAN GO WRONG? WE'RE THE BEST THAT MONEY CAN BUY... AND WHAT WE DO BEST IS KILLIN'!
NOTHIN' THAT WALKS, CRAWLS OR FLIES IS GONNA GET PAST US...
...IN ONE PIECE...
HEY! I THOUGHT I HEARD SOMETHIN'!
WELL, I DON'T SEE NOTHIN'!
PSSTT... FIVER! WHAT ABOUT YOU? SEE ANYTHING YET?
IN THIS PEA-SOUP? YOU GOT TO BE KIDDIN'!
KATHAK
WHAT THE--?
KRAK

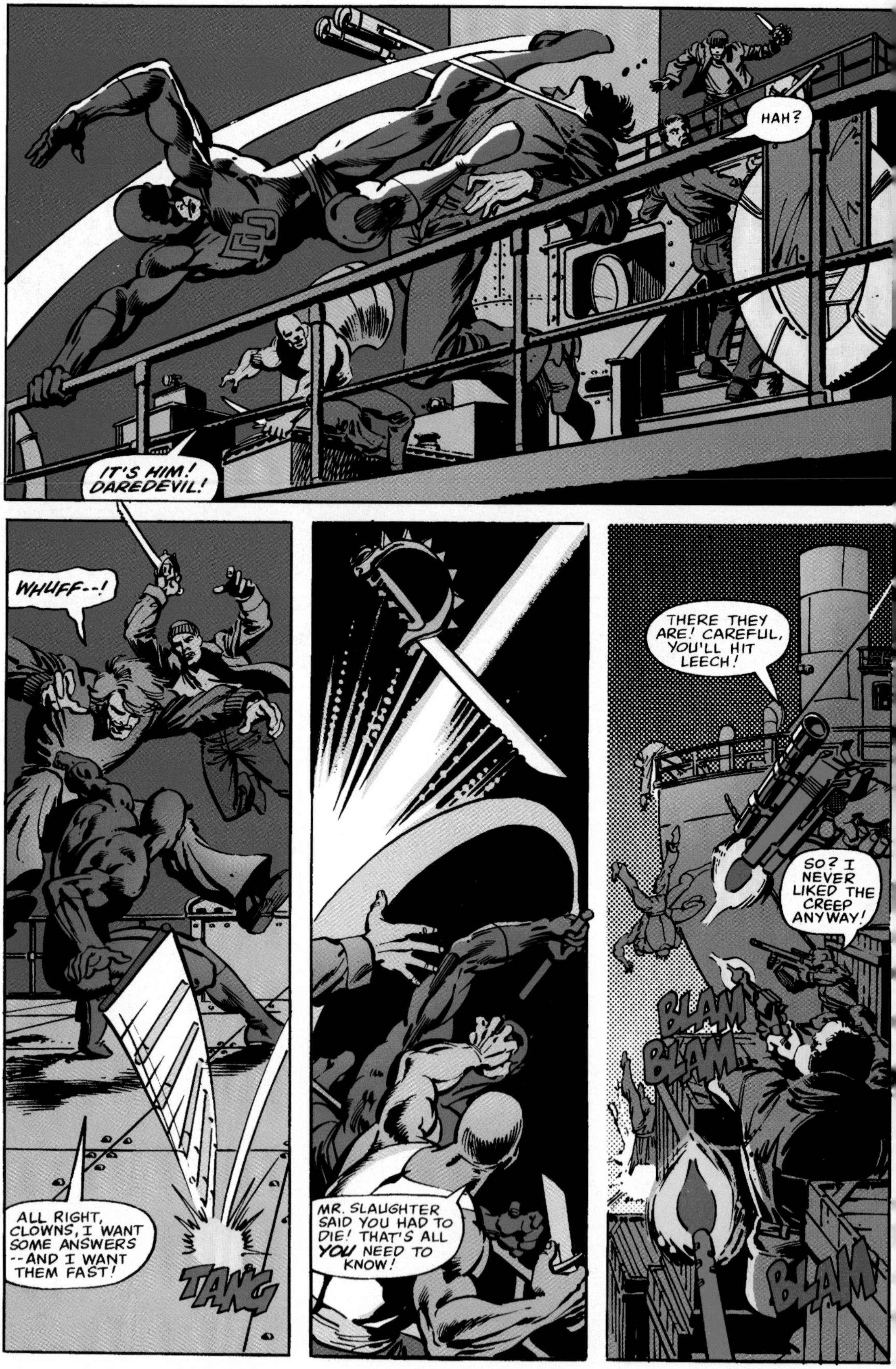
HAH?
IT'S HIM! DAREDEVIL!
WHUFF--!
ALL RIGHT, CLOWNS, I WANT SOME ANSWERS --AND I WANT THEM FAST!
TANG
MR. SLAUGHTER SAID YOU HAD TO DIE! THAT'S ALL YOU NEED TO KNOW!
THERE THEY ARE! CAREFUL, YOU'LL HIT LEECH!
SO? I NEVER LIKED THE CREEP ANYWAY!
BLAM
BLAM
BLAM

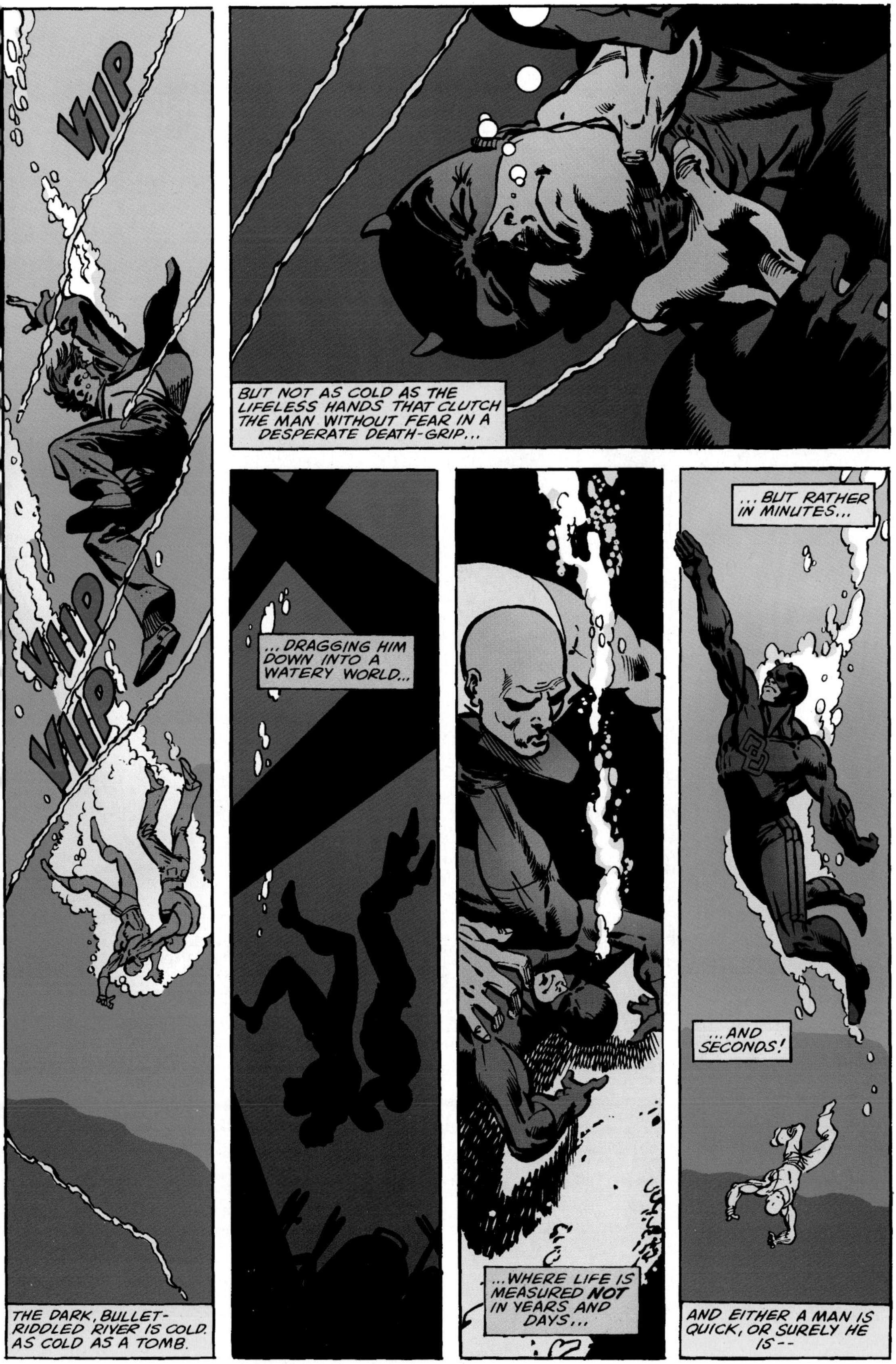
VIIP
VIIP
VIIP
THE DARK, BULLET-RIDDLED RIVER IS COLD. AS COLD AS A TOMB.
BUT NOT AS COLD AS THE LIFELESS HANDS THAT CLUTCH THE MAN WITHOUT FEAR IN A DESPERATE DEATH-GRIP...
...DRAGGING HIM DOWN INTO A WATERY WORLD...
...WHERE LIFE IS MEASURED NOT IN YEARS AND DAYS...
...BUT RATHER IN MINUTES...
...AND SECONDS!
AND EITHER A MAN IS QUICK, OR SURELY HE IS--

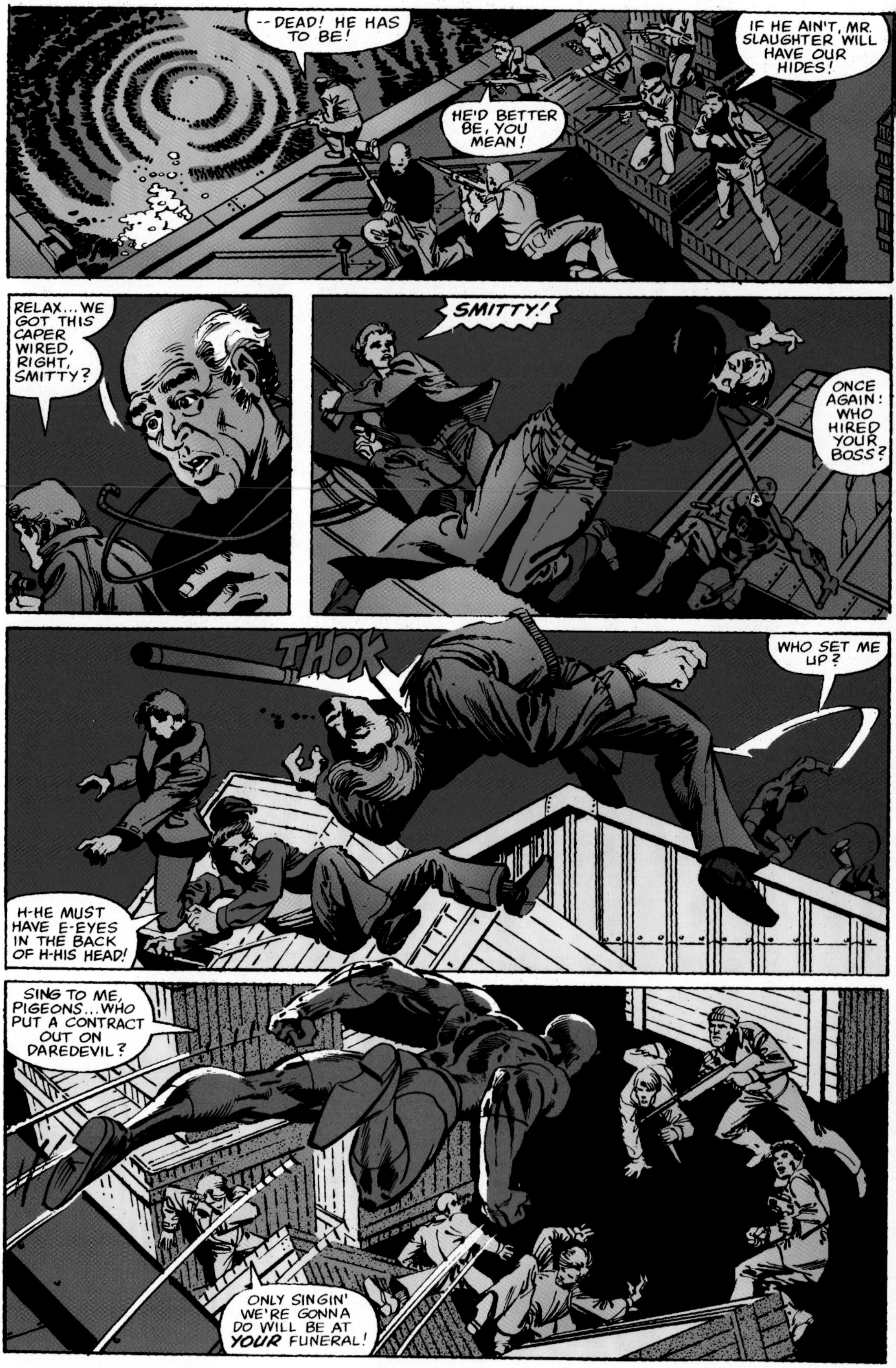
--DEAD! HE HAS TO BE!
HE'D BETTER BE, YOU MEAN!
IF HE AIN'T, MR. SLAUGHTER WILL HAVE OUR HIDES!
RELAX... WE GOT THIS CAPER WIRED, RIGHT, SMITTY?
SMITTY!
ONCE AGAIN: WHO HIRED YOUR BOSS?
THOK
WHO SET ME UP?
H-HE MUST HAVE E-EYES IN THE BACK OF H-HIS HEAD!
SING TO ME, PIGEONS... WHO PUT A CONTRACT OUT ON DAREDEVIL?
ONLY SINGIN' WE'RE GONNA DO WILL BE AT *YOUR* FUNERAL!

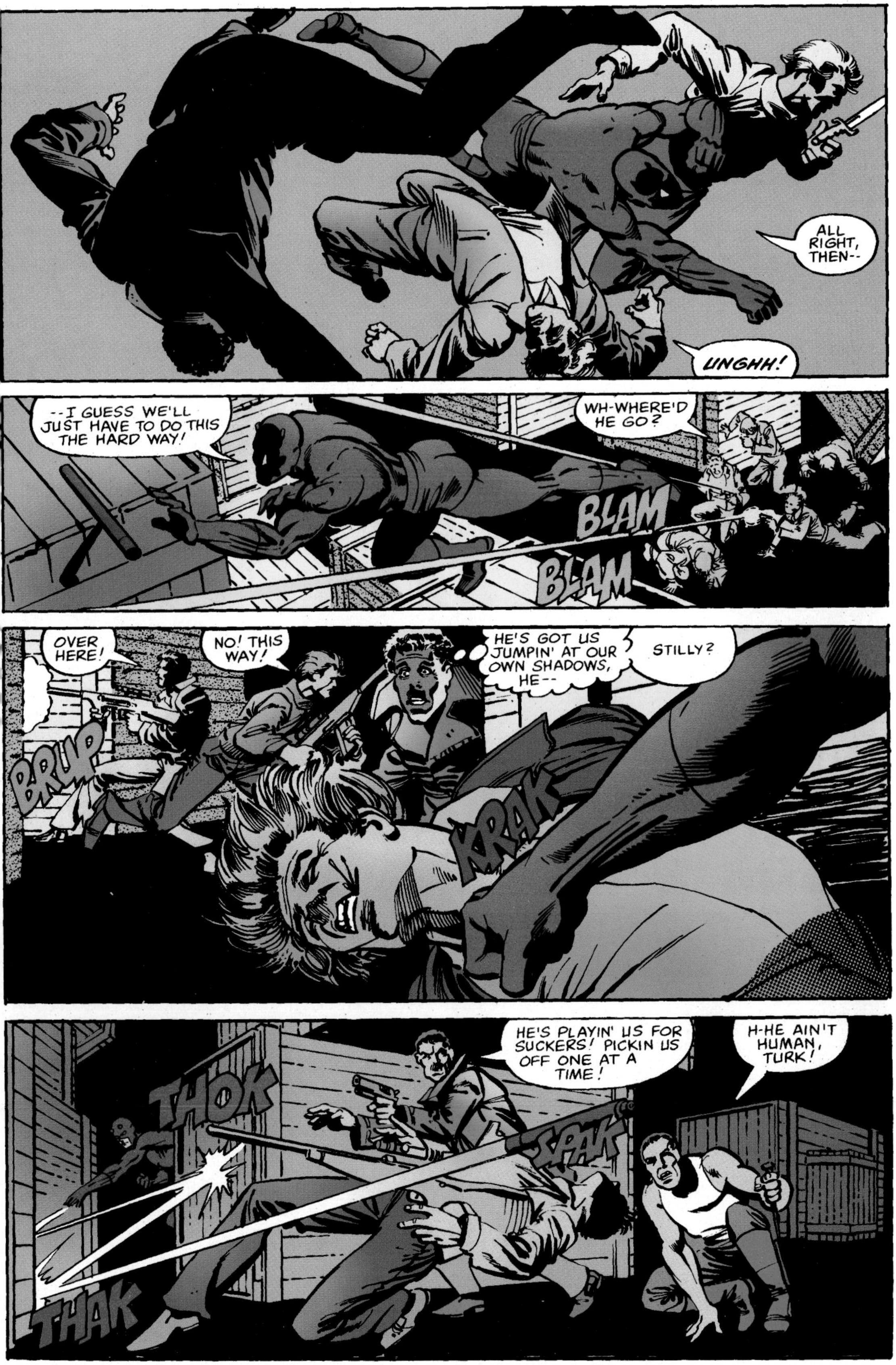
ALL RIGHT, THEN--
UNGHH!
--I GUESS WE'LL JUST HAVE TO DO THIS THE HARD WAY!
WH-WHERE'D HE GO?
BLAM
BLAM
OVER HERE!
NO! THIS WAY!
HE'S GOT US JUMPIN' AT OUR OWN SHADOWS, HE--
STILLY?
BRUP
KRAK
HE'S PLAYIN' US FOR SUCKERS! PICKIN US OFF ONE AT A TIME!
H-HE AIN'T HUMAN, TURK!
THOK
SPAK
THAK

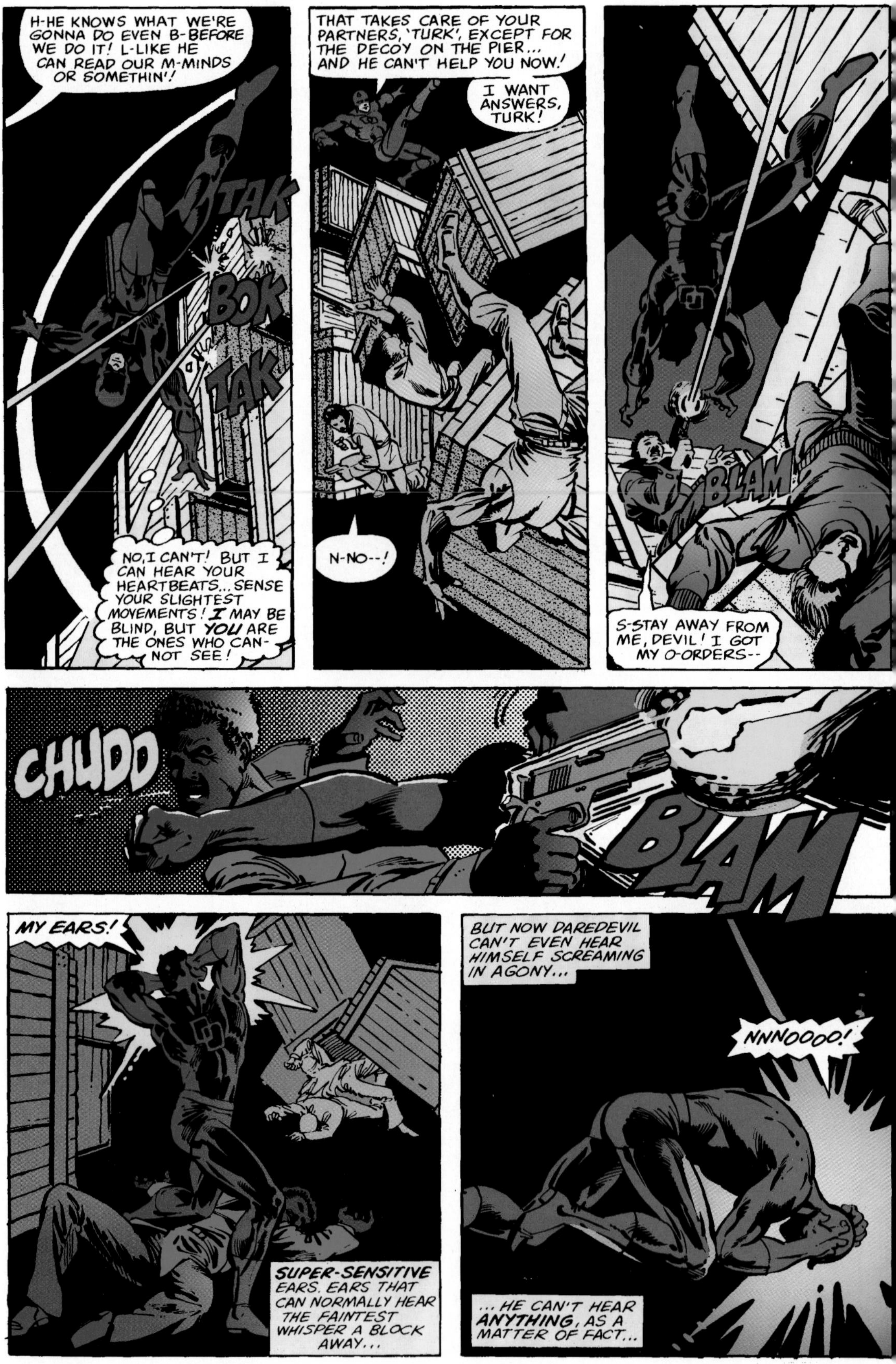
H-HE KNOWS WHAT WE'RE GONNA DO EVEN B-BEFORE WE DO IT! L-LIKE HE CAN READ OUR M-MINDS OR SOMETHIN'!
TAK
BOK
TAK
NO, I CAN'T! BUT I CAN HEAR YOUR HEARTBEATS... SENSE YOUR SLIGHTEST MOVEMENTS! I MAY BE BLIND, BUT YOU ARE THE ONES WHO CAN-NOT SEE!
THAT TAKES CARE OF YOUR PARTNERS, 'TURK', EXCEPT FOR THE DECOY ON THE PIER... AND HE CAN'T HELP YOU NOW!
I WANT ANSWERS, TURK!
N-NO--!
BLAM
S-STAY AWAY FROM ME, DEVIL! I GOT MY O-ORDERS--
CHUDD
BLAM
MY EARS!
SUPER-SENSITIVE EARS. EARS THAT CAN NORMALLY HEAR THE FAINTEST WHISPER A BLOCK AWAY...
BUT NOW DAREDEVIL CAN'T EVEN HEAR HIMSELF SCREAMING IN AGONY...
NNNOOOO!
...HE CAN'T HEAR ANYTHING, AS A MATTER OF FACT...

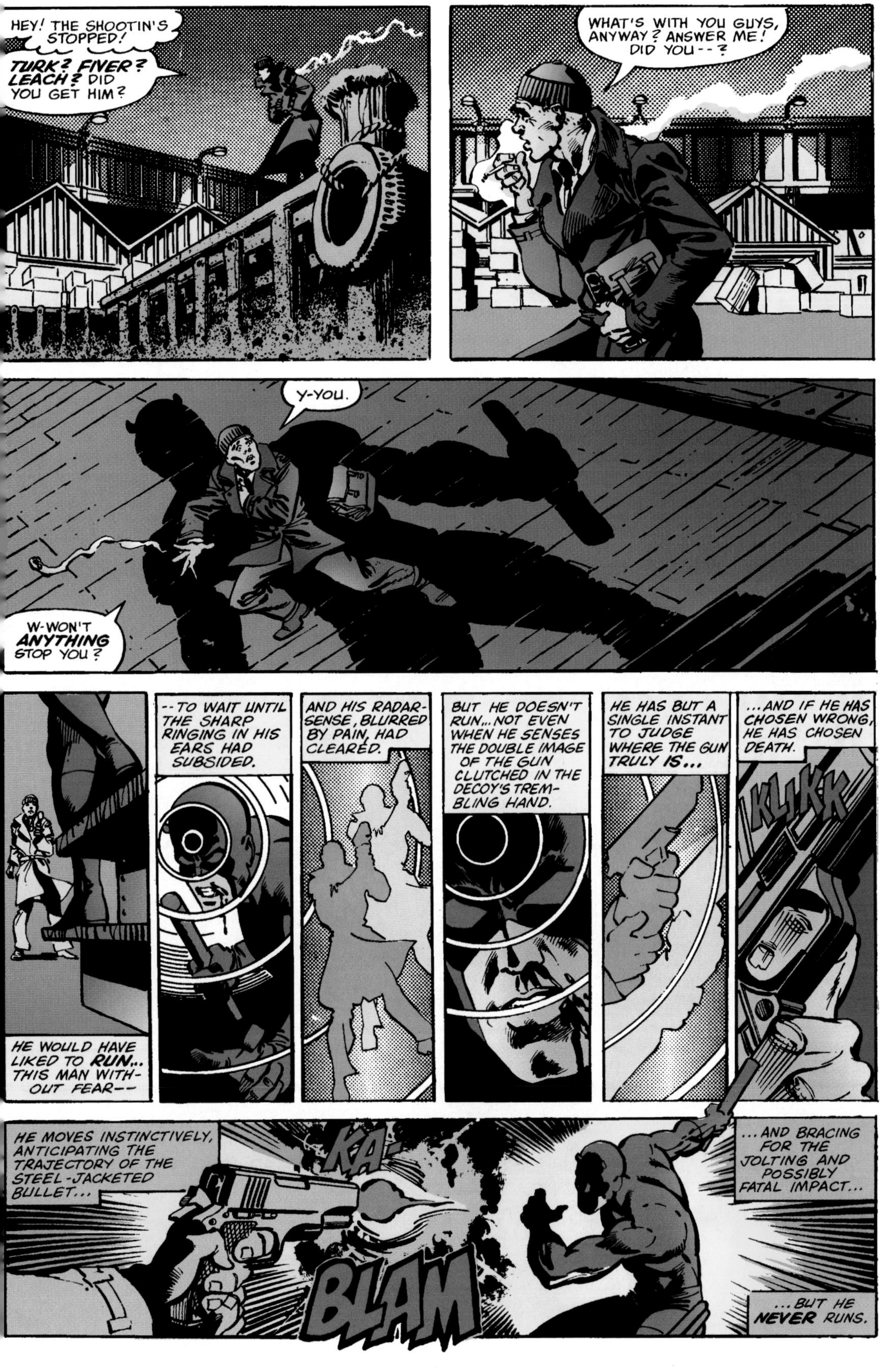
HEY! THE SHOOTIN'S STOPPED!
TURK? FIVER? LEACH? DID YOU GET HIM?
WHAT'S WITH YOU GUYS, ANYWAY? ANSWER ME! DID YOU--?
Y-YOU.
W-WON'T ANYTHING STOP YOU?
HE WOULD HAVE LIKED TO RUN... THIS MAN WITHOUT FEAR--
--TO WAIT UNTIL THE SHARP RINGING IN HIS EARS HAD SUBSIDED.
AND HIS RADAR-SENSE, BLURRED BY PAIN, HAD CLEARED.
BUT HE DOESN'T RUN... NOT EVEN WHEN HE SENSES THE DOUBLE IMAGE OF THE GUN CLUTCHED IN THE DECOY'S TREMBLING HAND.
HE HAS BUT A SINGLE INSTANT TO JUDGE WHERE THE GUN TRULY IS...
...AND IF HE HAS CHOSEN WRONG, HE HAS CHOSEN DEATH.
KLIKK
HE MOVES INSTINCTIVELY, ANTICIPATING THE TRAJECTORY OF THE STEEL-JACKETED BULLET...
KA-BLAM
...AND BRACING FOR THE JOLTING AND POSSIBLY FATAL IMPACT...
...BUT HE NEVER RUNS.

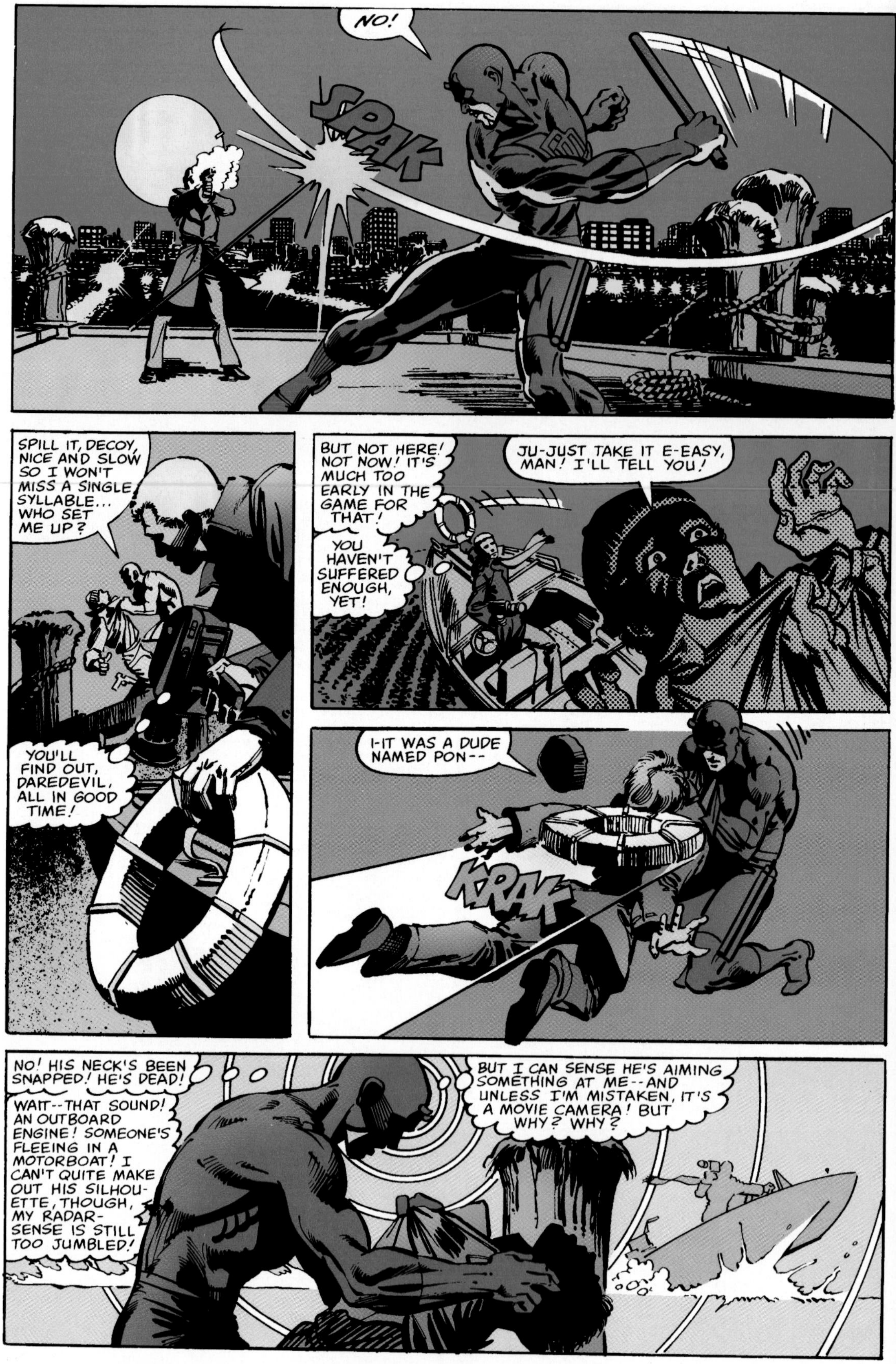
NO!
SPAK
SPILL IT, DECOY, NICE AND SLOW SO I WON'T MISS A SINGLE SYLLABLE... WHO SET ME UP?
YOU'LL FIND OUT, DAREDEVIL, ALL IN GOOD TIME!
BUT NOT HERE! NOT NOW! IT'S MUCH TOO EARLY IN THE GAME FOR THAT!
YOU HAVEN'T SUFFERED ENOUGH, YET!
JU-JUST TAKE IT E-EASY, MAN! I'LL TELL YOU!
I-IT WAS A DUDE NAMED PON--
KRAK
NO! HIS NECK'S BEEN SNAPPED! HE'S DEAD!
WAIT--THAT SOUND! AN OUTBOARD ENGINE! SOMEONE'S FLEEING IN A MOTORBOAT! I CAN'T QUITE MAKE OUT HIS SILHOUETTE, THOUGH, MY RADAR-SENSE IS STILL TOO JUMBLED!
BUT I CAN SENSE HE'S AIMING SOMETHING AT ME--AND UNLESS I'M MISTAKEN, IT'S A MOVIE CAMERA! BUT WHY? WHY?

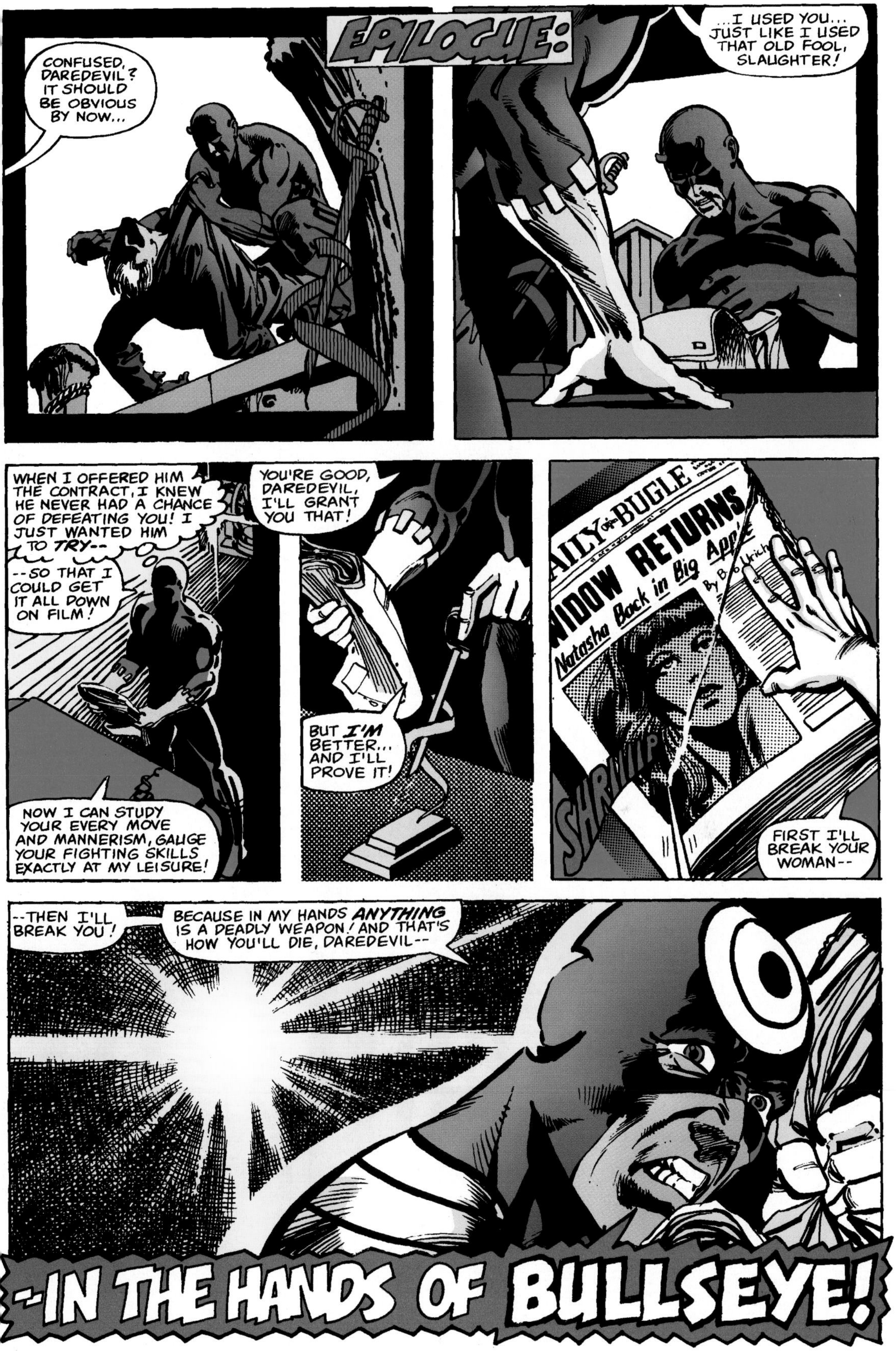
EPILOGUE:
CONFUSED, DAREDEVIL? IT SHOULD BE OBVIOUS BY NOW...
...I USED YOU... JUST LIKE I USED THAT OLD FOOL, SLAUGHTER!
WHEN I OFFERED HIM THE CONTRACT, I KNEW HE NEVER HAD A CHANCE OF DEFEATING YOU! I JUST WANTED HIM TO TRY--
--SO THAT I COULD GET IT ALL DOWN ON FILM!
NOW I CAN STUDY YOUR EVERY MOVE AND MANNERISM, GAUGE YOUR FIGHTING SKILLS EXACTLY AT MY LEISURE!
YOU'RE GOOD, DAREDEVIL, I'LL GRANT YOU THAT!
BUT I'M BETTER... AND I'LL PROVE IT!
DAILY BUGLE
WIDOW RETURNS
Natasha Back in Big Apple
SHRUUP
FIRST I'LL BREAK YOUR WOMAN--
--THEN I'LL BREAK YOU!
BECAUSE IN MY HANDS ANYTHING IS A DEADLY WEAPON! AND THAT'S HOW YOU'LL DIE, DAREDEVIL--
--IN THE HANDS OF BULLSEYE!

PRESENTING A MIGHTY MARVEL BONUS PAGE-- THE *SECRETS* OF DAREDEVIL'S BILLY CLUB!

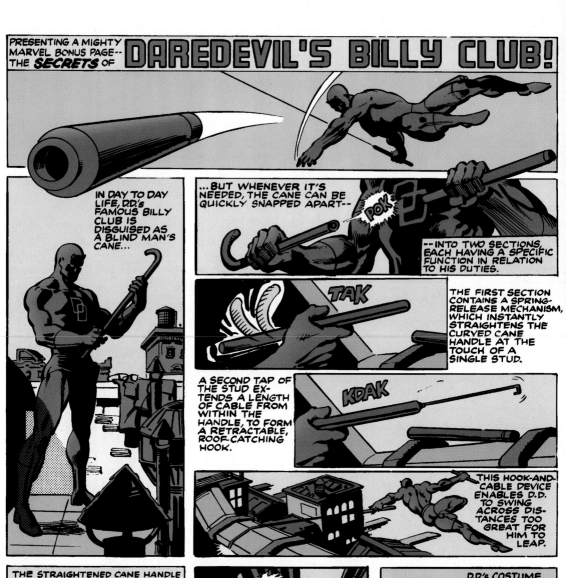

IN DAY TO DAY LIFE, D.D.'s FAMOUS BILLY CLUB IS DISGUISED AS A BLIND MAN'S CANE...

...BUT WHENEVER IT'S NEEDED, THE CANE CAN BE QUICKLY SNAPPED APART--

POK

--INTO TWO SECTIONS, EACH HAVING A SPECIFIC FUNCTION IN RELATION TO HIS DUTIES.

TAK

THE FIRST SECTION CONTAINS A SPRING-RELEASE MECHANISM, WHICH INSTANTLY STRAIGHTENS THE CURVED CANE HANDLE AT THE TOUCH OF A SINGLE STUD.

A SECOND TAP OF THE STUD EXTENDS A LENGTH OF CABLE FROM WITHIN THE HANDLE, TO FORM A RETRACTABLE, ROOF-CATCHING HOOK.

KDAK

THIS HOOK-AND-CABLE DEVICE ENABLES D.D. TO SWING ACROSS DISTANCES TOO GREAT FOR HIM TO LEAP.

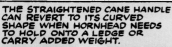

THE STRAIGHTENED CANE HANDLE CAN REVERT TO ITS CURVED SHAPE WHEN HORNHEAD NEEDS TO HOLD ONTO A LEDGE OR CARRY ADDED WEIGHT.

THOK!

THE REMAINING SECTION OF THE BILLY CLUB/CANE IS A SUPERBLY BALANCED PIECE OF STEEL-REINFORCED WOOD THAT D.D. THROWS WITH CONSUMMATE SKILL.

D.D.'s COSTUME FEATURES A LEG-HOLSTER, IN WHICH HE STORES BOTH SECTIONS OF THIS ELEGANT WEAPON.

DAREDEVIL #160

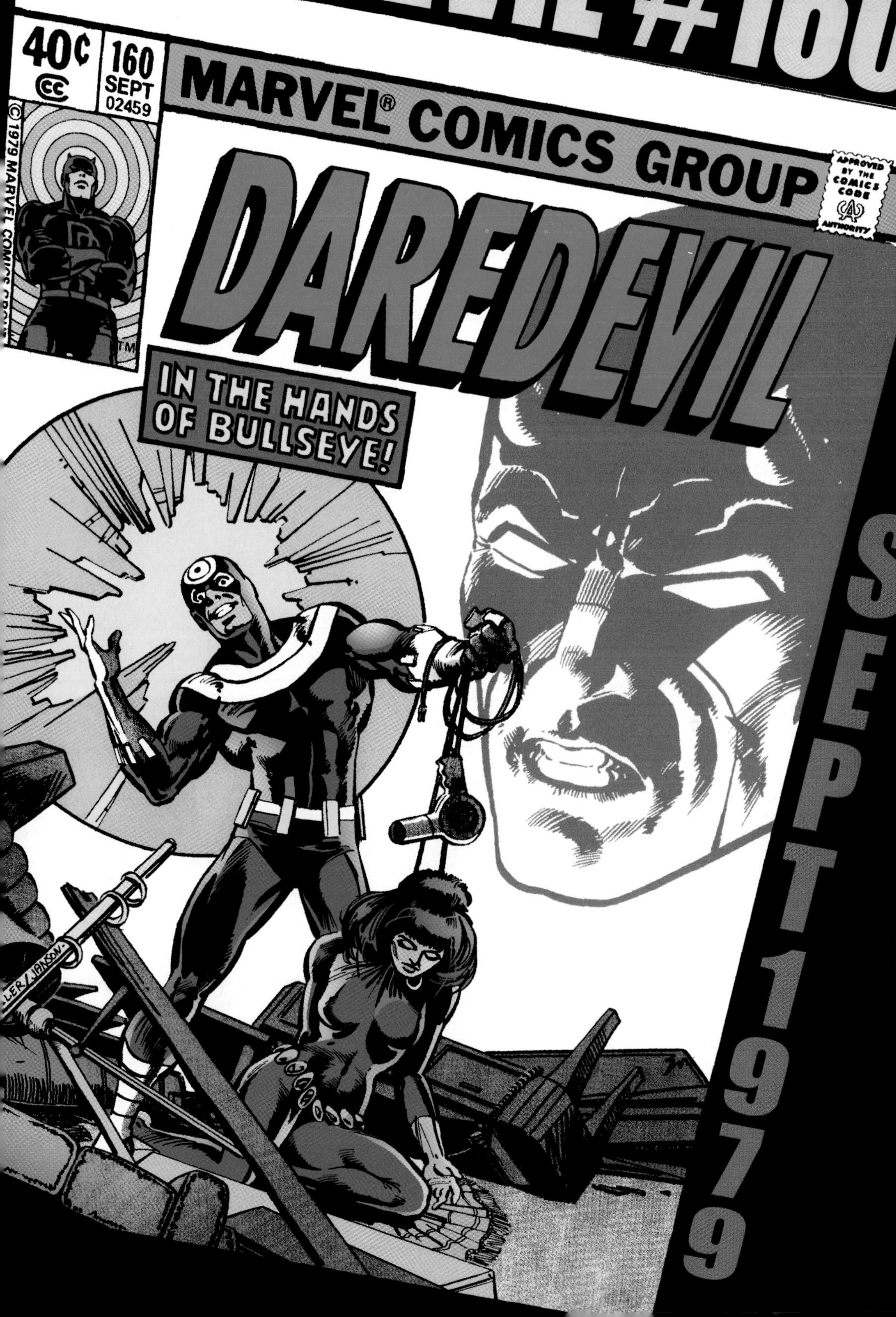
40¢
160
SEPT
02459
© 1979 MARVEL COMICS GROUP
MARVEL® COMICS GROUP
APPROVED BY THE COMICS CODE AUTHORITY
DAREDEVIL
IN THE HANDS OF BULLSEYE!

SEPT 1979

He dwells in eternal night—but the blackness is filled with sounds and scents other men cannot perceive. Though attorney MATT MURDOCK is *blind*, his other senses function with *superhuman sharpness*—his *radar sense* guides him over every obstacle! He stalks the streets by night, a red-garbed foe of evil!

Stan Lee PRESENTS: DAREDEVIL, THE MAN WITHOUT FEAR!®

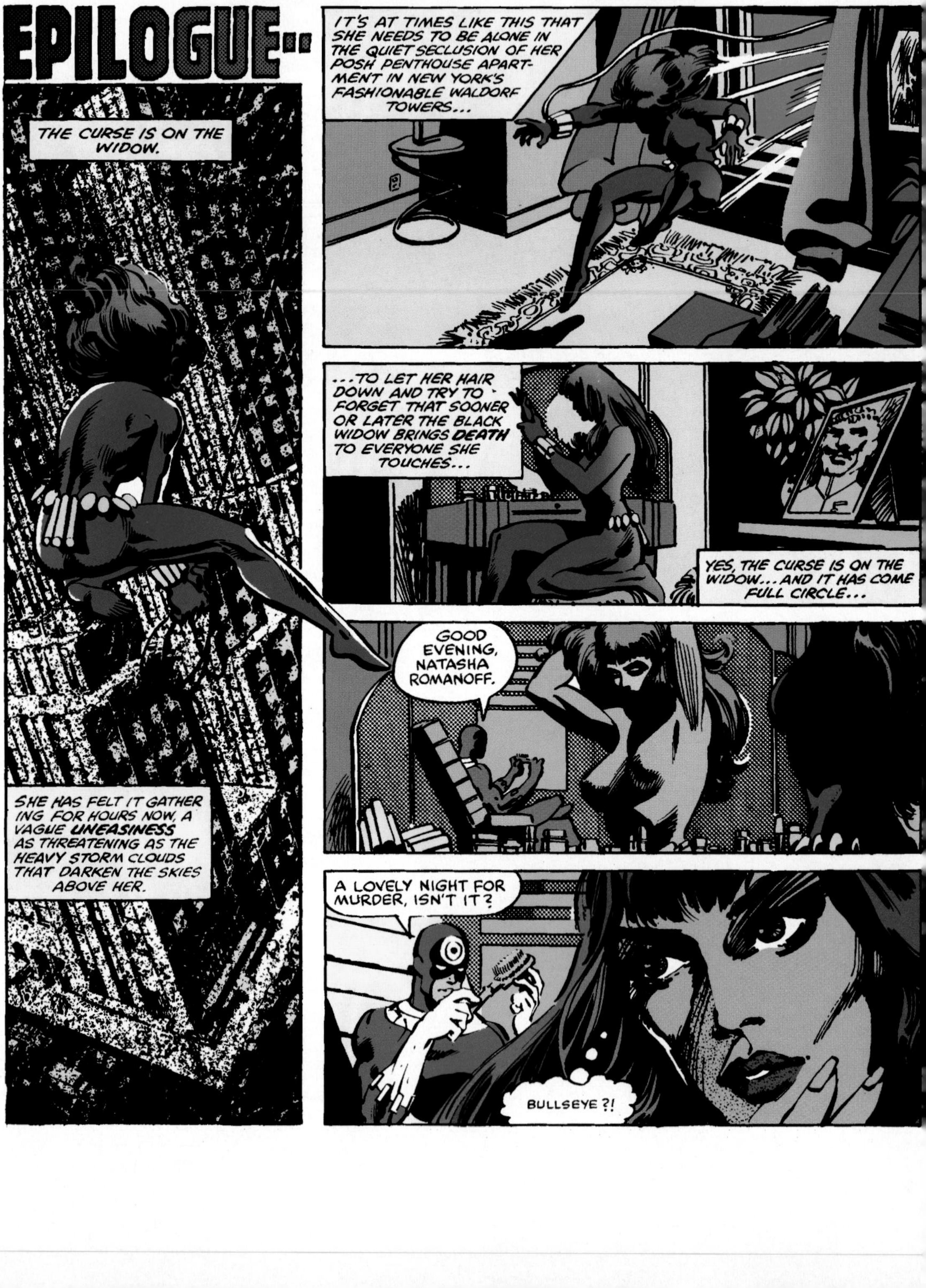

EPILOGUE..
THE CURSE IS ON THE WIDOW.
IT'S AT TIMES LIKE THIS THAT SHE NEEDS TO BE ALONE IN THE QUIET SECLUSION OF HER POSH PENTHOUSE APARTMENT IN NEW YORK'S FASHIONABLE WALDORF TOWERS...
...TO LET HER HAIR DOWN AND TRY TO FORGET THAT SOONER OR LATER THE BLACK WIDOW BRINGS DEATH TO EVERYONE SHE TOUCHES...
YES, THE CURSE IS ON THE WIDOW... AND IT HAS COME FULL CIRCLE...
SHE HAS FELT IT GATHERING FOR HOURS NOW, A VAGUE UNEASINESS AS THREATENING AS THE HEAVY STORM CLOUDS THAT DARKEN THE SKIES ABOVE HER.
GOOD EVENING, NATASHA ROMANOFF.
A LOVELY NIGHT FOR MURDER, ISN'T IT?
BULLSEYE ?!

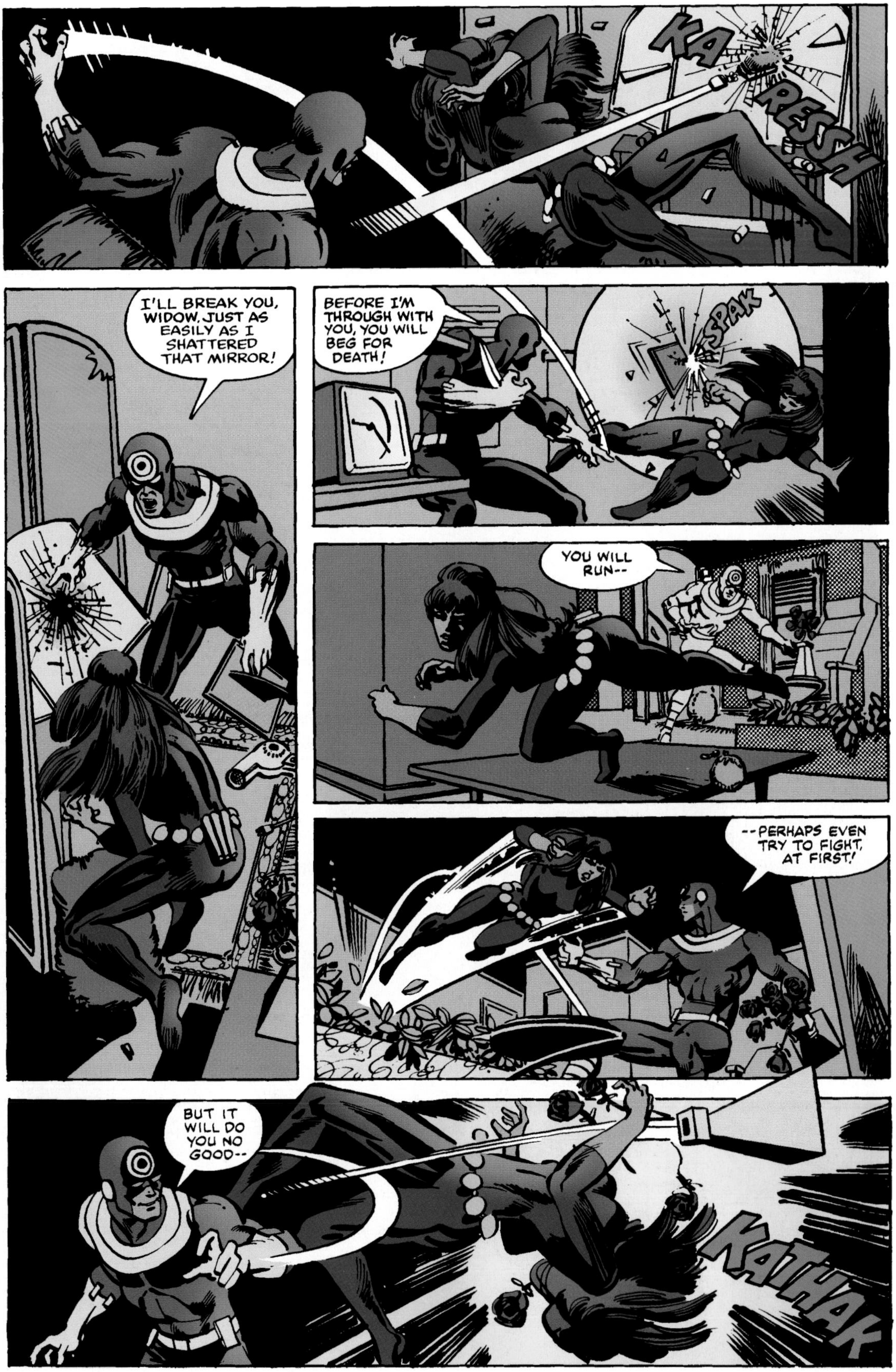
KA
RESSH
I'LL BREAK YOU, WIDOW. JUST AS EASILY AS I SHATTERED THAT MIRROR!
BEFORE I'M THROUGH WITH YOU, YOU WILL BEG FOR DEATH!
SPAK
YOU WILL RUN--
--PERHAPS EVEN TRY TO FIGHT, AT FIRST!
BUT IT WILL DO YOU NO GOOD--
KATHAK

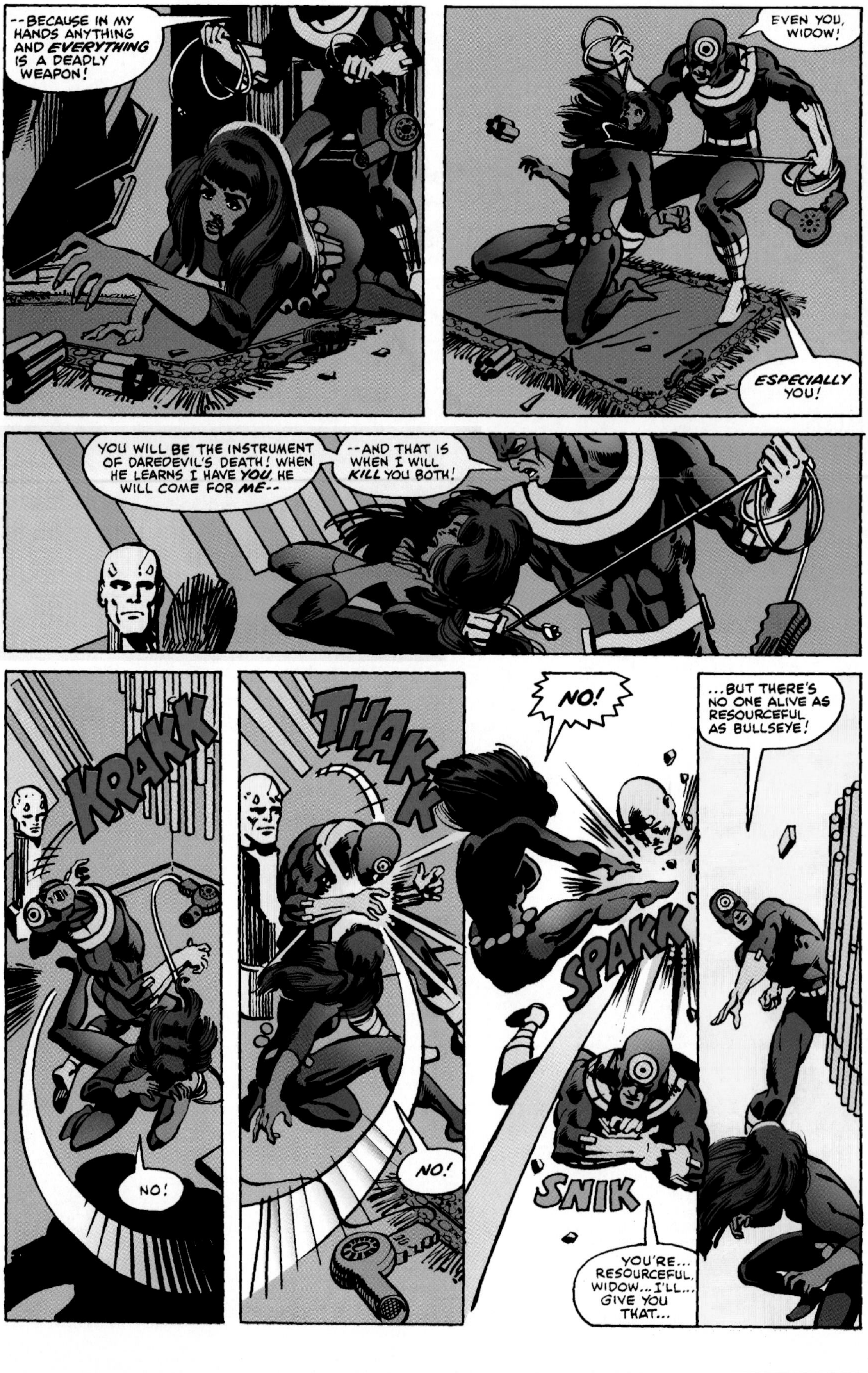
--BECAUSE IN MY HANDS ANYTHING AND *EVERYTHING* IS A DEADLY WEAPON!
EVEN YOU, WIDOW!
ESPECIALLY YOU!
YOU WILL BE THE INSTRUMENT OF DAREDEVIL'S DEATH! WHEN HE LEARNS I HAVE *YOU*, HE WILL COME FOR *ME*--
--AND THAT IS WHEN I WILL *KILL* YOU BOTH!
KRAKK
NO!
THAKK
NO!
NO!
SPAKK
SNIK
YOU'RE... RESOURCEFUL, WIDOW... I'LL... GIVE YOU THAT...
...BUT THERE'S NO ONE ALIVE AS RESOURCEFUL AS BULLSEYE!

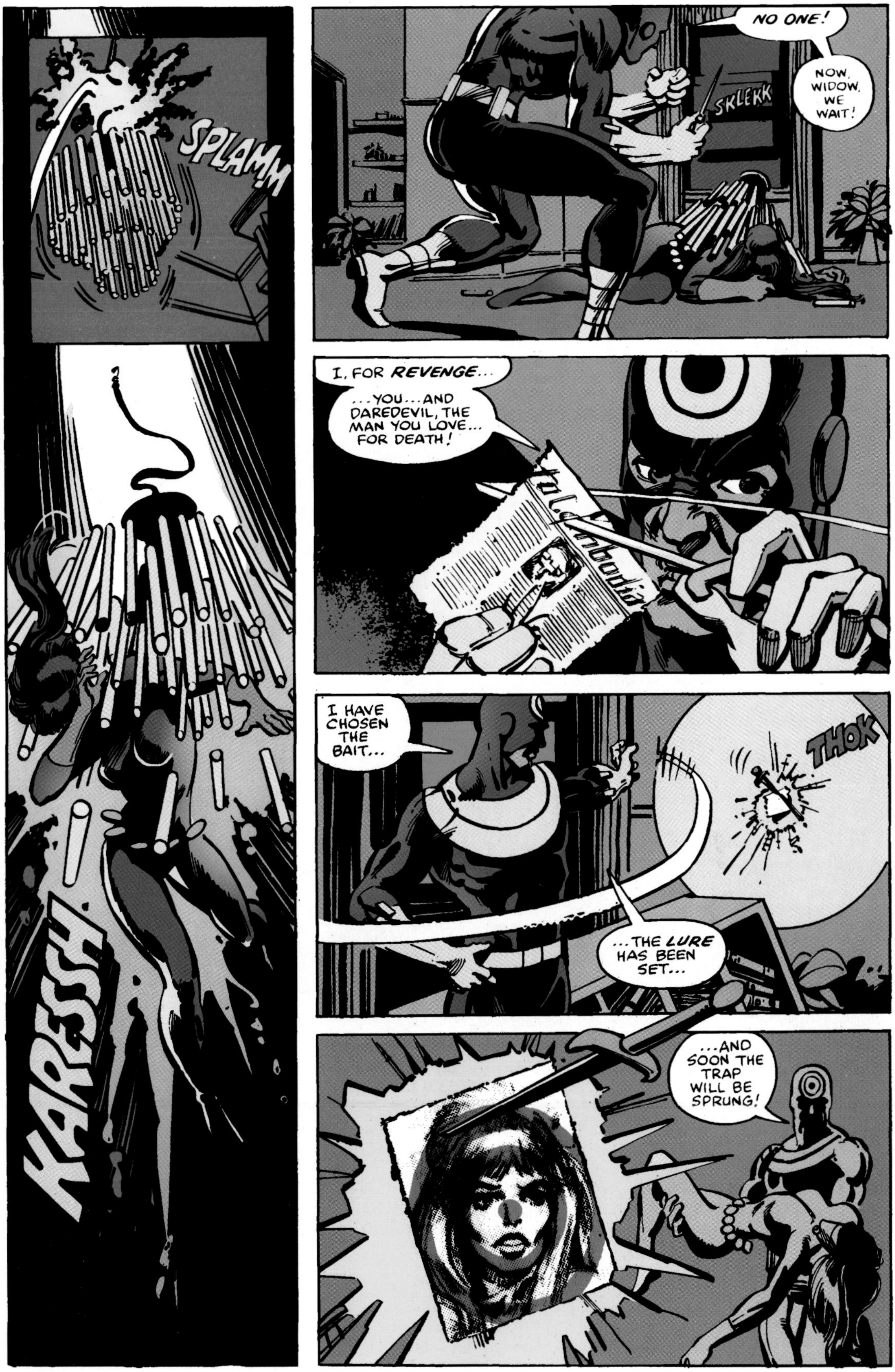

SPLAMM
KARESSH
NO ONE!
NOW, WIDOW, WE WAIT!
SKLEKK
I, FOR REVENGE...
...YOU...AND DAREDEVIL, THE MAN YOU LOVE... FOR DEATH!
I HAVE CHOSEN THE BAIT...
THOK
...THE LURE HAS BEEN SET...
...AND SOON THE TRAP WILL BE SPRUNG!

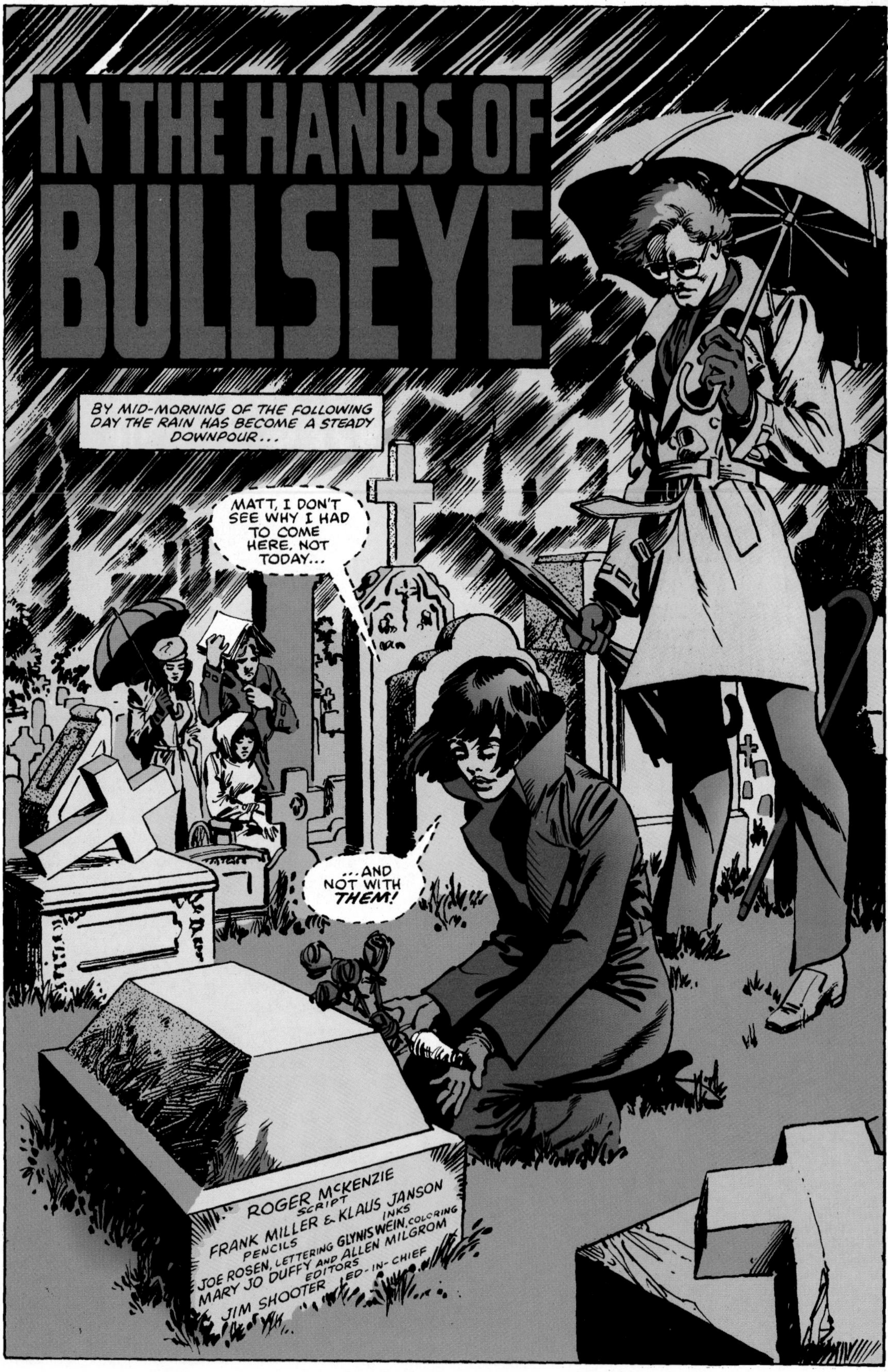
IN THE HANDS OF BULLSEYE
BY MID-MORNING OF THE FOLLOWING DAY THE RAIN HAS BECOME A STEADY DOWNPOUR...
MATT, I DON'T SEE WHY I HAD TO COME HERE, NOT TODAY...
...AND NOT WITH THEM!
ROGER McKENZIE SCRIPT
FRANK MILLER & KLAUS JANSON PENCILS INKS
JOE ROSEN, LETTERING GLYNIS WEIN, COLORING
MARY JO DUFFY AND ALLEN MILGROM EDITORS
JIM SHOOTER ED-IN-CHIEF

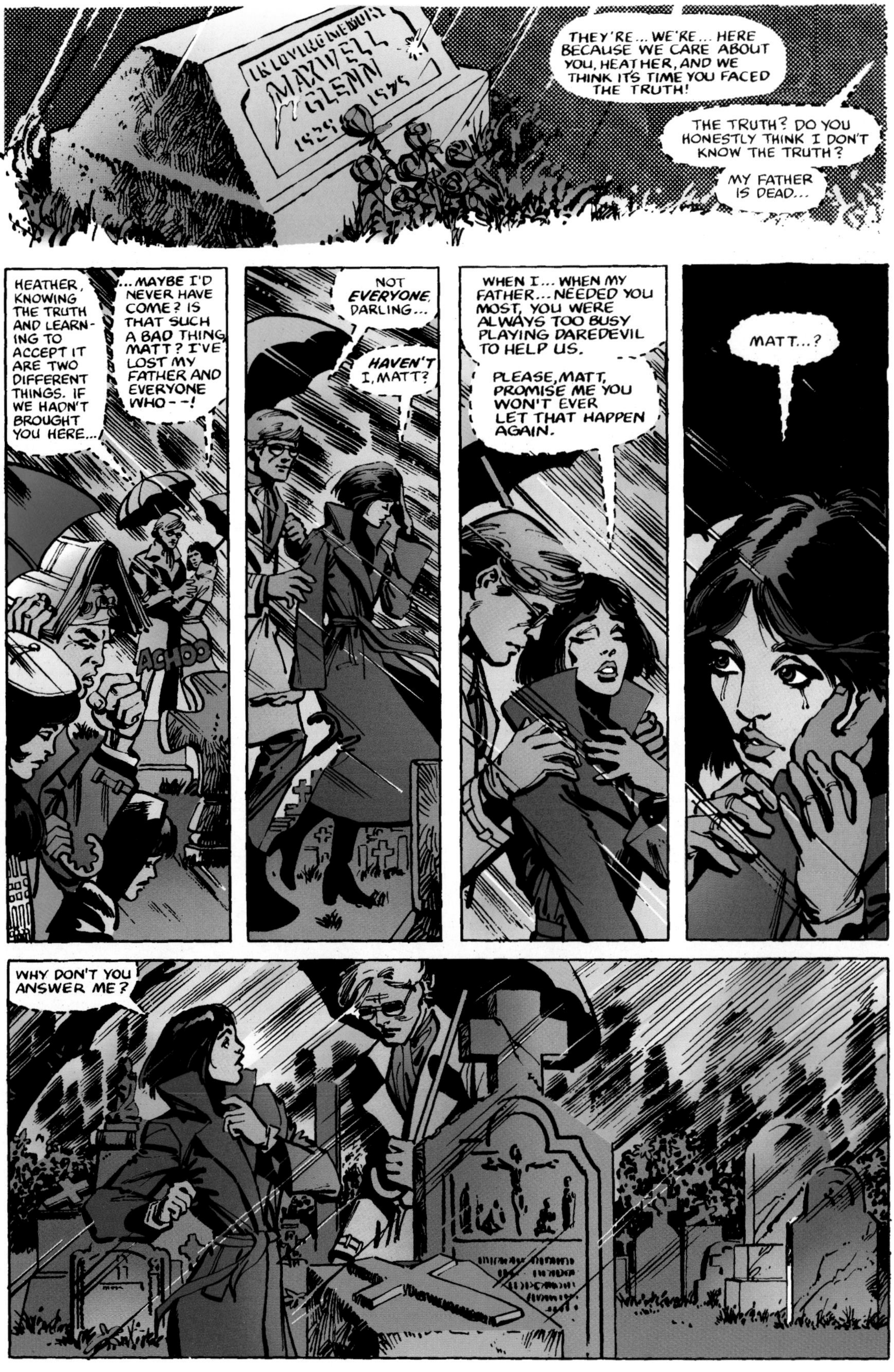
MAXWELL
GLENN
THEY'RE... WE'RE... HERE BECAUSE WE CARE ABOUT YOU, HEATHER, AND WE THINK IT'S TIME YOU FACED THE TRUTH!
THE TRUTH? DO YOU HONESTLY THINK I DON'T KNOW THE TRUTH?
MY FATHER IS DEAD...
HEATHER, KNOWING THE TRUTH AND LEARNING TO ACCEPT IT ARE TWO DIFFERENT THINGS. IF WE HADN'T BROUGHT YOU HERE...
...MAYBE I'D NEVER HAVE COME? IS THAT SUCH A BAD THING MATT? I'VE LOST MY FATHER AND EVERYONE WHO--!
ACHOO
NOT EVERYONE, DARLING...
HAVEN'T I, MATT?
WHEN I... WHEN MY FATHER... NEEDED YOU MOST, YOU WERE ALWAYS TOO BUSY PLAYING DAREDEVIL TO HELP US.
PLEASE, MATT, PROMISE ME YOU WON'T EVER LET THAT HAPPEN AGAIN.
MATT...?
WHY DON'T YOU ANSWER ME?

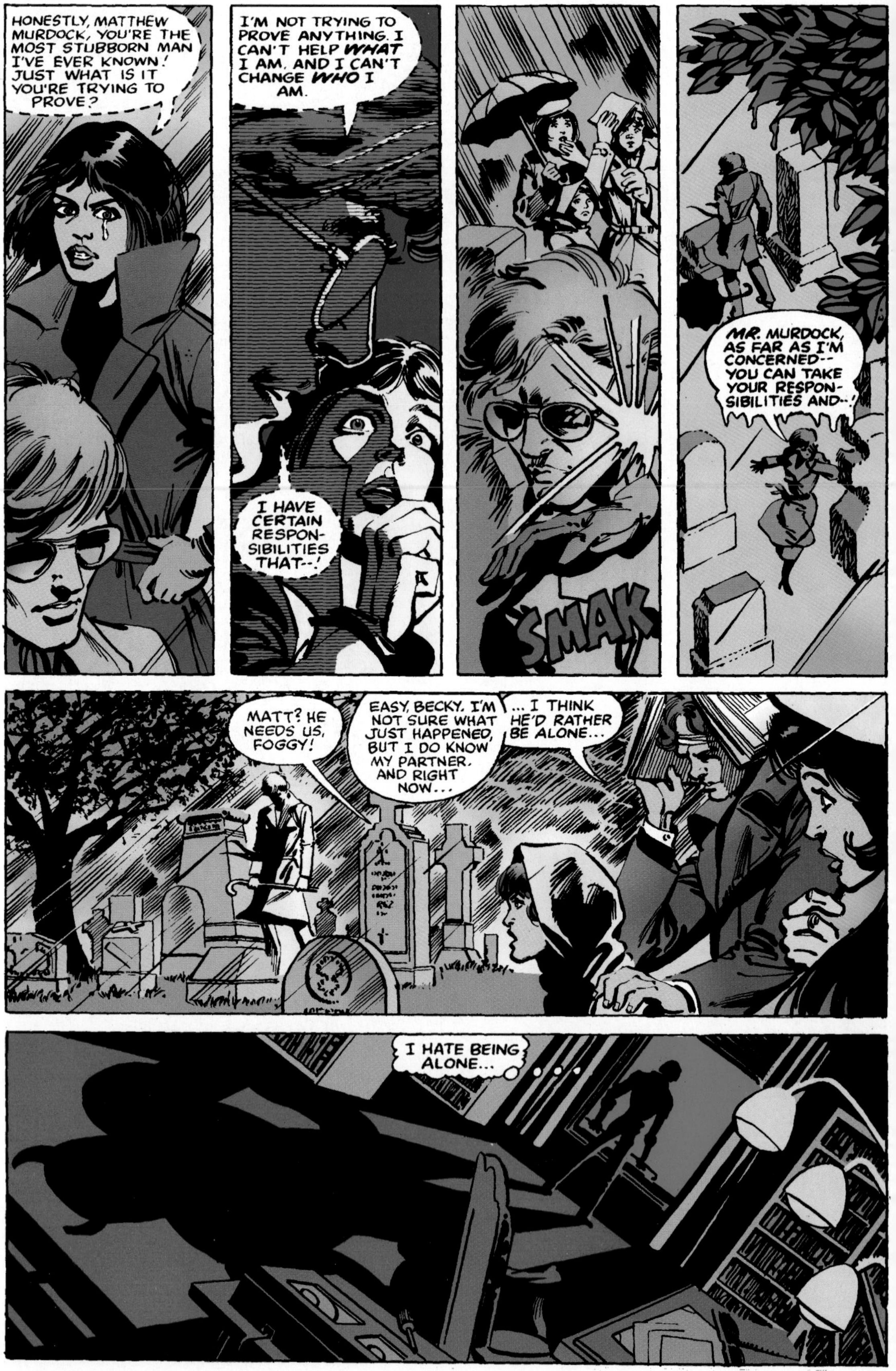
HONESTLY, MATTHEW MURDOCK, YOU'RE THE MOST STUBBORN MAN I'VE EVER KNOWN! JUST WHAT IS IT YOU'RE TRYING TO PROVE?
I'M NOT TRYING TO PROVE ANYTHING. I CAN'T HELP WHAT I AM, AND I CAN'T CHANGE WHO I AM.
I HAVE CERTAIN RESPON-SIBILITIES THAT--!
SMAK
MR. MURDOCK, AS FAR AS I'M CONCERNED-- YOU CAN TAKE YOUR RESPON-SIBILITIES AND--!
MATT? HE NEEDS US, FOGGY!
EASY, BECKY. I'M NOT SURE WHAT JUST HAPPENED, BUT I DO KNOW MY PARTNER. AND RIGHT NOW...
... I THINK HE'D RATHER BE ALONE...
I HATE BEING ALONE...

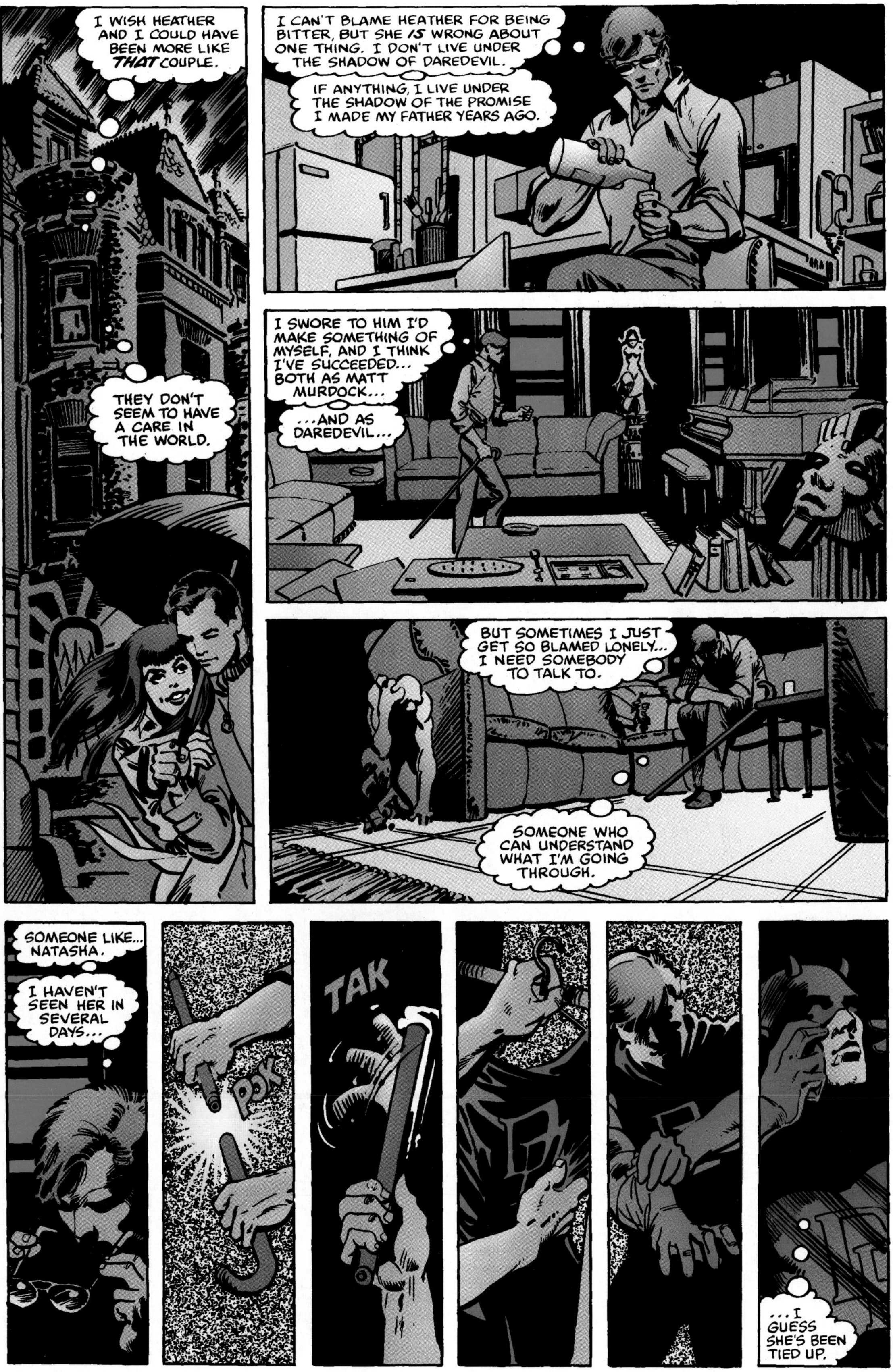
I WISH HEATHER AND I COULD HAVE BEEN MORE LIKE THAT COUPLE.
THEY DON'T SEEM TO HAVE A CARE IN THE WORLD.
I CAN'T BLAME HEATHER FOR BEING BITTER, BUT SHE IS WRONG ABOUT ONE THING. I DON'T LIVE UNDER THE SHADOW OF DAREDEVIL.
IF ANYTHING, I LIVE UNDER THE SHADOW OF THE PROMISE I MADE MY FATHER YEARS AGO.
I SWORE TO HIM I'D MAKE SOMETHING OF MYSELF, AND I THINK I'VE SUCCEEDED... BOTH AS MATT MURDOCK...
...AND AS DAREDEVIL...
BUT SOMETIMES I JUST GET SO BLAMED LONELY... I NEED SOMEBODY TO TALK TO.
SOMEONE WHO CAN UNDERSTAND WHAT I'M GOING THROUGH.
SOMEONE LIKE... NATASHA.
I HAVEN'T SEEN HER IN SEVERAL DAYS...
POK
TAK
...I GUESS SHE'S BEEN TIED UP.

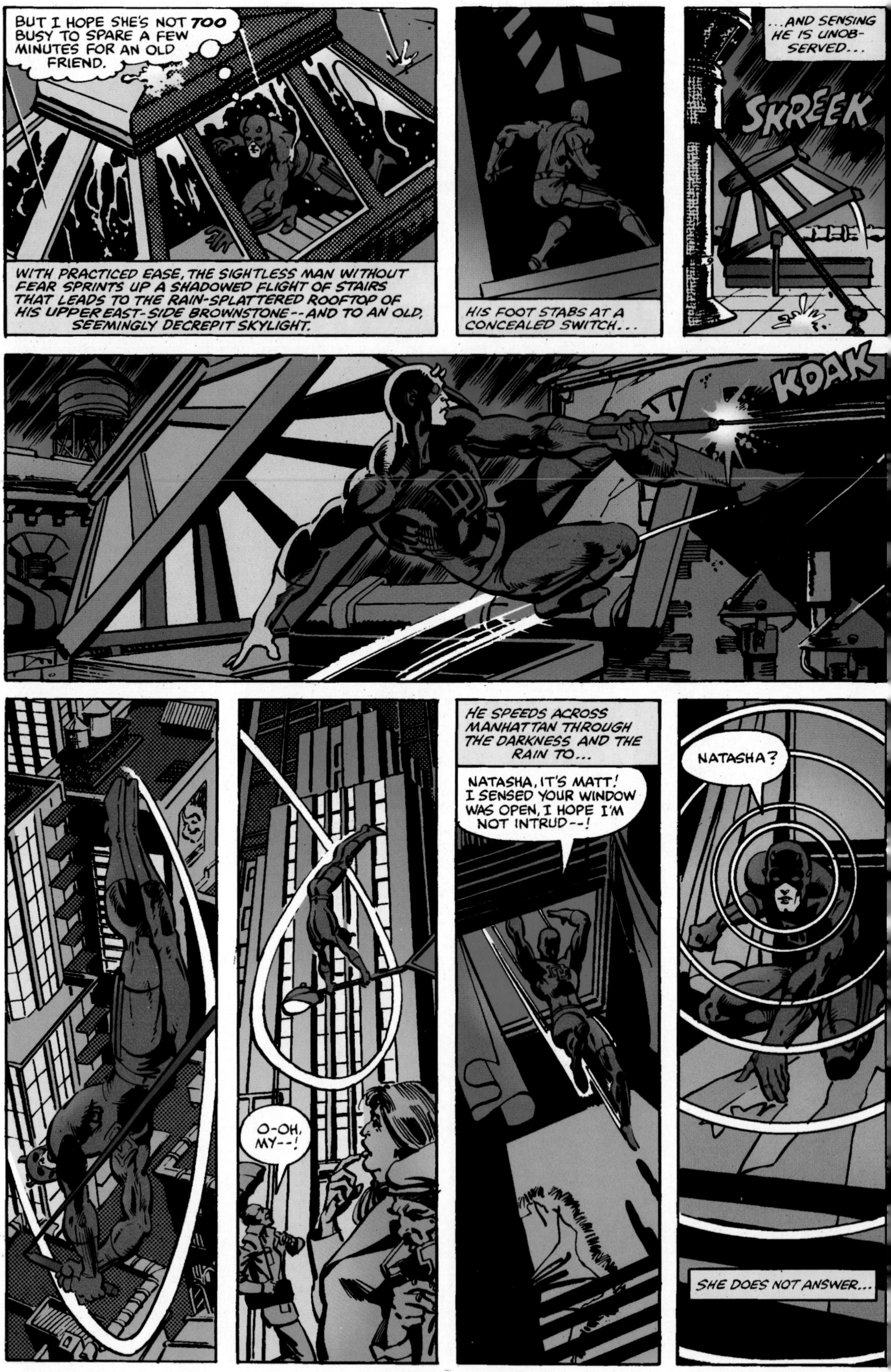
BUT I HOPE SHE'S NOT TOO BUSY TO SPARE A FEW MINUTES FOR AN OLD FRIEND.
WITH PRACTICED EASE, THE SIGHTLESS MAN WITHOUT FEAR SPRINTS UP A SHADOWED FLIGHT OF STAIRS THAT LEADS TO THE RAIN-SPLATTERED ROOFTOP OF HIS UPPER EAST-SIDE BROWNSTONE--AND TO AN OLD, SEEMINGLY DECREPIT SKYLIGHT.
HIS FOOT STABS AT A CONCEALED SWITCH...
...AND SENSING HE IS UNOBSERVED...
SKREEK
KDAK
O-OH, MY--!
HE SPEEDS ACROSS MANHATTAN THROUGH THE DARKNESS AND THE RAIN TO...
NATASHA, IT'S MATT! I SENSED YOUR WINDOW WAS OPEN, I HOPE I'M NOT INTRUD--!
NATASHA?
SHE DOES NOT ANSWER...

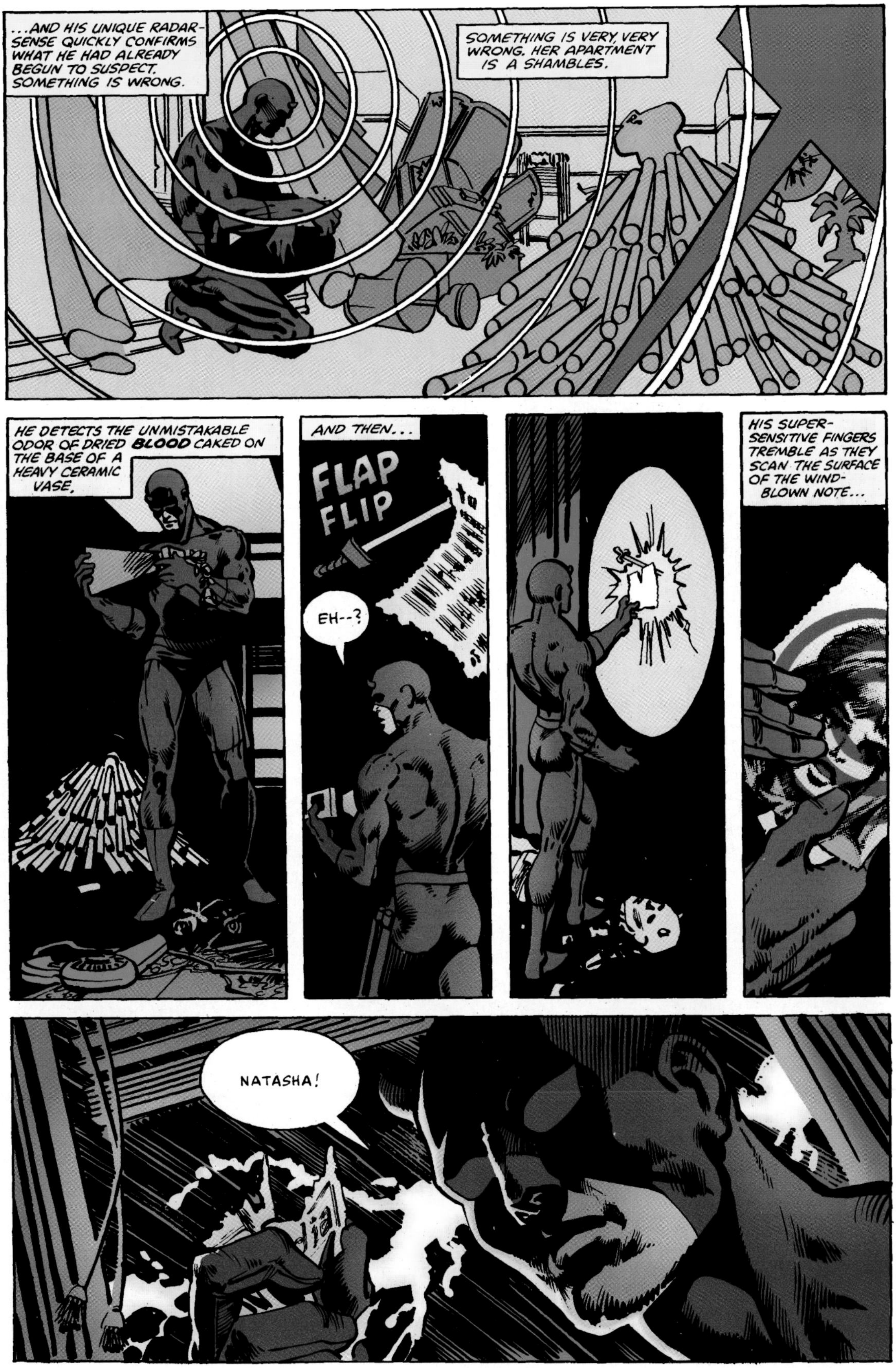
...AND HIS UNIQUE RADAR-SENSE QUICKLY CONFIRMS WHAT HE HAD ALREADY BEGUN TO SUSPECT. SOMETHING IS WRONG.
SOMETHING IS VERY, VERY WRONG. HER APARTMENT IS A SHAMBLES.
HE DETECTS THE UNMISTAKABLE ODOR OF DRIED BLOOD CAKED ON THE BASE OF A HEAVY CERAMIC VASE.
AND THEN...
FLAP
FLIP
EH--?
HIS SUPER-SENSITIVE FINGERS TREMBLE AS THEY SCAN THE SURFACE OF THE WIND-BLOWN NOTE...
NATASHA!

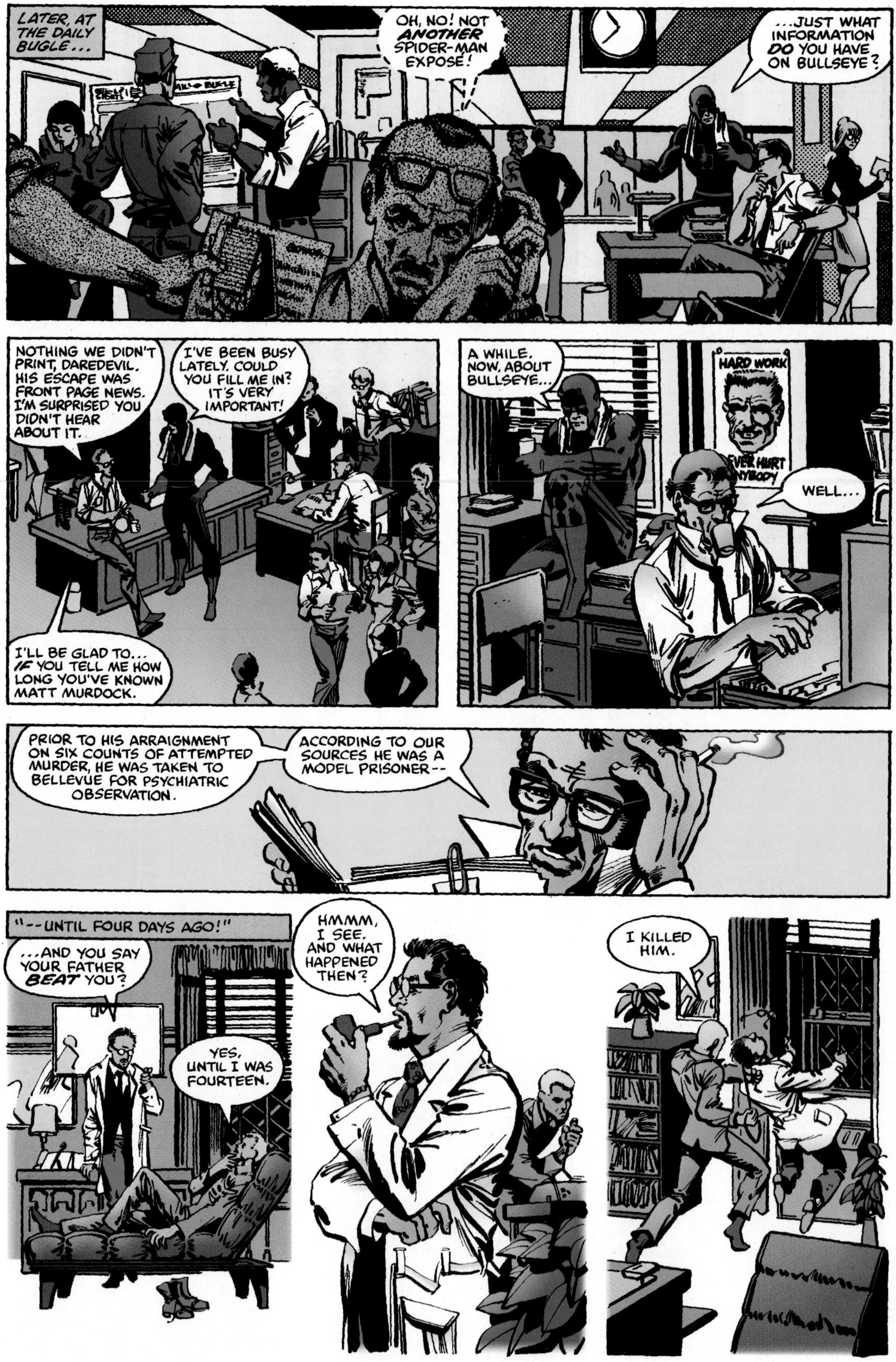
LATER, AT THE DAILY BUGLE...
OH, NO! NOT ANOTHER SPIDER-MAN EXPOSE!
...JUST WHAT INFORMATION DO YOU HAVE ON BULLSEYE?
NOTHING WE DIDN'T PRINT, DAREDEVIL. HIS ESCAPE WAS FRONT PAGE NEWS. I'M SURPRISED YOU DIDN'T HEAR ABOUT IT.
I'VE BEEN BUSY LATELY. COULD YOU FILL ME IN? IT'S VERY IMPORTANT!
I'LL BE GLAD TO... IF YOU TELL ME HOW LONG YOU'VE KNOWN MATT MURDOCK.
A WHILE. NOW, ABOUT BULLSEYE...
HARD WORK
WELL...
PRIOR TO HIS ARRAIGNMENT ON SIX COUNTS OF ATTEMPTED MURDER, HE WAS TAKEN TO BELLEVUE FOR PSYCHIATRIC OBSERVATION.
ACCORDING TO OUR SOURCES HE WAS A MODEL PRISONER--
"--UNTIL FOUR DAYS AGO!"
...AND YOU SAY YOUR FATHER BEAT YOU?
YES, UNTIL I WAS FOURTEEN.
HMMM, I SEE. AND WHAT HAPPENED THEN?
I KILLED HIM.

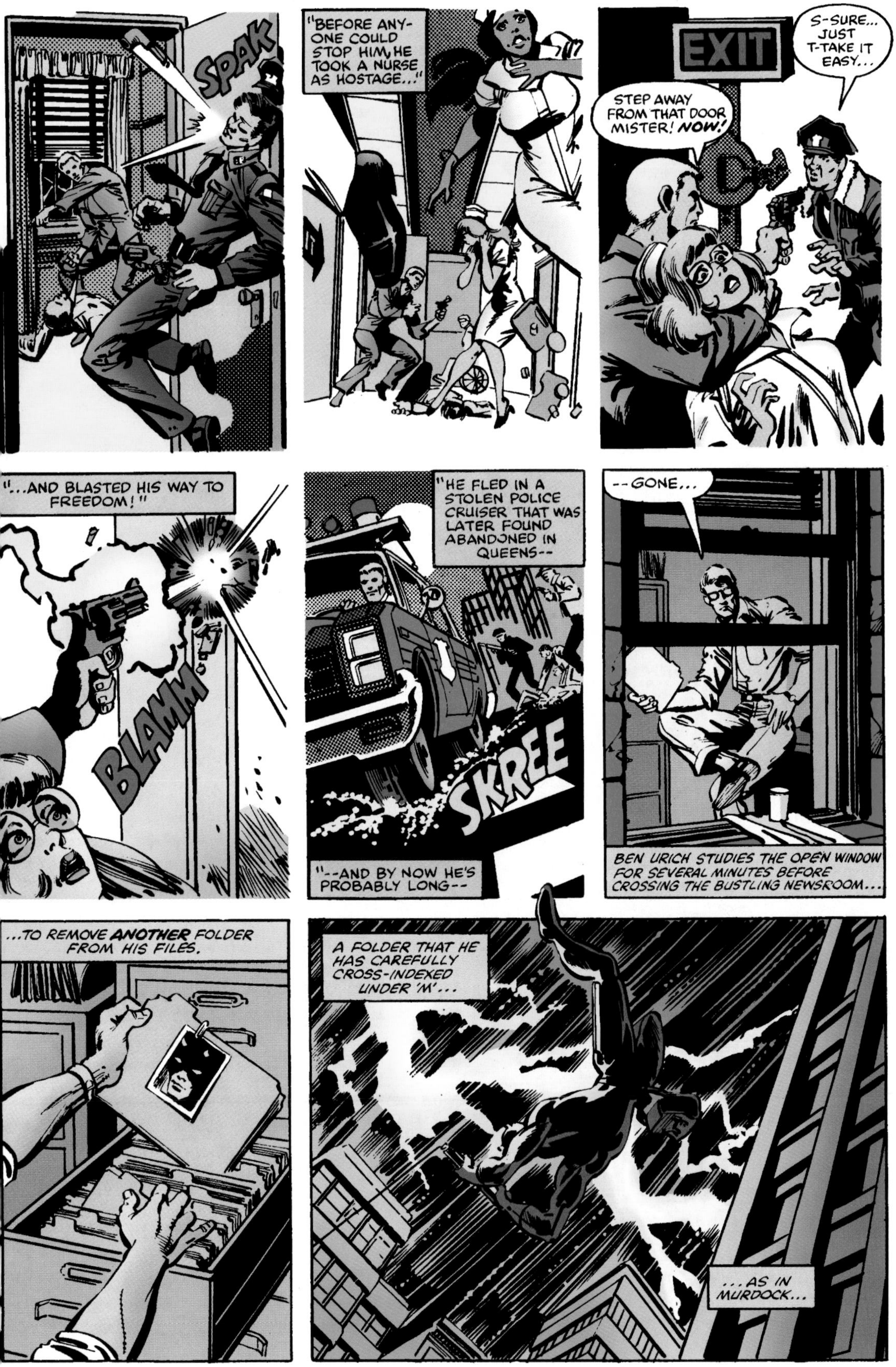
SPAK
"BEFORE ANY-ONE COULD STOP HIM, HE TOOK A NURSE AS HOSTAGE..."
EXIT
S-SURE... JUST T-TAKE IT EASY...
STEP AWAY FROM THAT DOOR MISTER! NOW!
"...AND BLASTED HIS WAY TO FREEDOM!"
BLAMM
"HE FLED IN A STOLEN POLICE CRUISER THAT WAS LATER FOUND ABANDONED IN QUEENS--
SKREE
"--AND BY NOW HE'S PROBABLY LONG--
--GONE...
BEN URICH STUDIES THE OPEN WINDOW FOR SEVERAL MINUTES BEFORE CROSSING THE BUSTLING NEWSROOM...
...TO REMOVE ANOTHER FOLDER FROM HIS FILES.
A FOLDER THAT HE HAS CAREFULLY CROSS-INDEXED UNDER 'M'...
...AS IN MURDOCK...

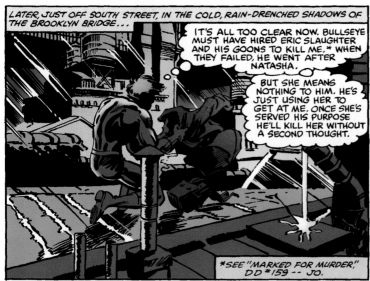

LATER, JUST OFF SOUTH STREET, IN THE COLD, RAIN-DRENCHED SHADOWS OF THE BROOKLYN BRIDGE...

IT'S ALL TOO CLEAR NOW. BULLSEYE MUST HAVE HIRED ERIC SLAUGHTER AND HIS GOONS TO KILL ME.* WHEN THEY FAILED, HE WENT AFTER NATASHA.

BUT SHE MEANS NOTHING TO HIM, HE'S JUST USING HER TO GET AT ME. ONCE SHE'S SERVED HIS PURPOSE HE'LL KILL HER WITHOUT A SECOND THOUGHT.

*SEE "MARKED FOR MURDER," DD #159 -- JO.

THIS HAS BECOME A GAME TO HIM. A SICK LITTLE GAME OF REVENGE. HE *WANTS* ME TO FIND HIM.

AND, SO HELP ME, HE WON'T BE DISAPPOINTED. I'LL SCOUR EVERY UNDERWORLD DIVE IN THIS CITY UNTIL I DO!

BAR JOSIE'S GRILL

WELL, WELL... "LARK" LOGAN. GOT A MINUTE TO SING FOR YOUR SUPPER, STOOLIE?

THEY'RE SQUARING OFF IN THE CENTER OF THE RING!

MISTER, I GOT ALL THE TIME IN THE WORLD--

--BUT NOT FOR YOU *OR* YOUR INSULTS!

AND THERE'S THE BELL!

MAKE TIME, STOOLIE. I NEED ANSWERS.

SO? WHO DON'T?

WHAT CAN YOU TELL ME ABOUT A MAN CALLED BULLSEYE?

WHAT A STRUGGLE!

BULLSEYE, HUH? LET ME THINK...

YOU DO THAT, STOOLIE. THINK REAL HARD. I'M SURE *SOMETHING* WILL COME TO YOU.

HEY, MITHITHIPPI--!

YEAH...I'M BEGINNIN' TO SEE WHAT YOU MEAN!

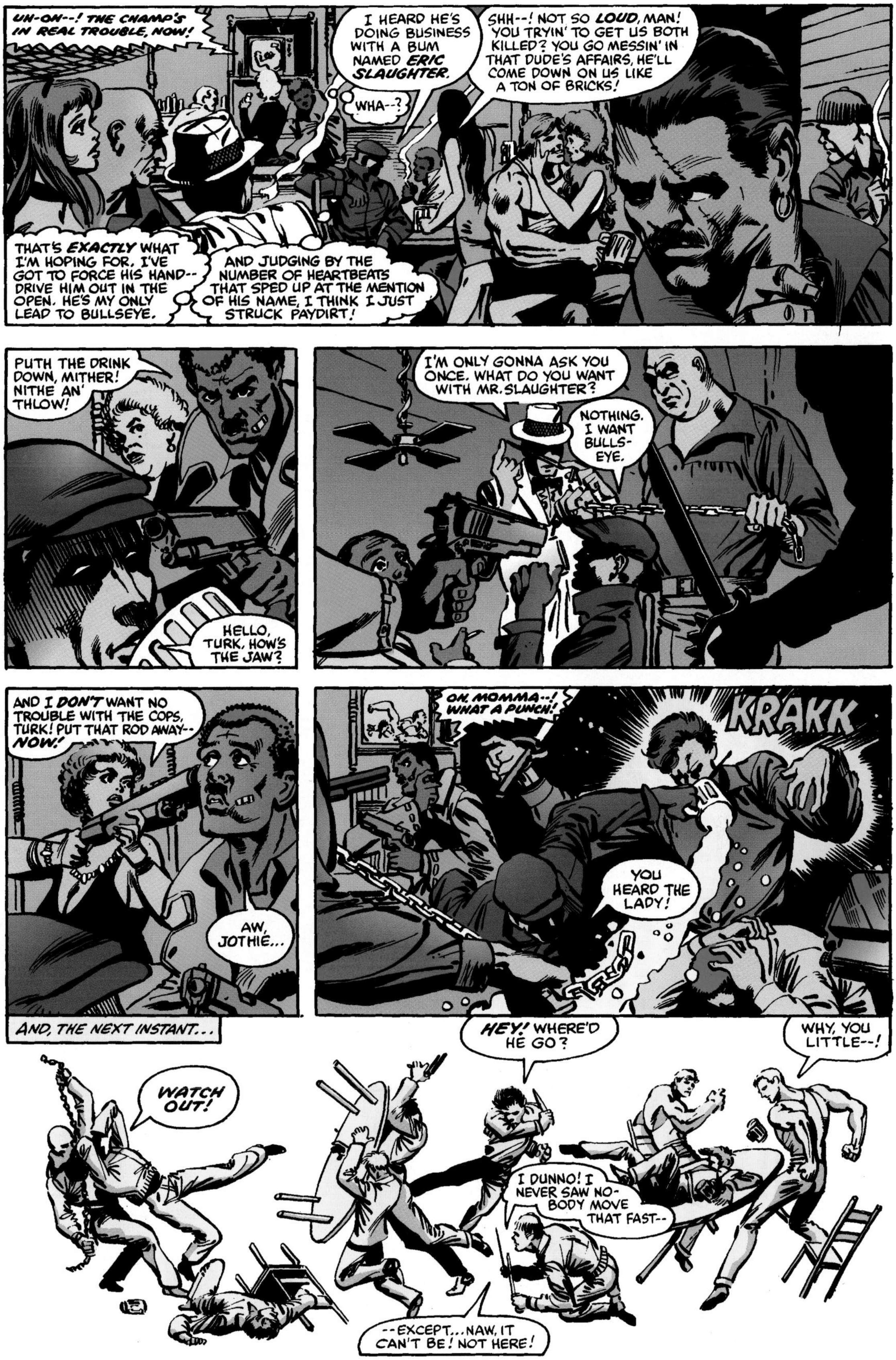
UH-OH--! THE CHAMP'S IN REAL TROUBLE, NOW!
I HEARD HE'S DOING BUSINESS WITH A BUM NAMED ERIC SLAUGHTER.
WHA--?
SHH--! NOT SO LOUD, MAN! YOU TRYIN' TO GET US BOTH KILLED? YOU GO MESSIN' IN THAT DUDE'S AFFAIRS, HE'LL COME DOWN ON US LIKE A TON OF BRICKS!
THAT'S EXACTLY WHAT I'M HOPING FOR. I'VE GOT TO FORCE HIS HAND-- DRIVE HIM OUT IN THE OPEN. HE'S MY ONLY LEAD TO BULLSEYE.
AND JUDGING BY THE NUMBER OF HEARTBEATS THAT SPED UP AT THE MENTION OF HIS NAME, I THINK I JUST STRUCK PAYDIRT!
PUTH THE DRINK DOWN, MITHER! NITHE AN' THLOW!
HELLO, TURK, HOW'S THE JAW?
I'M ONLY GONNA ASK YOU ONCE. WHAT DO YOU WANT WITH MR. SLAUGHTER?
NOTHING. I WANT BULLS-EYE.
AND I DON'T WANT NO TROUBLE WITH THE COPS, TURK! PUT THAT ROD AWAY-- NOW!
AW, JOTHIE...
OH, MOMMA--! WHAT A PUNCH!
KRAKK
YOU HEARD THE LADY!
AND, THE NEXT INSTANT...
WATCH OUT!
HEY! WHERE'D HE GO?
WHY, YOU LITTLE--!
I DUNNO! I NEVER SAW NO-BODY MOVE THAT FAST--
--EXCEPT...NAW, IT CAN'T BE! NOT HERE!

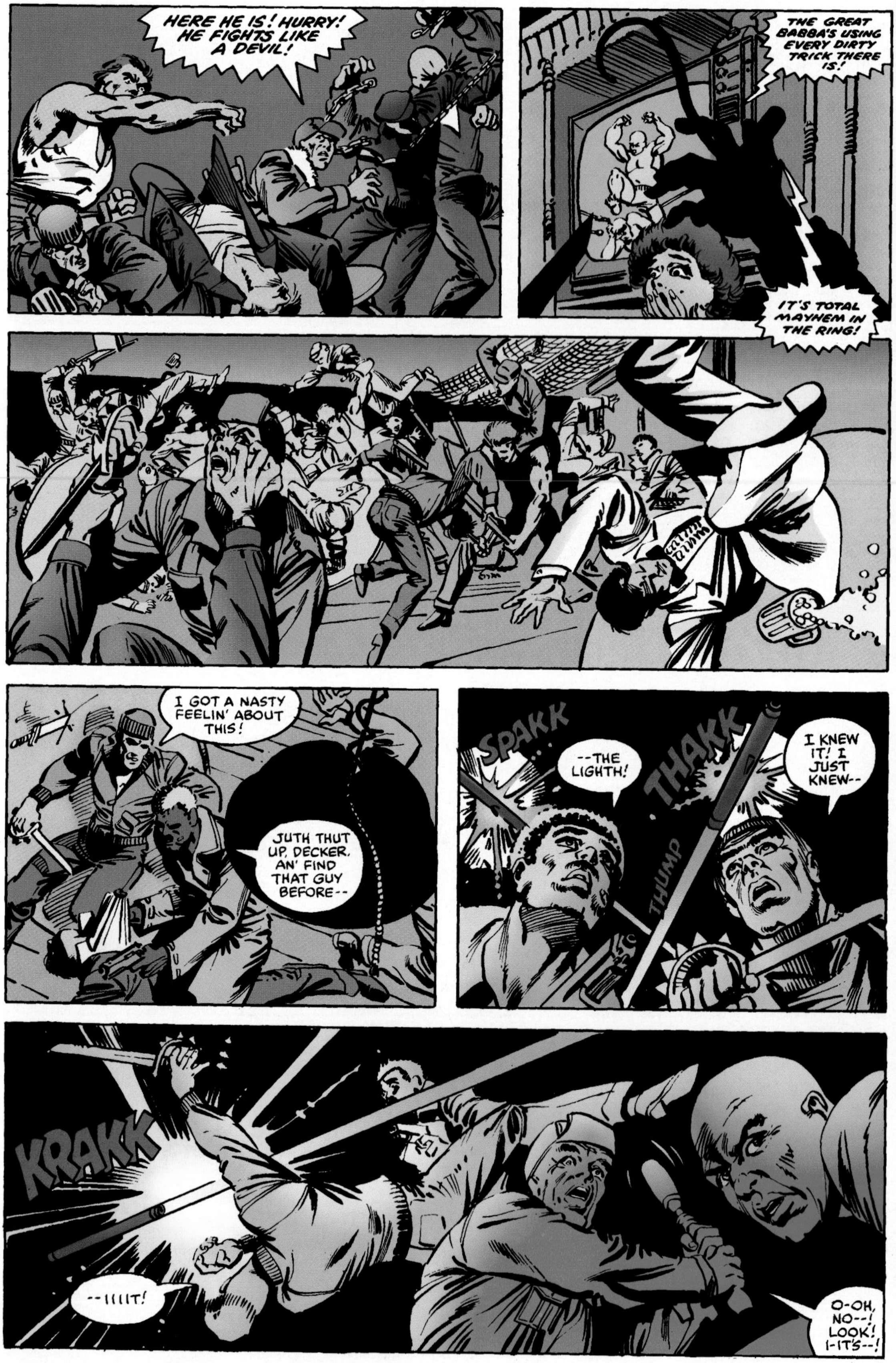
HERE HE IS! HURRY! HE FIGHTS LIKE A DEVIL!
THE GREAT BABBA'S USING EVERY DIRTY TRICK THERE IS!
IT'S TOTAL MAYHEM IN THE RING!
I GOT A NASTY FEELIN' ABOUT THIS!
JUTH THUT UP, DECKER. AN' FIND THAT GUY BEFORE--
SPAKK
--THE LIGHTH!
THAKK
THUMP
I KNEW IT! I JUST KNEW--
KRAKK
--IIIIT!
O-OH, NO--! LOOK! I-IT'S--!

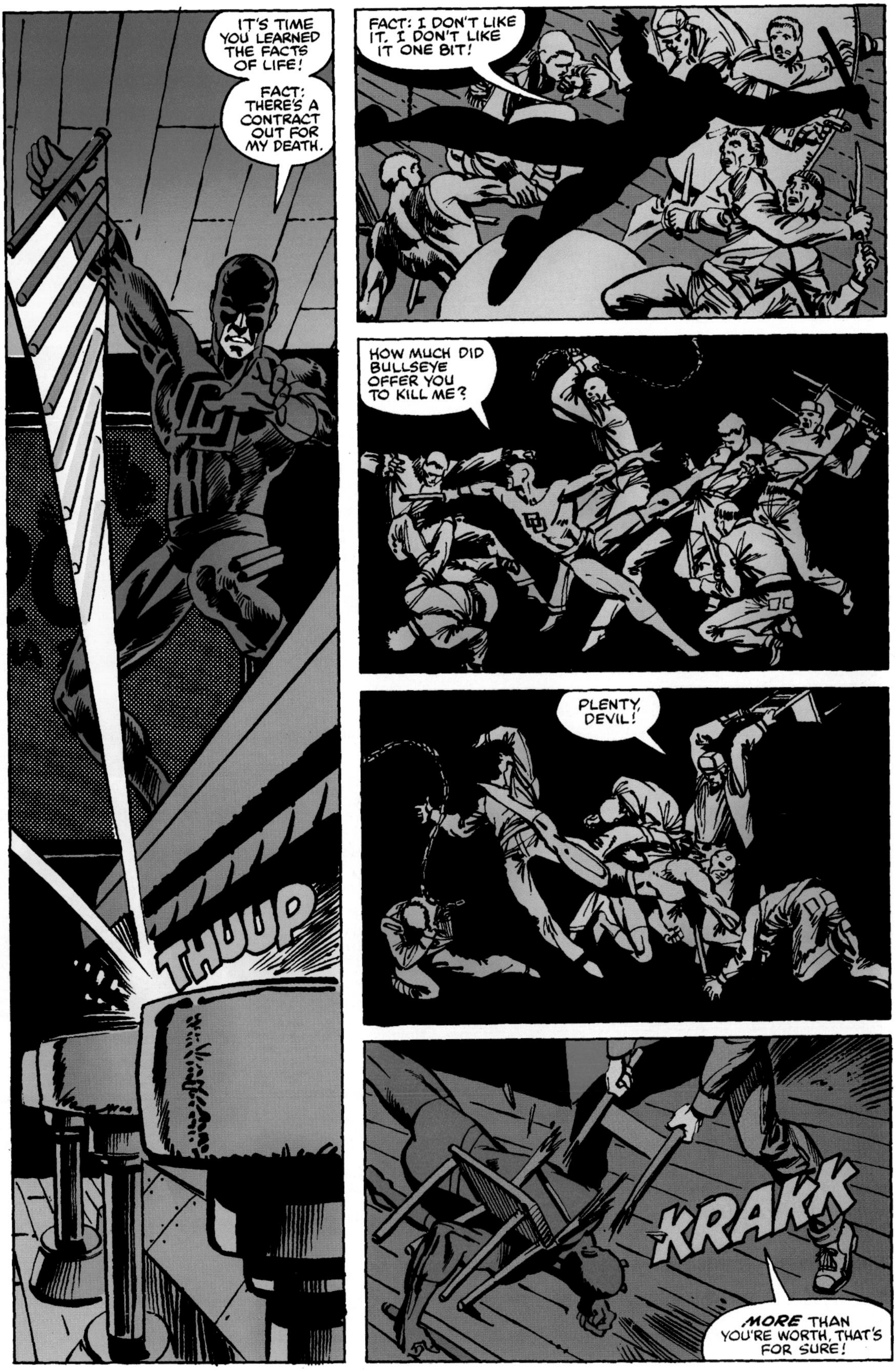
IT'S TIME YOU LEARNED THE FACTS OF LIFE!
FACT: THERE'S A CONTRACT OUT FOR MY DEATH.
THUUP
FACT: I DON'T LIKE IT. I DON'T LIKE IT ONE BIT!
HOW MUCH DID BULLSEYE OFFER YOU TO KILL ME?
PLENTY, DEVIL!
KRAKK
MORE THAN YOU'RE WORTH, THAT'S FOR SURE!

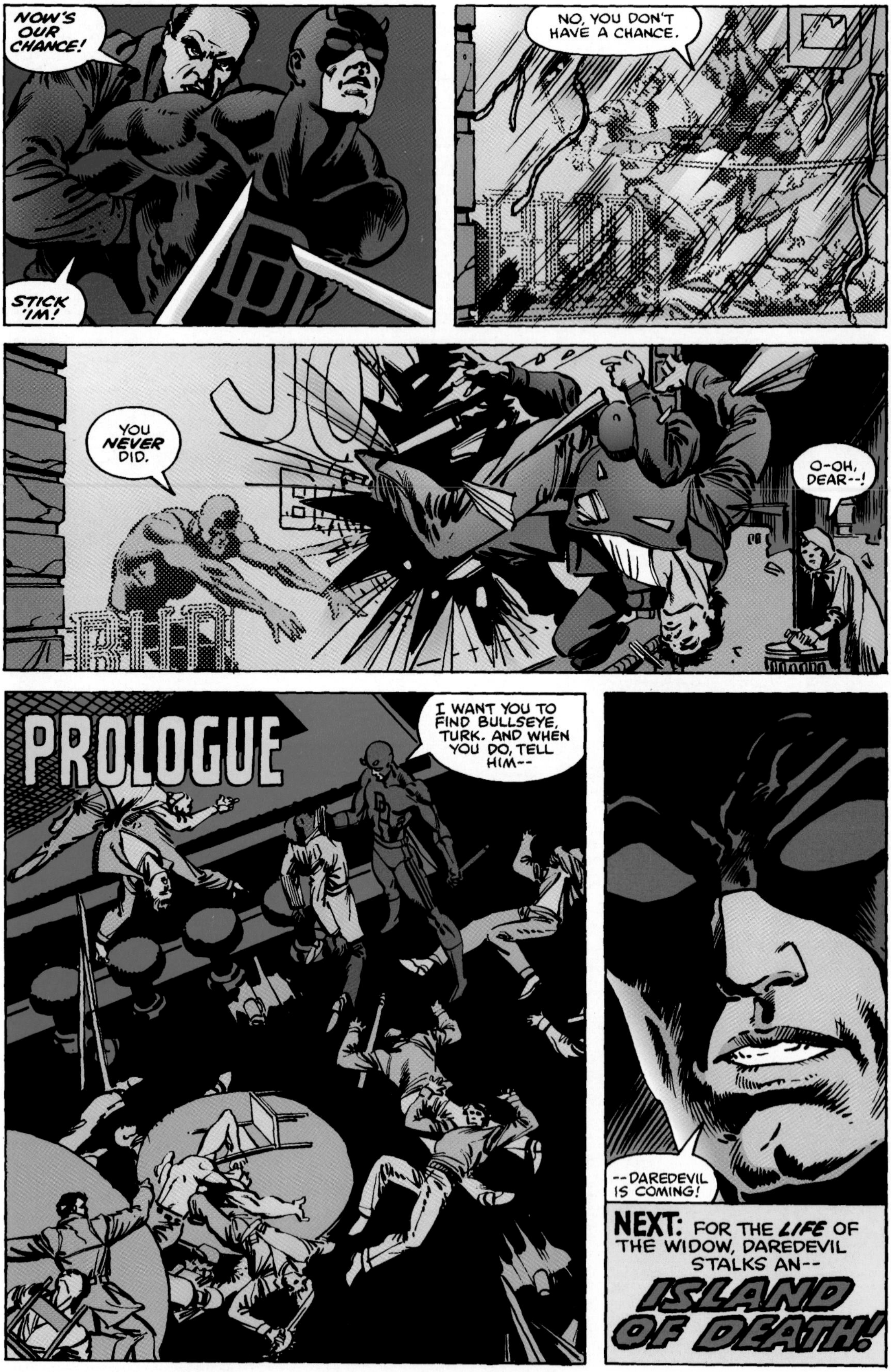
NOW'S OUR CHANCE!
STICK 'IM!
NO, YOU DON'T HAVE A CHANCE.
YOU NEVER DID.
O-OH, DEAR--!
PROLOGUE
I WANT YOU TO FIND BULLSEYE, TURK. AND WHEN YOU DO, TELL HIM--
--DAREDEVIL IS COMING!
NEXT: FOR THE LIFE OF THE WIDOW, DAREDEVIL STALKS AN--
ISLAND OF DEATH!

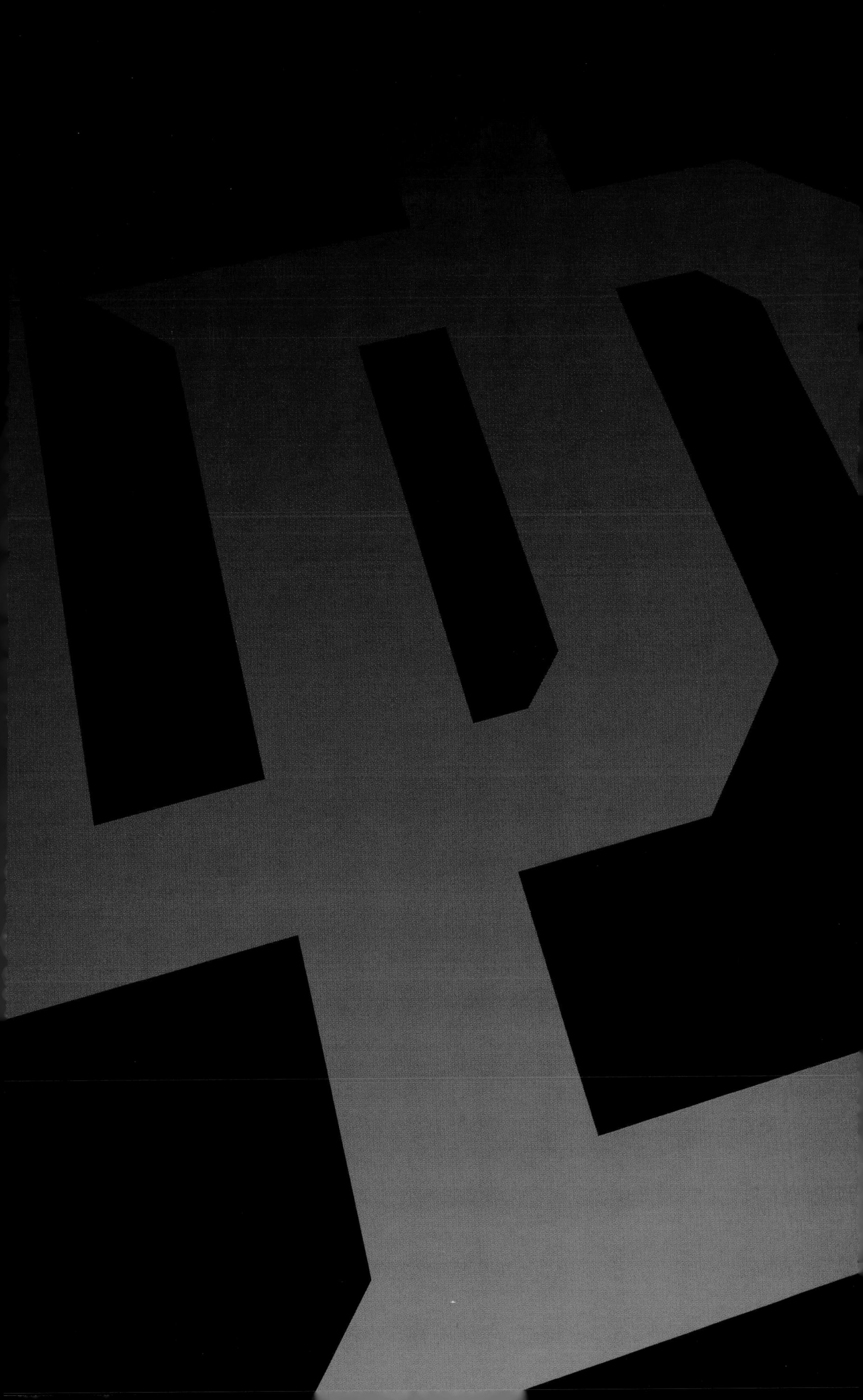

DAREDEVIL #161

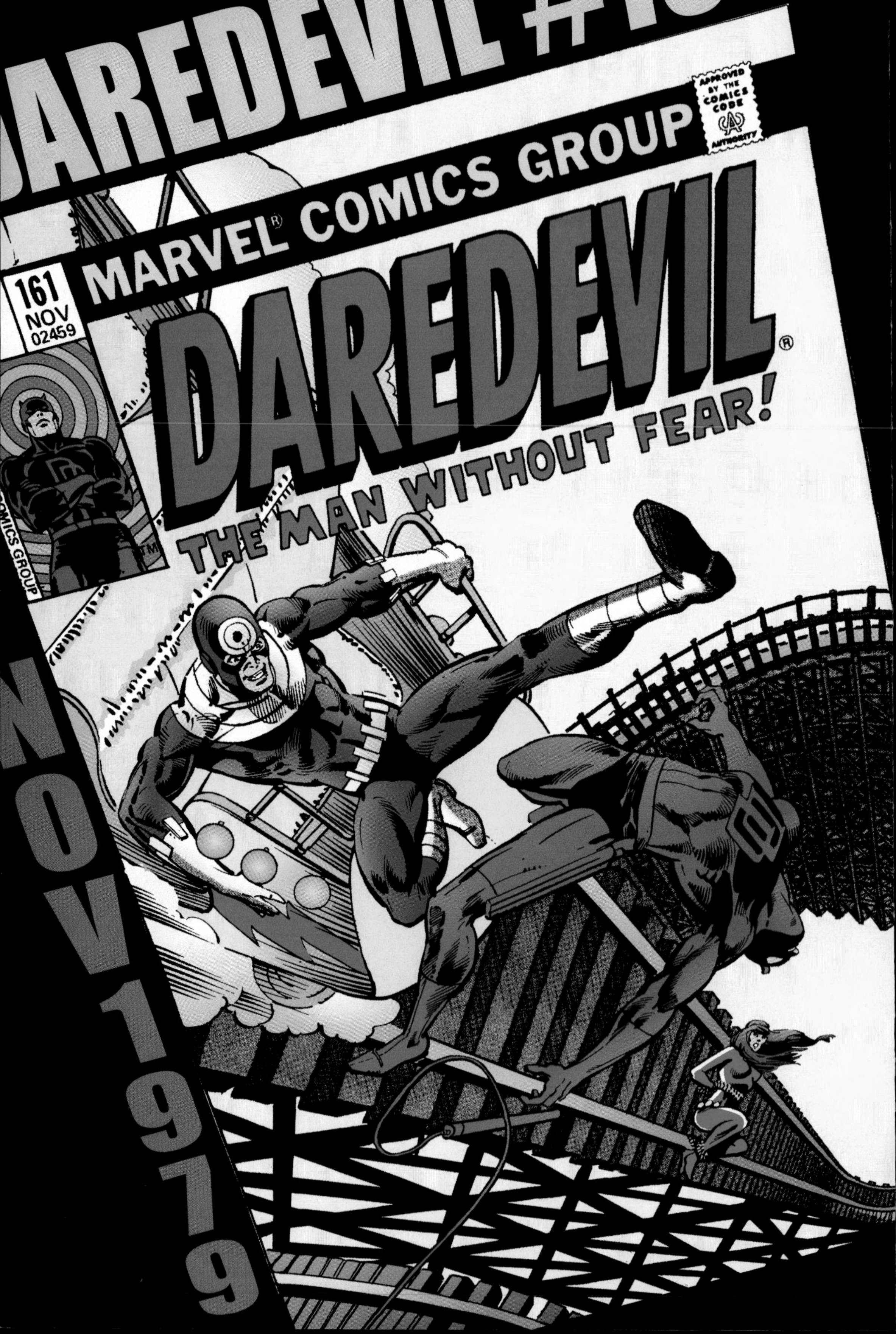
MARVEL® COMICS GROUP
APPROVED BY THE COMICS CODE AUTHORITY
161 NOV 02459
DAREDEVIL®
THE MAN WITHOUT FEAR!

NOV 1979

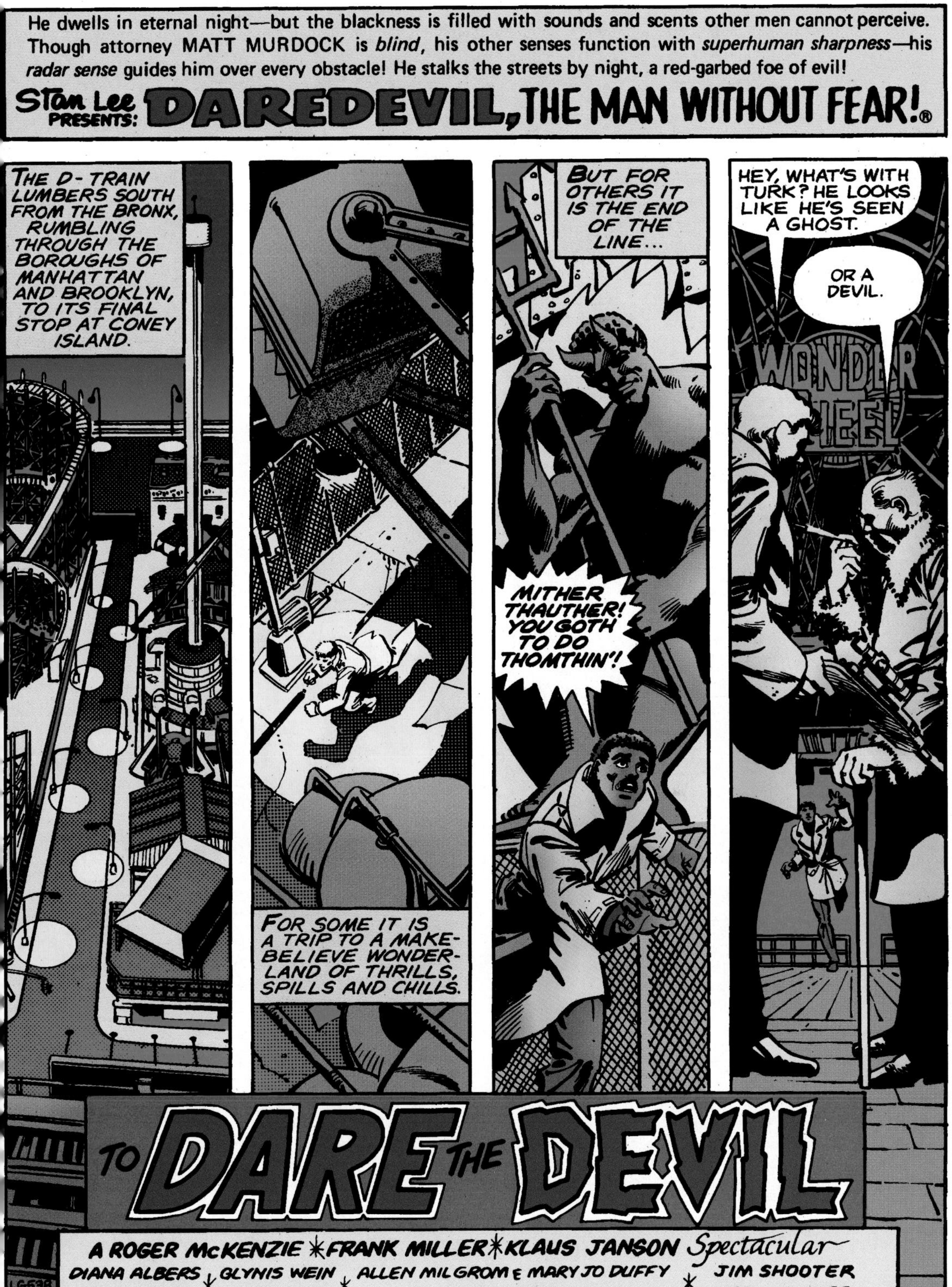
He dwells in eternal night—but the blackness is filled with sounds and scents other men cannot perceive. Though attorney MATT MURDOCK is blind, his other senses function with superhuman sharpness—his radar sense guides him over every obstacle! He stalks the streets by night, a red-garbed foe of evil!
Stan Lee PRESENTS: DAREDEVIL, THE MAN WITHOUT FEAR!®
THE D-TRAIN LUMBERS SOUTH FROM THE BRONX, RUMBLING THROUGH THE BOROUGHS OF MANHATTAN AND BROOKLYN, TO ITS FINAL STOP AT CONEY ISLAND.
FOR SOME IT IS A TRIP TO A MAKE-BELIEVE WONDERLAND OF THRILLS, SPILLS AND CHILLS.
BUT FOR OTHERS IT IS THE END OF THE LINE...
MITHER THAUTHER! YOU GOTH TO DO THOMTHIN'!
HEY, WHAT'S WITH TURK? HE LOOKS LIKE HE'S SEEN A GHOST.
OR A DEVIL.
TO DARE THE DEVIL
A ROGER McKENZIE * FRANK MILLER * KLAUS JANSON Spectacular
DIANA ALBERS LETTERER * GLYNIS WEIN COLORIST * ALLEN MILGROM & MARY JO DUFFY EDITORS * JIM SHOOTER ED.-IN-CHIEF
LG538

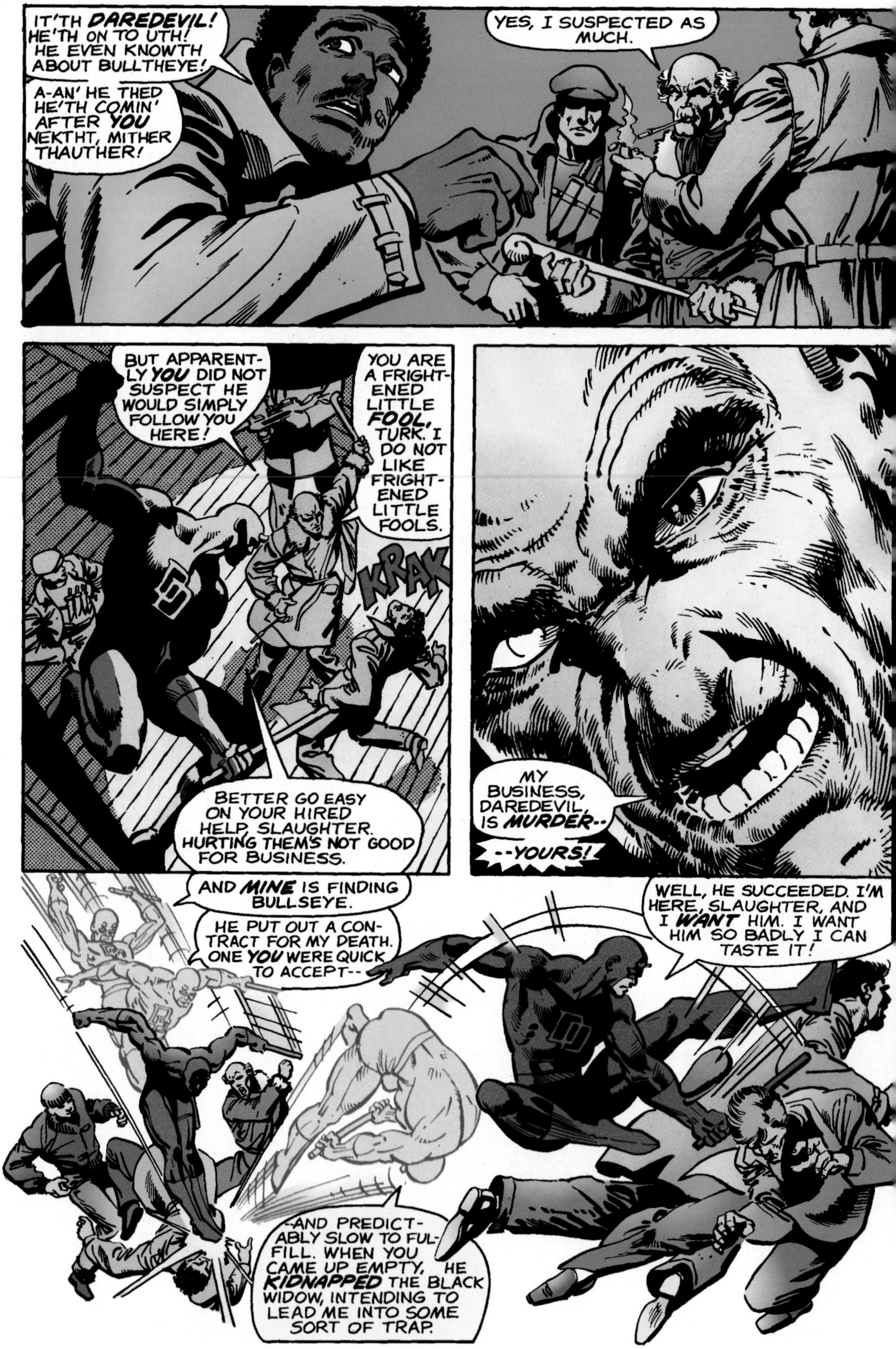
IT'TH DAREDEVIL! HE'TH ON TO UTH! HE EVEN KNOWTH ABOUT BULLTHEYE!
A-AN' HE THED HE'TH COMIN' AFTER YOU NEKTHT, MITHER THAUTHER!
YES, I SUSPECTED AS MUCH.
BUT APPARENTLY YOU DID NOT SUSPECT HE WOULD SIMPLY FOLLOW YOU HERE!
YOU ARE A FRIGHTENED LITTLE FOOL, TURK. I DO NOT LIKE FRIGHTENED LITTLE FOOLS.
KRAK
BETTER GO EASY ON YOUR HIRED HELP, SLAUGHTER. HURTING THEM'S NOT GOOD FOR BUSINESS.
MY BUSINESS, DAREDEVIL, IS MURDER--
--YOURS!
AND MINE IS FINDING BULLSEYE.
HE PUT OUT A CONTRACT FOR MY DEATH. ONE YOU WERE QUICK TO ACCEPT--
--AND PREDICTABLY SLOW TO FULFILL. WHEN YOU CAME UP EMPTY, HE KIDNAPPED THE BLACK WIDOW, INTENDING TO LEAD ME INTO SOME SORT OF TRAP.
WELL, HE SUCCEEDED. I'M HERE, SLAUGHTER, AND I WANT HIM. I WANT HIM SO BADLY I CAN TASTE IT!

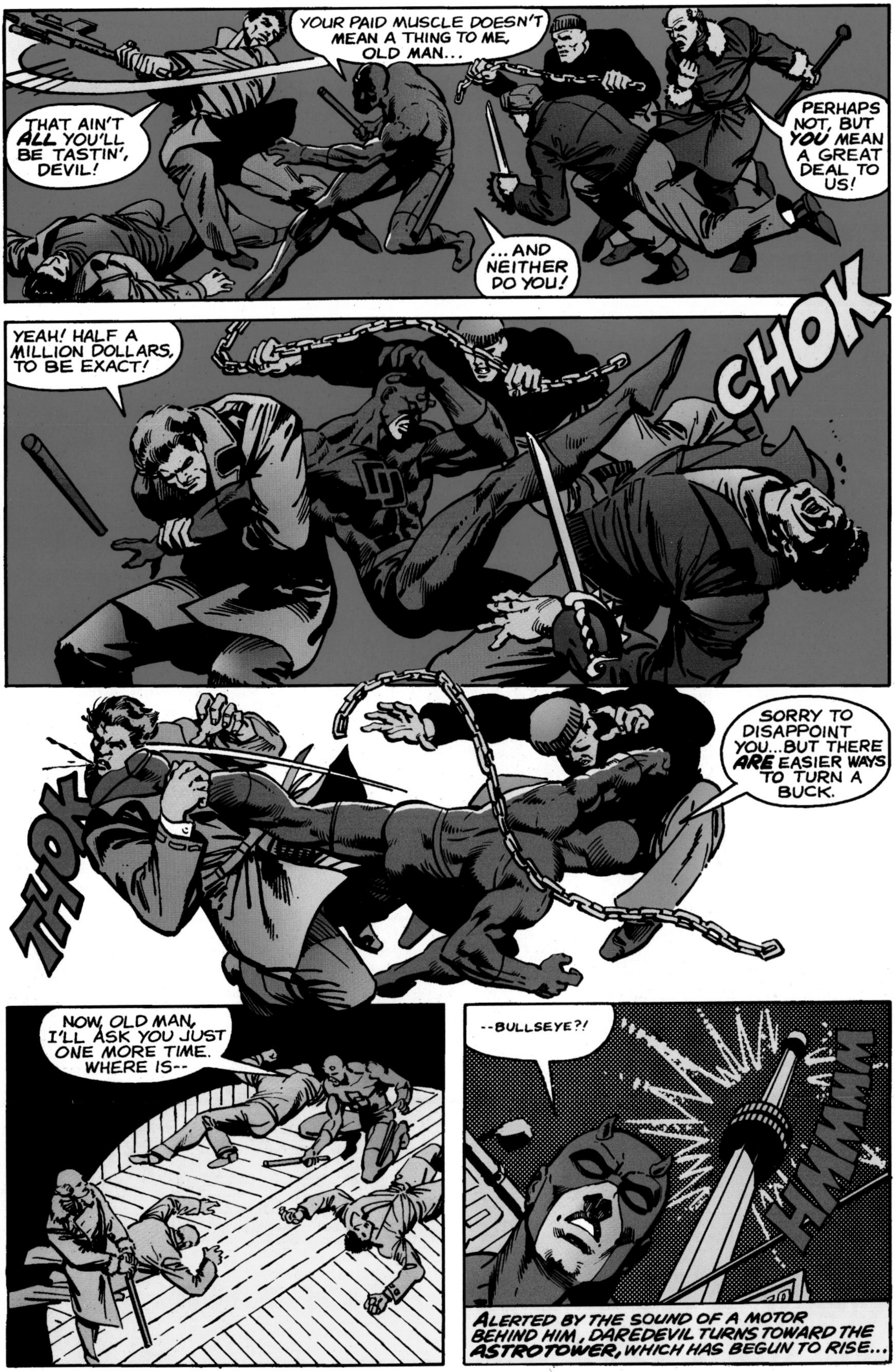
YOUR PAID MUSCLE DOESN'T MEAN A THING TO ME, OLD MAN...
THAT AIN'T ALL YOU'LL BE TASTIN', DEVIL!
PERHAPS NOT, BUT YOU MEAN A GREAT DEAL TO US!
...AND NEITHER DO YOU!
YEAH! HALF A MILLION DOLLARS, TO BE EXACT!
CHOK
SORRY TO DISAPPOINT YOU...BUT THERE ARE EASIER WAYS TO TURN A BUCK.
THOK
NOW, OLD MAN, I'LL ASK YOU JUST ONE MORE TIME. WHERE IS--
--BULLSEYE?!
HMMMM
ALERTED BY THE SOUND OF A MOTOR BEHIND HIM, DAREDEVIL TURNS TOWARD THE ASTROTOWER, WHICH HAS BEGUN TO RISE...

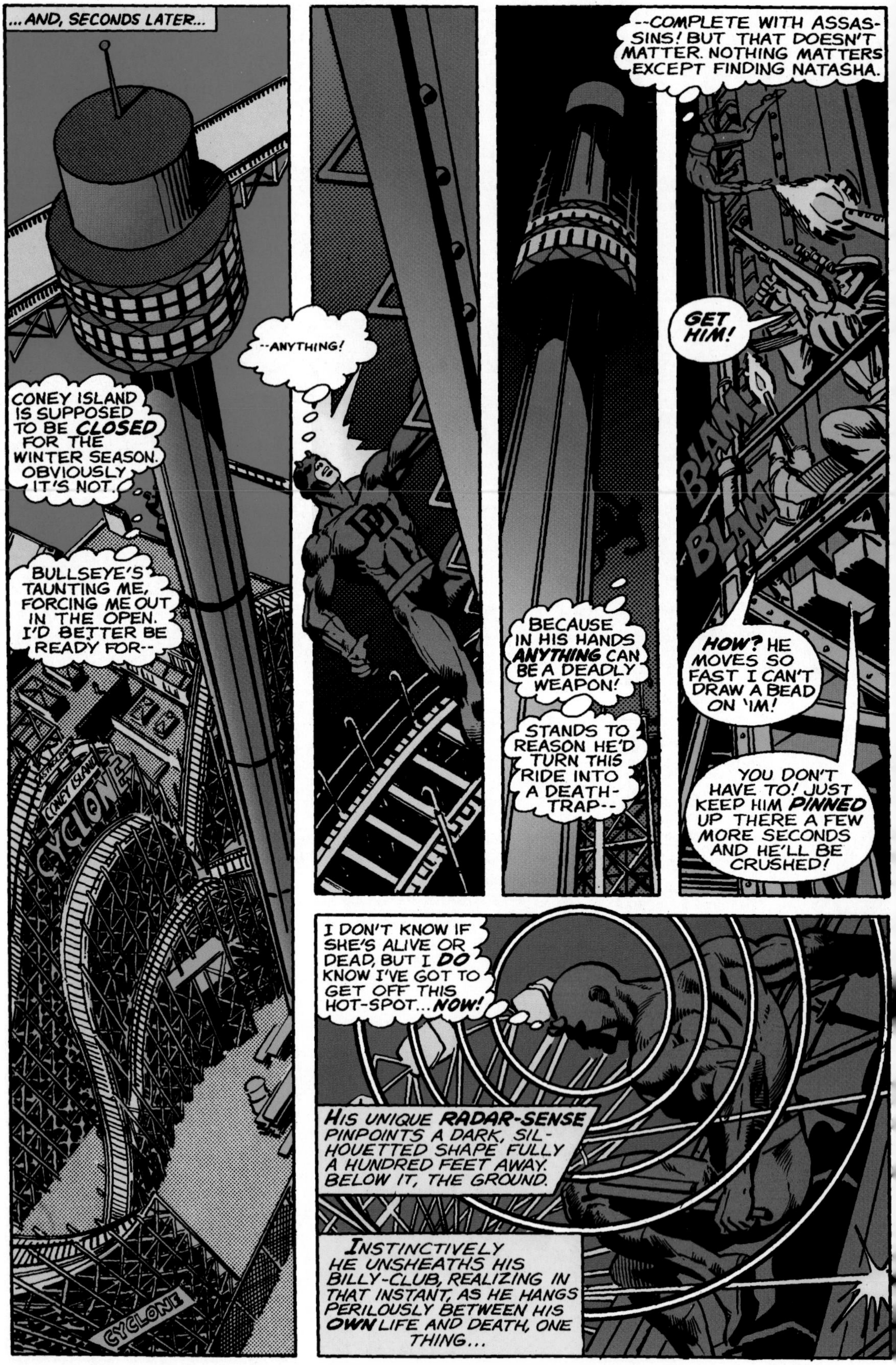
...AND, SECONDS LATER...
CONEY ISLAND IS SUPPOSED TO BE CLOSED FOR THE WINTER SEASON. OBVIOUSLY IT'S NOT.
BULLSEYE'S TAUNTING ME, FORCING ME OUT IN THE OPEN. I'D BETTER BE READY FOR--
CONEY ISLAND
CYCLONE
CYCLONE
--ANYTHING!
BECAUSE IN HIS HANDS ANYTHING CAN BE A DEADLY WEAPON!
STANDS TO REASON HE'D TURN THIS RIDE INTO A DEATH-TRAP--
--COMPLETE WITH ASSASSINS! BUT THAT DOESN'T MATTER. NOTHING MATTERS EXCEPT FINDING NATASHA.
GET HIM!
BLAM
BLAM
HOW? HE MOVES SO FAST I CAN'T DRAW A BEAD ON 'IM!
YOU DON'T HAVE TO! JUST KEEP HIM PINNED UP THERE A FEW MORE SECONDS AND HE'LL BE CRUSHED!
I DON'T KNOW IF SHE'S ALIVE OR DEAD, BUT I DO KNOW I'VE GOT TO GET OFF THIS HOT-SPOT... NOW!
HIS UNIQUE RADAR-SENSE PINPOINTS A DARK, SILHOUETTED SHAPE FULLY A HUNDRED FEET AWAY. BELOW IT, THE GROUND.
INSTINCTIVELY HE UNSHEATHS HIS BILLY-CLUB, REALIZING IN THAT INSTANT, AS HE HANGS PERILOUSLY BETWEEN HIS OWN LIFE AND DEATH, ONE THING...

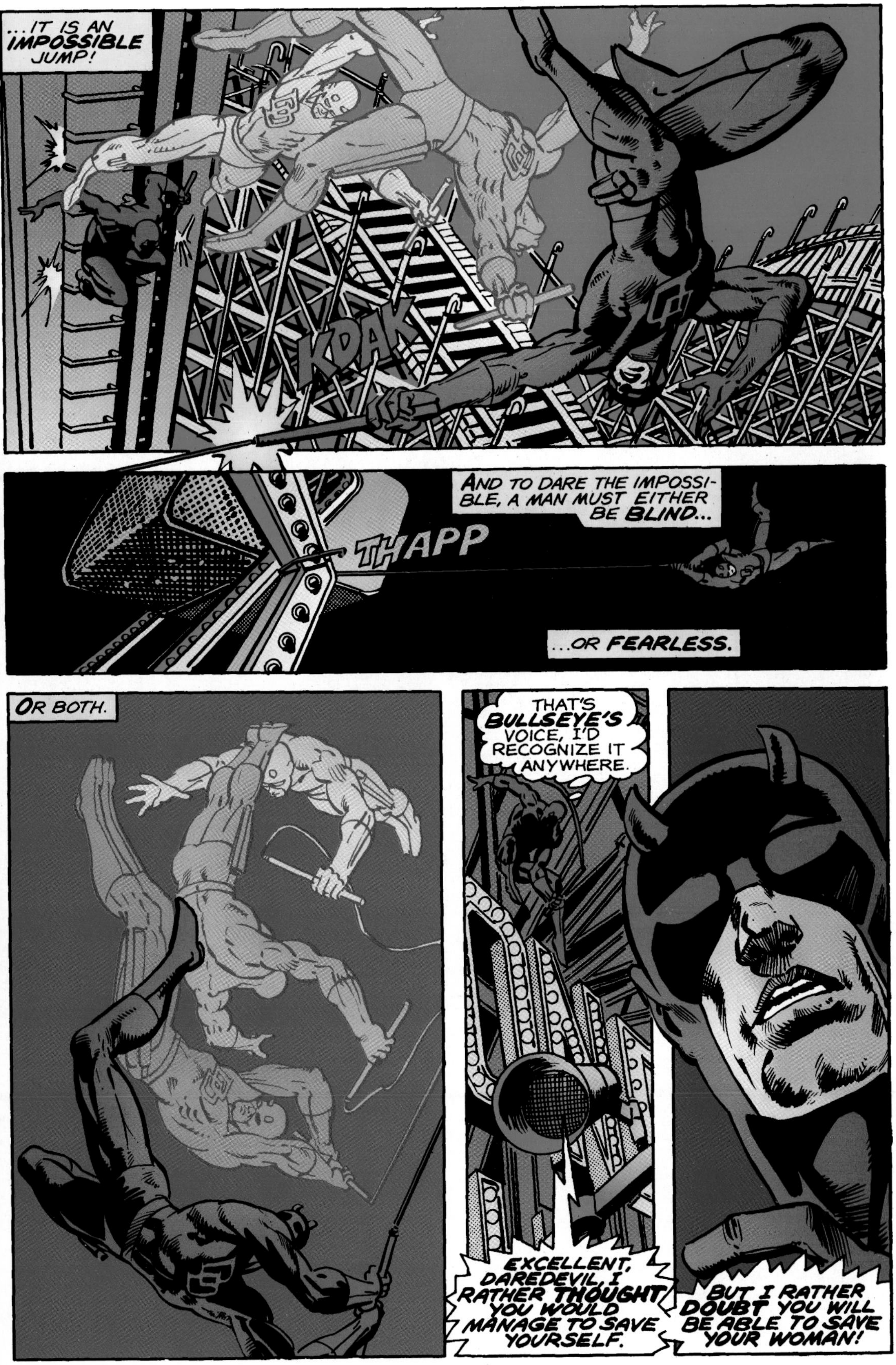
...IT IS AN IMPOSSIBLE JUMP!
KDAK
AND TO DARE THE IMPOSSIBLE, A MAN MUST EITHER BE BLIND...
THAPP
...OR FEARLESS.
OR BOTH.
THAT'S BULLSEYE'S VOICE, I'D RECOGNIZE IT ANYWHERE.
EXCELLENT, DAREDEVIL, I RATHER THOUGHT YOU WOULD MANAGE TO SAVE YOURSELF.
BUT I RATHER DOUBT YOU WILL BE ABLE TO SAVE YOUR WOMAN!

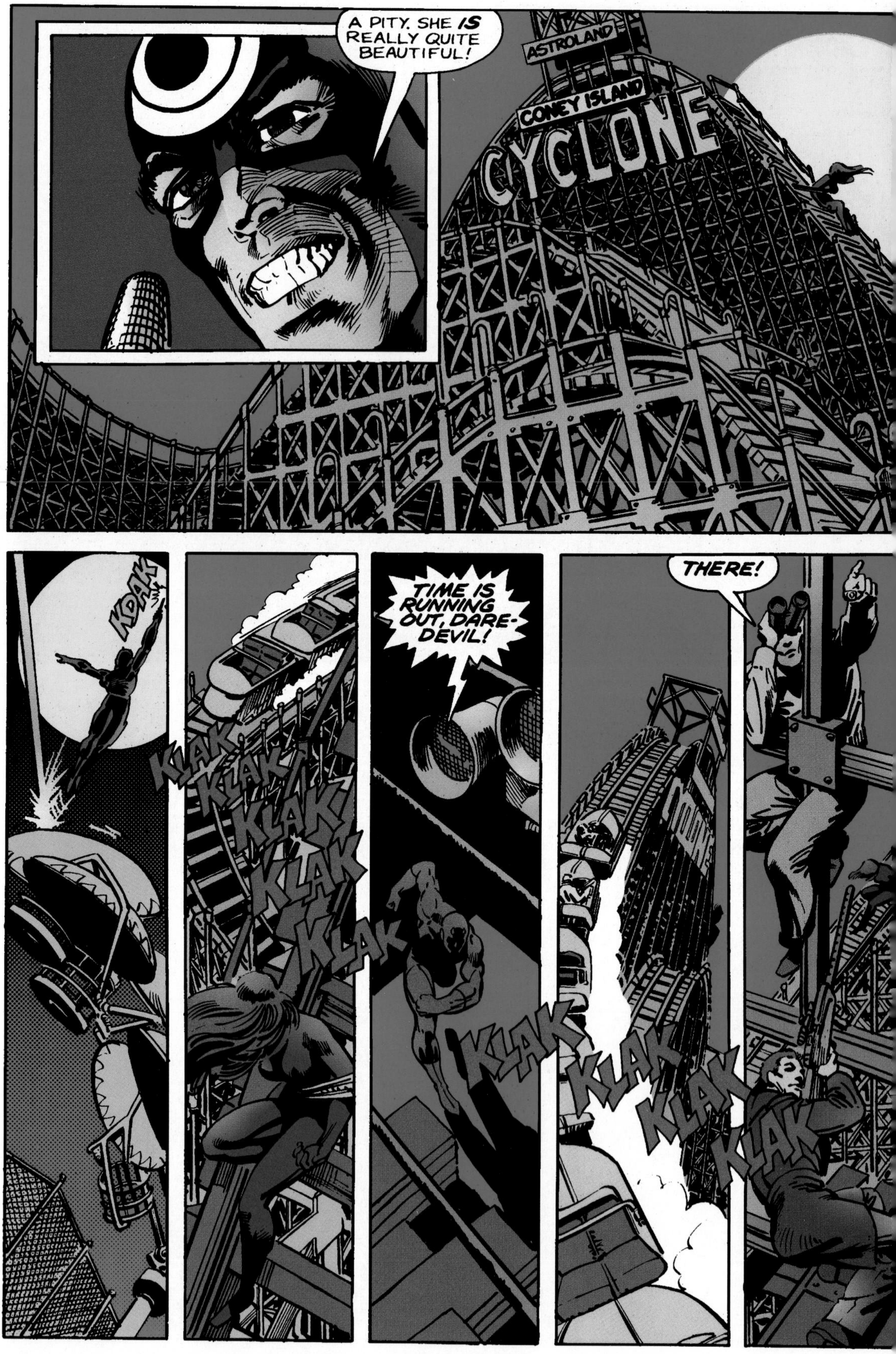
A PITY. SHE *IS* REALLY QUITE BEAUTIFUL!
ASTROLAND
CONEY ISLAND
CYCLONE
KDAK
KLAK KLAK KLAK KLAK KLAK
TIME IS RUNNING OUT, DARE-DEVIL!
KLAK KLAK KLAK KLAK
THERE!

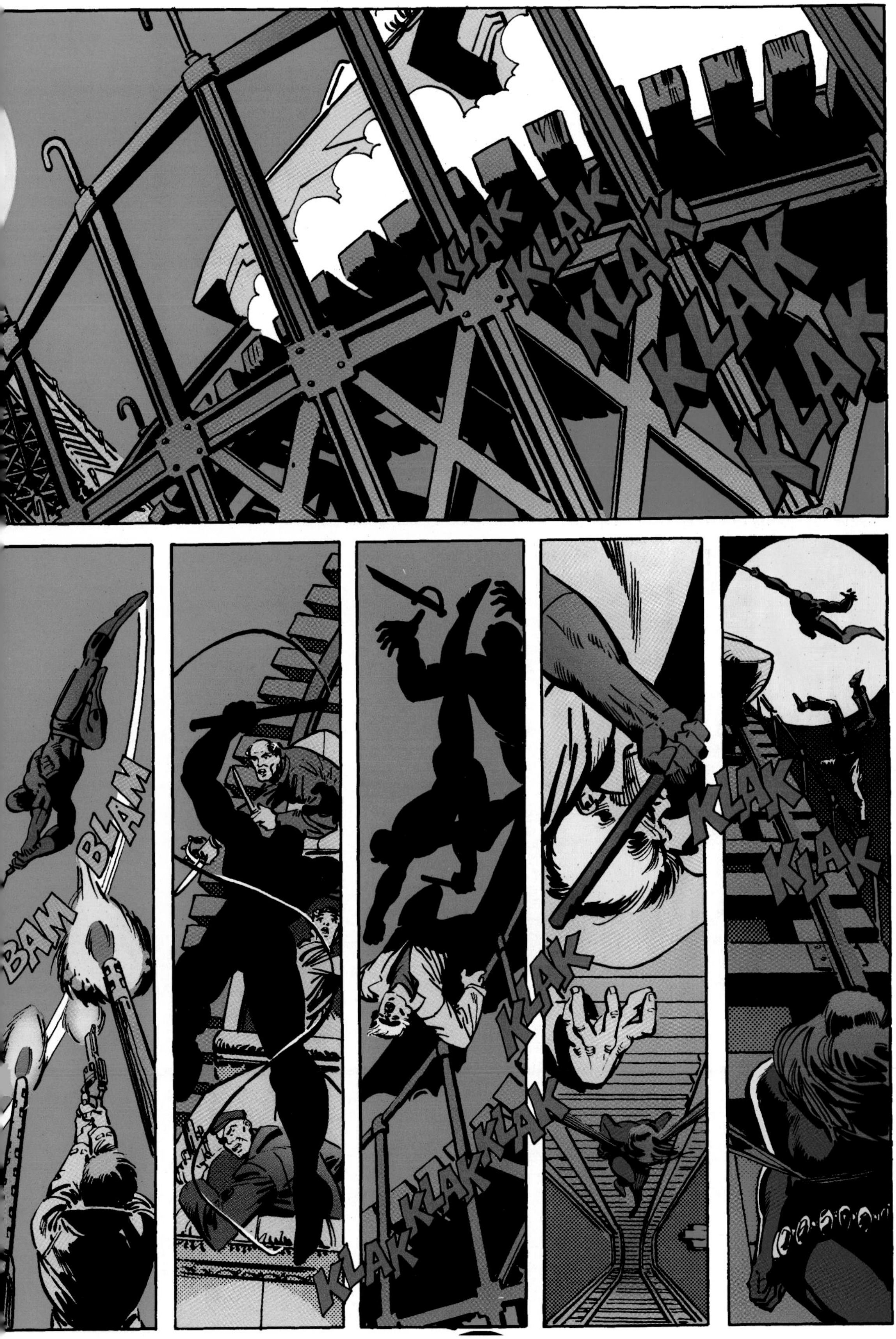
KLAK KLAK KLAK KLAK KLAK KLAK
BLAM
BAM
KLAK KLAK KLAK KLAK KLAK
KLAK KLAK

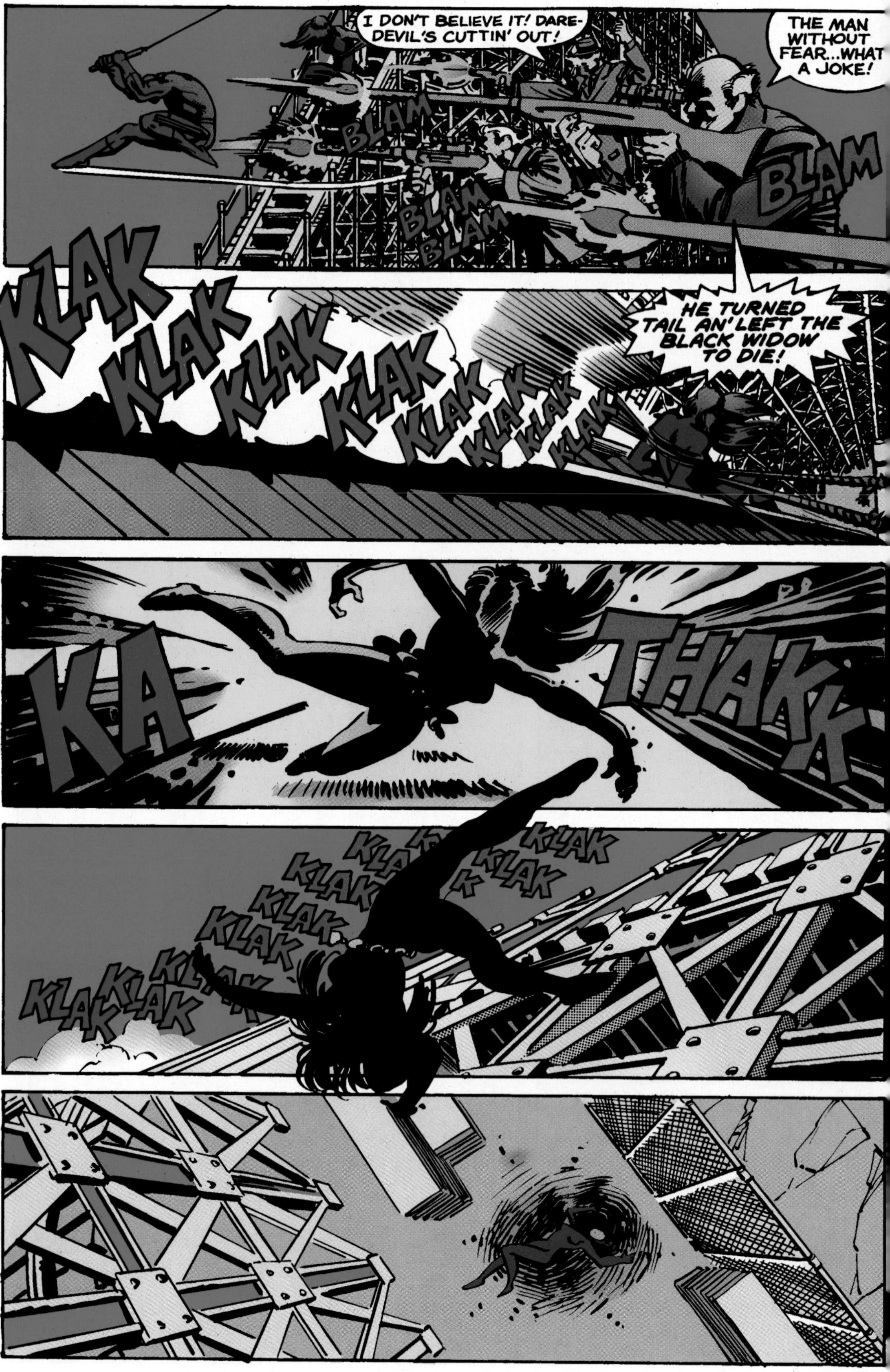
I DON'T BELIEVE IT! DAREDEVIL'S CUTTIN' OUT!
THE MAN WITHOUT FEAR...WHAT A JOKE!
BLAM
BLAM
BLAM BLAM
BLAM
HE TURNED TAIL AN' LEFT THE BLACK WIDOW TO DIE!
KLAK KLAK KLAK KLAK KLAK KLAK KLAK KLAK
KA THAKK
KLAK KLAK KLAK KLAK KLAK KLAK KLAK KLAK KLAK

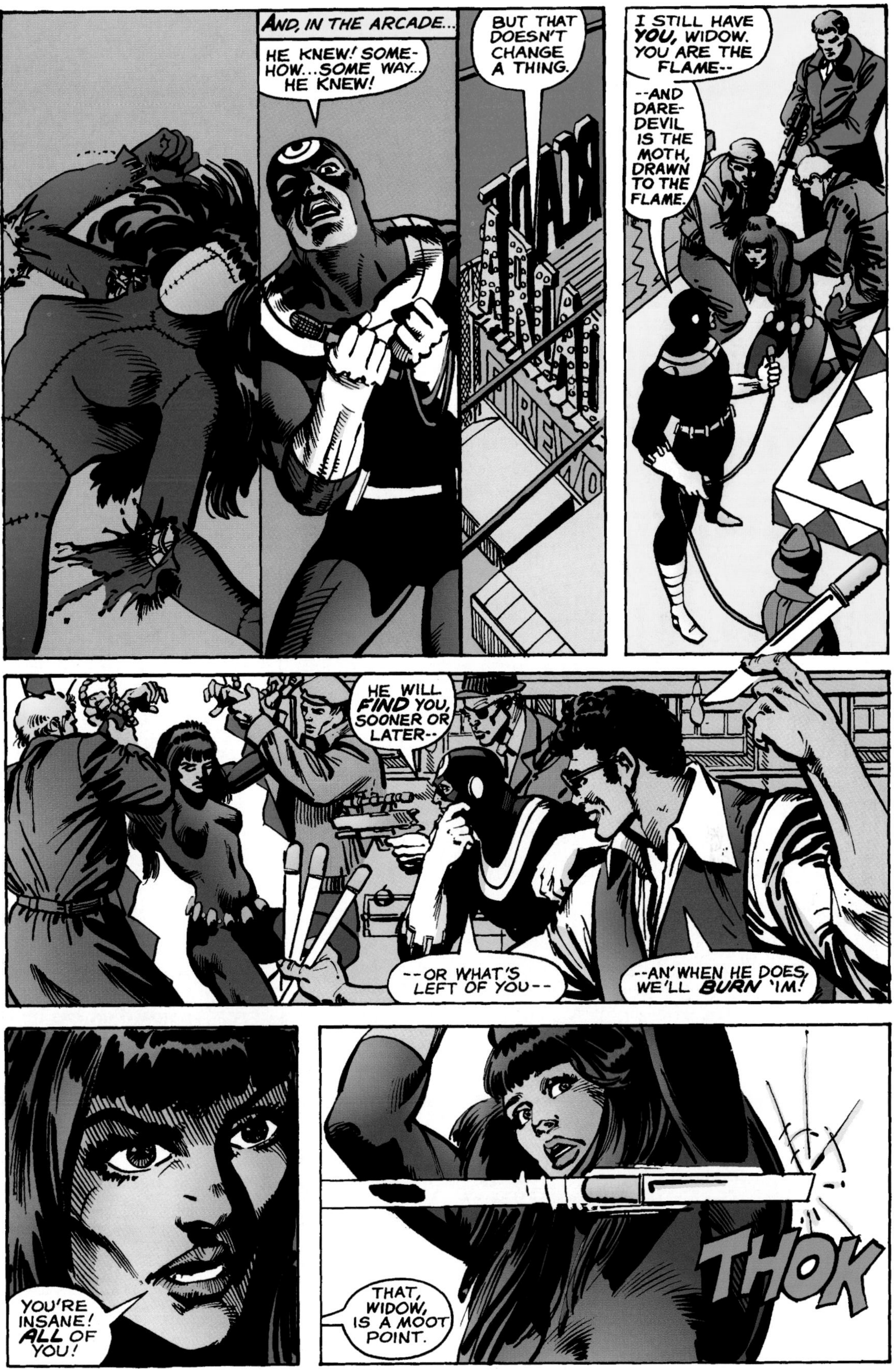
AND, IN THE ARCADE...
HE KNEW! SOME-HOW...SOME WAY... HE KNEW!
BUT THAT DOESN'T CHANGE A THING.
I STILL HAVE YOU, WIDOW. YOU ARE THE FLAME--
--AND DARE-DEVIL IS THE MOTH, DRAWN TO THE FLAME.
HE WILL FIND YOU, SOONER OR LATER--
--OR WHAT'S LEFT OF YOU--
--AN' WHEN HE DOES, WE'LL BURN 'IM!
YOU'RE INSANE! ALL OF YOU!
THAT, WIDOW, IS A MOOT POINT.
THOK

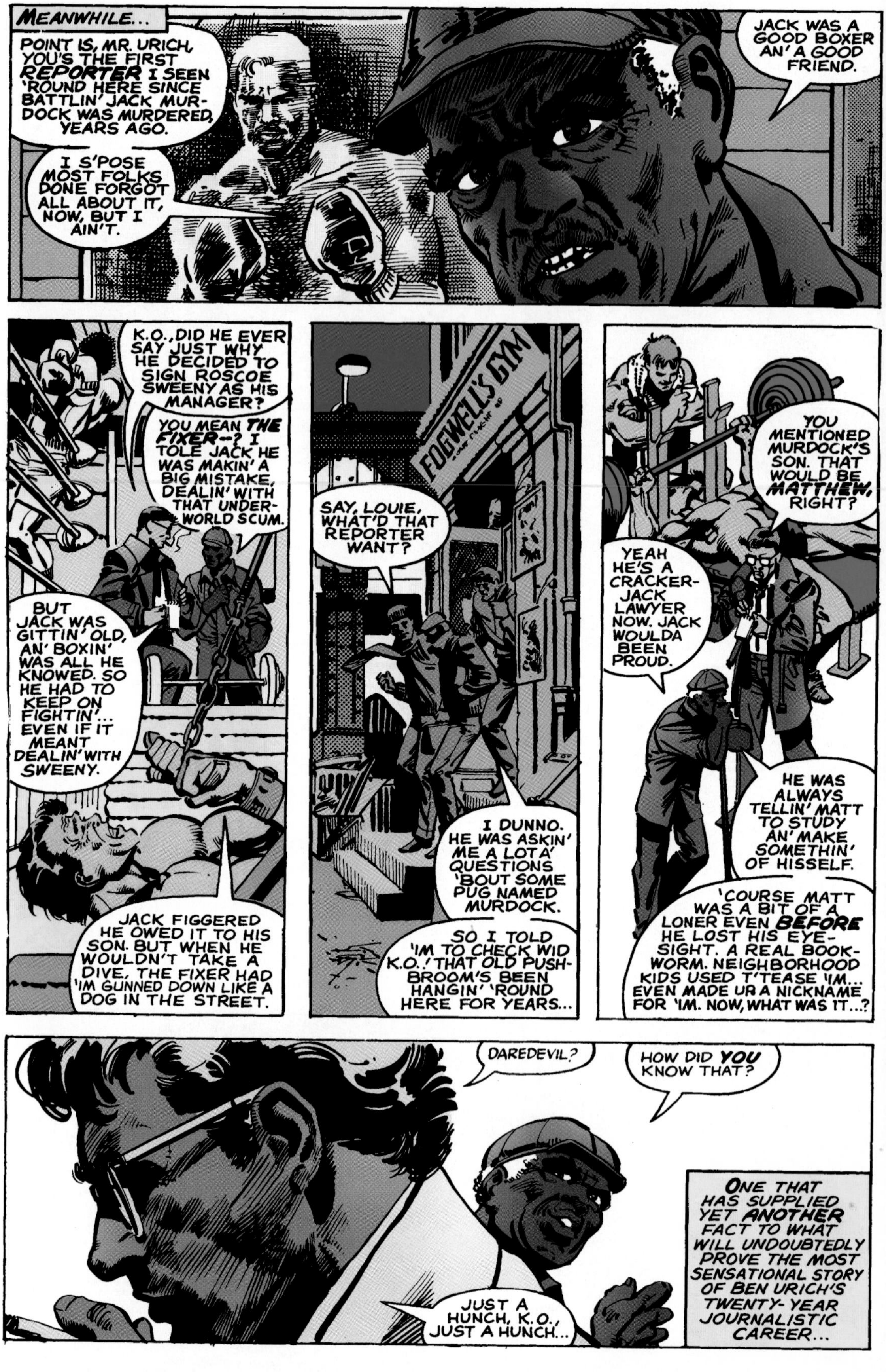
MEANWHILE...
POINT IS, MR. URICH, YOU'S THE FIRST REPORTER I SEEN 'ROUND HERE SINCE BATTLIN' JACK MURDOCK WAS MURDERED, YEARS AGO.
I S'POSE MOST FOLKS DONE FORGOT ALL ABOUT IT, NOW, BUT I AIN'T.
JACK WAS A GOOD BOXER AN' A GOOD FRIEND.
K.O., DID HE EVER SAY JUST WHY HE DECIDED TO SIGN ROSCOE SWEENY AS HIS MANAGER?
YOU MEAN THE FIXER--? I TOLE JACK HE WAS MAKIN' A BIG MISTAKE, DEALIN' WITH THAT UNDER-WORLD SCUM.
BUT JACK WAS GITTIN' OLD, AN' BOXIN' WAS ALL HE KNOWED. SO HE HAD TO KEEP ON FIGHTIN'... EVEN IF IT MEANT DEALIN' WITH SWEENY.
JACK FIGGERED HE OWED IT TO HIS SON. BUT WHEN HE WOULDN'T TAKE A DIVE, THE FIXER HAD 'IM GUNNED DOWN LIKE A DOG IN THE STREET.
FOGWELL'S GYM
SAY, LOUIE, WHAT'D THAT REPORTER WANT?
I DUNNO. HE WAS ASKIN' ME A LOTA' QUESTIONS 'BOUT SOME PUG NAMED MURDOCK.
SO I TOLD 'IM TO CHECK WID K.O.! THAT OLD PUSH-BROOM'S BEEN HANGIN' 'ROUND HERE FOR YEARS...
YOU MENTIONED MURDOCK'S SON. THAT WOULD BE MATTHEW, RIGHT?
YEAH HE'S A CRACKER-JACK LAWYER NOW. JACK WOULDA BEEN PROUD.
HE WAS ALWAYS TELLIN' MATT TO STUDY AN' MAKE SOMETHIN' OF HISSELF.
'COURSE MATT WAS A BIT OF A LONER EVEN BEFORE HE LOST HIS EYE-SIGHT. A REAL BOOK-WORM. NEIGHBORHOOD KIDS USED T'TEASE 'IM... EVEN MADE UP A NICKNAME FOR 'IM. NOW, WHAT WAS IT...?
DAREDEVIL?
HOW DID YOU KNOW THAT?
JUST A HUNCH, K.O., JUST A HUNCH...
ONE THAT HAS SUPPLIED YET ANOTHER FACT TO WHAT WILL UNDOUBTEDLY PROVE THE MOST SENSATIONAL STORY OF BEN URICH'S TWENTY-YEAR JOURNALISTIC CAREER...

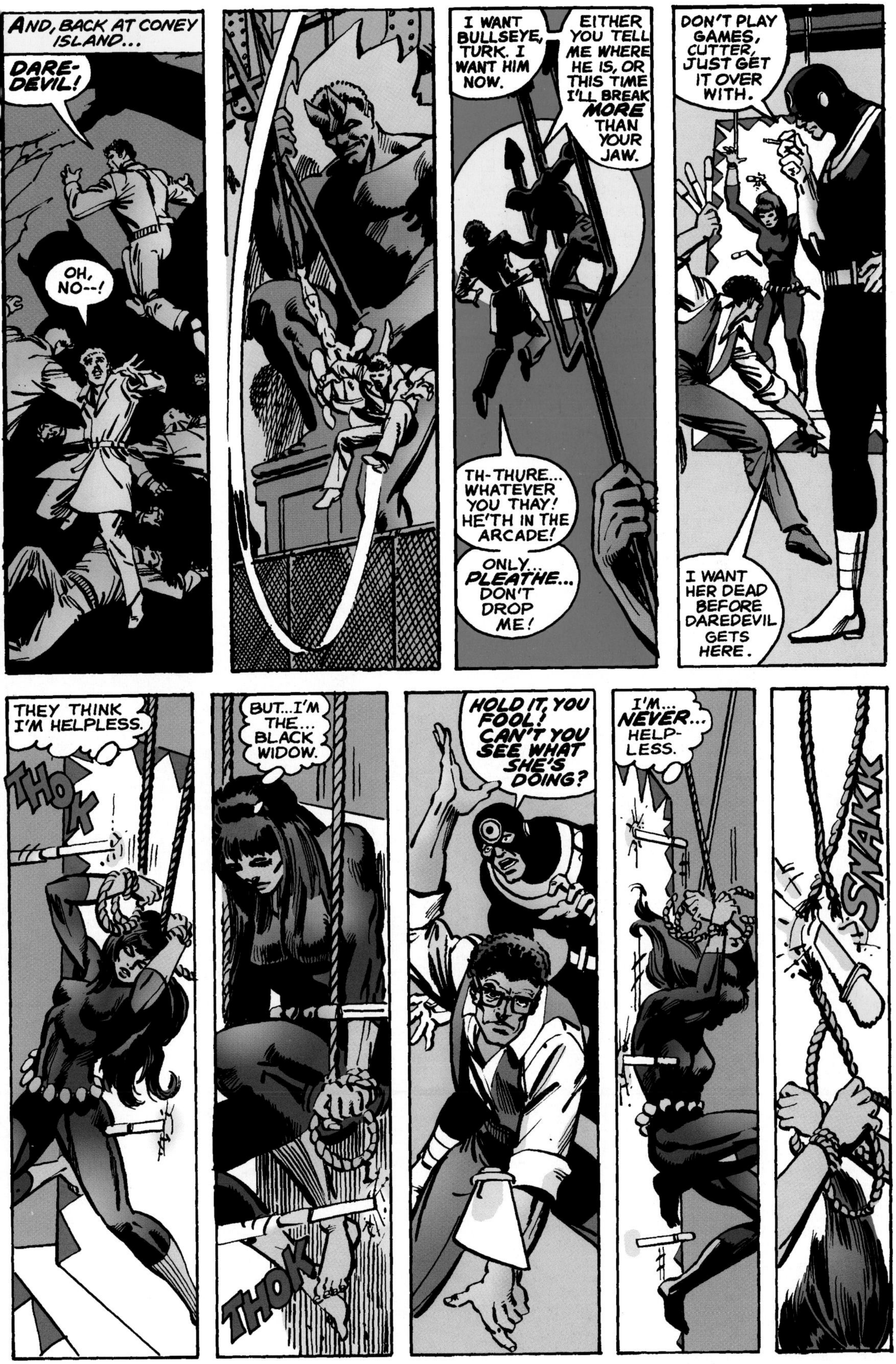
AND, BACK AT CONEY ISLAND...
DARE-DEVIL!
OH, NO--!
I WANT BULLSEYE, TURK. I WANT HIM NOW.
EITHER YOU TELL ME WHERE HE IS, OR THIS TIME I'LL BREAK MORE THAN YOUR JAW.
TH-THURE... WHATEVER YOU THAY! HE'TH IN THE ARCADE!
ONLY... PLEATHE... DON'T DROP ME!
DON'T PLAY GAMES, CUTTER, JUST GET IT OVER WITH.
I WANT HER DEAD BEFORE DAREDEVIL GETS HERE.
THEY THINK I'M HELPLESS.
THOK
BUT...I'M THE... BLACK WIDOW.
THOK
HOLD IT, YOU FOOL! CAN'T YOU SEE WHAT SHE'S DOING?
I'M... NEVER... HELP-LESS.
SNAKK

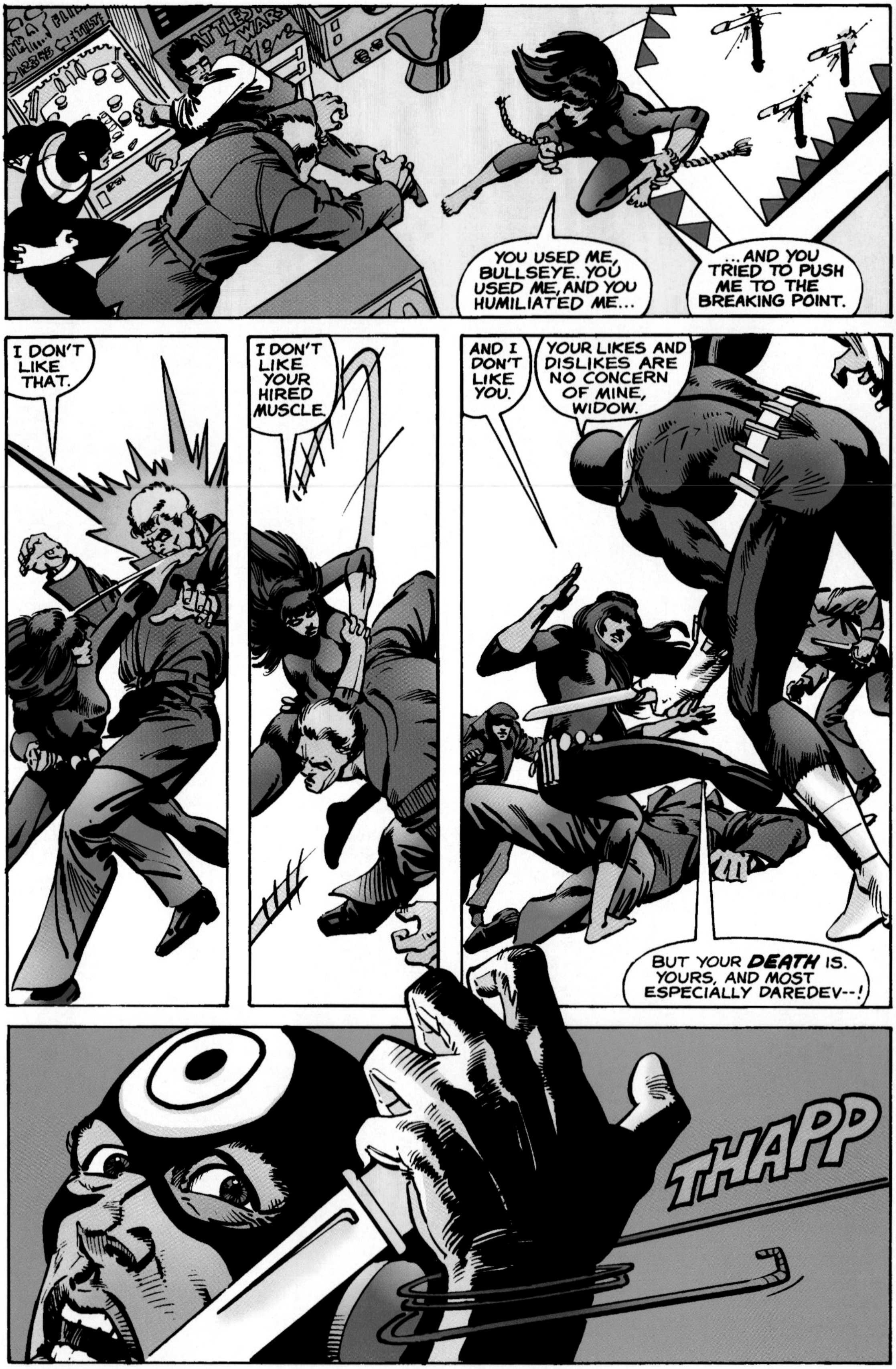
YOU USED ME, BULLSEYE. YOU USED ME, AND YOU HUMILIATED ME...
...AND YOU TRIED TO PUSH ME TO THE BREAKING POINT.
I DON'T LIKE THAT.
I DON'T LIKE YOUR HIRED MUSCLE.
AND I DON'T LIKE YOU.
YOUR LIKES AND DISLIKES ARE NO CONCERN OF MINE, WIDOW.
BUT YOUR DEATH IS. YOURS, AND MOST ESPECIALLY DAREDEV--!
THAPP

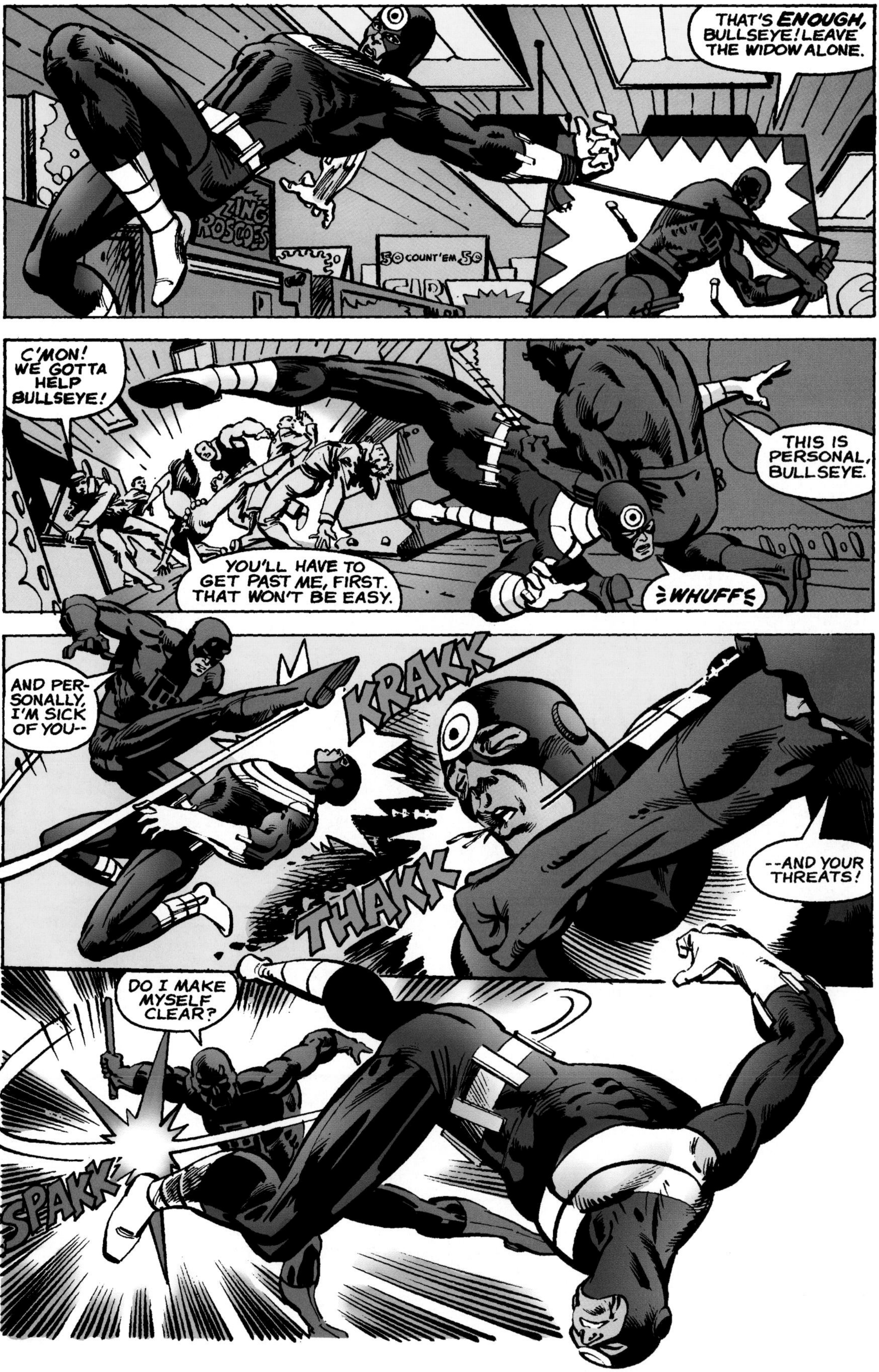
THAT'S ENOUGH, BULLSEYE! LEAVE THE WIDOW ALONE.
ZING
ROSCOES
50 COUNT'EM 50
C'MON! WE GOTTA HELP BULLSEYE!
THIS IS PERSONAL, BULLSEYE.
YOU'LL HAVE TO GET PAST ME, FIRST. THAT WON'T BE EASY.
WHUFF
AND PERSONALLY, I'M SICK OF YOU--
KRAKK
THAKK
--AND YOUR THREATS!
DO I MAKE MYSELF CLEAR?
SPAKK

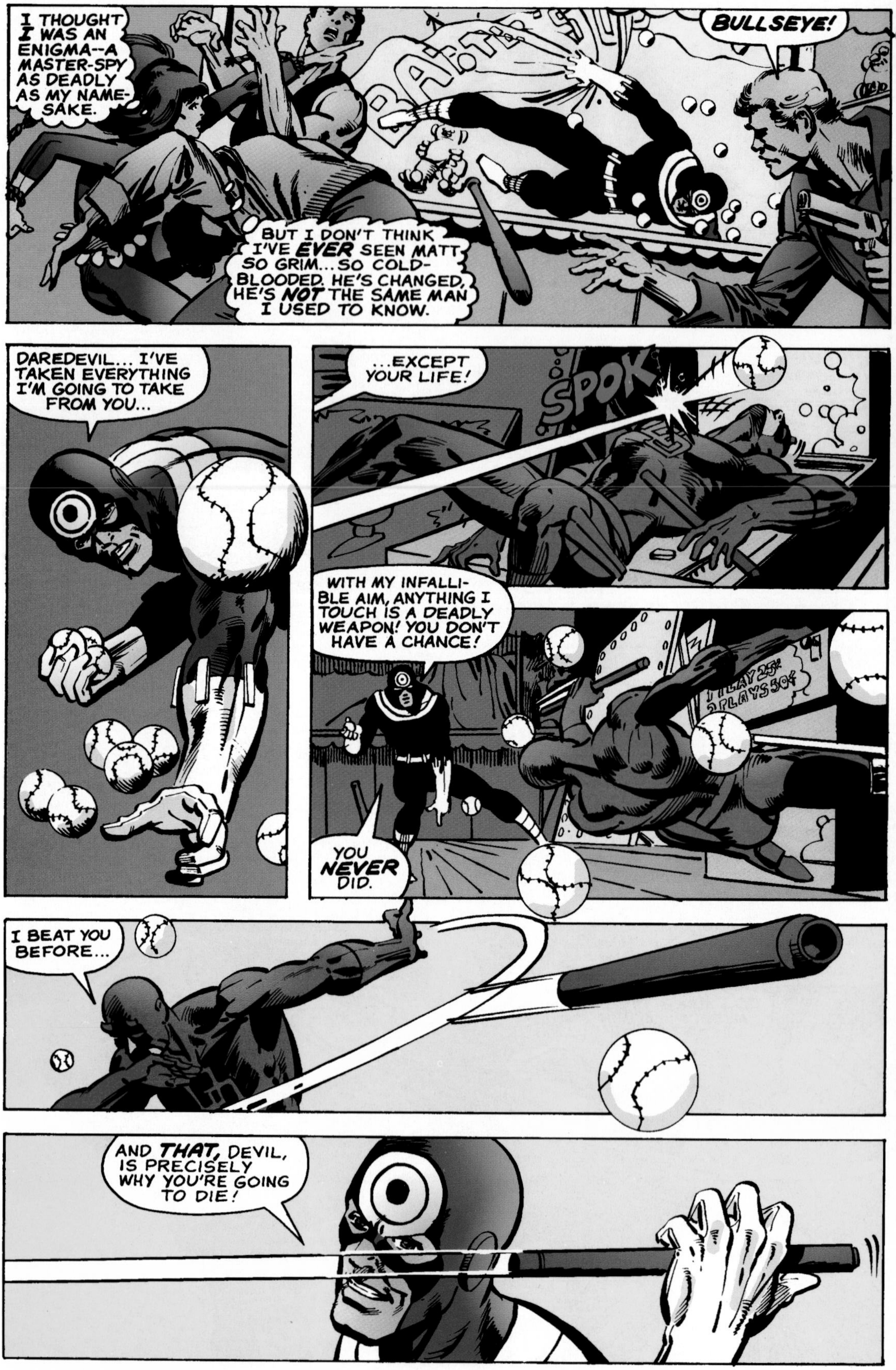
I THOUGHT I WAS AN ENIGMA--A MASTER-SPY AS DEADLY AS MY NAME-SAKE.
BULLSEYE!
BUT I DON'T THINK I'VE EVER SEEN MATT SO GRIM... SO COLD-BLOODED. HE'S CHANGED, HE'S NOT THE SAME MAN I USED TO KNOW.
DAREDEVIL... I'VE TAKEN EVERYTHING I'M GOING TO TAKE FROM YOU...
...EXCEPT YOUR LIFE!
SPOK
WITH MY INFALLI-BLE AIM, ANYTHING I TOUCH IS A DEADLY WEAPON! YOU DON'T HAVE A CHANCE!
YOU NEVER DID.
I BEAT YOU BEFORE...
AND THAT, DEVIL, IS PRECISELY WHY YOU'RE GOING TO DIE!

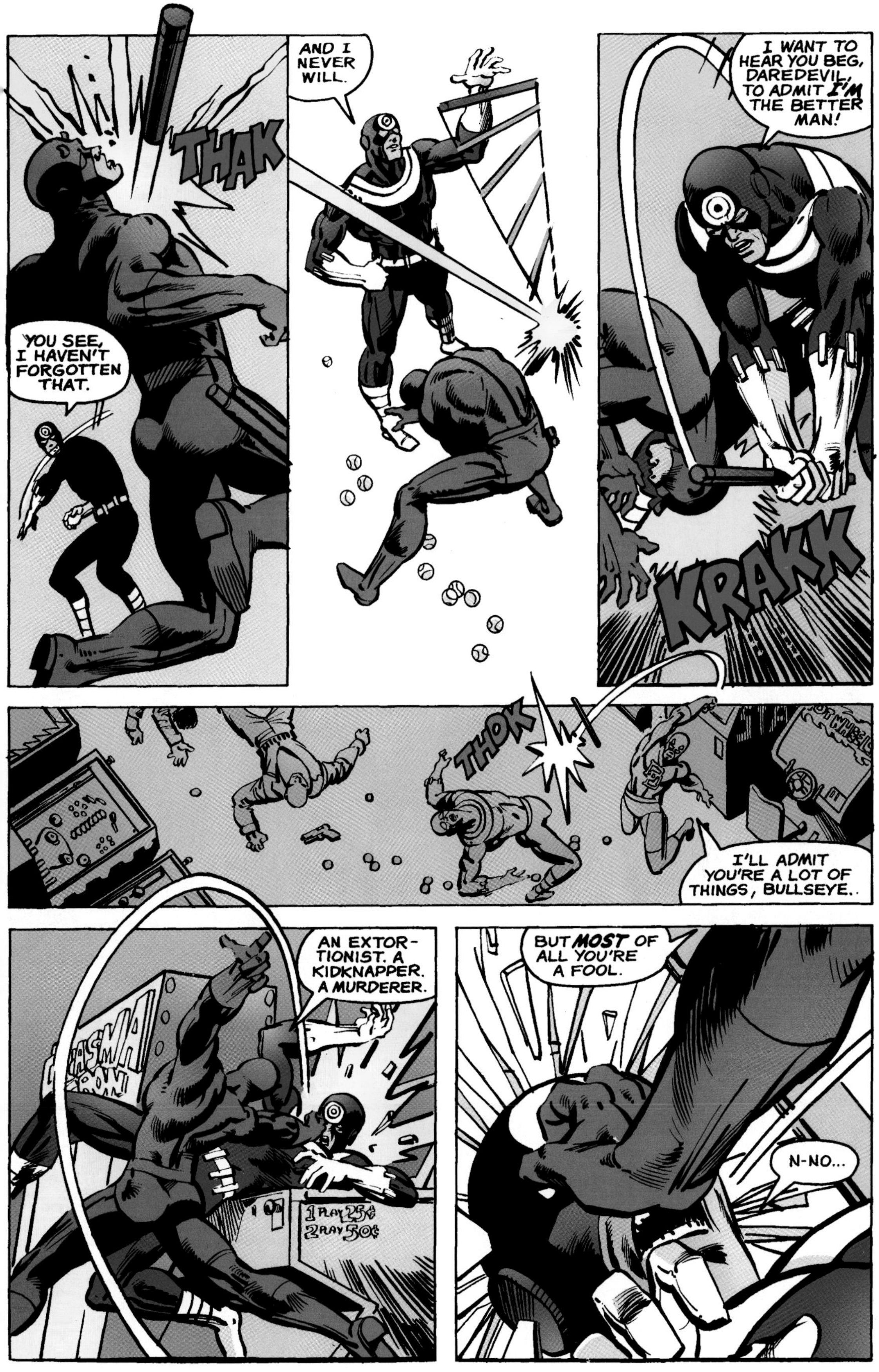
THAK
YOU SEE, I HAVEN'T FORGOTTEN THAT.
AND I NEVER WILL.
I WANT TO HEAR YOU BEG, DAREDEVIL, TO ADMIT I'M THE BETTER MAN!
KRAKK
THOK
I'LL ADMIT YOU'RE A LOT OF THINGS, BULLSEYE..
AN EXTOR-TIONIST. A KIDNAPPER. A MURDERER.
1 PLAY 25¢
2 PLAY 50¢
BUT MOST OF ALL YOU'RE A FOOL.
N-NO...

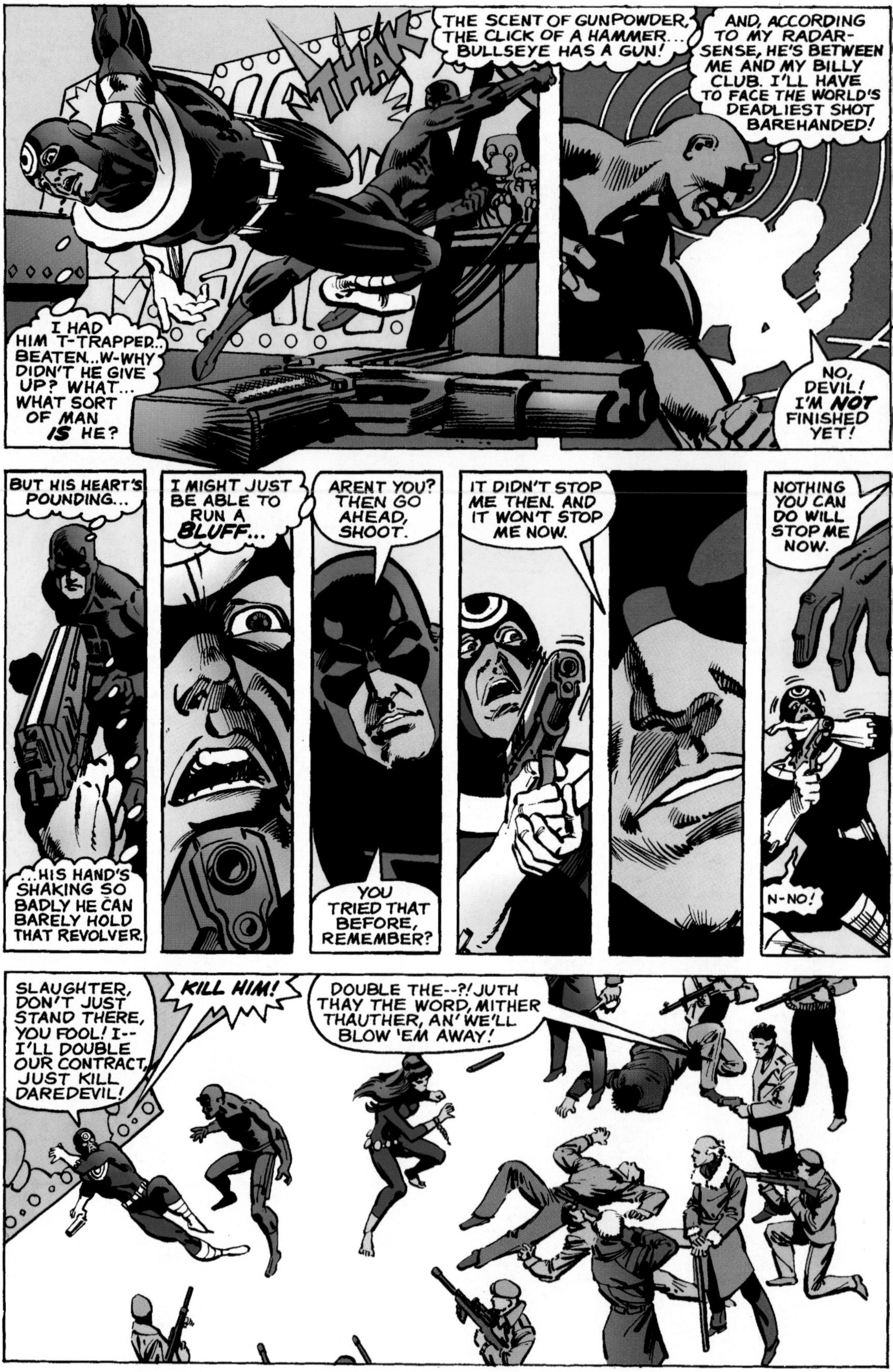
THAK
THE SCENT OF GUNPOWDER, THE CLICK OF A HAMMER... BULLSEYE HAS A GUN!
AND, ACCORDING TO MY RADAR-SENSE, HE'S BETWEEN ME AND MY BILLY CLUB. I'LL HAVE TO FACE THE WORLD'S DEADLIEST SHOT BAREHANDED!
I HAD HIM T-TRAPPED.. BEATEN...W-WHY DIDN'T HE GIVE UP? WHAT... WHAT SORT OF MAN IS HE?
NO, DEVIL! I'M NOT FINISHED YET!
BUT HIS HEART'S POUNDING...
...HIS HAND'S SHAKING SO BADLY HE CAN BARELY HOLD THAT REVOLVER.
I MIGHT JUST BE ABLE TO RUN A BLUFF...
ARENT YOU? THEN GO AHEAD, SHOOT.
YOU TRIED THAT BEFORE, REMEMBER?
IT DIDN'T STOP ME THEN. AND IT WON'T STOP ME NOW.
NOTHING YOU CAN DO WILL STOP ME NOW.
N-NO!
SLAUGHTER, DON'T JUST STAND THERE, YOU FOOL! I-- I'LL DOUBLE OUR CONTRACT, JUST KILL DAREDEVIL!
KILL HIM!
DOUBLE THE--?! JUTH THAY THE WORD, MITHER THAUTHER, AN' WE'LL BLOW 'EM AWAY!

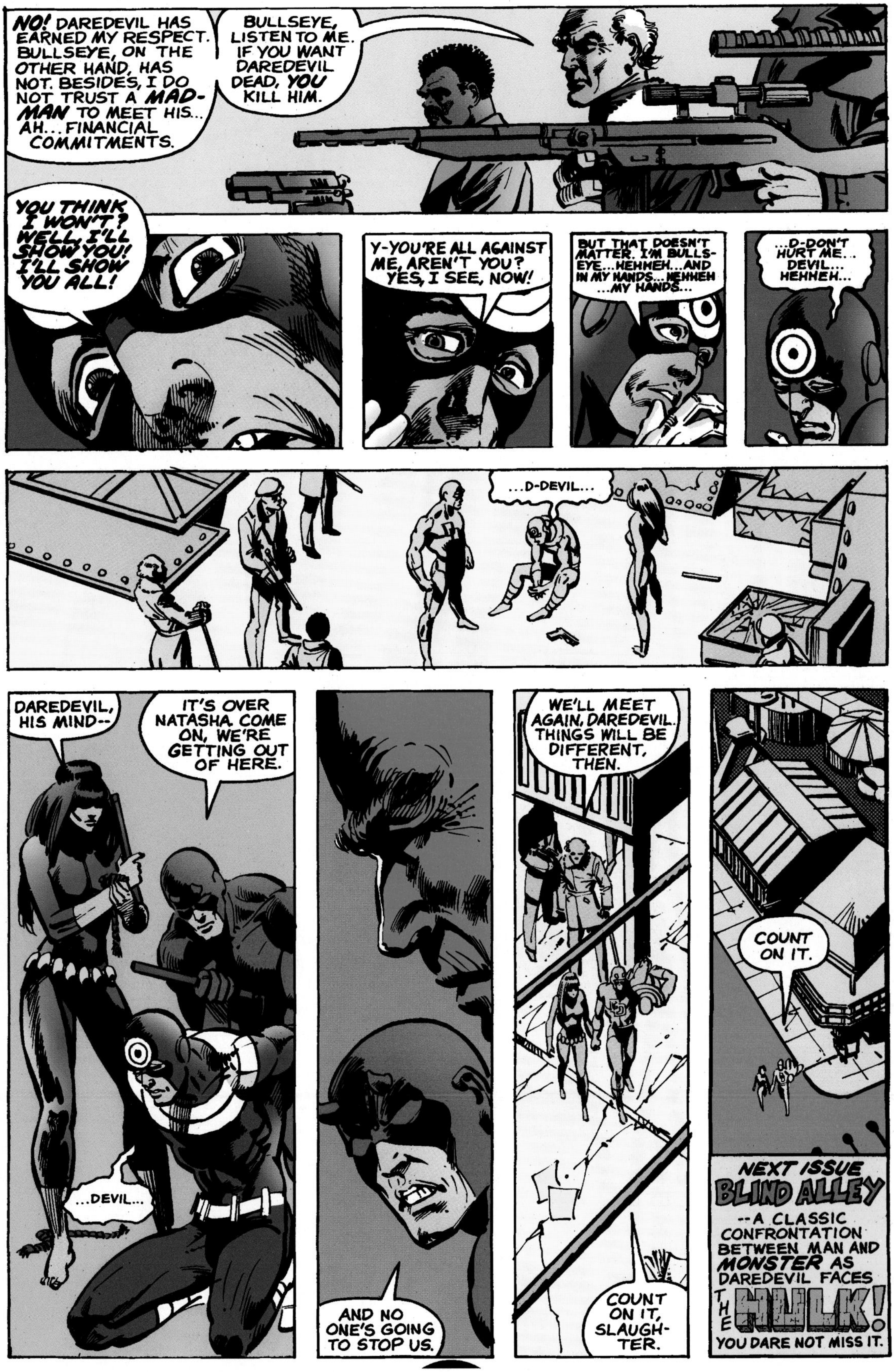
NO! DAREDEVIL HAS EARNED MY RESPECT. BULLSEYE, ON THE OTHER HAND, HAS NOT. BESIDES, I DO NOT TRUST A MAD-MAN TO MEET HIS... AH... FINANCIAL COMMITMENTS.
BULLSEYE, LISTEN TO ME. IF YOU WANT DAREDEVIL DEAD, YOU KILL HIM.
YOU THINK I WON'T? WELL, I'LL SHOW YOU! I'LL SHOW YOU ALL!
Y-YOU'RE ALL AGAINST ME, AREN'T YOU? YES, I SEE, NOW!
BUT THAT DOESN'T MATTER. I'M BULLS-EYE... HEHHEH... AND IN MY HANDS... HEHHEH ...MY HANDS...
...D-DON'T HURT ME... DEVIL... HEHHEH...
...D-DEVIL...
DAREDEVIL, HIS MIND--
IT'S OVER NATASHA. COME ON, WE'RE GETTING OUT OF HERE.
...DEVIL...
AND NO ONE'S GOING TO STOP US.
WE'LL MEET AGAIN, DAREDEVIL. THINGS WILL BE DIFFERENT, THEN.
COUNT ON IT, SLAUGH-TER.
COUNT ON IT.
NEXT ISSUE
BLIND ALLEY
--A CLASSIC CONFRONTATION BETWEEN MAN AND MONSTER AS DAREDEVIL FACES THE HULK!
YOU DARE NOT MISS IT.

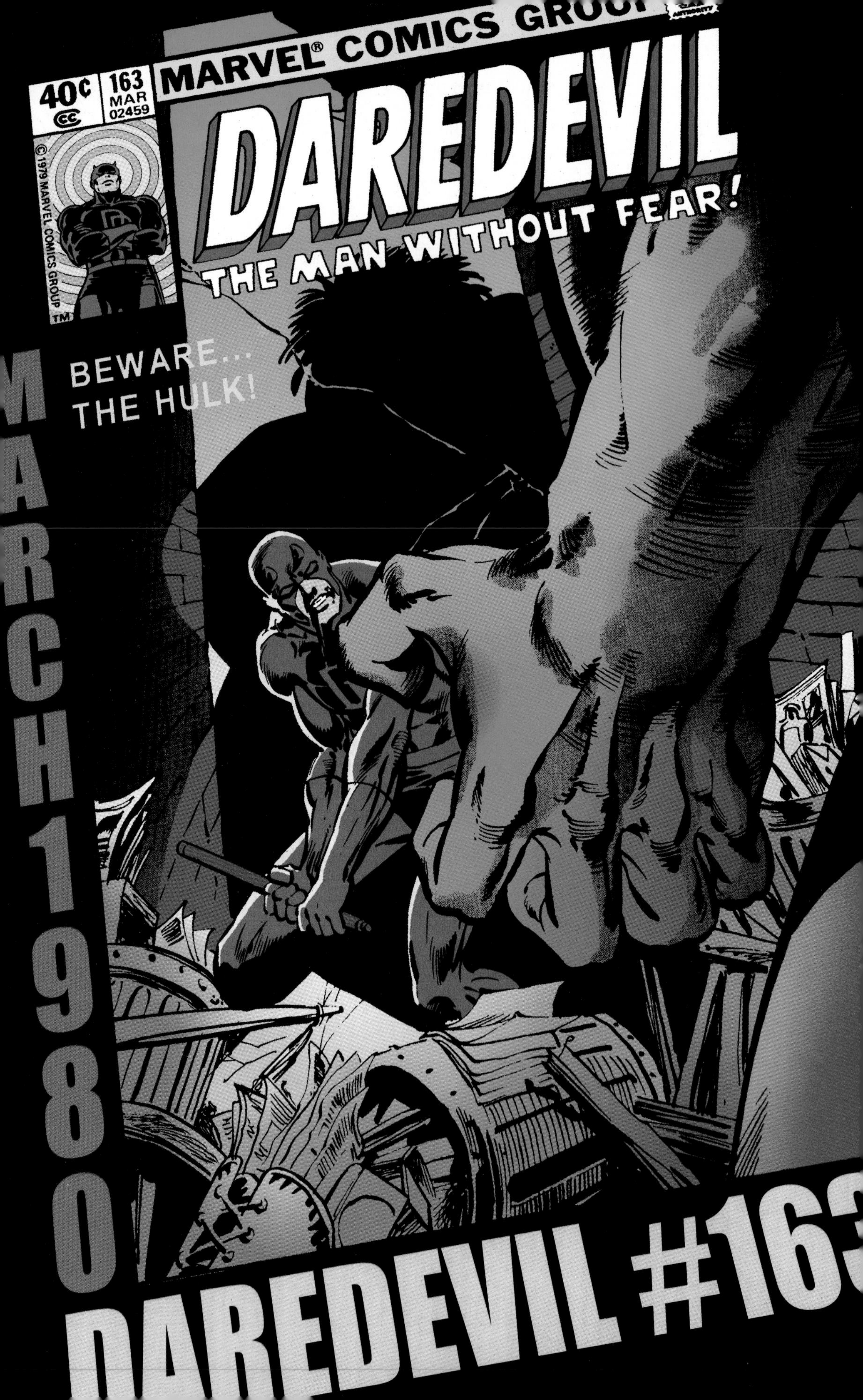
MARVEL® COMICS GROU
40¢
163
MAR
02459
©1979 MARVEL COMICS GROUP
TM
DAREDEVIL
THE MAN WITHOUT FEAR!
BEWARE...
THE HULK!
MARCH 1980
DAREDEVIL #16

He dwells in eternal night—but the blackness is filled with sounds and scents other men cannot perceive. Though attorney MATT MURDOCK is *blind*, his other senses function with *superhuman sharpness*—his *radar sense* guides him over every obstacle! He stalks the streets by night, a red-garbed foe of evil!

Stan Lee PRESENTS: DAREDEVIL, THE MAN WITHOUT FEAR! ™

THE OCCASION IS A HUNDRED DOLLAR A PLATE FUNDRAISER, LAUNCHING THE RE-ELECTION CAMPAIGN OF DISTRICT ATTORNEY BLAKE TOWER.

Monster Sighted in Manhattan

A green behemoth may be hiding somewhere in New York City. State and local police...

BUT THE MAIN TOPIC OF CONVERSATION THIS EVENING CENTERS AROUND A MISUNDERSTOOD MAN-MONSTER...

THE HULK IS A UNIQUE CASE, JUDGE COFFIN. I DON'T BELIEVE FORCE WILL SOLVE THE PROBLEM.

THE BUGLE HAS ALWAYS BEEN PROGRESSIVE, STARK. MY PAPER WAS THE *FIRST* TO EXPOSE THE SPIDER-MAN MENACE.

FRANKLY, JAMESON, PRINTING, UNSUBSTANTIATED RUMORS STRIKES ME AS *IRRESPONSIBLE* JOURNALISM.

FORCE IS THE *ONLY* SOLUTION, TOWER!

IRRE--?!

MURDOCK, YOU DEFENDED THE HULK ONCE.

WHAT DO YOU THINK?

I *DOUBT* ANY LAWYER WHO WOULD REPRESENT THAT BRUTE *CAN* THINK.

UH, MATT, I'M SURE HIS HONOR DIDN'T MEAN--!

...AND THEN THE PRIEST SAYS TO THE RABBI...

DON'T BE RIDICULOUS, TOWER! I MEANT *EVERY* WORD!

HELLO, MATTHEW.

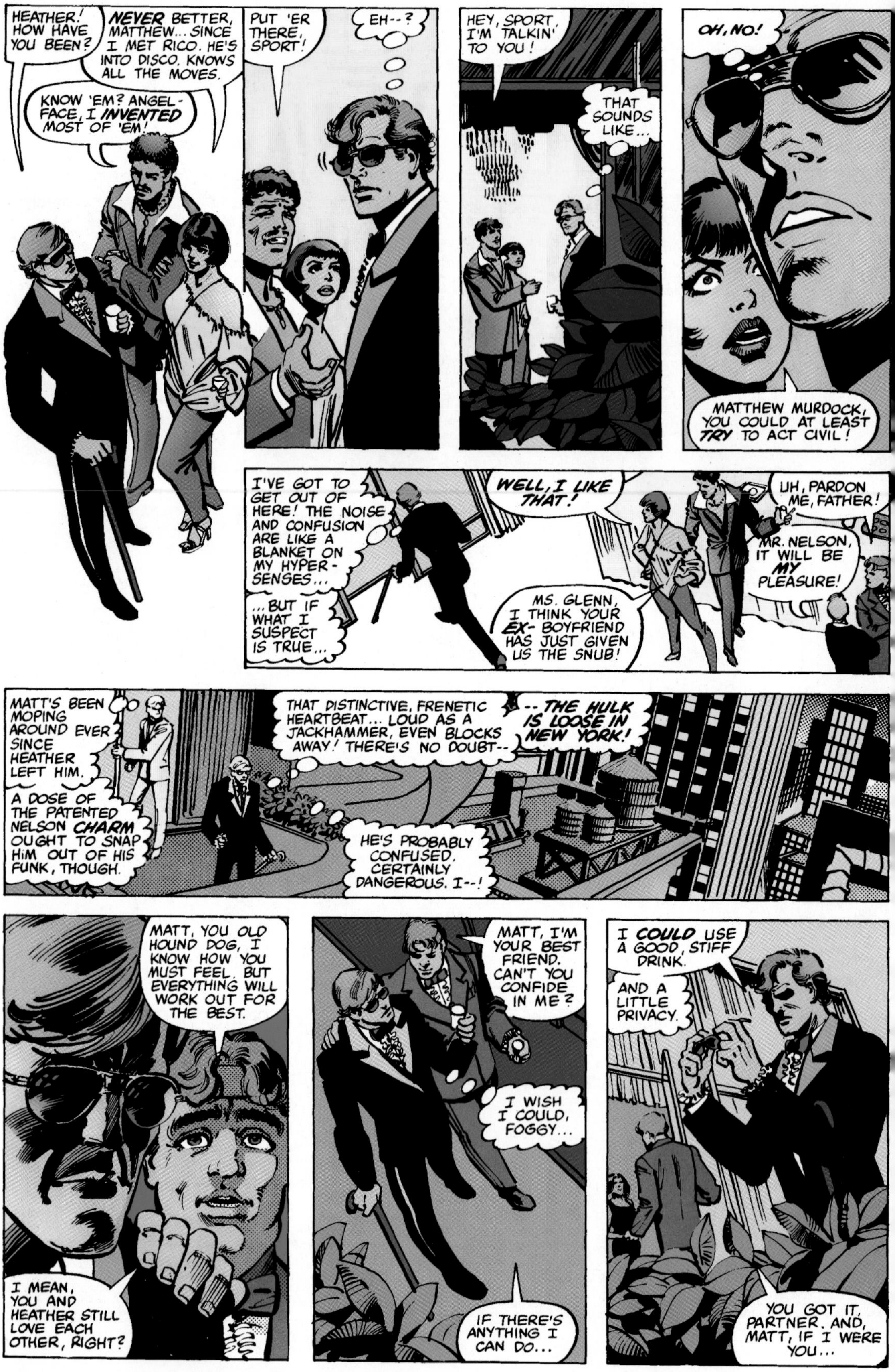
HEATHER! HOW HAVE YOU BEEN?
NEVER BETTER, MATTHEW... SINCE I MET RICO. HE'S INTO DISCO. KNOWS ALL THE MOVES.
KNOW 'EM? ANGEL-FACE, I INVENTED MOST OF 'EM!
PUT 'ER THERE, SPORT!
EH--?
HEY, SPORT, I'M TALKIN' TO YOU!
THAT SOUNDS LIKE...
OH, NO!
MATTHEW MURDOCK, YOU COULD AT LEAST TRY TO ACT CIVIL!
I'VE GOT TO GET OUT OF HERE! THE NOISE AND CONFUSION ARE LIKE A BLANKET ON MY HYPER-SENSES...
...BUT IF WHAT I SUSPECT IS TRUE...
WELL, I LIKE THAT!
MS. GLENN, I THINK YOUR EX- BOYFRIEND HAS JUST GIVEN US THE SNUB!
UH, PARDON ME, FATHER!
MR. NELSON, IT WILL BE MY PLEASURE!
MATT'S BEEN MOPING AROUND EVER SINCE HEATHER LEFT HIM.
A DOSE OF THE PATENTED NELSON CHARM OUGHT TO SNAP HIM OUT OF HIS FUNK, THOUGH.
THAT DISTINCTIVE, FRENETIC HEARTBEAT... LOUD AS A JACKHAMMER, EVEN BLOCKS AWAY! THERE'S NO DOUBT--
--THE HULK IS LOOSE IN NEW YORK!
HE'S PROBABLY CONFUSED. CERTAINLY DANGEROUS. I--!
MATT, YOU OLD HOUND DOG, I KNOW HOW YOU MUST FEEL. BUT EVERYTHING WILL WORK OUT FOR THE BEST.
I MEAN, YOU AND HEATHER STILL LOVE EACH OTHER, RIGHT?
MATT, I'M YOUR BEST FRIEND. CAN'T YOU CONFIDE IN ME?
I WISH I COULD, FOGGY...
IF THERE'S ANYTHING I CAN DO...
I COULD USE A GOOD, STIFF DRINK.
AND A LITTLE PRIVACY.
YOU GOT IT, PARTNER. AND, MATT, IF I WERE YOU...

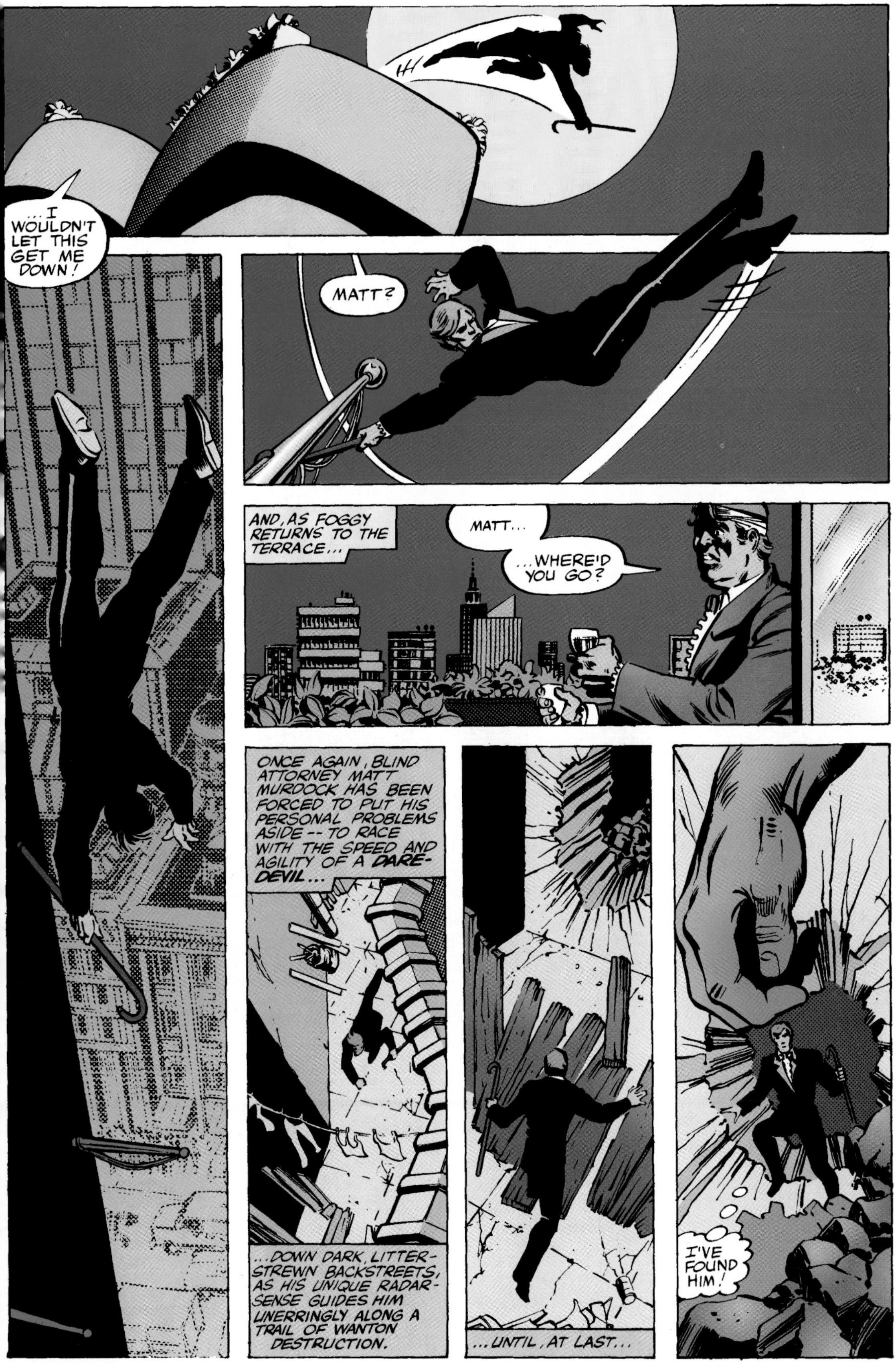
...I WOULDN'T LET THIS GET ME DOWN!
MATT?
AND, AS FOGGY RETURNS TO THE TERRACE...
MATT...
...WHERE'D YOU GO?
ONCE AGAIN, BLIND ATTORNEY MATT MURDOCK HAS BEEN FORCED TO PUT HIS PERSONAL PROBLEMS ASIDE -- TO RACE WITH THE SPEED AND AGILITY OF A DARE-DEVIL...
...DOWN DARK, LITTER-STREWN BACKSTREETS, AS HIS UNIQUE RADAR-SENSE GUIDES HIM UNERRINGLY ALONG A TRAIL OF WANTON DESTRUCTION.
...UNTIL, AT LAST...
I'VE FOUND HIM!

THE HULK! I'D ALMOST FORGOTTEN HOW BIG HE IS!

IT'S INCREDIBLE... THAT GAMMA RADIATION MUTATED DR. ROBERT BRUCE BANNER INTO THE MOST TRAGIC... UNPREDICTABLE... AND *POWERFUL* CREATURE TO EVER WALK THE FACE OF THE EARTH!

THUMP THUMP

THUMP THUMP

SOMEWAY, I HAVE TO REACH THE MAN INSIDE THE MONSTER... BEFORE IT'S TOO LATE!

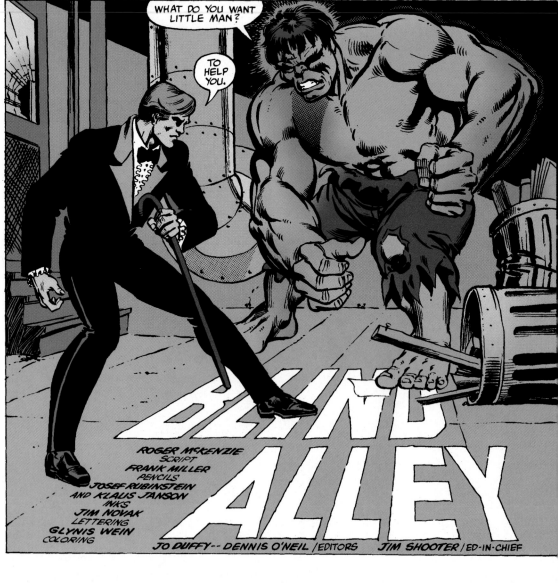

WHAT DO YOU WANT LITTLE MAN?

TO HELP YOU.

BLIND ALLEY

ROGER McKENZIE
SCRIPT
FRANK MILLER
PENCILS
JOSEF RUBINSTEIN
AND KLAUS JANSON
INKS
JIM NOVAK
LETTERING
GLYNIS WEIN
COLORING

JO DUFFY -- DENNIS O'NEIL / EDITORS   JIM SHOOTER / ED-IN-CHIEF

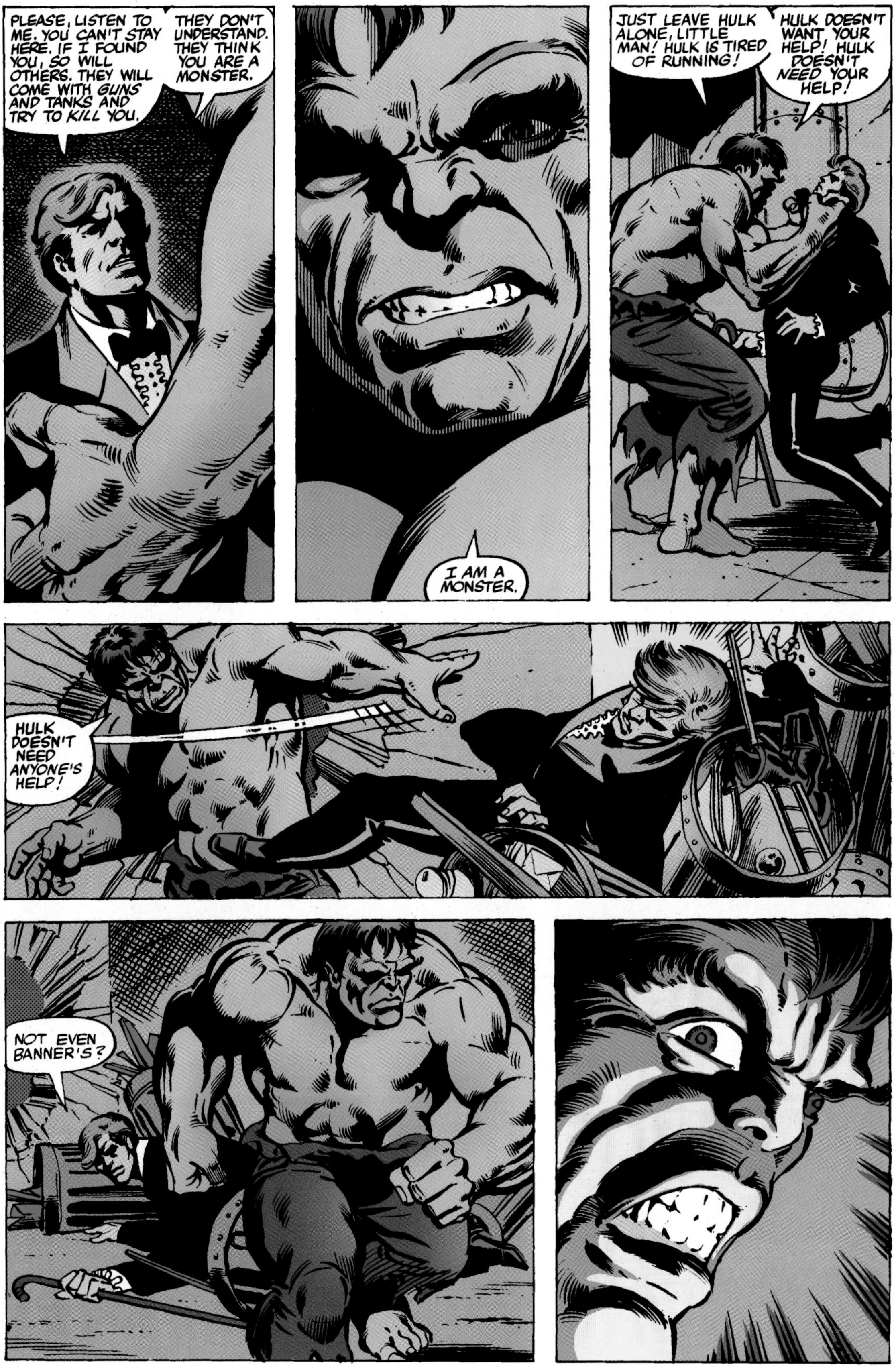

PLEASE, LISTEN TO ME. YOU CAN'T STAY HERE. IF I FOUND YOU, SO WILL OTHERS. THEY WILL COME WITH GUNS AND TANKS AND TRY TO KILL YOU.
THEY DON'T UNDERSTAND. THEY THINK YOU ARE A MONSTER.
I AM A MONSTER.
JUST LEAVE HULK ALONE, LITTLE MAN! HULK IS TIRED OF RUNNING!
HULK DOESN'T WANT YOUR HELP! HULK DOESN'T NEED YOUR HELP!
HULK DOESN'T NEED ANYONE'S HELP!
NOT EVEN BANNER'S?

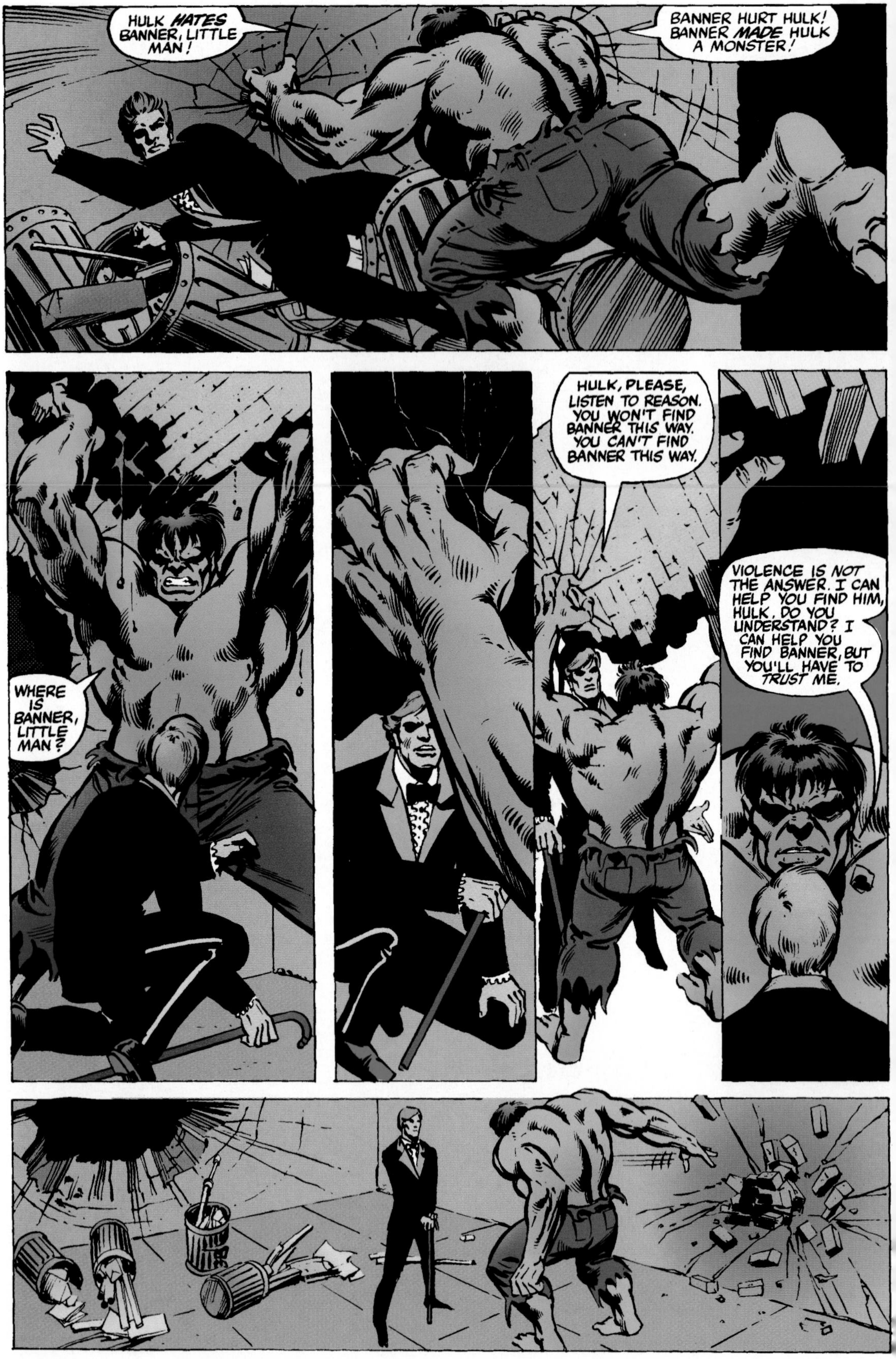
HULK *HATES* BANNER, LITTLE MAN!
BANNER HURT HULK! BANNER *MADE* HULK A MONSTER!
WHERE IS BANNER, LITTLE MAN?
HULK, PLEASE, LISTEN TO REASON. YOU WON'T FIND BANNER THIS WAY. YOU CAN'T FIND BANNER THIS WAY.
VIOLENCE IS *NOT* THE ANSWER. I CAN HELP YOU FIND HIM, HULK. DO YOU UNDERSTAND? I CAN HELP YOU FIND BANNER, BUT YOU'LL HAVE TO *TRUST* ME.

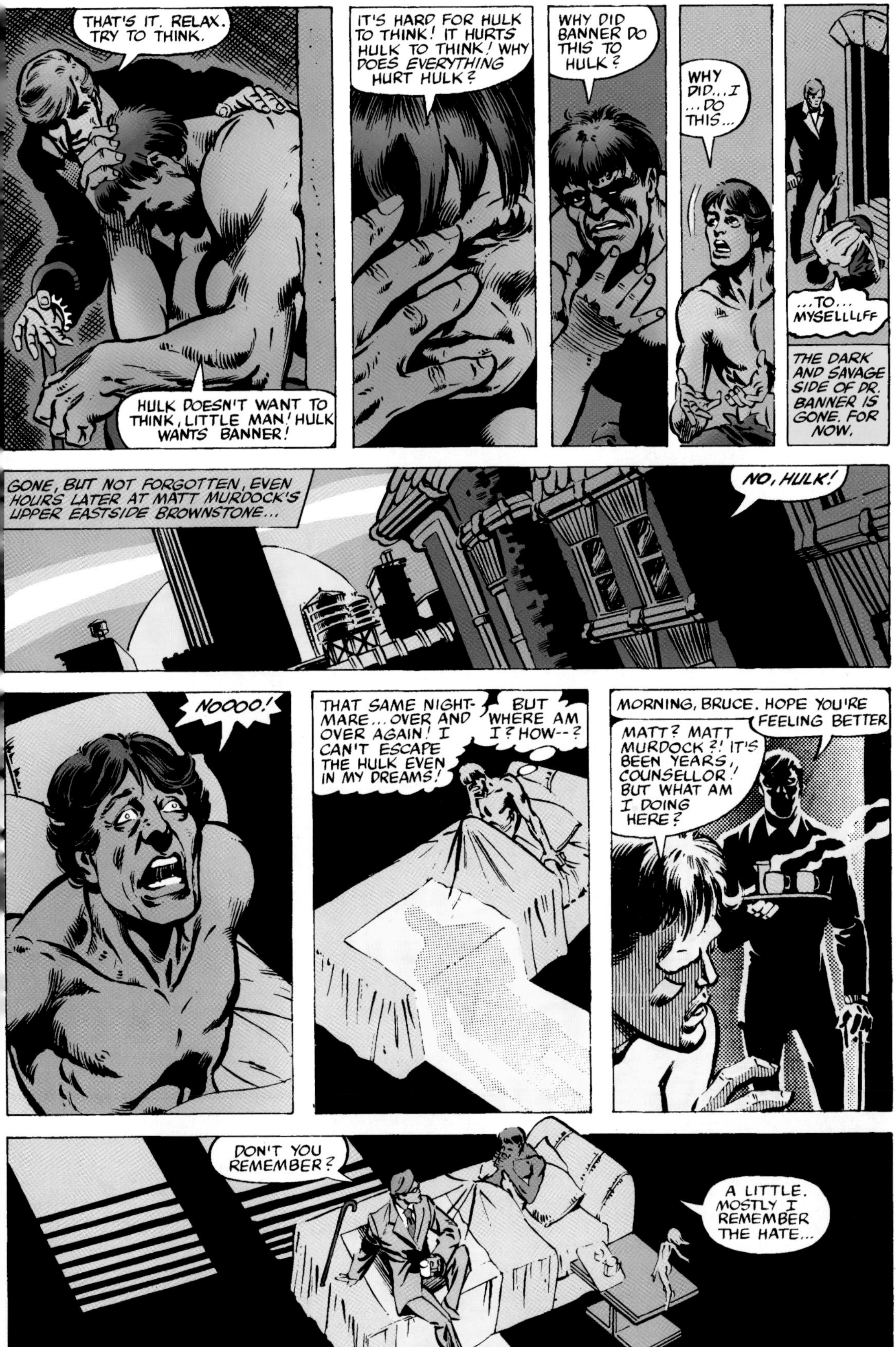
THAT'S IT. RELAX. TRY TO THINK.
HULK DOESN'T WANT TO THINK, LITTLE MAN! HULK WANTS BANNER!
IT'S HARD FOR HULK TO THINK! IT HURTS HULK TO THINK! WHY DOES EVERYTHING HURT HULK?
WHY DID BANNER DO THIS TO HULK?
WHY DID...I ...DO THIS...
...TO... MYSELLLLFF
THE DARK AND SAVAGE SIDE OF DR. BANNER IS GONE. FOR NOW.
GONE, BUT NOT FORGOTTEN, EVEN HOURS LATER AT MATT MURDOCK'S UPPER EASTSIDE BROWNSTONE...
NO, HULK!
NOOOO!
THAT SAME NIGHTMARE...OVER AND OVER AGAIN! I CAN'T ESCAPE THE HULK EVEN IN MY DREAMS!
BUT WHERE AM I? HOW--?
MORNING, BRUCE. HOPE YOU'RE FEELING BETTER
MATT? MATT MURDOCK?! IT'S BEEN YEARS, COUNSELLOR! BUT WHAT AM I DOING HERE?
DON'T YOU REMEMBER?
A LITTLE. MOSTLY I REMEMBER THE HATE...

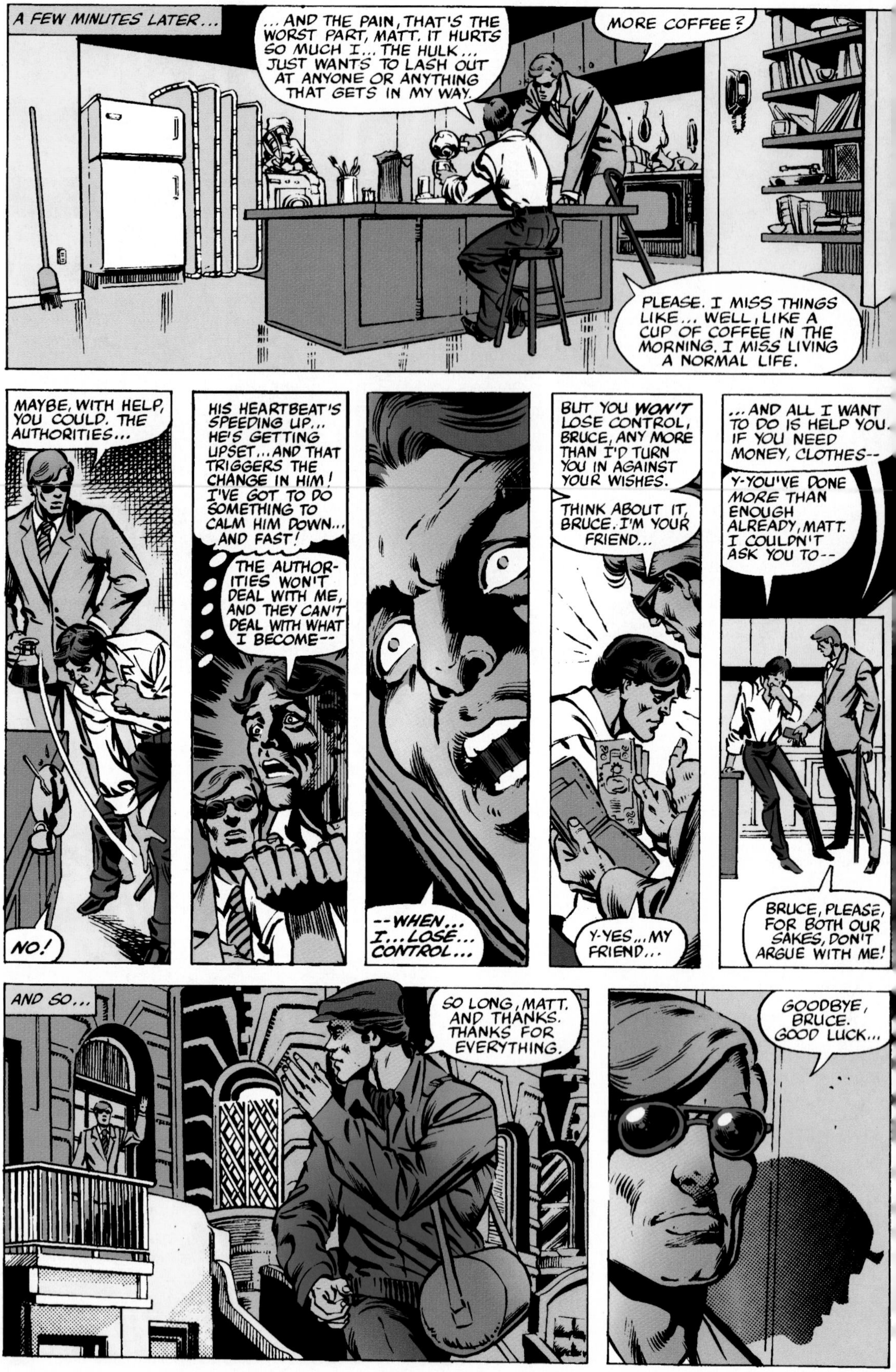

A FEW MINUTES LATER...
...AND THE PAIN, THAT'S THE WORST PART, MATT. IT HURTS SO MUCH I... THE HULK... JUST WANTS TO LASH OUT AT ANYONE OR ANYTHING THAT GETS IN MY WAY.
MORE COFFEE?
PLEASE. I MISS THINGS LIKE... WELL, LIKE A CUP OF COFFEE IN THE MORNING. I MISS LIVING A NORMAL LIFE.
MAYBE, WITH HELP, YOU COULD. THE AUTHORITIES...
NO!
HIS HEARTBEAT'S SPEEDING UP... HE'S GETTING UPSET... AND THAT TRIGGERS THE CHANGE IN HIM! I'VE GOT TO DO SOMETHING TO CALM HIM DOWN... AND FAST!
THE AUTHORITIES WON'T DEAL WITH ME, AND THEY CAN'T DEAL WITH WHAT I BECOME--
--WHEN... I... LOSE... CONTROL...
BUT YOU WON'T LOSE CONTROL, BRUCE, ANY MORE THAN I'D TURN YOU IN AGAINST YOUR WISHES.
THINK ABOUT IT, BRUCE. I'M YOUR FRIEND...
Y-YES... MY FRIEND...
...AND ALL I WANT TO DO IS HELP YOU. IF YOU NEED MONEY, CLOTHES--
Y-YOU'VE DONE MORE THAN ENOUGH ALREADY, MATT. I COULDN'T ASK YOU TO--
BRUCE, PLEASE, FOR BOTH OUR SAKES, DON'T ARGUE WITH ME!
AND SO...
SO LONG, MATT. AND THANKS. THANKS FOR EVERYTHING.
GOODBYE, BRUCE. GOOD LUCK...

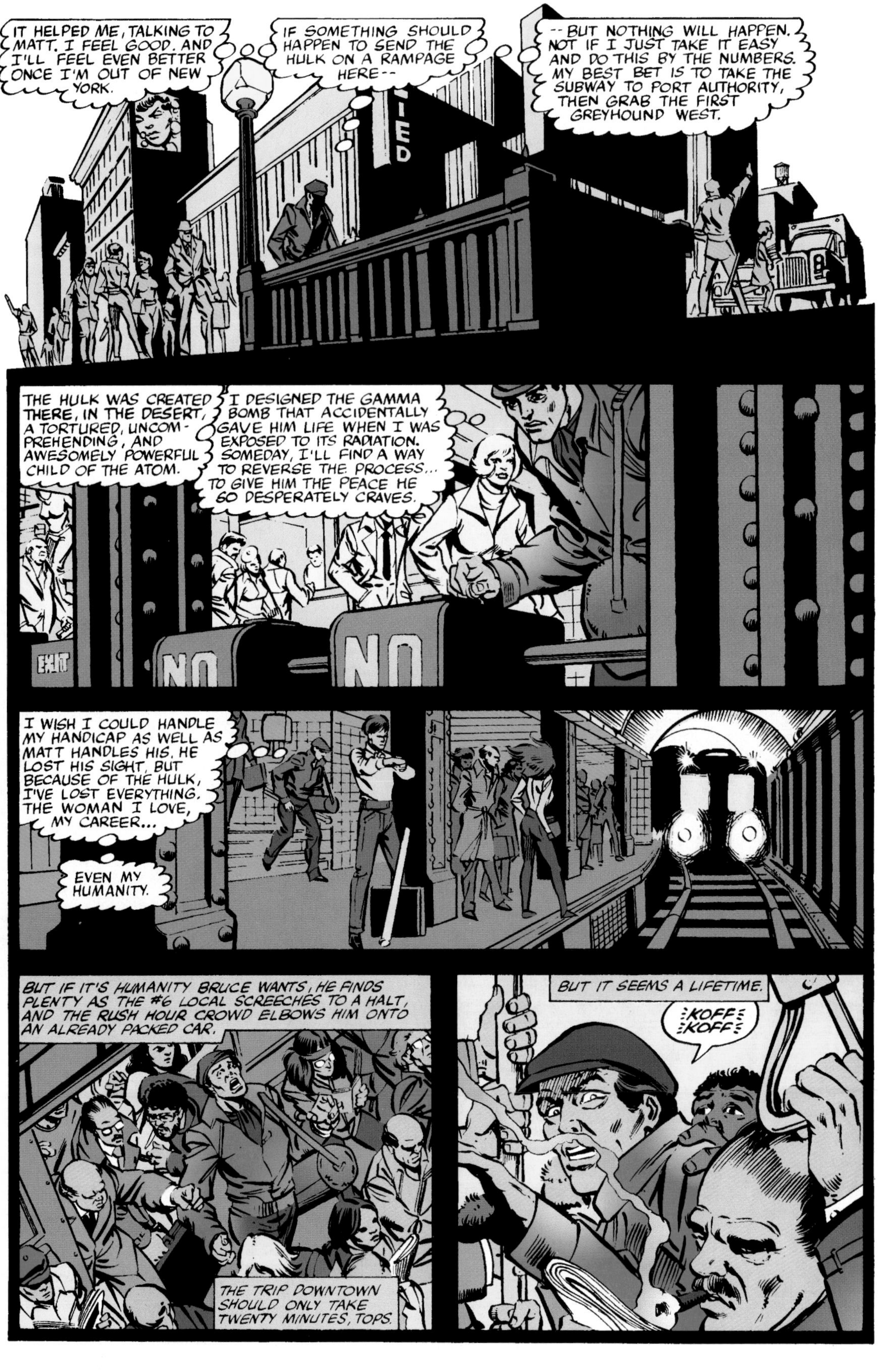
IT HELPED ME, TALKING TO MATT. I FEEL GOOD. AND I'LL FEEL EVEN BETTER ONCE I'M OUT OF NEW YORK.
IF SOMETHING SHOULD HAPPEN TO SEND THE HULK ON A RAMPAGE HERE--
--BUT NOTHING WILL HAPPEN. NOT IF I JUST TAKE IT EASY AND DO THIS BY THE NUMBERS. MY BEST BET IS TO TAKE THE SUBWAY TO PORT AUTHORITY, THEN GRAB THE FIRST GREYHOUND WEST.
THE HULK WAS CREATED THERE, IN THE DESERT, A TORTURED, UNCOMPREHENDING, AND AWESOMELY POWERFUL CHILD OF THE ATOM.
I DESIGNED THE GAMMA BOMB THAT ACCIDENTALLY GAVE HIM LIFE WHEN I WAS EXPOSED TO ITS RADIATION. SOMEDAY, I'LL FIND A WAY TO REVERSE THE PROCESS... TO GIVE HIM THE PEACE HE SO DESPERATELY CRAVES.
EXIT
NO
NO
I WISH I COULD HANDLE MY HANDICAP AS WELL AS MATT HANDLES HIS. HE LOST HIS SIGHT, BUT BECAUSE OF THE HULK, I'VE LOST EVERYTHING. THE WOMAN I LOVE, MY CAREER...
EVEN MY HUMANITY.
BUT IF IT'S HUMANITY BRUCE WANTS, HE FINDS PLENTY AS THE #6 LOCAL SCREECHES TO A HALT, AND THE RUSH HOUR CROWD ELBOWS HIM ONTO AN ALREADY PACKED CAR.
THE TRIP DOWNTOWN SHOULD ONLY TAKE TWENTY MINUTES, TOPS.
BUT IT SEEMS A LIFETIME.
KOFF KOFF

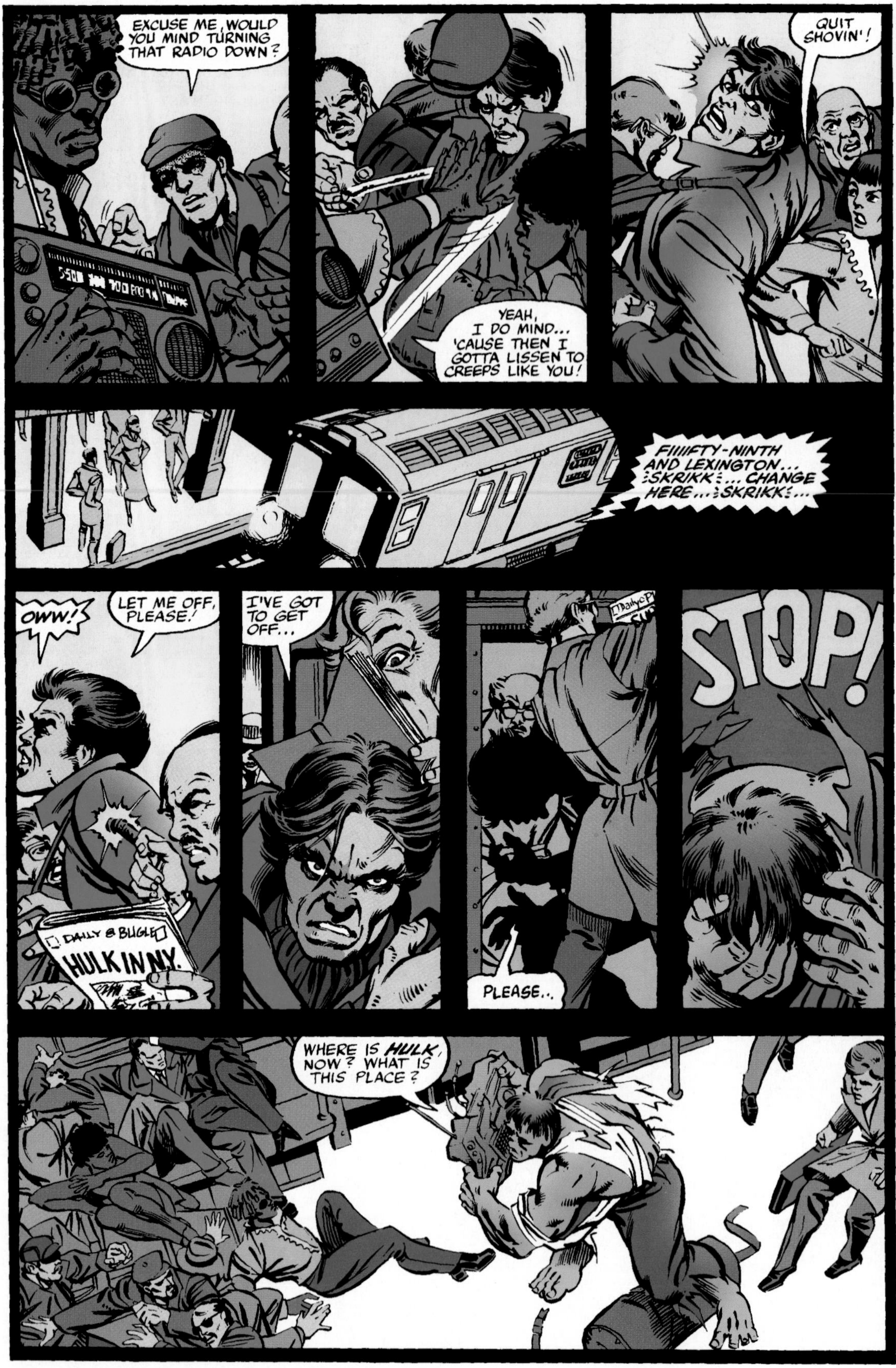
EXCUSE ME, WOULD YOU MIND TURNING THAT RADIO DOWN?
YEAH, I DO MIND... 'CAUSE THEN I GOTTA LISSEN TO CREEPS LIKE YOU!
QUIT SHOVIN'!
FIIIIFTY-NINTH AND LEXINGTON... SKRIKK... CHANGE HERE... SKRIKK...
OWW!
LET ME OFF, PLEASE!
DAILY BUGLE
HULK IN N.Y.
I'VE GOT TO GET OFF...
PLEASE...
STOP!
WHERE IS HULK, NOW? WHAT IS THIS PLACE?

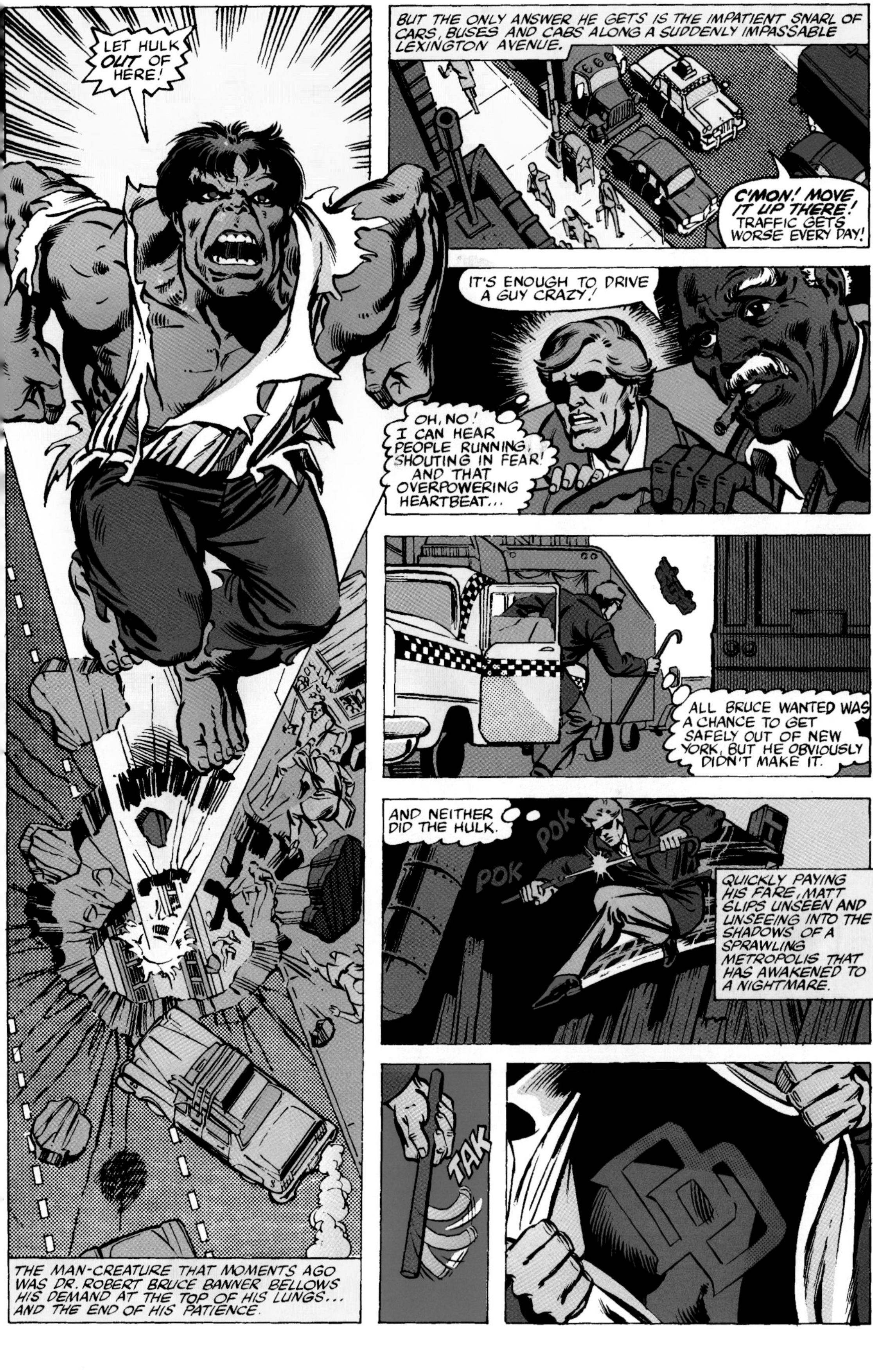
LET HULK OUT OF HERE!
THE MAN-CREATURE THAT MOMENTS AGO WAS DR. ROBERT BRUCE BANNER BELLOWS HIS DEMAND AT THE TOP OF HIS LUNGS... AND THE END OF HIS PATIENCE.
BUT THE ONLY ANSWER HE GETS IS THE IMPATIENT SNARL OF CARS, BUSES AND CABS ALONG A SUDDENLY IMPASSABLE LEXINGTON AVENUE.
C'MON! MOVE IT UP THERE! TRAFFIC GETS WORSE EVERY DAY!
IT'S ENOUGH TO DRIVE A GUY CRAZY!
OH, NO! I CAN HEAR PEOPLE RUNNING, SHOUTING IN FEAR! AND THAT OVERPOWERING HEARTBEAT...
ALL BRUCE WANTED WAS A CHANCE TO GET SAFELY OUT OF NEW YORK, BUT HE OBVIOUSLY DIDN'T MAKE IT.
AND NEITHER DID THE HULK.
POK
POK
QUICKLY PAYING HIS FARE, MATT SLIPS UNSEEN AND UNSEEING INTO THE SHADOWS OF A SPRAWLING METROPOLIS THAT HAS AWAKENED TO A NIGHTMARE.
TAK

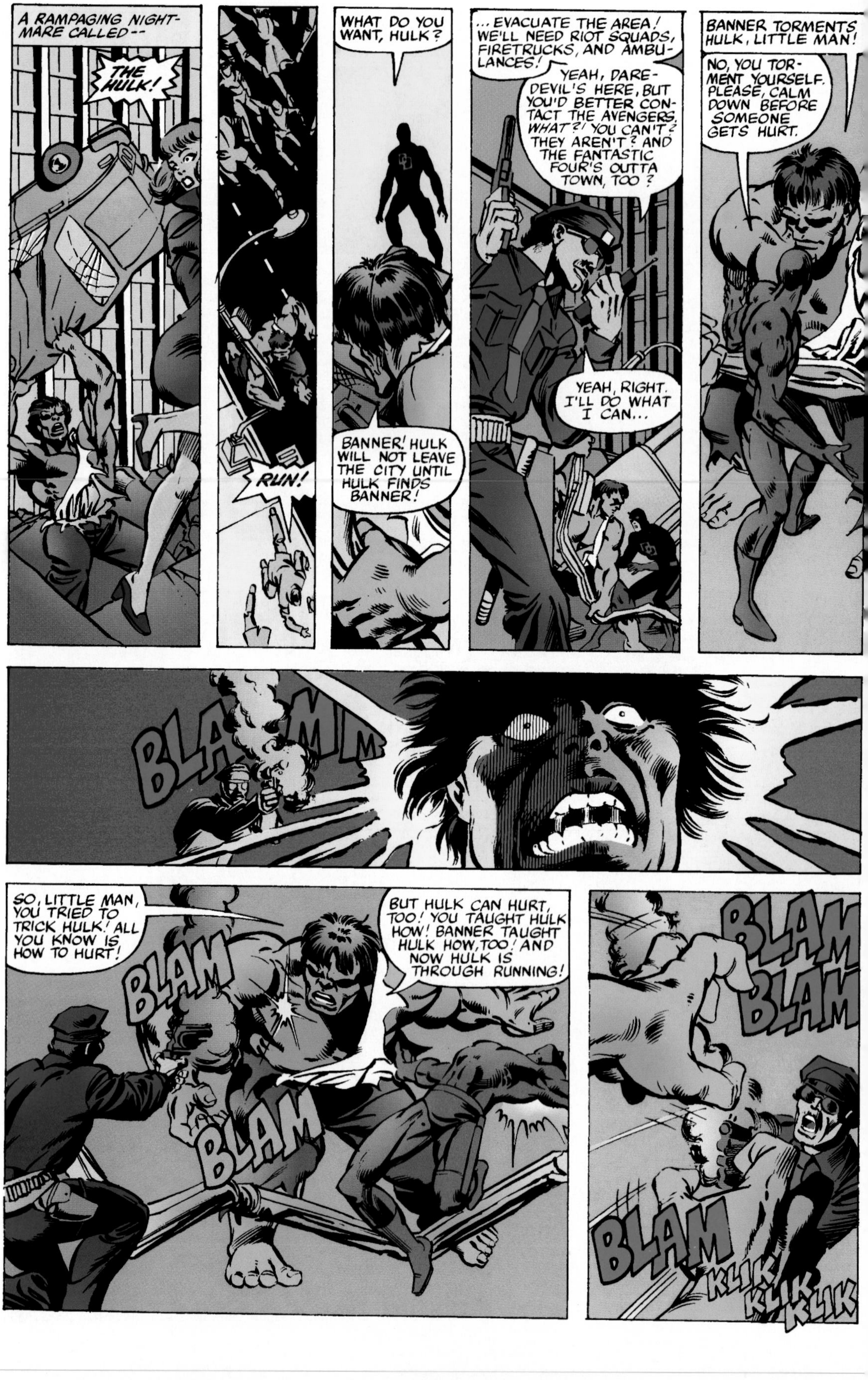
A RAMPAGING NIGHT-MARE CALLED--
THE HULK!
RUN!
WHAT DO YOU WANT, HULK?
BANNER! HULK WILL NOT LEAVE THE CITY UNTIL HULK FINDS BANNER!
...EVACUATE THE AREA! WE'LL NEED RIOT SQUADS, FIRETRUCKS, AND AMBULANCES!
YEAH, DARE-DEVIL'S HERE, BUT YOU'D BETTER CONTACT THE AVENGERS. WHAT?! YOU CAN'T? THEY AREN'T? AND THE FANTASTIC FOUR'S OUTTA TOWN, TOO?
YEAH, RIGHT. I'LL DO WHAT I CAN...
BANNER TORMENTS HULK, LITTLE MAN!
NO, YOU TORMENT YOURSELF. PLEASE, CALM DOWN BEFORE SOMEONE GETS HURT.
BLAMM
SO, LITTLE MAN, YOU TRIED TO TRICK HULK! ALL YOU KNOW IS HOW TO HURT!
BUT HULK CAN HURT, TOO! YOU TAUGHT HULK HOW! BANNER TAUGHT HULK HOW, TOO! AND NOW HULK IS THROUGH RUNNING!
BLAM
BLAM
BLAM
BLAM
BLAM
KLIK KLIK KLIK

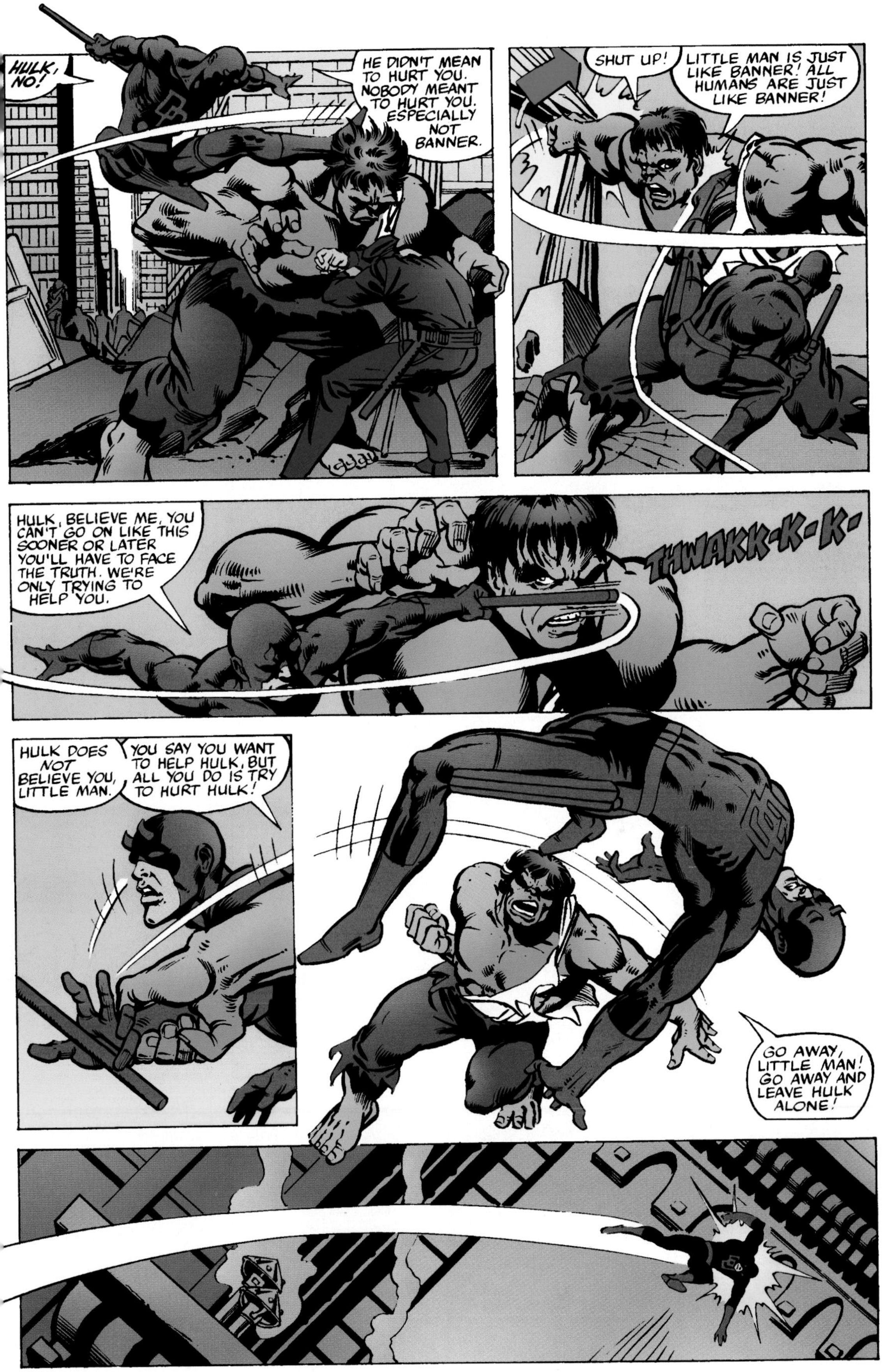
HULK, NO!
HE DIDN'T MEAN TO HURT YOU. NOBODY MEANT TO HURT YOU. ESPECIALLY NOT BANNER.
SHUT UP!
LITTLE MAN IS JUST LIKE BANNER! ALL HUMANS ARE JUST LIKE BANNER!
HULK, BELIEVE ME, YOU CAN'T GO ON LIKE THIS SOONER OR LATER YOU'LL HAVE TO FACE THE TRUTH. WE'RE ONLY TRYING TO HELP YOU.
THWAKK-K-K-
HULK DOES NOT BELIEVE YOU, LITTLE MAN.
YOU SAY YOU WANT TO HELP HULK, BUT ALL YOU DO IS TRY TO HURT HULK!
GO AWAY, LITTLE MAN! GO AWAY AND LEAVE HULK ALONE!

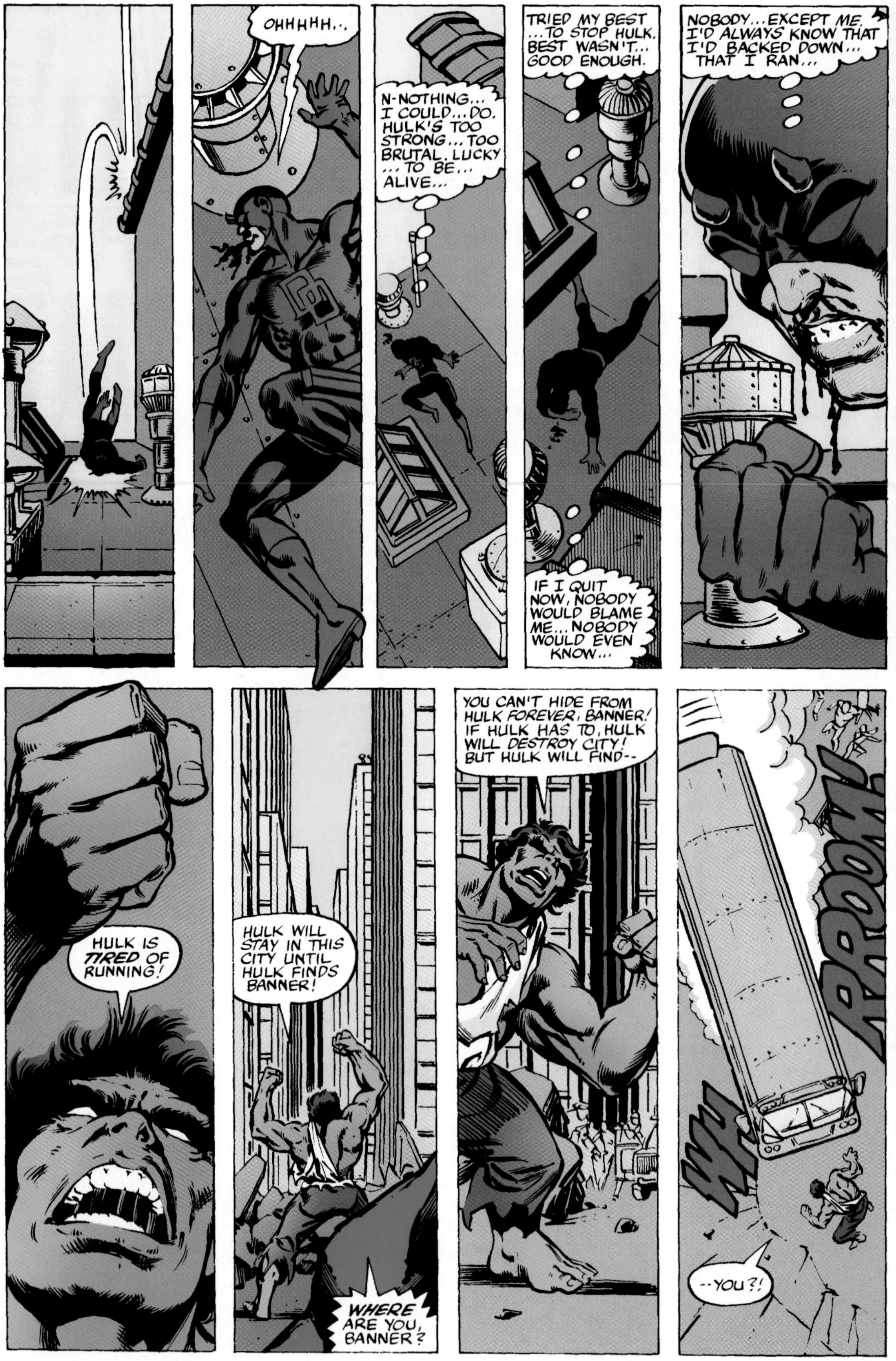
OHHHHH...
N-NOTHING... I COULD...DO. HULK'S TOO STRONG...TOO BRUTAL. LUCKY ...TO BE... ALIVE...
TRIED MY BEST ...TO STOP HULK. BEST WASN'T... GOOD ENOUGH.
IF I QUIT NOW, NOBODY WOULD BLAME ME...NOBODY WOULD EVEN KNOW...
NOBODY...EXCEPT ME. I'D ALWAYS KNOW THAT I'D BACKED DOWN... THAT I RAN...
HULK IS TIRED OF RUNNING!
HULK WILL STAY IN THIS CITY UNTIL HULK FINDS BANNER!
WHERE ARE YOU, BANNER?
YOU CAN'T HIDE FROM HULK FOREVER, BANNER! IF HULK HAS TO, HULK WILL DESTROY CITY! BUT HULK WILL FIND--
KRROOM!
--YOU?!

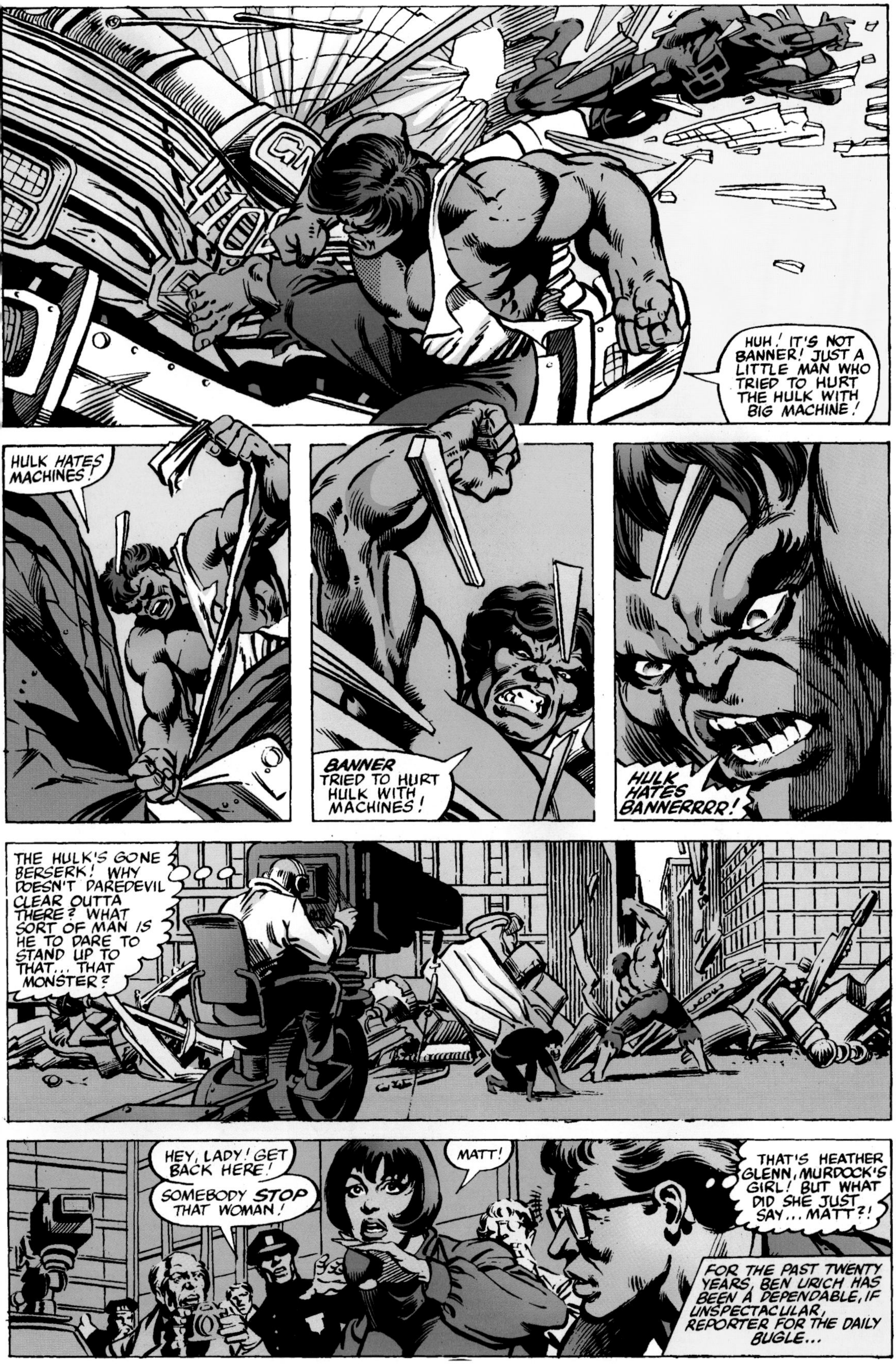
HUH! IT'S NOT BANNER! JUST A LITTLE MAN WHO TRIED TO HURT THE HULK WITH BIG MACHINE!
HULK HATES MACHINES!
BANNER TRIED TO HURT HULK WITH MACHINES!
HULK HATES BANNERRRR!
THE HULK'S GONE BERSERK! WHY DOESN'T DAREDEVIL CLEAR OUTTA THERE? WHAT SORT OF MAN IS HE TO DARE TO STAND UP TO THAT... THAT MONSTER?
HEY, LADY! GET BACK HERE!
SOMEBODY STOP THAT WOMAN!
MATT!
THAT'S HEATHER GLENN, MURDOCK'S GIRL! BUT WHAT DID SHE JUST SAY... MATT?!
FOR THE PAST TWENTY YEARS, BEN URICH HAS BEEN A DEPENDABLE, IF UNSPECTACULAR, REPORTER FOR THE DAILY BUGLE...

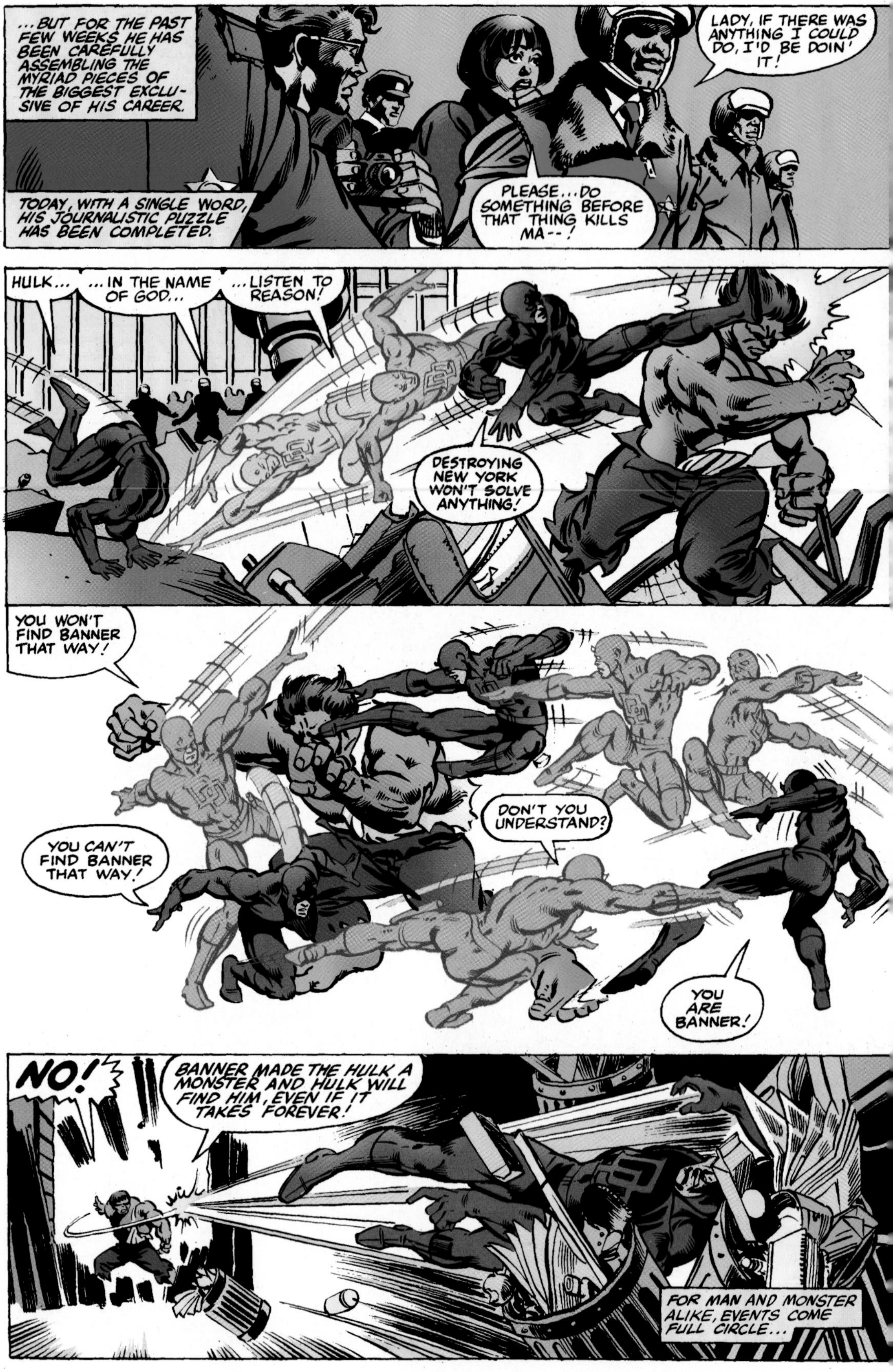
...BUT FOR THE PAST FEW WEEKS HE HAS BEEN CAREFULLY ASSEMBLING THE MYRIAD PIECES OF THE BIGGEST EXCLUSIVE OF HIS CAREER.
TODAY, WITH A SINGLE WORD, HIS JOURNALISTIC PUZZLE HAS BEEN COMPLETED.
PLEASE...DO SOMETHING BEFORE THAT THING KILLS MA--!
LADY, IF THERE WAS ANYTHING I COULD DO, I'D BE DOIN' IT!
HULK...
...IN THE NAME OF GOD...
...LISTEN TO REASON!
DESTROYING NEW YORK WON'T SOLVE ANYTHING!
YOU WON'T FIND BANNER THAT WAY!
YOU CAN'T FIND BANNER THAT WAY!
DON'T YOU UNDERSTAND?
YOU ARE BANNER!
NO!
BANNER MADE THE HULK A MONSTER AND HULK WILL FIND HIM, EVEN IF IT TAKES FOREVER!
FOR MAN AND MONSTER ALIKE, EVENTS COME FULL CIRCLE...

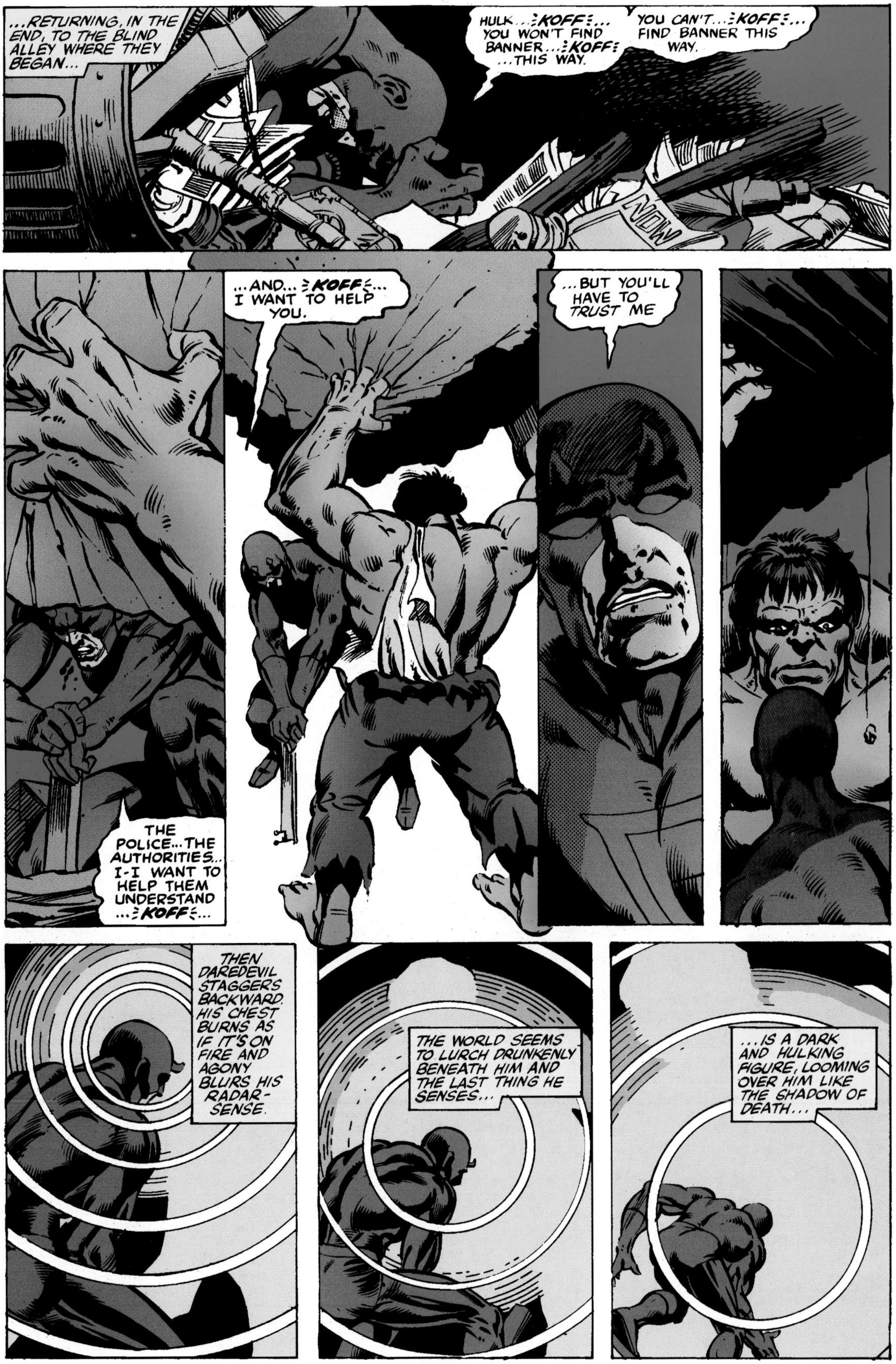
...RETURNING, IN THE END, TO THE BLIND ALLEY WHERE THEY BEGAN...
HULK... KOFF... YOU WON'T FIND BANNER... KOFF... ...THIS WAY.
YOU CAN'T... KOFF... FIND BANNER THIS WAY.
THE POLICE... THE AUTHORITIES... I-I WANT TO HELP THEM UNDERSTAND ... KOFF...
...AND... KOFF... I WANT TO HELP YOU.
...BUT YOU'LL HAVE TO TRUST ME
THEN DAREDEVIL STAGGERS BACKWARD. HIS CHEST BURNS AS IF IT'S ON FIRE AND AGONY BLURS HIS RADAR-SENSE.
THE WORLD SEEMS TO LURCH DRUNKENLY BENEATH HIM AND THE LAST THING HE SENSES...
...IS A DARK AND HULKING FIGURE, LOOMING OVER HIM LIKE THE SHADOW OF DEATH...

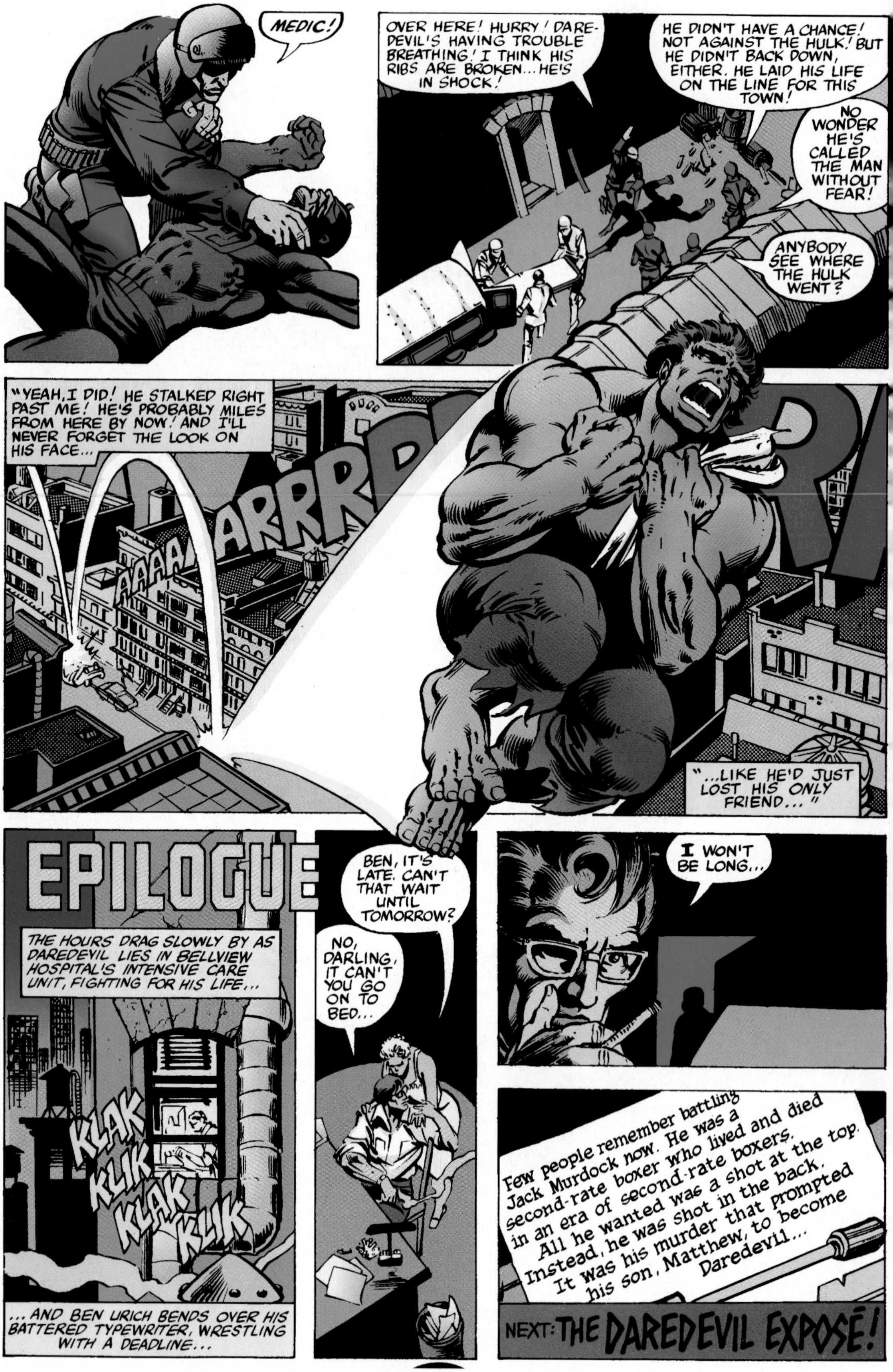
MEDIC!
OVER HERE! HURRY! DAREDEVIL'S HAVING TROUBLE BREATHING! I THINK HIS RIBS ARE BROKEN... HE'S IN SHOCK!
HE DIDN'T HAVE A CHANCE! NOT AGAINST THE HULK! BUT HE DIDN'T BACK DOWN, EITHER. HE LAID HIS LIFE ON THE LINE FOR THIS TOWN!
NO WONDER HE'S CALLED THE MAN WITHOUT FEAR!
ANYBODY SEE WHERE THE HULK WENT?
"YEAH, I DID! HE STALKED RIGHT PAST ME! HE'S PROBABLY MILES FROM HERE BY NOW! AND I'LL NEVER FORGET THE LOOK ON HIS FACE...
AAAAARRRRR
"...LIKE HE'D JUST LOST HIS ONLY FRIEND..."
EPILOGUE
THE HOURS DRAG SLOWLY BY AS DAREDEVIL LIES IN BELLVIEW HOSPITAL'S INTENSIVE CARE UNIT, FIGHTING FOR HIS LIFE...
KLAK KLIK KLAK KLIK
...AND BEN URICH BENDS OVER HIS BATTERED TYPEWRITER, WRESTLING WITH A DEADLINE...
BEN, IT'S LATE. CAN'T THAT WAIT UNTIL TOMORROW?
NO, DARLING, IT CAN'T. YOU GO ON TO BED...
I WON'T BE LONG...
Few people remember battling Jack Murdock now. He was a second-rate boxer who lived and died in an era of second-rate boxers. All he wanted was a shot at the top. Instead, he was shot in the back. It was his murder that prompted his son, Matthew, to become Daredevil...
NEXT: THE DAREDEVIL EXPOSÉ!

DAREDEVIL #164

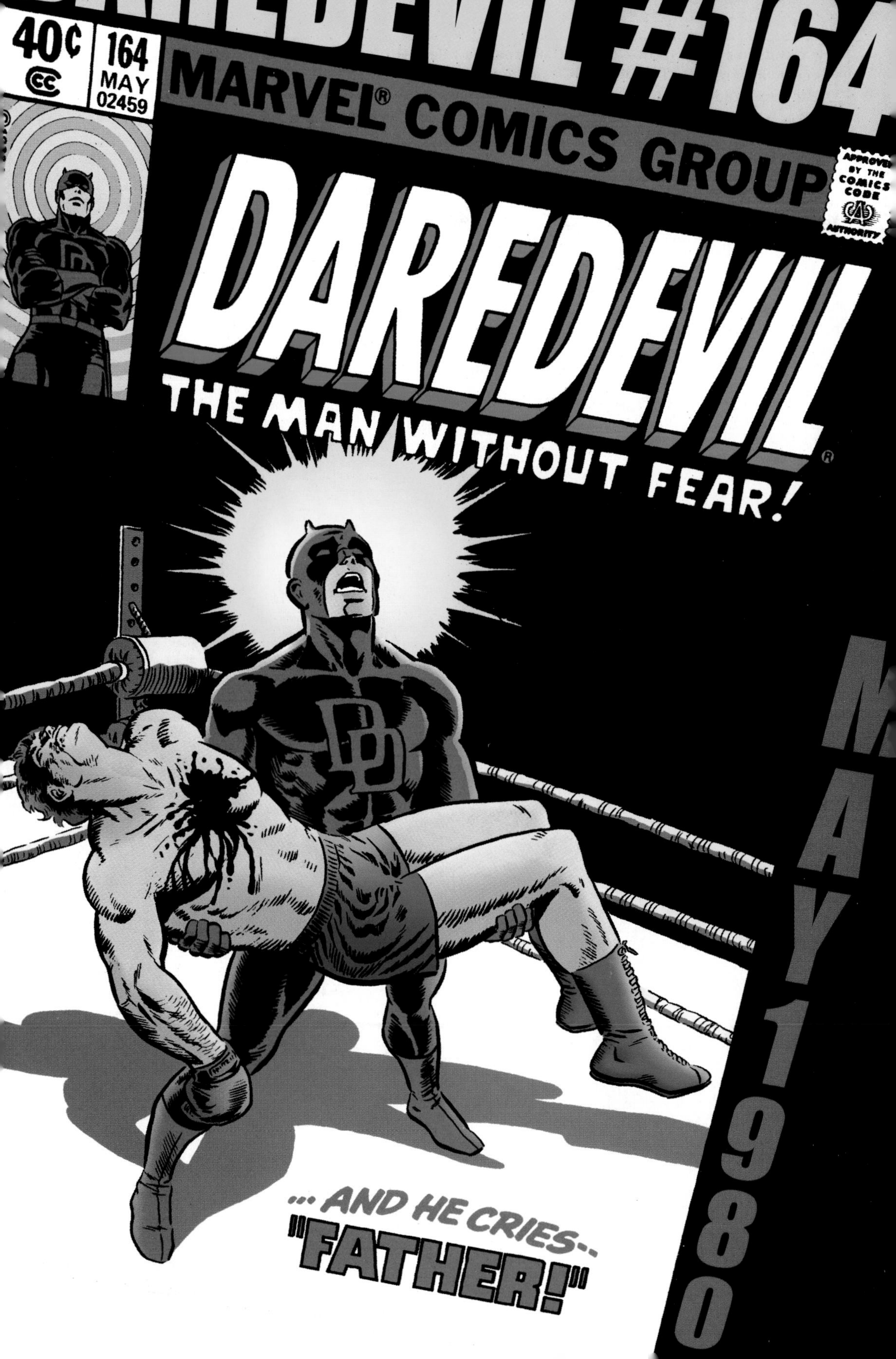
40¢
CC
164
MAY
02459
MARVEL® COMICS GROUP
APPROVED BY THE COMICS CODE AUTHORITY
DAREDEVIL
THE MAN WITHOUT FEAR!
...AND HE CRIES--
"FATHER!"

MAY 1980

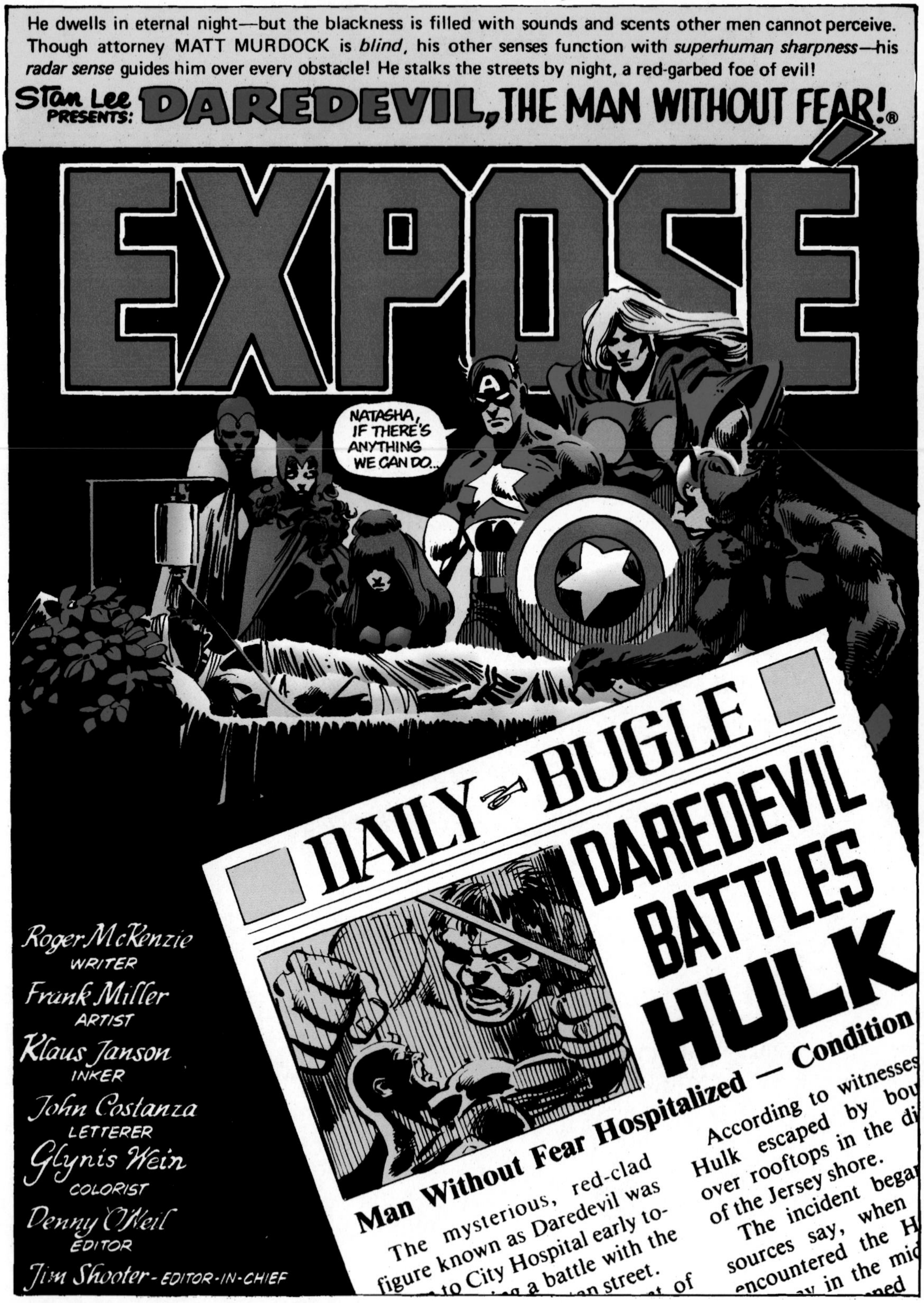

He dwells in eternal night—but the blackness is filled with sounds and scents other men cannot perceive. Though attorney MATT MURDOCK is *blind*, his other senses function with *superhuman sharpness*—his *radar sense* guides him over every obstacle! He stalks the streets by night, a red-garbed foe of evil!
Stan Lee PRESENTS: DAREDEVIL, THE MAN WITHOUT FEAR!®
EXPOSÉ
NATASHA, IF THERE'S ANYTHING WE CAN DO...
DAILY BUGLE
DAREDEVIL BATTLES HULK
Man Without Fear Hospitalized — Condition
The mysterious, red-clad figure known as Daredevil was
to City Hospital early to-
a battle with the
According to witnesses
Hulk escaped by
over rooftops in the
of the Jersey shore.
The incident
sources say, when
encountered the
Roger McKenzie WRITER
Frank Miller ARTIST
Klaus Janson INKER
John Costanza LETTERER
Glynis Wein COLORIST
Denny O'Neil EDITOR
Jim Shooter - EDITOR-IN-CHIEF

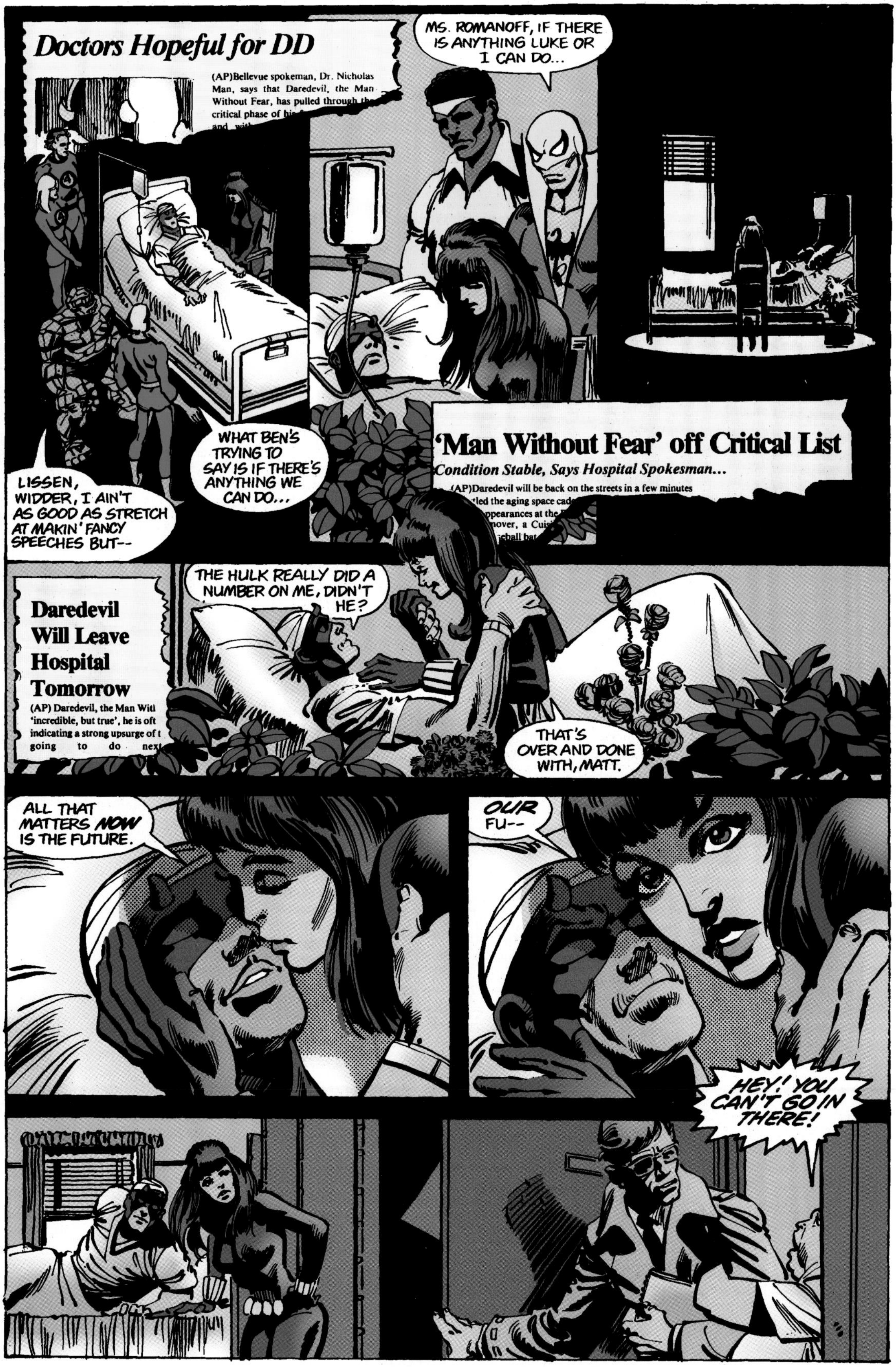

Doctors Hopeful for DD
(AP)Bellevue spokeman, Dr. Nicholas Man, says that Daredevil, the Man Without Fear, has pulled through the critical phase of his
MS. ROMANOFF, IF THERE IS ANYTHING LUKE OR I CAN DO...
LISSEN, WIDDER, I AIN'T AS GOOD AS STRETCH AT MAKIN' FANCY SPEECHES BUT--
WHAT BEN'S TRYING TO SAY IS IF THERE'S ANYTHING WE CAN DO...
'Man Without Fear' off Critical List
Condition Stable, Says Hospital Spokesman...
(AP)Daredevil will be back on the streets in a few minutes
Daredevil Will Leave Hospital Tomorrow
(AP) Daredevil, the Man Wit
'incredible, but true', he is oft
indicating a strong upsurge of t
going to do next
THE HULK REALLY DID A NUMBER ON ME, DIDN'T HE?
THAT'S OVER AND DONE WITH, MATT.
ALL THAT MATTERS NOW IS THE FUTURE.
OUR FU--
HEY! YOU CAN'T GO IN THERE!

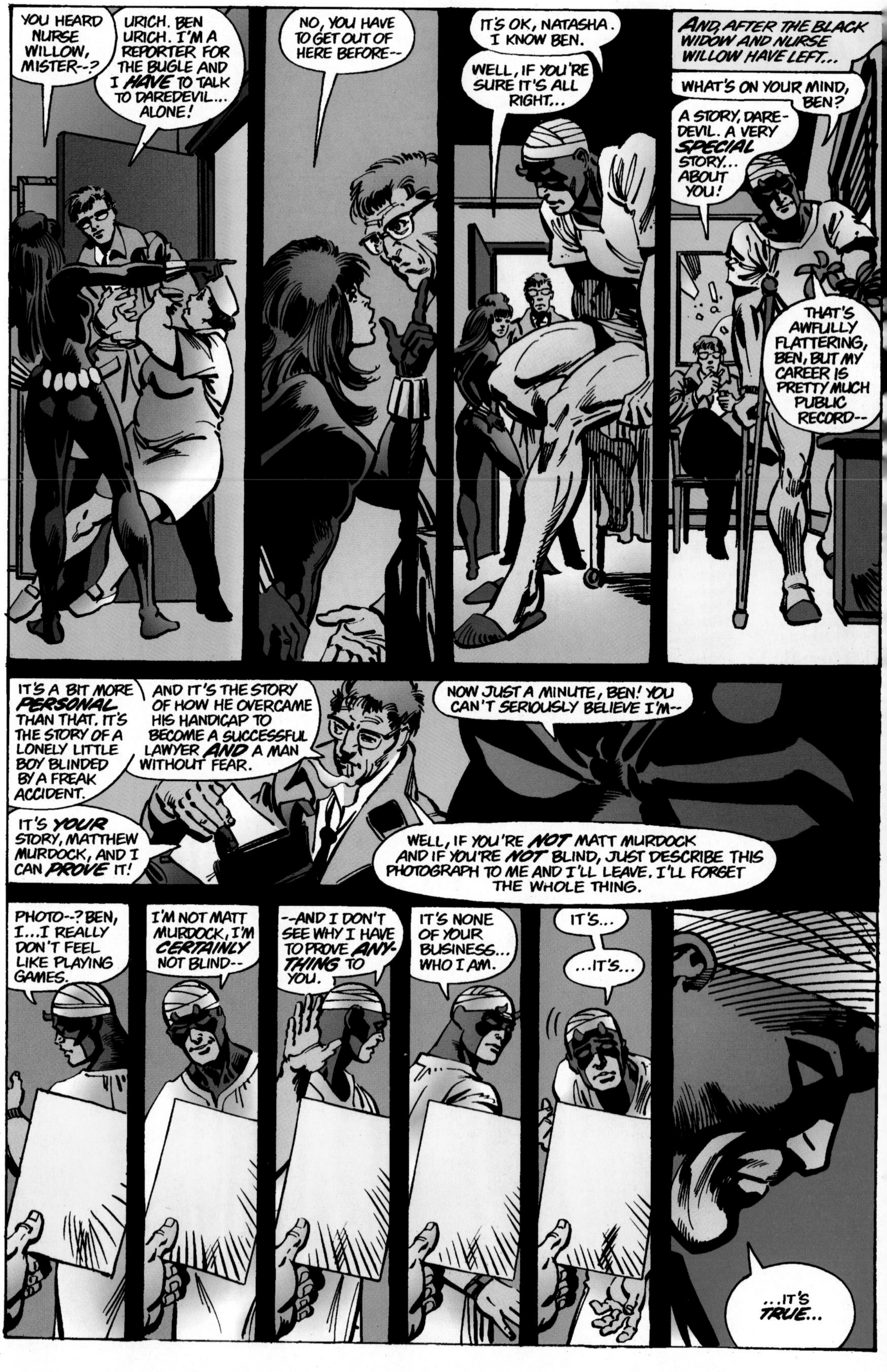
YOU HEARD NURSE WILLOW, MISTER--?
URICH. BEN URICH. I'M A REPORTER FOR THE BUGLE AND I HAVE TO TALK TO DAREDEVIL... ALONE!
NO, YOU HAVE TO GET OUT OF HERE BEFORE--
IT'S OK, NATASHA. I KNOW BEN.
WELL, IF YOU'RE SURE IT'S ALL RIGHT...
AND, AFTER THE BLACK WIDOW AND NURSE WILLOW HAVE LEFT...
WHAT'S ON YOUR MIND, BEN?
A STORY, DAREDEVIL. A VERY SPECIAL STORY... ABOUT YOU!
THAT'S AWFULLY FLATTERING, BEN, BUT MY CAREER IS PRETTY MUCH PUBLIC RECORD--
IT'S A BIT MORE PERSONAL THAN THAT. IT'S THE STORY OF A LONELY LITTLE BOY BLINDED BY A FREAK ACCIDENT.
AND IT'S THE STORY OF HOW HE OVERCAME HIS HANDICAP TO BECOME A SUCCESSFUL LAWYER AND A MAN WITHOUT FEAR.
IT'S YOUR STORY, MATTHEW MURDOCK, AND I CAN PROVE IT!
NOW JUST A MINUTE, BEN! YOU CAN'T SERIOUSLY BELIEVE I'M--
WELL, IF YOU'RE NOT MATT MURDOCK AND IF YOU'RE NOT BLIND, JUST DESCRIBE THIS PHOTOGRAPH TO ME AND I'LL LEAVE. I'LL FORGET THE WHOLE THING.
PHOTO--? BEN, I...I REALLY DON'T FEEL LIKE PLAYING GAMES.
I'M NOT MATT MURDOCK, I'M CERTAINLY NOT BLIND--
--AND I DON'T SEE WHY I HAVE TO PROVE ANYTHING TO YOU.
IT'S NONE OF YOUR BUSINESS... WHO I AM.
IT'S...
...IT'S...
...IT'S TRUE...

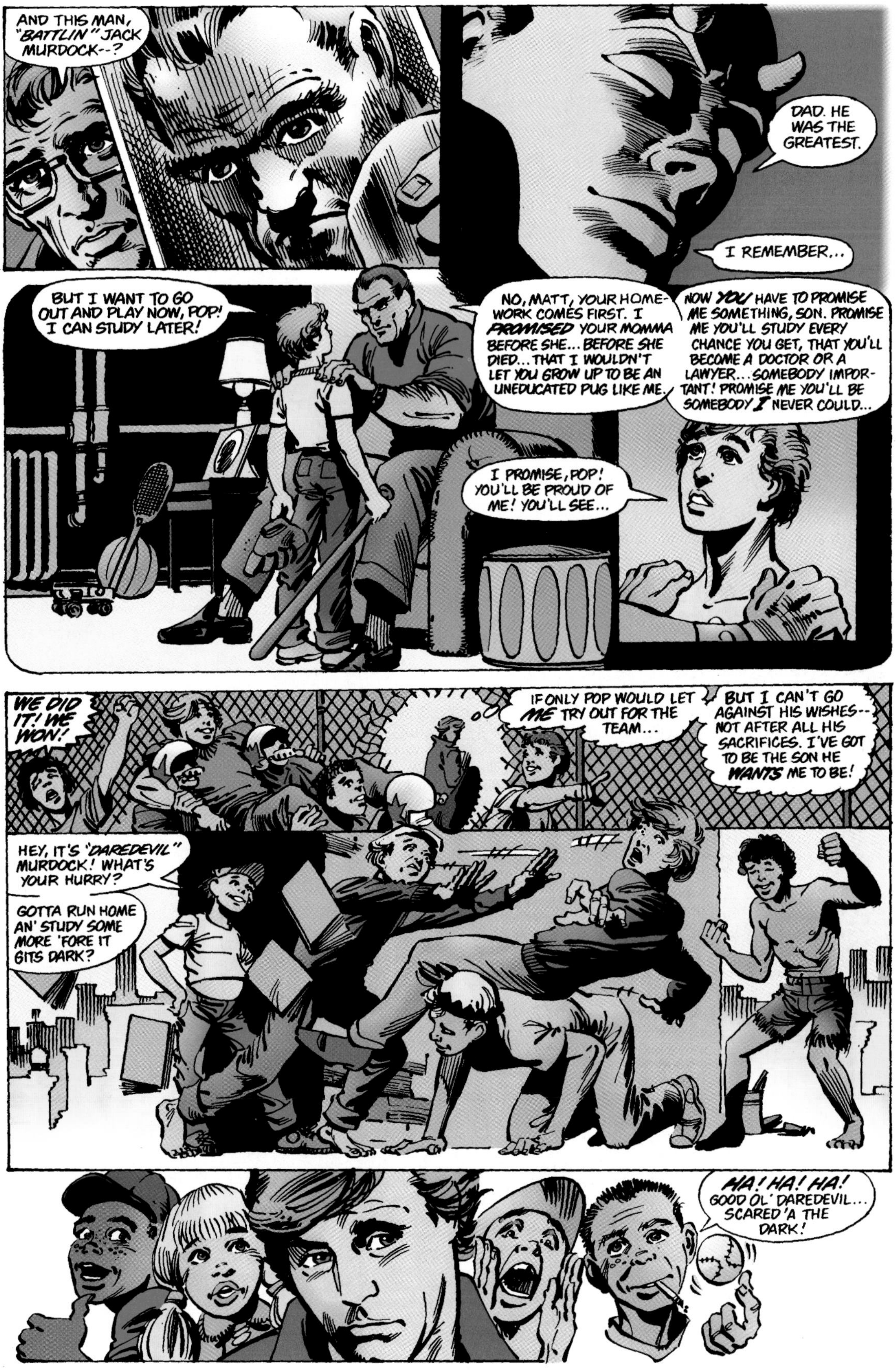
AND THIS MAN, "BATTLIN" JACK MURDOCK--?
DAD. HE WAS THE GREATEST.
I REMEMBER...
BUT I WANT TO GO OUT AND PLAY NOW, POP! I CAN STUDY LATER!
NO, MATT, YOUR HOMEWORK COMES FIRST. I PROMISED YOUR MOMMA BEFORE SHE... BEFORE SHE DIED... THAT I WOULDN'T LET YOU GROW UP TO BE AN UNEDUCATED PUG LIKE ME.
NOW YOU HAVE TO PROMISE ME SOMETHING, SON. PROMISE ME YOU'LL STUDY EVERY CHANCE YOU GET, THAT YOU'LL BECOME A DOCTOR OR A LAWYER... SOMEBODY IMPORTANT! PROMISE ME YOU'LL BE SOMEBODY I NEVER COULD...
I PROMISE, POP! YOU'LL BE PROUD OF ME! YOU'LL SEE...
WE DID IT! WE WON!
IF ONLY POP WOULD LET ME TRY OUT FOR THE TEAM...
BUT I CAN'T GO AGAINST HIS WISHES-- NOT AFTER ALL HIS SACRIFICES. I'VE GOT TO BE THE SON HE WANTS ME TO BE!
HEY, IT'S "DAREDEVIL" MURDOCK! WHAT'S YOUR HURRY?
GOTTA RUN HOME AN' STUDY SOME MORE 'FORE IT GITS DARK?
HA! HA! HA! GOOD OL' DAREDEVIL... SCARED 'A THE DARK!

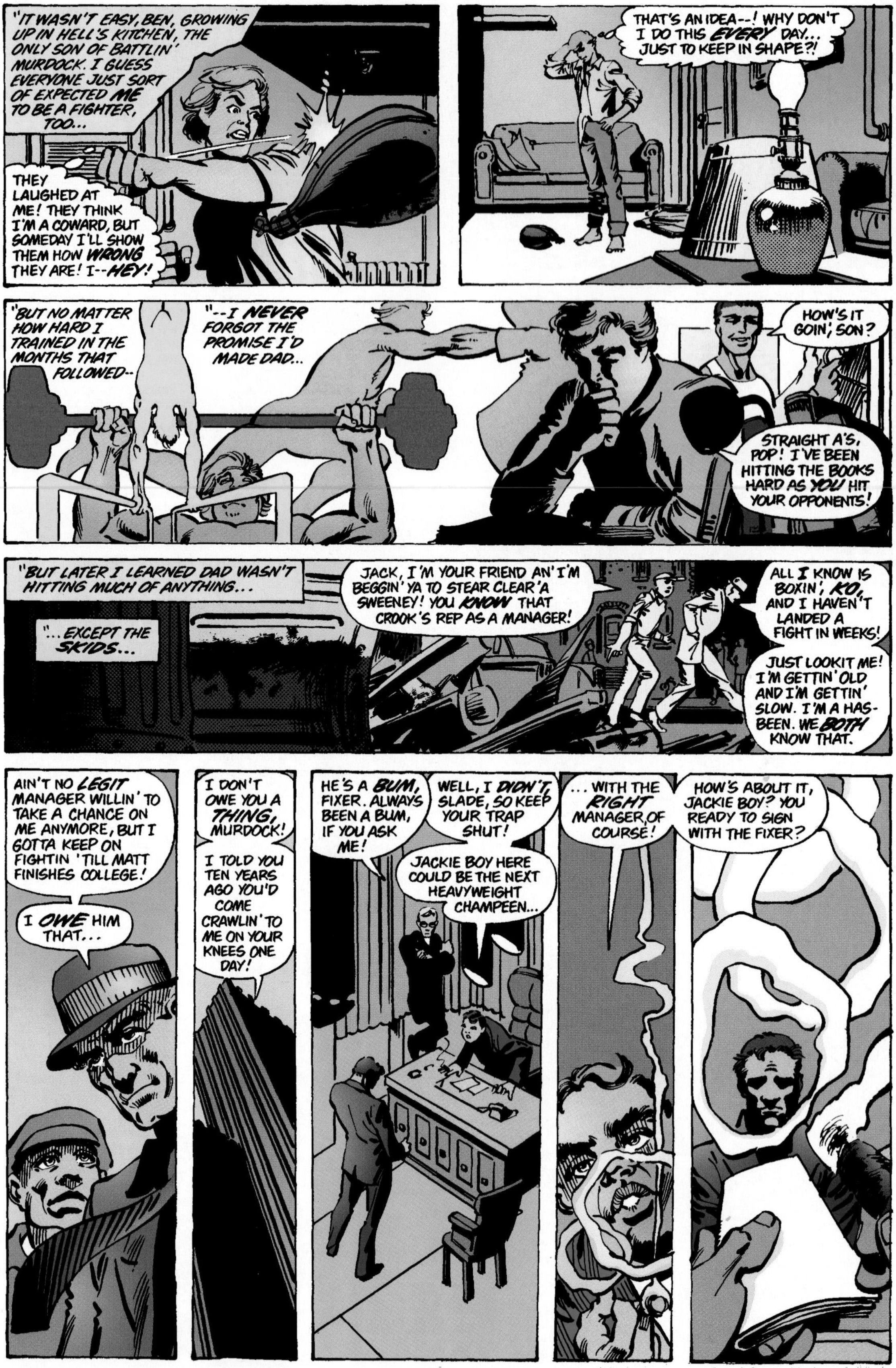
"IT WASN'T EASY, BEN, GROWING UP IN HELL'S KITCHEN, THE ONLY SON OF BATTLIN' MURDOCK. I GUESS EVERYONE JUST SORT OF EXPECTED ME TO BE A FIGHTER, TOO...
THEY LAUGHED AT ME! THEY THINK I'M A COWARD, BUT SOMEDAY I'LL SHOW THEM HOW WRONG THEY ARE! I--HEY!
THAT'S AN IDEA--! WHY DON'T I DO THIS EVERY DAY... JUST TO KEEP IN SHAPE?!
"BUT NO MATTER HOW HARD I TRAINED IN THE MONTHS THAT FOLLOWED--
"--I NEVER FORGOT THE PROMISE I'D MADE DAD...
HOW'S IT GOIN', SON?
STRAIGHT A'S, POP! I'VE BEEN HITTING THE BOOKS HARD AS YOU HIT YOUR OPPONENTS!
"BUT LATER I LEARNED DAD WASN'T HITTING MUCH OF ANYTHING...
"... EXCEPT THE SKIDS...
JACK, I'M YOUR FRIEND AN' I'M BEGGIN' YA TO STEAR CLEAR 'A SWEENEY! YOU KNOW THAT CROOK'S REP AS A MANAGER!
ALL I KNOW IS BOXIN', KO, AND I HAVEN'T LANDED A FIGHT IN WEEKS!
JUST LOOKIT ME! I'M GETTIN' OLD AND I'M GETTIN' SLOW. I'M A HAS-BEEN. WE BOTH KNOW THAT.
AIN'T NO LEGIT MANAGER WILLIN' TO TAKE A CHANCE ON ME ANYMORE, BUT I GOTTA KEEP ON FIGHTIN 'TILL MATT FINISHES COLLEGE!
I OWE HIM THAT...
I DON'T OWE YOU A THING, MURDOCK!
I TOLD YOU TEN YEARS AGO YOU'D COME CRAWLIN' TO ME ON YOUR KNEES ONE DAY!
HE'S A BUM, FIXER. ALWAYS BEEN A BUM, IF YOU ASK ME!
WELL, I DIDN'T, SLADE, SO KEEP YOUR TRAP SHUT!
JACKIE BOY HERE COULD BE THE NEXT HEAVYWEIGHT CHAMPEEN...
... WITH THE RIGHT MANAGER, OF COURSE!
HOW'S ABOUT IT, JACKIE BOY? YOU READY TO SIGN WITH THE FIXER?

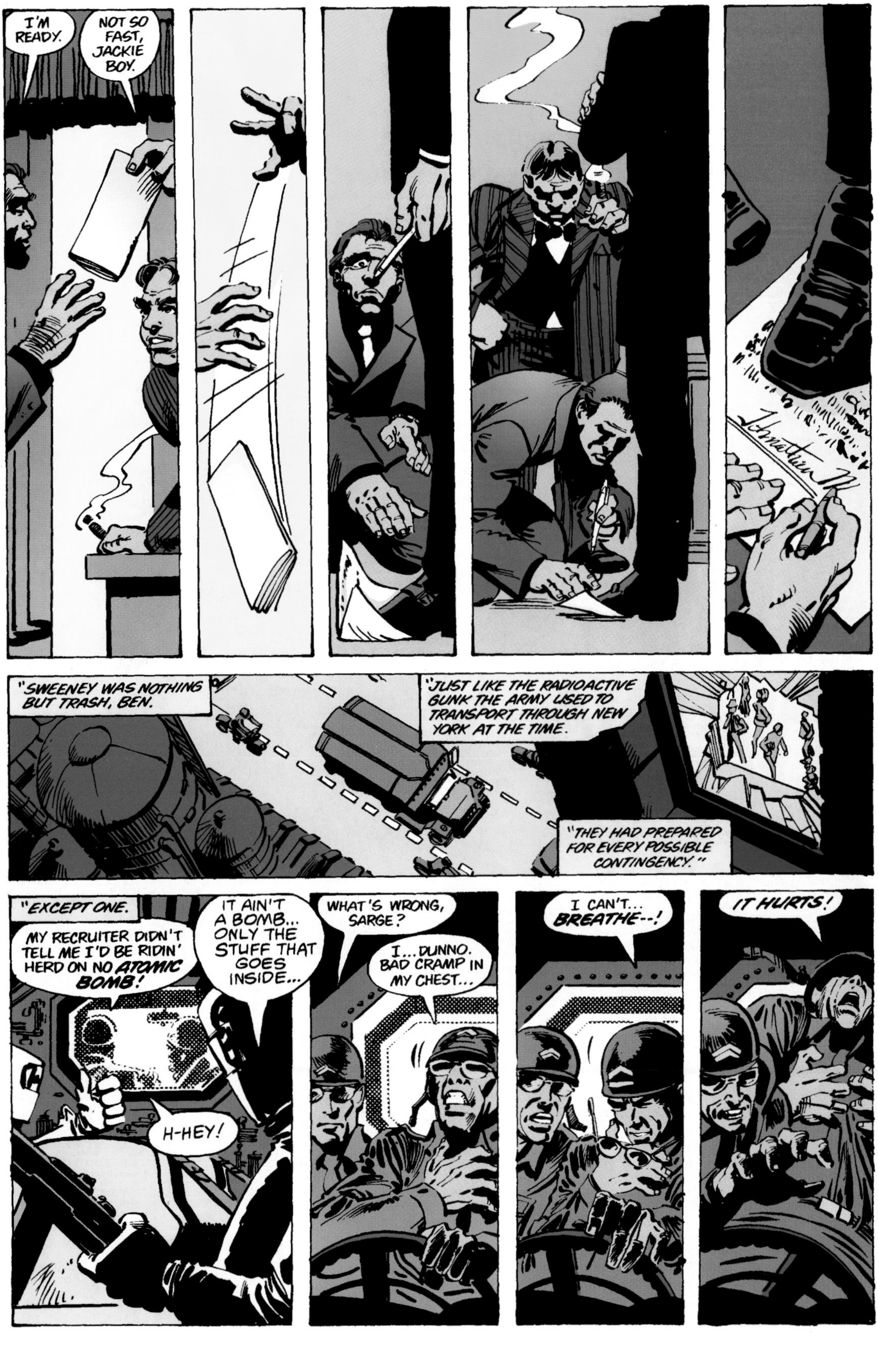
I'M READY.
NOT SO FAST, JACKIE BOY.
"SWEENEY WAS NOTHING BUT TRASH, BEN.
"JUST LIKE THE RADIOACTIVE GUNK THE ARMY USED TO TRANSPORT THROUGH NEW YORK AT THE TIME.
"THEY HAD PREPARED FOR EVERY POSSIBLE CONTINGENCY."
"EXCEPT ONE.
MY RECRUITER DIDN'T TELL ME I'D BE RIDIN' HERD ON NO ATOMIC BOMB!
IT AIN'T A BOMB... ONLY THE STUFF THAT GOES INSIDE...
H-HEY!
WHAT'S WRONG, SARGE?
I... DUNNO. BAD CRAMP IN MY CHEST...
I CAN'T... BREATHE--!
IT HURTS!

SCREEEEEEEE

"I REMEMBER WATCHING IN HORROR AS THE TRUCK SKIDDED OUT OF CONTROL TOWARD A HELPLESS OLD BLIND MAN.

GOTTA... *KOFF*... GET THIS CANNISTER... *KOFF*... AWAY FROM THE FLAMES-- OR IT'LL *BLOW--!*

"THE NEXT THING I KNEW I WAS LYING IN THE STREET. I HEARD SOMETHING HEAVY SHATTER RIGHT BESIDE ME...

"...AND WHEN I LOOKED UP...

"...I LOOKED INTO THE HEART OF A MAN-MADE SUN.

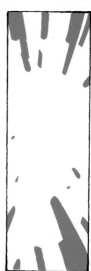
"IT WAS THE LAST THING I EVER SAW.

"I WOKE TO A HOSPITAL... AND DAD--

SON, THAT WAS A BRAVE THING YOU DID. I JUST HOPE... SOMEDAY... I CAN MAKE YOU AS *PROUD* OF ME AS I AM OF YOU...

"MY REHABILITATION WAS A SLOW, PAIN-FUL, AND AT TIMES FRUSTRATING ORDEAL. I DON'T THINK I COULD HAVE MADE IT WITHOUT THE LOVE AND SUPPORT OF PEOPLE LIKE DAD--

"--OR MY COLLEGE ROOMIE, FOGGY NELSON. THEY NEVER LET ME DOWN. NOT ONCE.

MATT, YOU OL' HOUND DOG, HOW DO YOU DO IT? I STUDY LIKE A DEMON, BUT *YOU* JUST BREEZE ALONG WITH TOP GRADES!

"AND, BEN, BECAUSE OF THE ACCIDENT, I WAS MORE DETERMINED THEN *EVER* TO GET MY LAW DEGREE. TO PROVE I COULD *STILL* BE A HUMAN BEING... DESPITE MY HANDICAP.

POP DESERVES THE CREDIT, FOGGY. HE HAD ME STUDY SO HARD WHEN I WAS YOUNGER THAT IT ALL SEEMS TO COME *EASY* FOR ME NOW.

AND I WOULDN'T BE SURPRISED IF THE *RADIA-TION* I ABSORBED DOESN'T HAVE SOMETHING TO DO WITH IT.

I'LL ALWAYS BE BLIND-- *NOTHING* CAN CHANGE THAT--BUT MY REMAINING SENSES ARE RAZOR SHARP.

"MY *TOUCH* IS SO SENSITIVE I CAN 'READ' AN ORDIN-ARY NEWSPAPER BY FEELING THE FAINT IMPRESS-IONS OF THE INK.

"AND I NEVER FORGET A SCENT ONCE I SMELL IT. I CAN RECOGNIZE ANY GIRL BY THE PERFUME SHE WEARS... ANY MAN BY HIS AFTERSHAVE.

"I CAN HEAR THE FAINTEST WHISPER, EVEN A PERSON'S *HEARTBEAT.*

"AND MY SENSE OF *TASTE* IS SO ACUTE I CAN EVEN TELL HOW MANY GRAINS OF SALT ARE ON A PRETZEL.

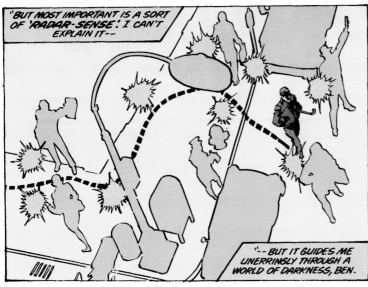

"BUT MOST IMPORTANT IS A SORT OF 'RADAR-SENSE'. I CAN'T EXPLAIN IT--

"-- BUT IT GUIDES ME UNERRINGLY THROUGH A WORLD OF DARKNESS, BEN.

SAY, SON... WANT ANY *HELP* CROSSING THE STREET?

NO THANKS, I CAN MAKE IT.

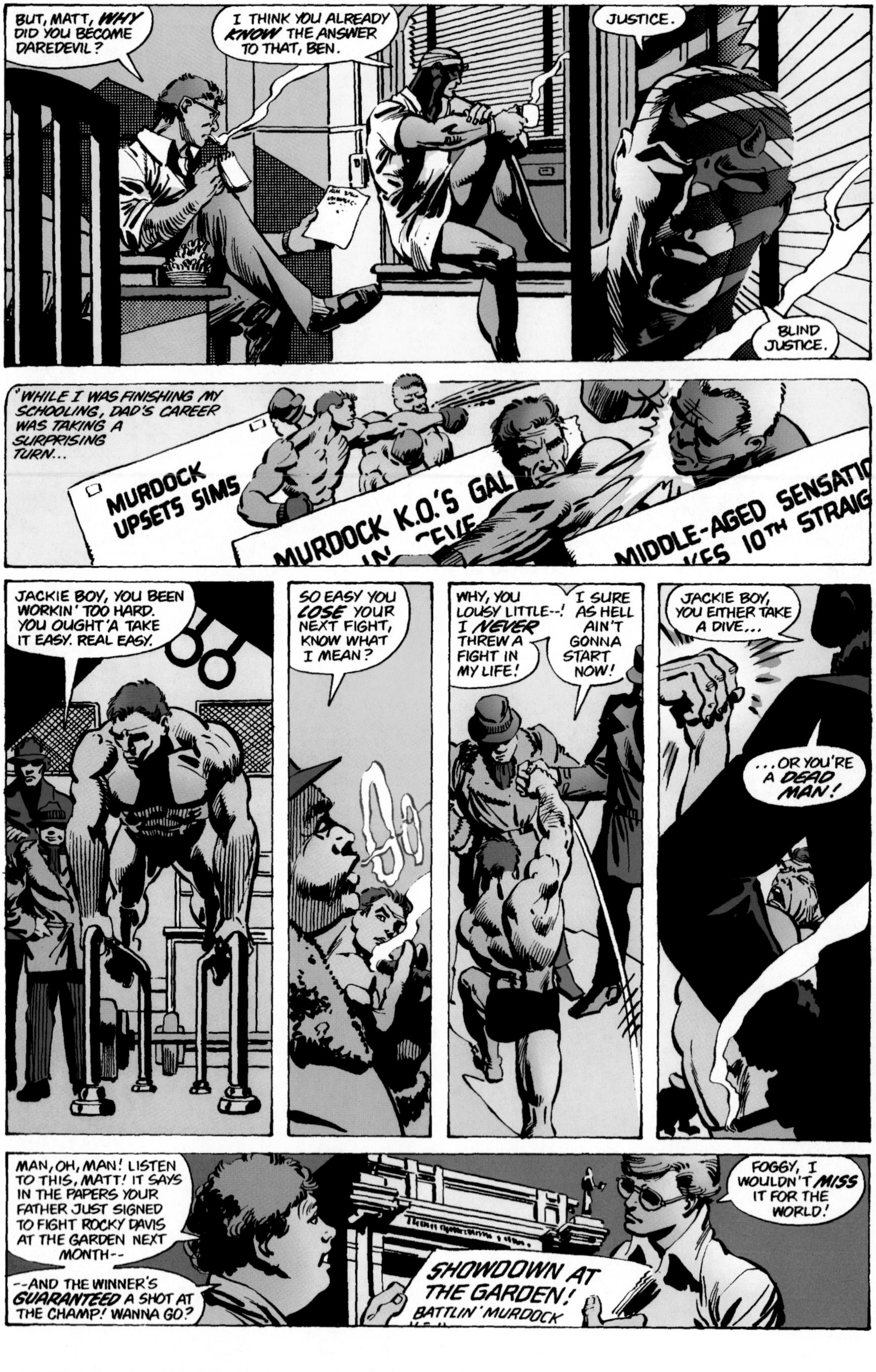

BUT, MATT, WHY DID YOU BECOME DAREDEVIL?
I THINK YOU ALREADY KNOW THE ANSWER TO THAT, BEN.
JUSTICE.
BLIND JUSTICE.
"WHILE I WAS FINISHING MY SCHOOLING, DAD'S CAREER WAS TAKING A SURPRISING TURN...
MURDOCK UPSETS SIMS
MURDOCK K.O.'S GAL
MIDDLE-AGED SENSATIO
JACKIE BOY, YOU BEEN WORKIN' TOO HARD. YOU OUGHT'A TAKE IT EASY. REAL EASY.
SO EASY YOU LOSE YOUR NEXT FIGHT, KNOW WHAT I MEAN?
WHY, YOU LOUSY LITTLE--! I NEVER THREW A FIGHT IN MY LIFE!
I SURE AS HELL AIN'T GONNA START NOW!
JACKIE BOY, YOU EITHER TAKE A DIVE...
...OR YOU'RE A DEAD MAN!
MAN, OH, MAN! LISTEN TO THIS, MATT! IT SAYS IN THE PAPERS YOUR FATHER JUST SIGNED TO FIGHT ROCKY DAVIS AT THE GARDEN NEXT MONTH--
--AND THE WINNER'S GUARANTEED A SHOT AT THE CHAMP! WANNA GO?
SHOWDOWN AT THE GARDEN!
BATTLIN' MURDOCK
FOGGY, I WOULDN'T MISS IT FOR THE WORLD!

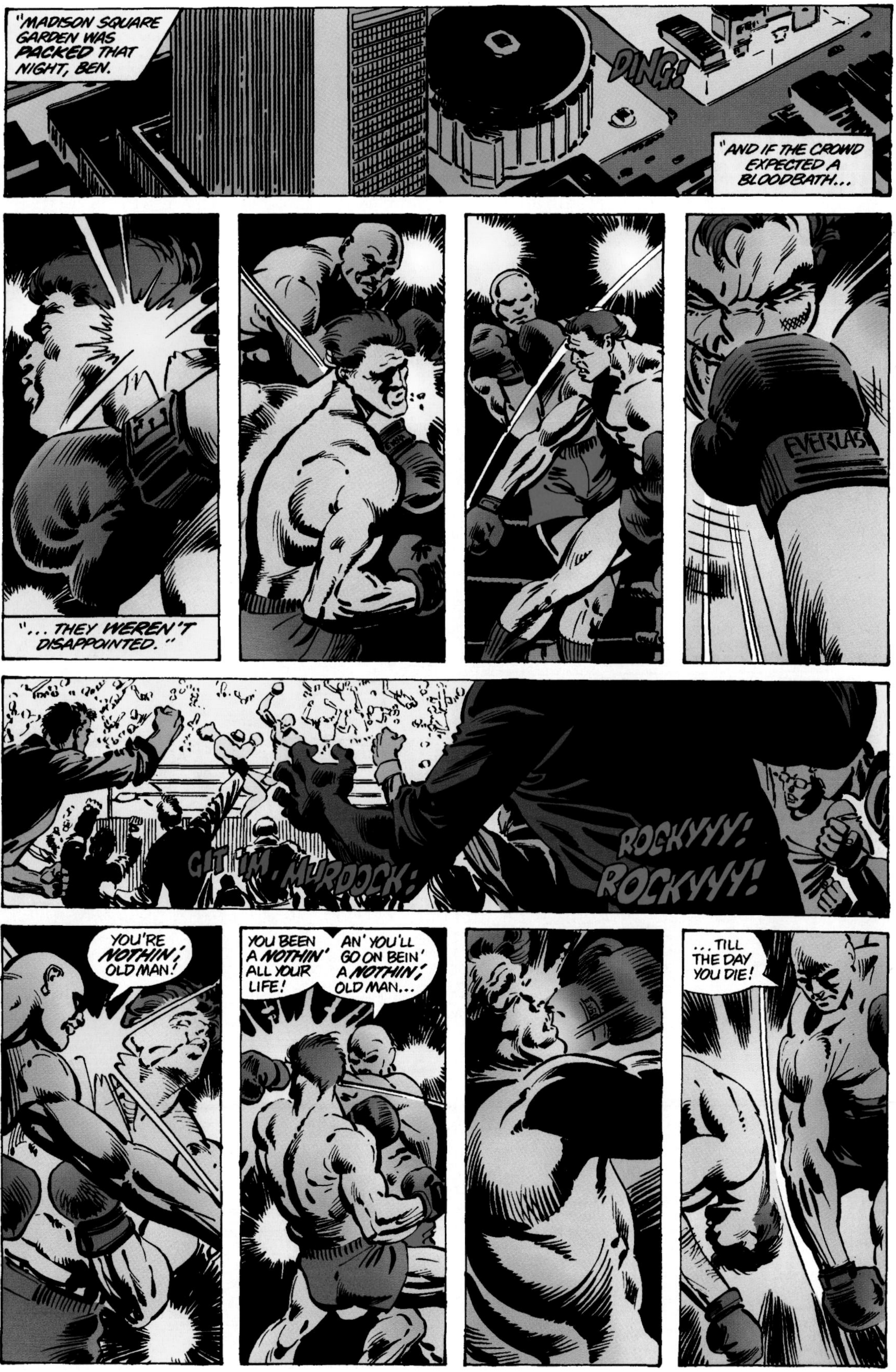
"MADISON SQUARE GARDEN WAS PACKED THAT NIGHT, BEN.
DING!
"AND IF THE CROWD EXPECTED A BLOODBATH...
"...THEY WEREN'T DISAPPOINTED."
EVERLAST
GIT 'IM, MURDOCK!
ROCKYYY! ROCKYYY!
YOU'RE NOTHIN', OLD MAN!
YOU BEEN A NOTHIN' ALL YOUR LIFE!
AN' YOU'LL GO ON BEIN' A NOTHIN', OLD MAN...
...TILL THE DAY YOU DIE!

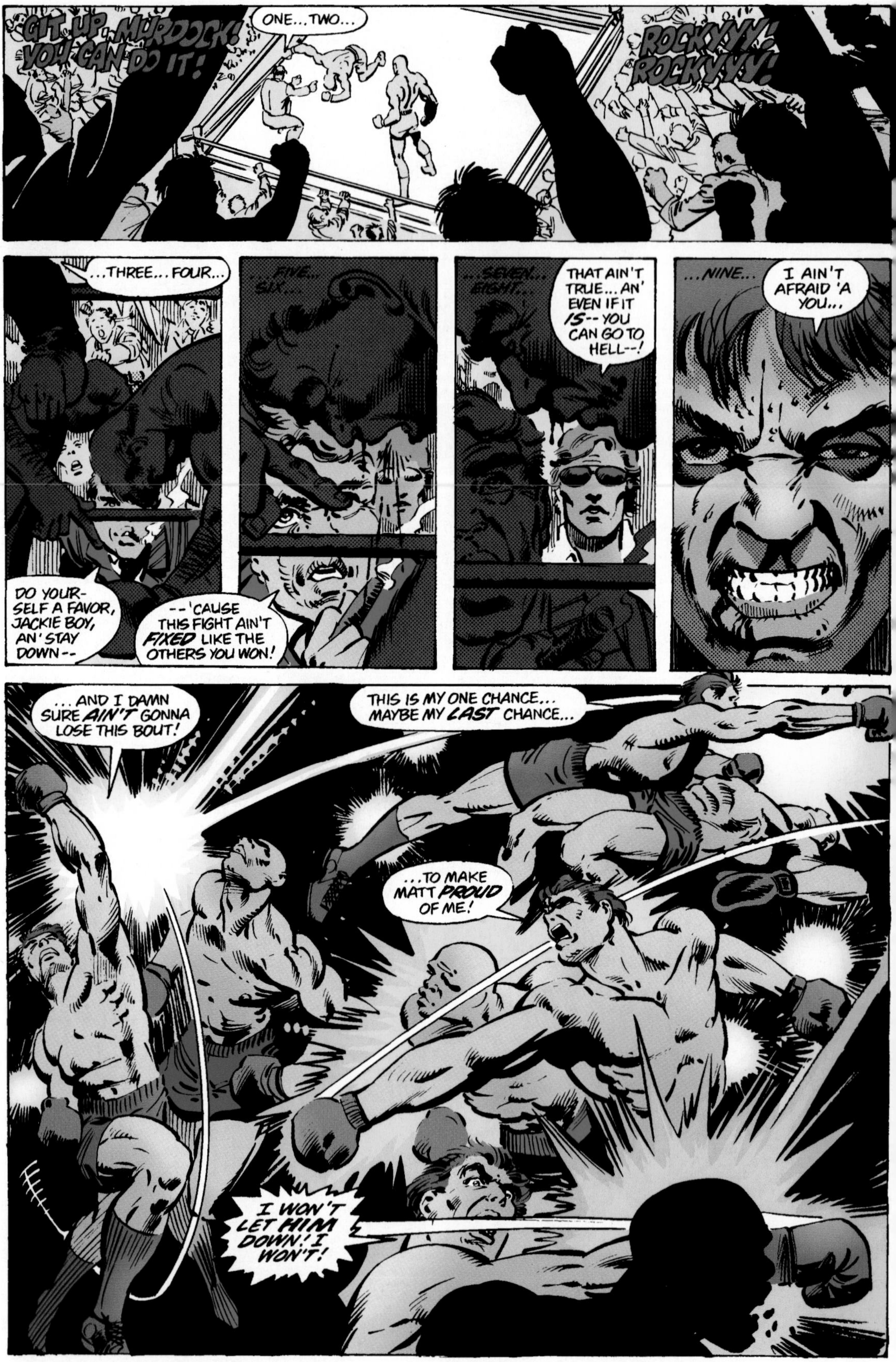
GIT UP, MURDOCK! YOU CAN DO IT!
ONE... TWO...
ROCKYYY! ROCKYYY!
...THREE... FOUR...
DO YOURSELF A FAVOR, JACKIE BOY, AN' STAY DOWN--
...FIVE... SIX...
--'CAUSE THIS FIGHT AIN'T FIXED LIKE THE OTHERS YOU WON!
...SEVEN... EIGHT...
THAT AIN'T TRUE... AN' EVEN IF IT IS--YOU CAN GO TO HELL--!
...NINE...
I AIN'T AFRAID 'A YOU...
...AND I DAMN SURE AIN'T GONNA LOSE THIS BOUT!
THIS IS MY ONE CHANCE... MAYBE MY LAST CHANCE...
...TO MAKE MATT PROUD OF ME!
I WON'T LET HIM DOWN! I WON'T!

THIS ONE'S FOR *YOU*, MATT!

"DAD *WON* THE FIGHT.

BLAM

"BUT HE LOST HIS LIFE...

THIS ONE'S FOR *YOU*, BUM!

EASY, SON--

--THERE'S NOTHIN' YOU CAN DO, MATT. CAN'T *NOBODY* DO NOTHIN'!

HELL, MATT, YOU THINK I DON'T KNOW HOW YOU FEEL? YOU THINK I DON'T HURT, TOO?

JACK AN' ME, WE WENT BACK A LONG WAYS.

I *TOLD* 'IM NOT TO MESS WITH SWEENEY.

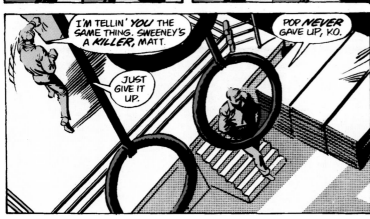

I'M TELLIN' *YOU* THE SAME THING. SWEENEY'S A *KILLER*, MATT.

JUST GIVE IT UP.

POP *NEVER* GAVE UP, K.O.

NEITHER WILL I.

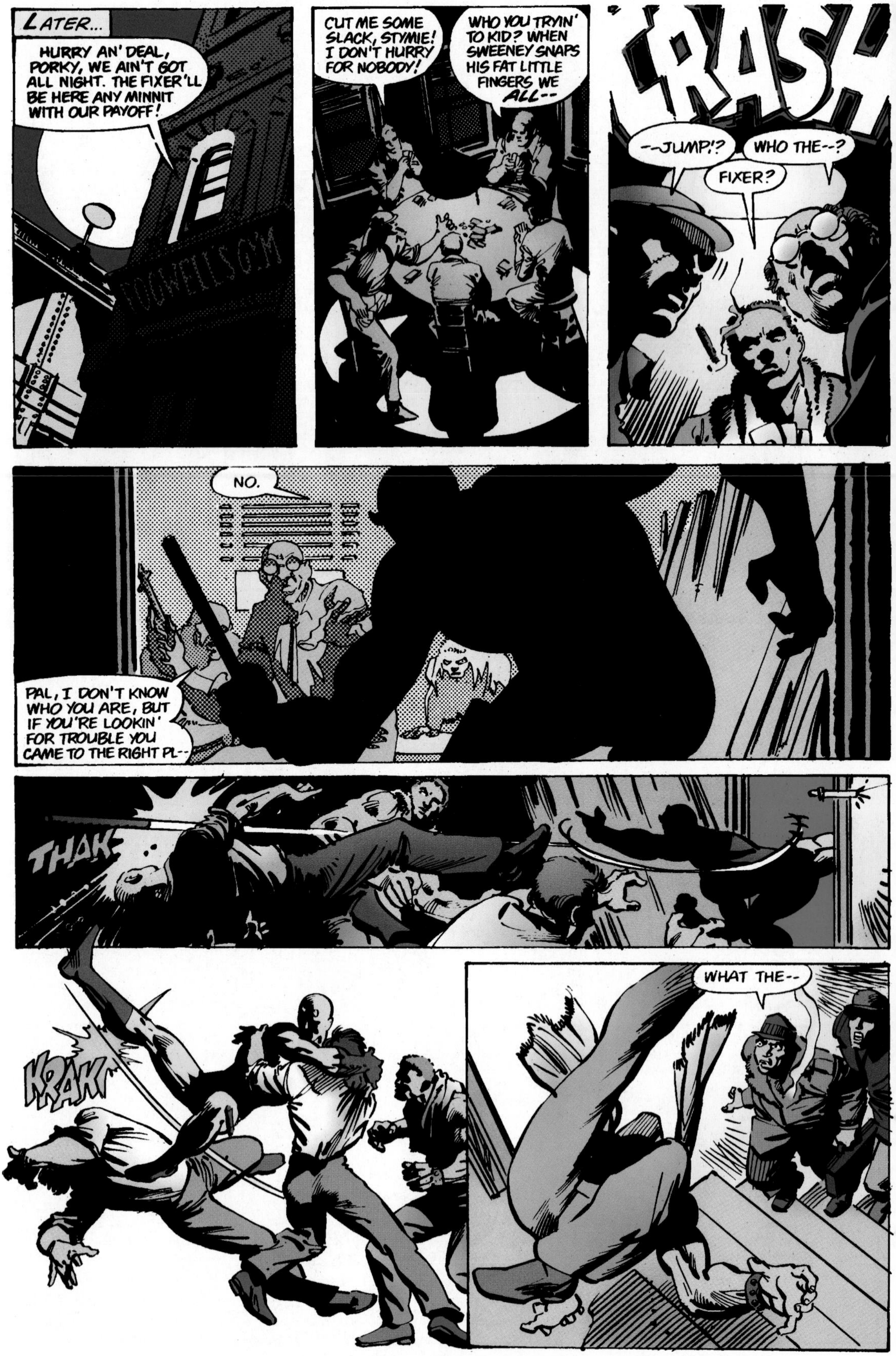
LATER...
HURRY AN' DEAL, PORKY, WE AIN'T GOT ALL NIGHT. THE FIXER'LL BE HERE ANY MINNIT WITH OUR PAYOFF!
CUT ME SOME SLACK, STYMIE! I DON'T HURRY FOR NOBODY!
WHO YOU TRYIN' TO KID? WHEN SWEENEY SNAPS HIS FAT LITTLE FINGERS WE ALL--
CRASH!
--JUMP!?
FIXER?
WHO THE--?
NO.
PAL, I DON'T KNOW WHO YOU ARE, BUT IF YOU'RE LOOKIN' FOR TROUBLE YOU CAME TO THE RIGHT PL--
THAK
KRAK!
WHAT THE--

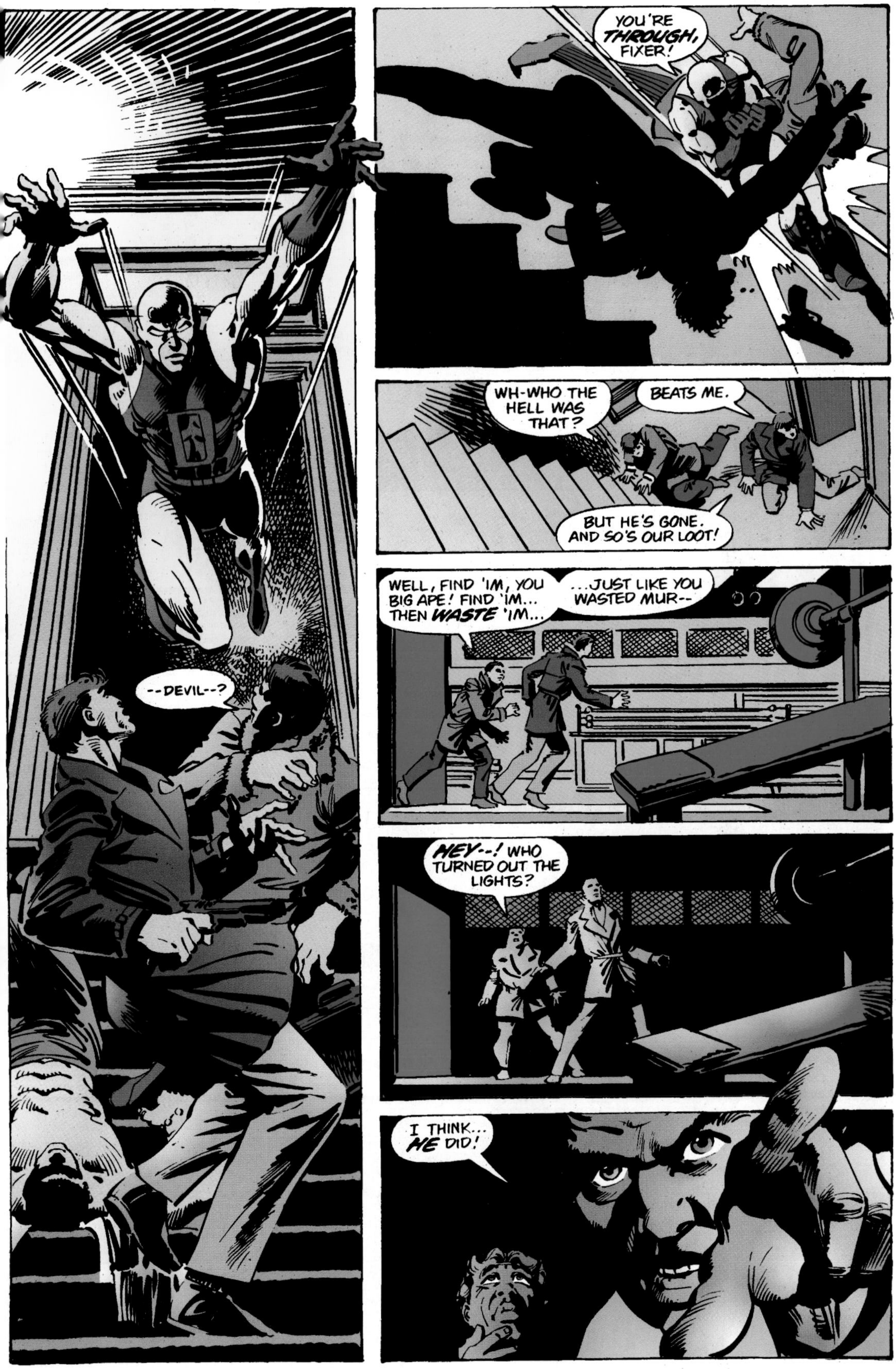
--DEVIL--?
YOU'RE THROUGH, FIXER!
WH-WHO THE HELL WAS THAT?
BEATS ME.
BUT HE'S GONE. AND SO'S OUR LOOT!
WELL, FIND 'IM, YOU BIG APE! FIND 'IM... THEN WASTE 'IM...
...JUST LIKE YOU WASTED MUR--
HEY--! WHO TURNED OUT THE LIGHTS?
I THINK... HE DID!

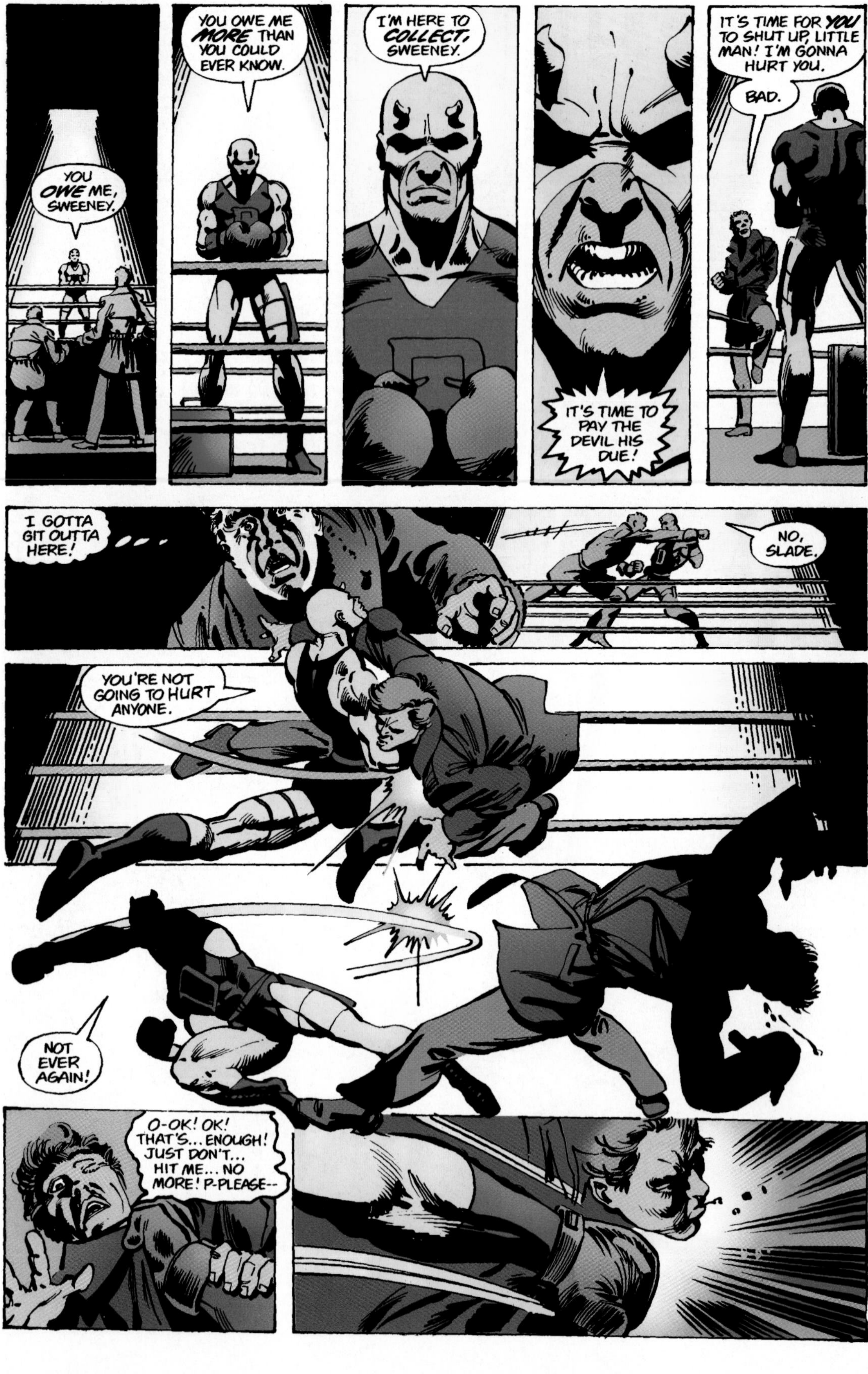
YOU OWE ME, SWEENEY.
YOU OWE ME MORE THAN YOU COULD EVER KNOW.
I'M HERE TO COLLECT, SWEENEY.
IT'S TIME TO PAY THE DEVIL HIS DUE!
IT'S TIME FOR YOU TO SHUT UP, LITTLE MAN! I'M GONNA HURT YOU.
BAD.
I GOTTA GIT OUTTA HERE!
NO, SLADE.
YOU'RE NOT GOING TO HURT ANYONE.
NOT EVER AGAIN!
O-OK! OK! THAT'S... ENOUGH! JUST DON'T... HIT ME... NO MORE! P-PLEASE--

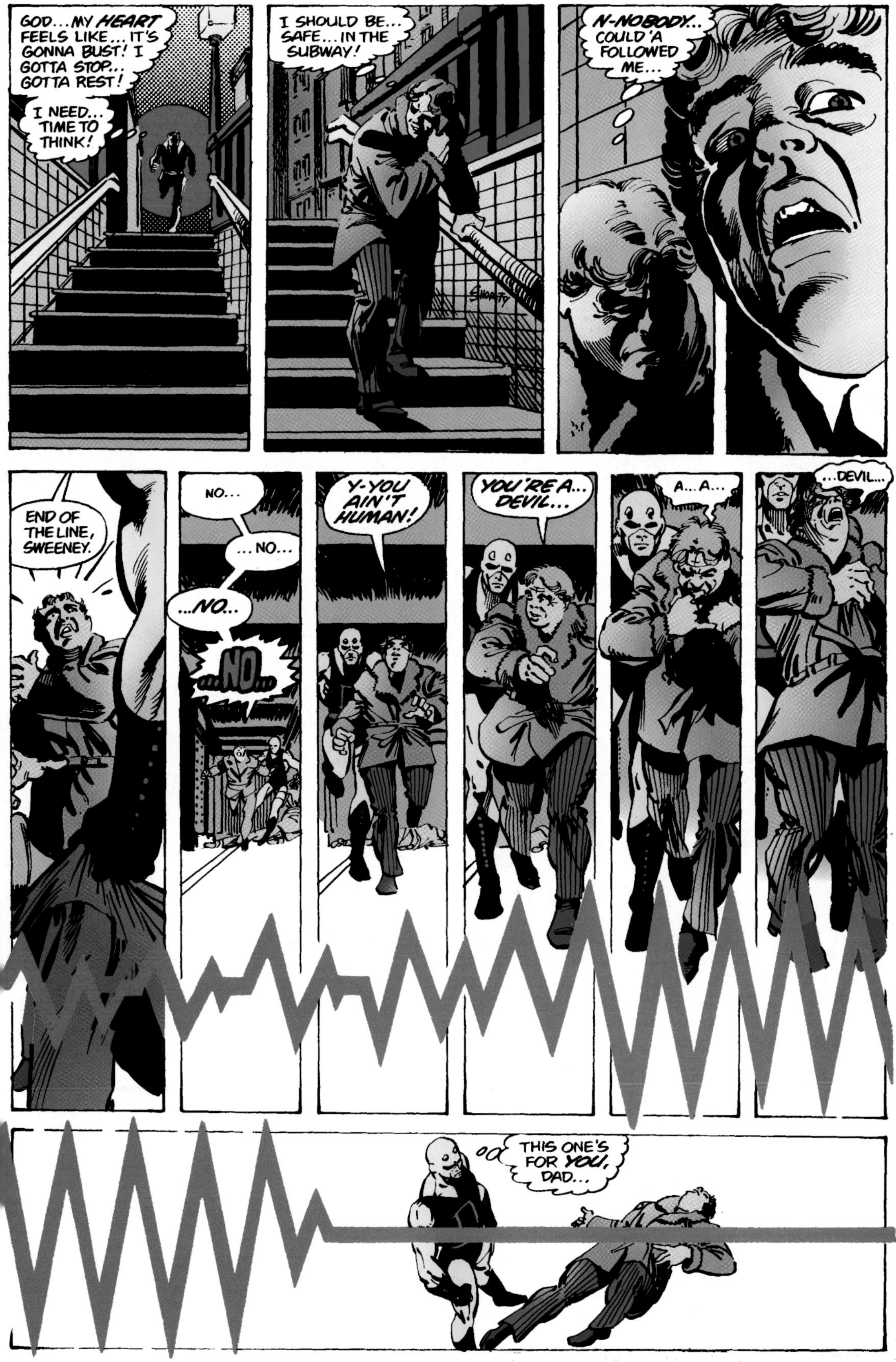
GOD... MY HEART FEELS LIKE... IT'S GONNA BUST! I GOTTA STOP... GOTTA REST!
I NEED... TIME TO THINK!
I SHOULD BE... SAFE... IN THE SUBWAY!
N-NOBODY... COULD'A FOLLOWED ME...
END OF THE LINE, SWEENEY.
NO...
...NO...
...NO...
...NO...
Y-YOU AIN'T HUMAN!
YOU'RE A... DEVIL...
A... A...
...DEVIL...
THIS ONE'S FOR YOU, DAD...

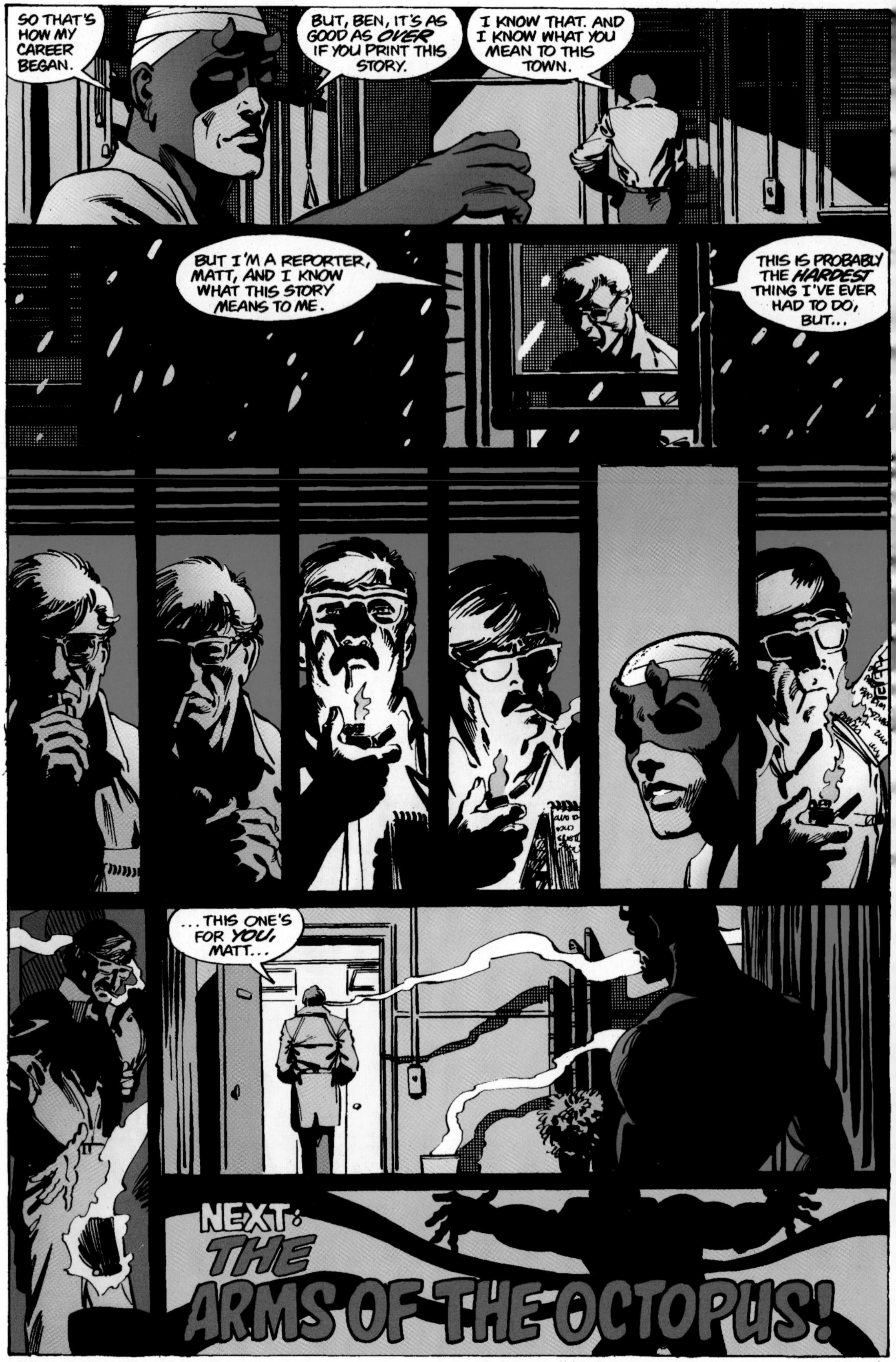
SO THAT'S HOW MY CAREER BEGAN.
BUT, BEN, IT'S AS GOOD AS OVER IF YOU PRINT THIS STORY.
I KNOW THAT. AND I KNOW WHAT YOU MEAN TO THIS TOWN.
BUT I'M A REPORTER, MATT, AND I KNOW WHAT THIS STORY MEANS TO ME.
THIS IS PROBABLY THE HARDEST THING I'VE EVER HAD TO DO, BUT...
...THIS ONE'S FOR YOU, MATT...
NEXT: THE ARMS OF THE OCTOPUS!

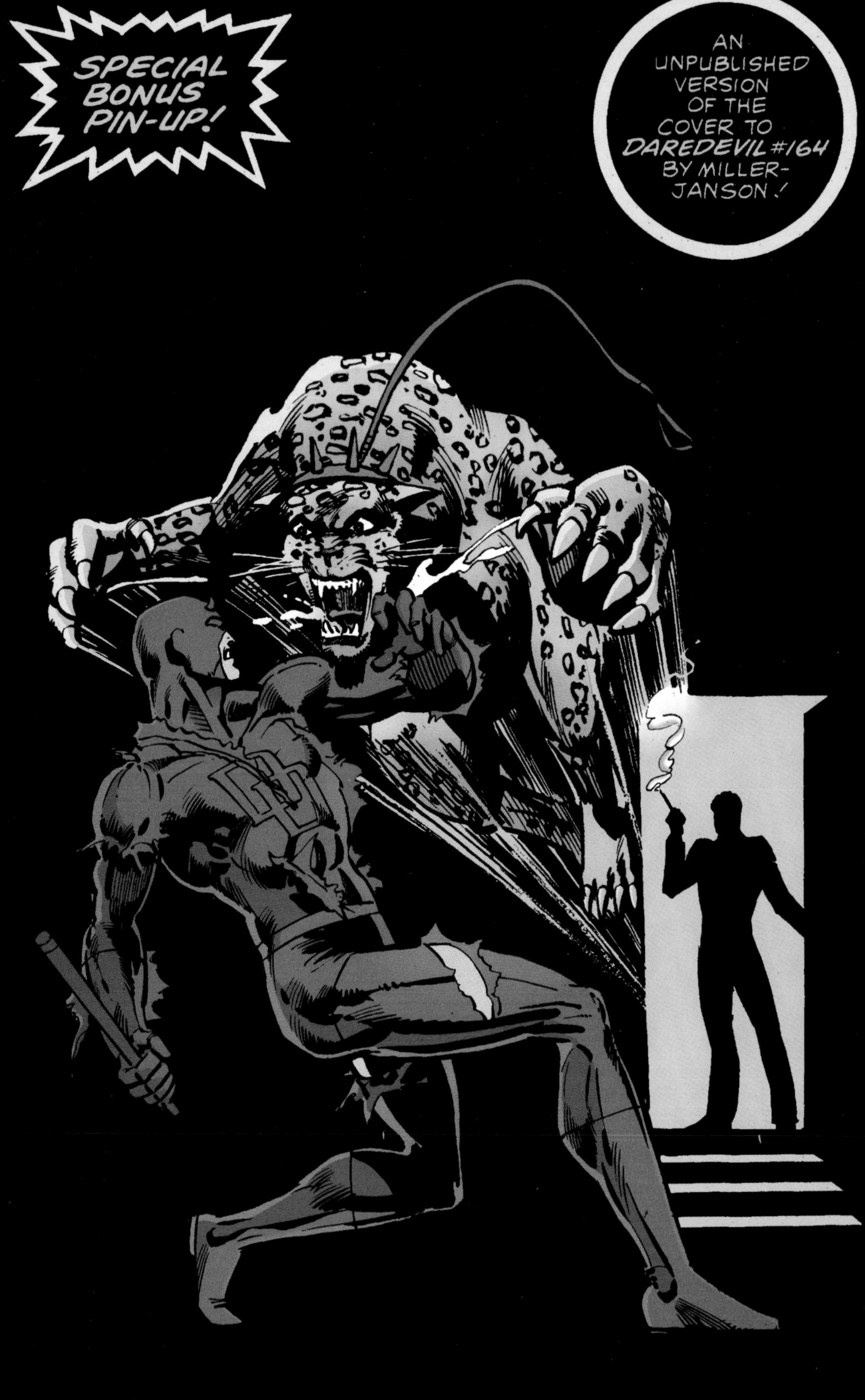
SPECIAL BONUS PIN-UP!
AN UNPUBLISHED VERSION OF THE COVER TO DAREDEVIL #164 BY MILLER-JANSON!

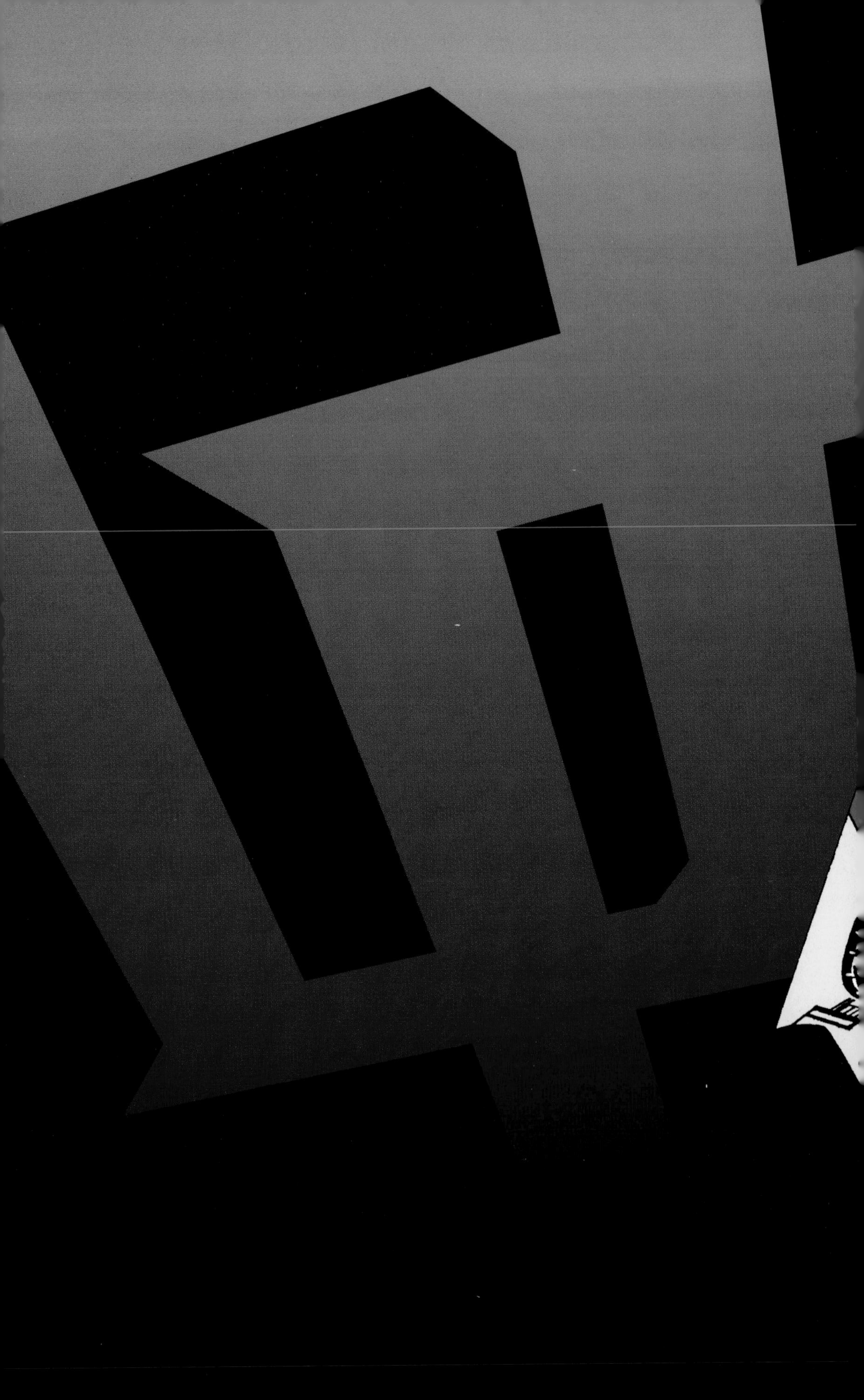

DAREDEVIL #165

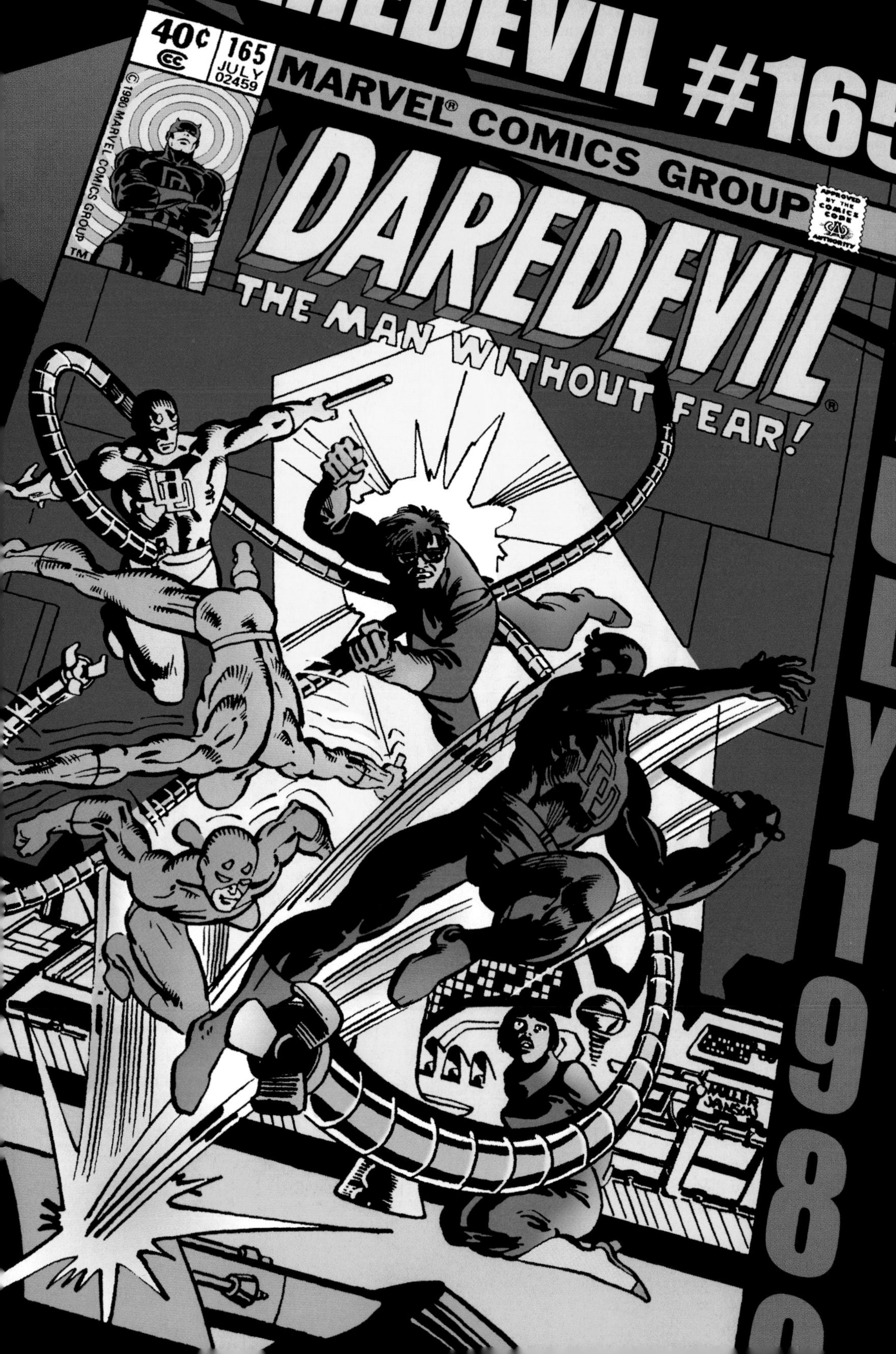
40¢
165
JULY
02459
© 1980 MARVEL COMICS GROUP
MARVEL® COMICS GROUP
APPROVED BY THE COMICS CODE AUTHORITY
DAREDEVIL
THE MAN WITHOUT FEAR!
MILLER
JANSON

JULY 1980

He dwells in eternal night—but the blackness is filled with sounds and scents other men cannot perceive. Though attorney MATT MURDOCK is *blind*, his other senses function with *superhuman sharpness*—his *radar sense* guides him over every obstacle! He stalks the streets by night, a red-garbed foe of evil!

Stan Lee PRESENTS: DAREDEVIL, THE MAN WITHOUT FEAR! ®

HIGH ABOVE THE BUSTLING CANYONS OF MANHATTAN THIS COOL MARCH EVENING, THE NOISE OF RUSH-HOUR TRAFFIC IS ONLY A DISTANT ECHO...

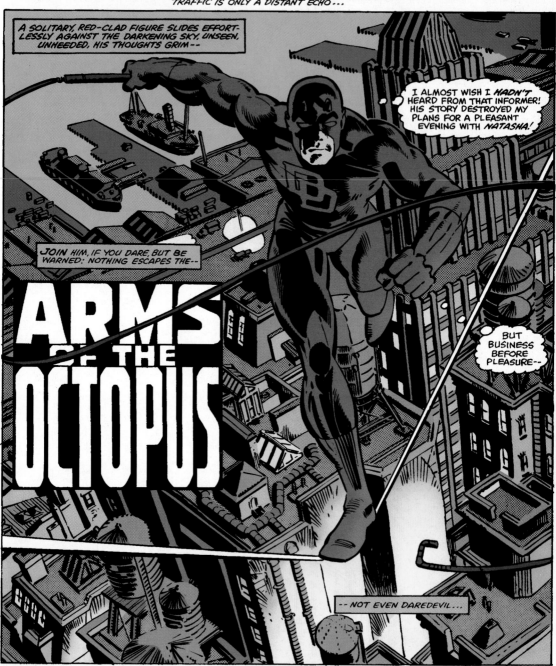

A SOLITARY, RED-CLAD FIGURE SLIDES EFFORT-LESSLY AGAINST THE DARKENING SKY, UNSEEN, UNHEEDED, HIS THOUGHTS GRIM--

I ALMOST WISH I *HADN'T* HEARD FROM THAT INFORMER! HIS STORY DESTROYED MY PLANS FOR A PLEASANT EVENING WITH *NATASHA!*

JOIN HIM, IF YOU DARE, BUT BE WARNED: NOTHING ESCAPES THE--

ARMS OF THE OCTOPUS

BUT BUSINESS BEFORE PLEASURE--

-- NOT EVEN DAREDEVIL...

ROGER McKENZIE & FRANK MILLER
SCRIPT / CO-PLOTTERS / PENCILS

KLAUS JANSON
INKS

JOE ROSEN
LETTERING

BOB SHAREN
COLORING

DENNY O'NEIL
EDITOR

JIM SHOOTER
EDITOR IN CHIEF

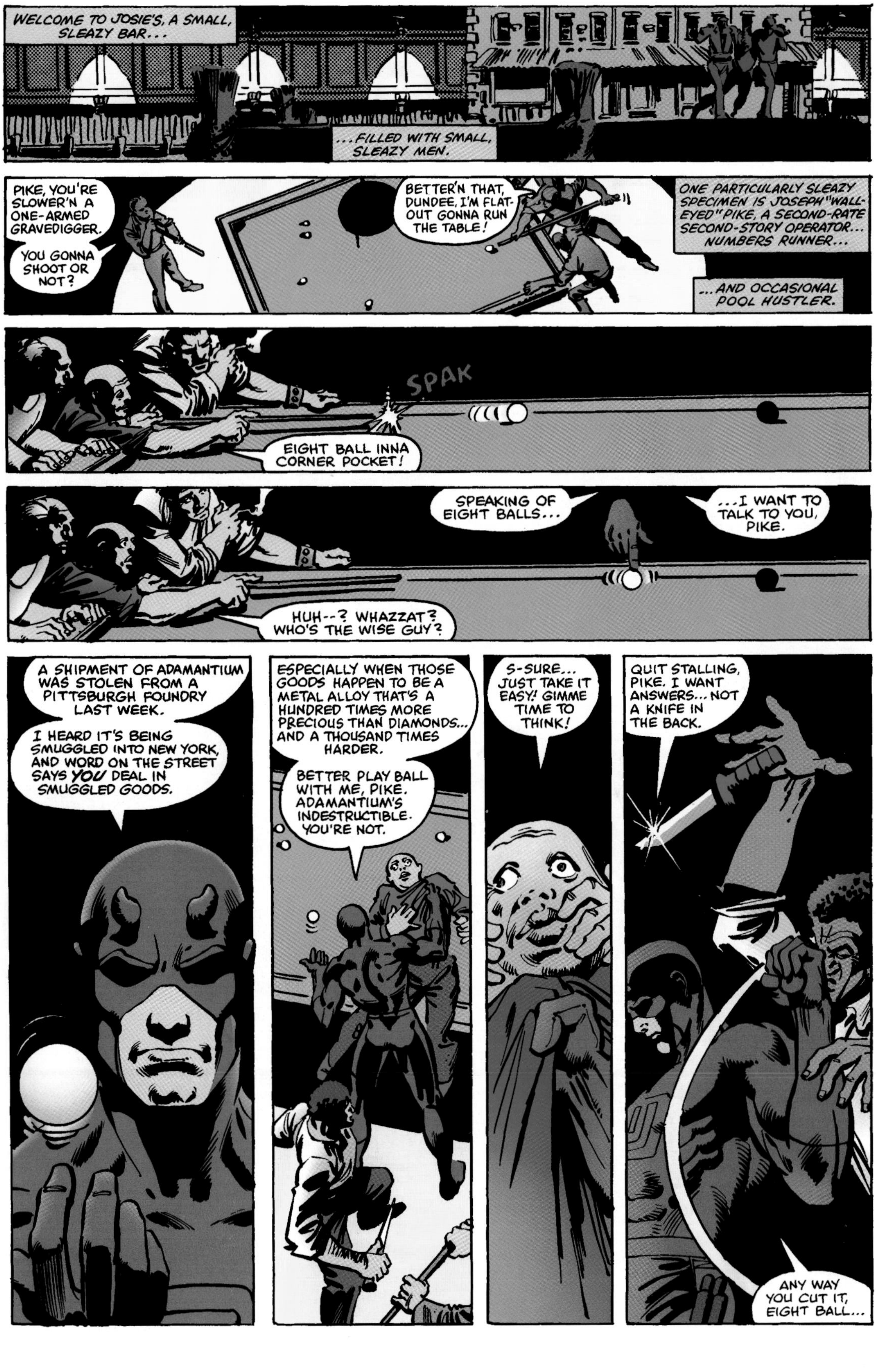

WELCOME TO JOSIE'S, A SMALL, SLEAZY BAR...
...FILLED WITH SMALL, SLEAZY MEN.
PIKE, YOU'RE SLOWER'N A ONE-ARMED GRAVEDIGGER.
YOU GONNA SHOOT OR NOT?
BETTER'N THAT, DUNDEE, I'M FLAT-OUT GONNA RUN THE TABLE!
ONE PARTICULARLY SLEAZY SPECIMEN IS JOSEPH "WALL-EYED" PIKE, A SECOND-RATE SECOND-STORY OPERATOR... NUMBERS RUNNER...
...AND OCCASIONAL POOL HUSTLER.
SPAK
EIGHT BALL INNA CORNER POCKET!
SPEAKING OF EIGHT BALLS...
...I WANT TO TALK TO YOU, PIKE.
HUH--? WHAZZAT? WHO'S THE WISE GUY?
A SHIPMENT OF ADAMANTIUM WAS STOLEN FROM A PITTSBURGH FOUNDRY LAST WEEK.
I HEARD IT'S BEING SMUGGLED INTO NEW YORK, AND WORD ON THE STREET SAYS YOU DEAL IN SMUGGLED GOODS.
ESPECIALLY WHEN THOSE GOODS HAPPEN TO BE A METAL ALLOY THAT'S A HUNDRED TIMES MORE PRECIOUS THAN DIAMONDS... AND A THOUSAND TIMES HARDER.
BETTER PLAY BALL WITH ME, PIKE. ADAMANTIUM'S INDESTRUCTIBLE. YOU'RE NOT.
S-SURE... JUST TAKE IT EASY! GIMME TIME TO THINK!
QUIT STALLING, PIKE. I WANT ANSWERS... NOT A KNIFE IN THE BACK.
ANY WAY YOU CUT IT, EIGHT BALL...

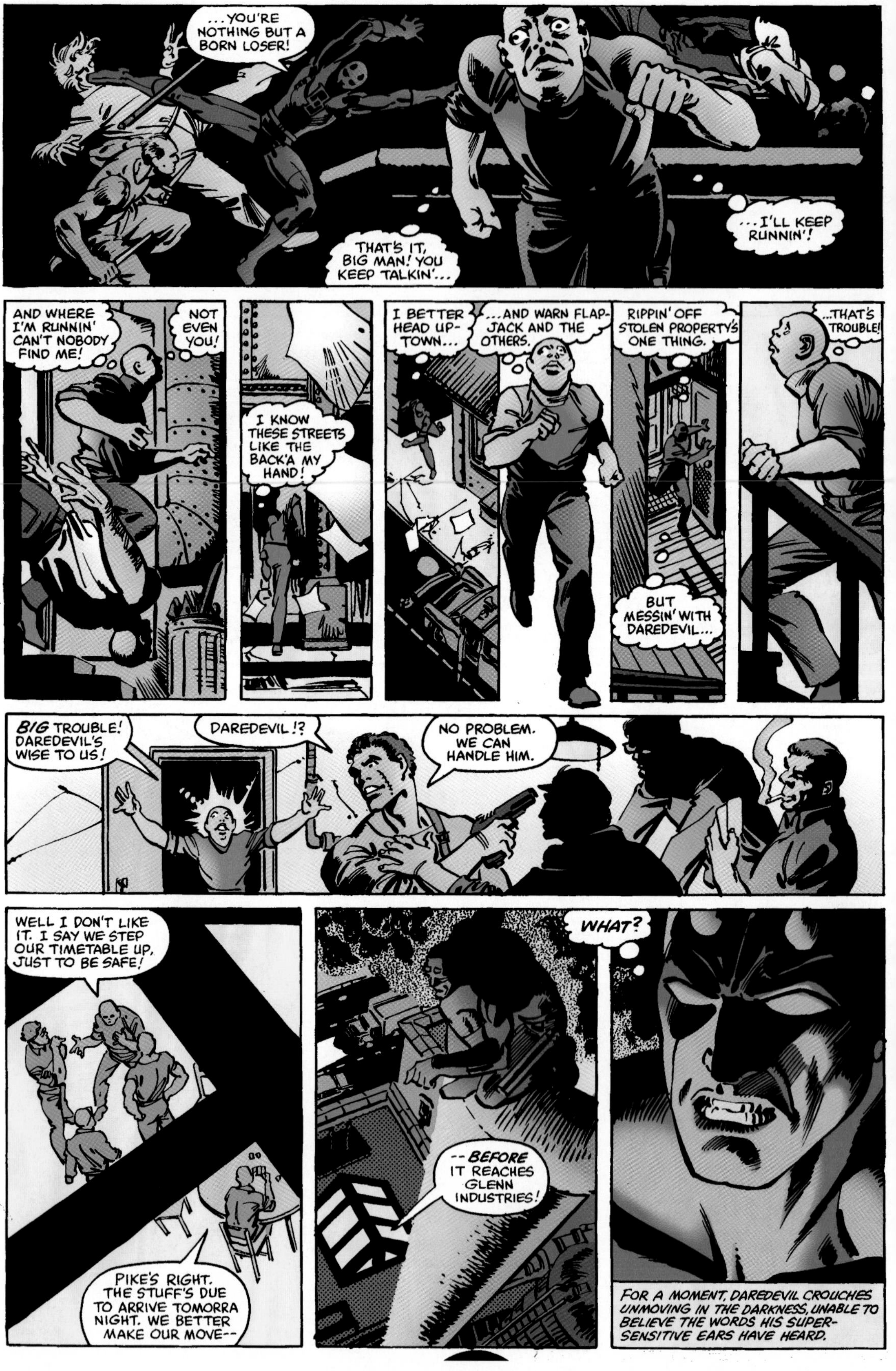
...YOU'RE NOTHING BUT A BORN LOSER!
THAT'S IT, BIG MAN! YOU KEEP TALKIN'...
...I'LL KEEP RUNNIN'!
AND WHERE I'M RUNNIN' CAN'T NOBODY FIND ME!
NOT EVEN YOU!
I KNOW THESE STREETS LIKE THE BACK'A MY HAND!
I BETTER HEAD UP-TOWN...
...AND WARN FLAP-JACK AND THE OTHERS.
RIPPIN' OFF STOLEN PROPERTY'S ONE THING.
BUT MESSIN' WITH DAREDEVIL...
...THAT'S TROUBLE!
BIG TROUBLE! DAREDEVIL'S WISE TO US!
DAREDEVIL!?
NO PROBLEM. WE CAN HANDLE HIM.
WELL I DON'T LIKE IT. I SAY WE STEP OUR TIMETABLE UP, JUST TO BE SAFE!
PIKE'S RIGHT. THE STUFF'S DUE TO ARRIVE TOMORRA NIGHT. WE BETTER MAKE OUR MOVE--
--BEFORE IT REACHES GLENN INDUSTRIES!
WHAT?
FOR A MOMENT, DAREDEVIL CROUCHES UNMOVING IN THE DARKNESS, UNABLE TO BELIEVE THE WORDS HIS SUPER-SENSITIVE EARS HAVE HEARD.

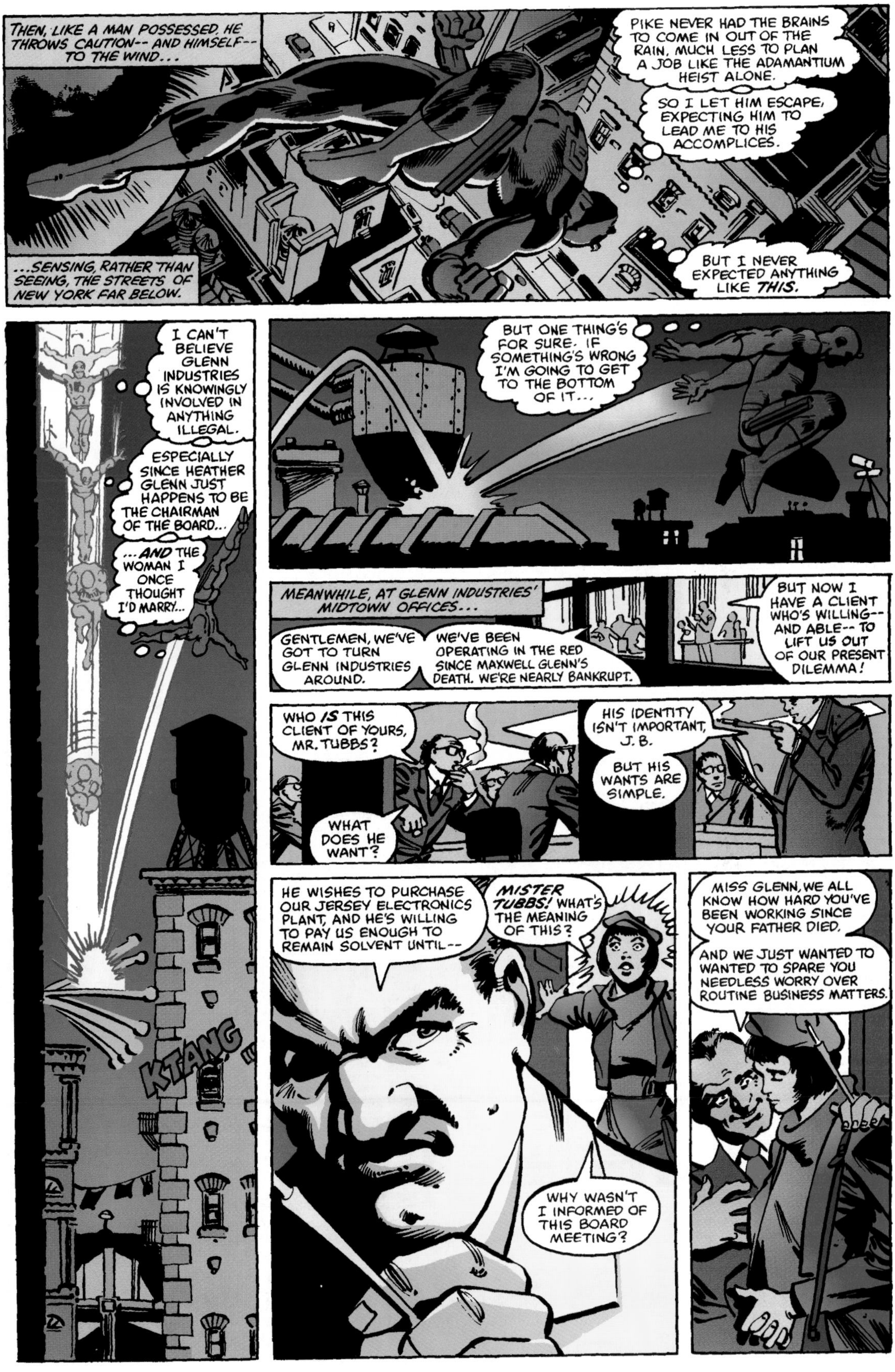
THEN, LIKE A MAN POSSESSED, HE THROWS CAUTION-- AND HIMSELF-- TO THE WIND...
PIKE NEVER HAD THE BRAINS TO COME IN OUT OF THE RAIN, MUCH LESS TO PLAN A JOB LIKE THE ADAMANTIUM HEIST ALONE.
SO I LET HIM ESCAPE, EXPECTING HIM TO LEAD ME TO HIS ACCOMPLICES.
...SENSING, RATHER THAN SEEING, THE STREETS OF NEW YORK FAR BELOW.
BUT I NEVER EXPECTED ANYTHING LIKE THIS.
I CAN'T BELIEVE GLENN INDUSTRIES IS KNOWINGLY INVOLVED IN ANYTHING ILLEGAL.
ESPECIALLY SINCE HEATHER GLENN JUST HAPPENS TO BE THE CHAIRMAN OF THE BOARD...
...AND THE WOMAN I ONCE THOUGHT I'D MARRY...
KTANG
BUT ONE THING'S FOR SURE. IF SOMETHING'S WRONG I'M GOING TO GET TO THE BOTTOM OF IT...
MEANWHILE, AT GLENN INDUSTRIES' MIDTOWN OFFICES...
GENTLEMEN, WE'VE GOT TO TURN GLENN INDUSTRIES AROUND.
WE'VE BEEN OPERATING IN THE RED SINCE MAXWELL GLENN'S DEATH. WE'RE NEARLY BANKRUPT.
BUT NOW I HAVE A CLIENT WHO'S WILLING-- AND ABLE-- TO LIFT US OUT OF OUR PRESENT DILEMMA!
WHO IS THIS CLIENT OF YOURS, MR. TUBBS?
WHAT DOES HE WANT?
HIS IDENTITY ISN'T IMPORTANT, J. B.
BUT HIS WANTS ARE SIMPLE.
HE WISHES TO PURCHASE OUR JERSEY ELECTRONICS PLANT, AND HE'S WILLING TO PAY US ENOUGH TO REMAIN SOLVENT UNTIL--
MISTER TUBBS! WHAT'S THE MEANING OF THIS?
WHY WASN'T I INFORMED OF THIS BOARD MEETING?
MISS GLENN, WE ALL KNOW HOW HARD YOU'VE BEEN WORKING SINCE YOUR FATHER DIED.
AND WE JUST WANTED TO WANTED TO SPARE YOU NEEDLESS WORRY OVER ROUTINE BUSINESS MATTERS.

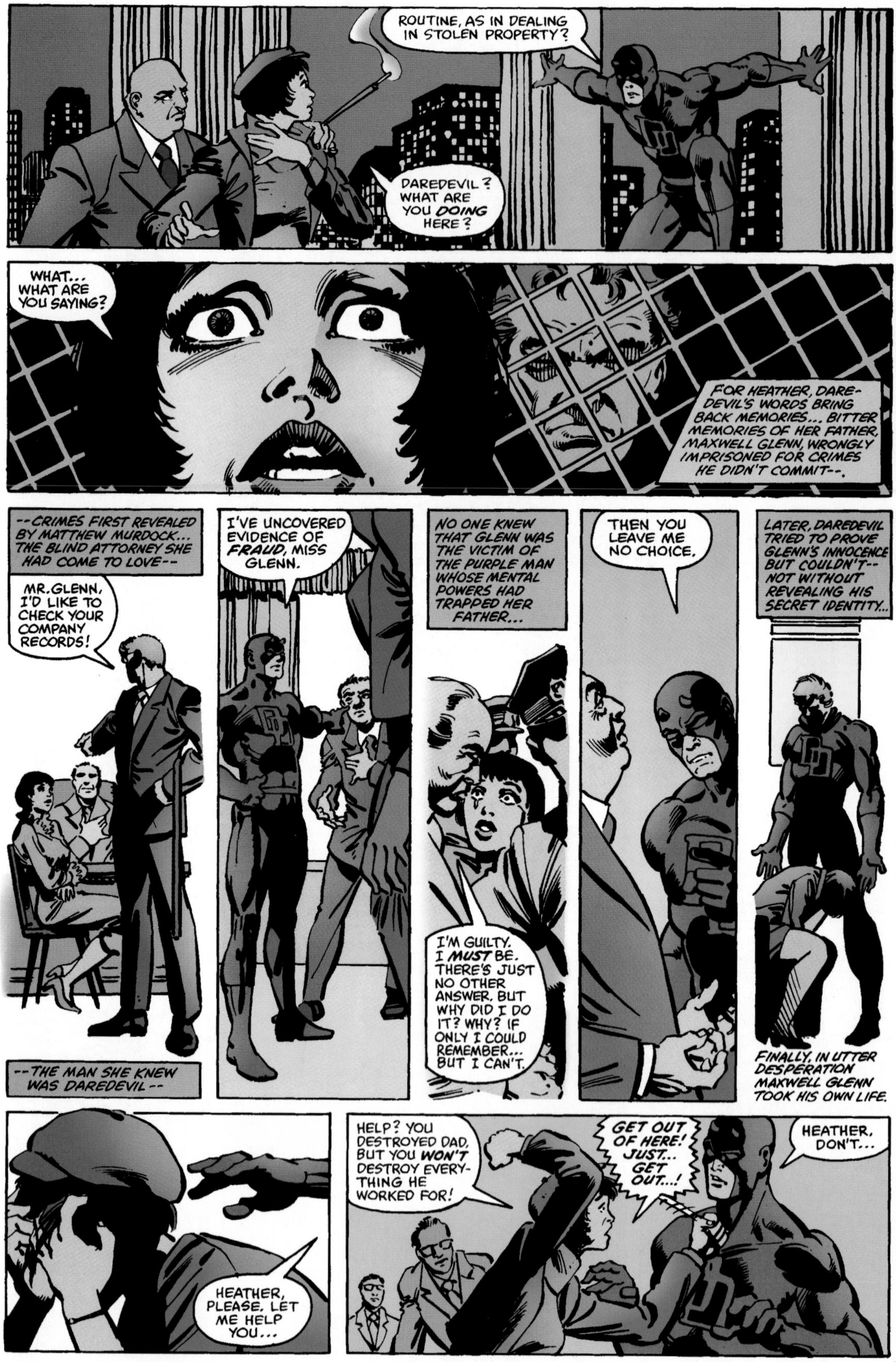
ROUTINE, AS IN DEALING IN STOLEN PROPERTY?
DAREDEVIL? WHAT ARE YOU DOING HERE?
WHAT... WHAT ARE YOU SAYING?
FOR HEATHER, DAREDEVIL'S WORDS BRING BACK MEMORIES... BITTER MEMORIES OF HER FATHER, MAXWELL GLENN, WRONGLY IMPRISONED FOR CRIMES HE DIDN'T COMMIT--.
--CRIMES FIRST REVEALED BY MATTHEW MURDOCK... THE BLIND ATTORNEY SHE HAD COME TO LOVE--
MR. GLENN, I'D LIKE TO CHECK YOUR COMPANY RECORDS!
--THE MAN SHE KNEW WAS DAREDEVIL--
I'VE UNCOVERED EVIDENCE OF FRAUD, MISS GLENN.
NO ONE KNEW THAT GLENN WAS THE VICTIM OF THE PURPLE MAN WHOSE MENTAL POWERS HAD TRAPPED HER FATHER...
I'M GUILTY. I MUST BE. THERE'S JUST NO OTHER ANSWER. BUT WHY DID I DO IT? WHY? IF ONLY I COULD REMEMBER... BUT I CAN'T.
THEN YOU LEAVE ME NO CHOICE.
LATER, DAREDEVIL TRIED TO PROVE GLENN'S INNOCENCE BUT COULDN'T-- NOT WITHOUT REVEALING HIS SECRET IDENTITY...
FINALLY, IN UTTER DESPERATION MAXWELL GLENN TOOK HIS OWN LIFE.
HEATHER, PLEASE. LET ME HELP YOU...
HELP? YOU DESTROYED DAD, BUT YOU WON'T DESTROY EVERYTHING HE WORKED FOR!
GET OUT OF HERE! JUST... GET OUT...!
HEATHER. DON'T...

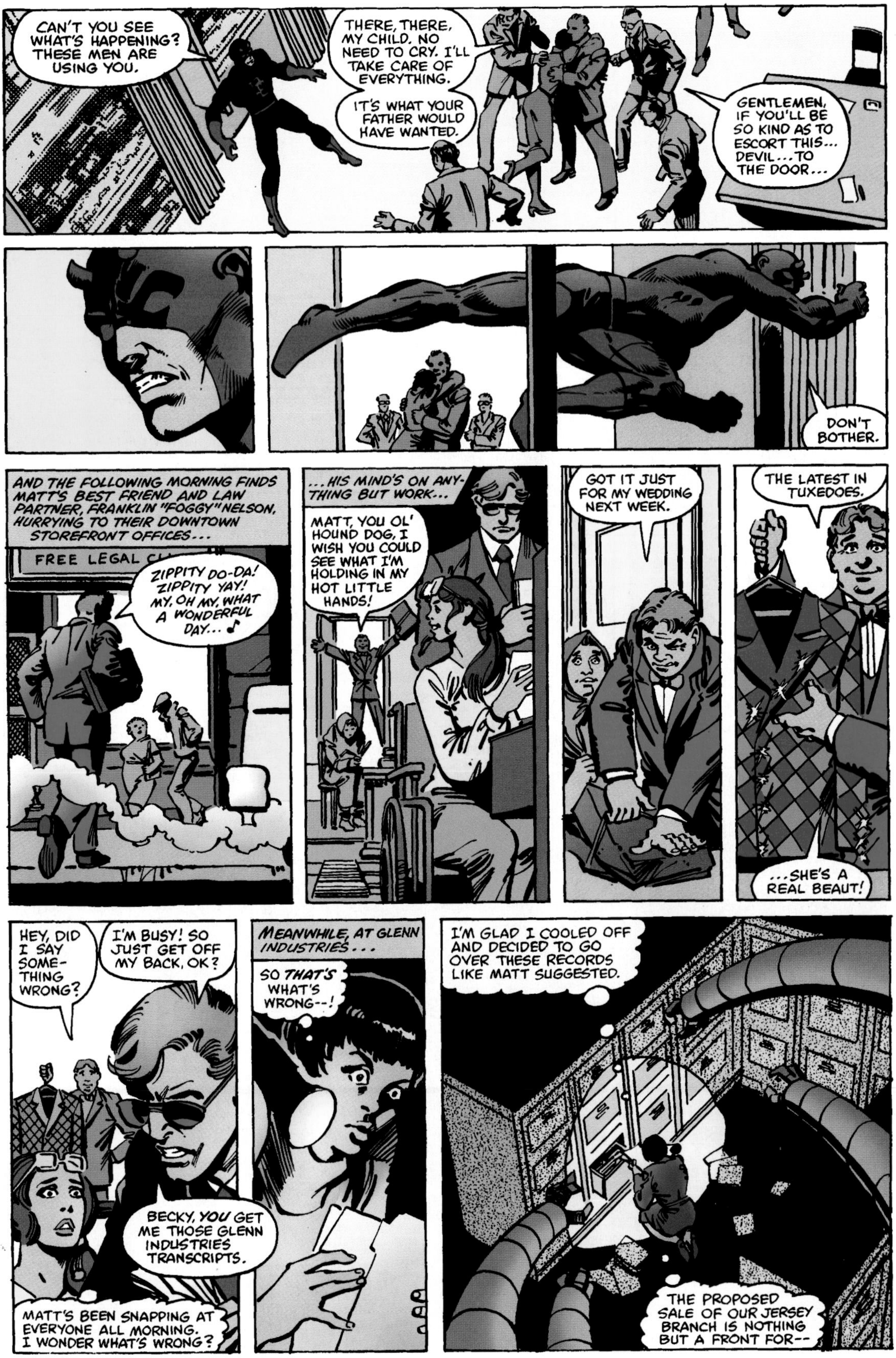
CAN'T YOU SEE WHAT'S HAPPENING? THESE MEN ARE USING YOU.
THERE, THERE, MY CHILD. NO NEED TO CRY. I'LL TAKE CARE OF EVERYTHING.
IT'S WHAT YOUR FATHER WOULD HAVE WANTED.
GENTLEMEN, IF YOU'LL BE SO KIND AS TO ESCORT THIS... DEVIL... TO THE DOOR...
DON'T BOTHER.
AND THE FOLLOWING MORNING FINDS MATT'S BEST FRIEND AND LAW PARTNER, FRANKLIN "FOGGY" NELSON, HURRYING TO THEIR DOWNTOWN STOREFRONT OFFICES...
ZIPPITY DO-DA! ZIPPITY YAY! MY, OH MY, WHAT A WONDERFUL DAY...
...HIS MIND'S ON ANYTHING BUT WORK...
MATT, YOU OL' HOUND DOG, I WISH YOU COULD SEE WHAT I'M HOLDING IN MY HOT LITTLE HANDS!
GOT IT JUST FOR MY WEDDING NEXT WEEK.
THE LATEST IN TUXEDOES.
...SHE'S A REAL BEAUT!
HEY, DID I SAY SOMETHING WRONG?
I'M BUSY! SO JUST GET OFF MY BACK, OK?
BECKY, YOU GET ME THOSE GLENN INDUSTRIES TRANSCRIPTS.
MATT'S BEEN SNAPPING AT EVERYONE ALL MORNING. I WONDER WHAT'S WRONG?
MEANWHILE, AT GLENN INDUSTRIES...
SO THAT'S WHAT'S WRONG--!
I'M GLAD I COOLED OFF AND DECIDED TO GO OVER THESE RECORDS LIKE MATT SUGGESTED.
THE PROPOSED SALE OF OUR JERSEY BRANCH IS NOTHING BUT A FRONT FOR--

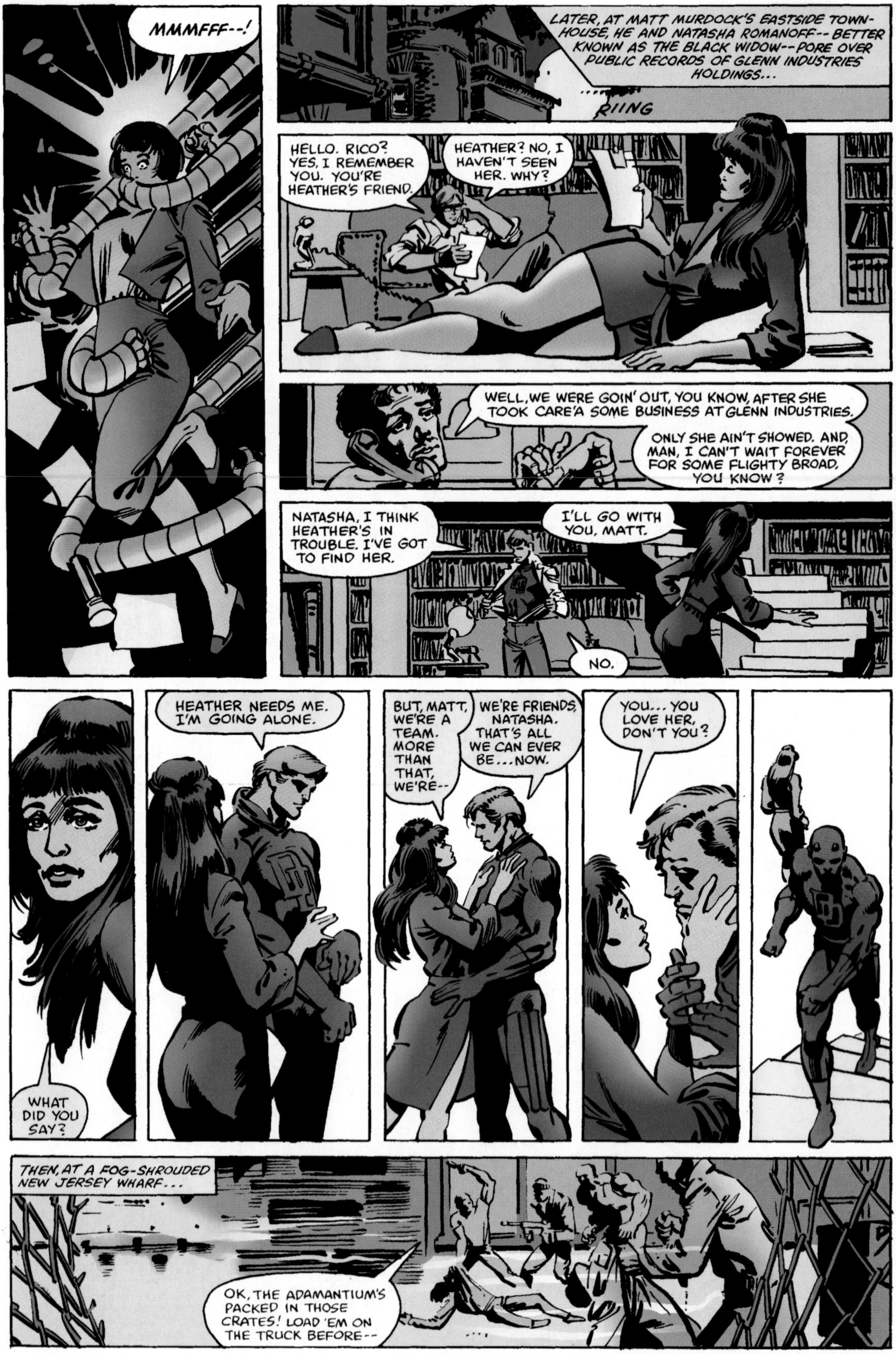
MMMFFF--!
LATER, AT MATT MURDOCK'S EASTSIDE TOWN-HOUSE, HE AND NATASHA ROMANOFF-- BETTER KNOWN AS THE BLACK WIDOW--PORE OVER PUBLIC RECORDS OF GLENN INDUSTRIES HOLDINGS...
RIING
HELLO. RICO? YES, I REMEMBER YOU. YOU'RE HEATHER'S FRIEND.
HEATHER? NO, I HAVEN'T SEEN HER. WHY?
WELL, WE WERE GOIN' OUT, YOU KNOW, AFTER SHE TOOK CARE'A SOME BUSINESS AT GLENN INDUSTRIES.
ONLY SHE AIN'T SHOWED. AND, MAN, I CAN'T WAIT FOREVER FOR SOME FLIGHTY BROAD, YOU KNOW?
NATASHA, I THINK HEATHER'S IN TROUBLE. I'VE GOT TO FIND HER.
I'LL GO WITH YOU, MATT.
NO.
WHAT DID YOU SAY?
HEATHER NEEDS ME. I'M GOING ALONE.
BUT, MATT, WE'RE A TEAM. MORE THAN THAT, WE'RE--
WE'RE FRIENDS, NATASHA. THAT'S ALL WE CAN EVER BE...NOW.
YOU... YOU LOVE HER, DON'T YOU?
THEN, AT A FOG-SHROUDED NEW JERSEY WHARF...
OK, THE ADAMANTIUM'S PACKED IN THOSE CRATES! LOAD 'EM ON THE TRUCK BEFORE--

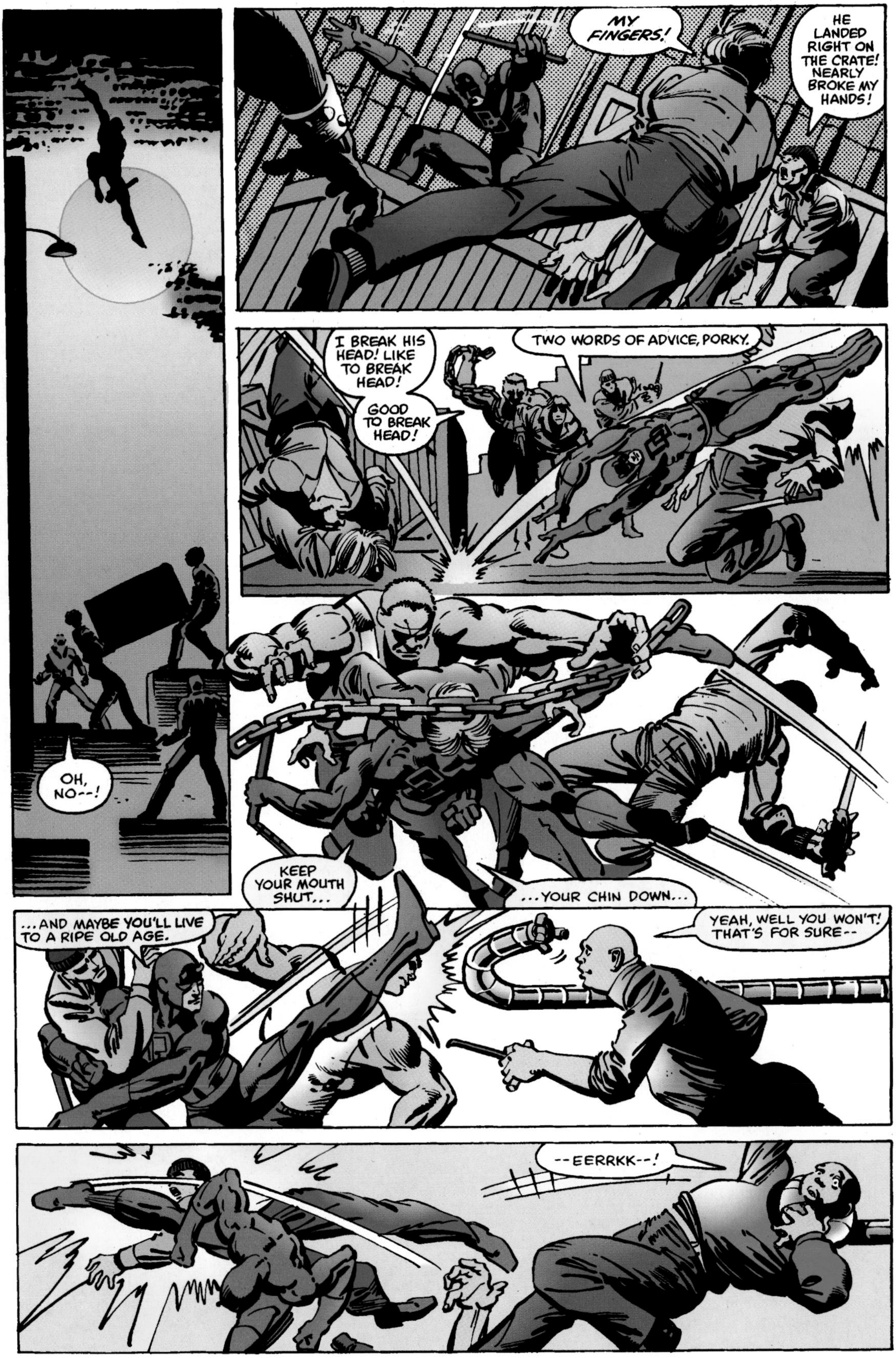
MY FINGERS!
HE LANDED RIGHT ON THE CRATE! NEARLY BROKE MY HANDS!
OH, NO--!
I BREAK HIS HEAD! LIKE TO BREAK HEAD!
GOOD TO BREAK HEAD!
TWO WORDS OF ADVICE, PORKY.
KEEP YOUR MOUTH SHUT...
...YOUR CHIN DOWN...
...AND MAYBE YOU'LL LIVE TO A RIPE OLD AGE.
YEAH, WELL YOU WON'T! THAT'S FOR SURE--
--EERRKK--!

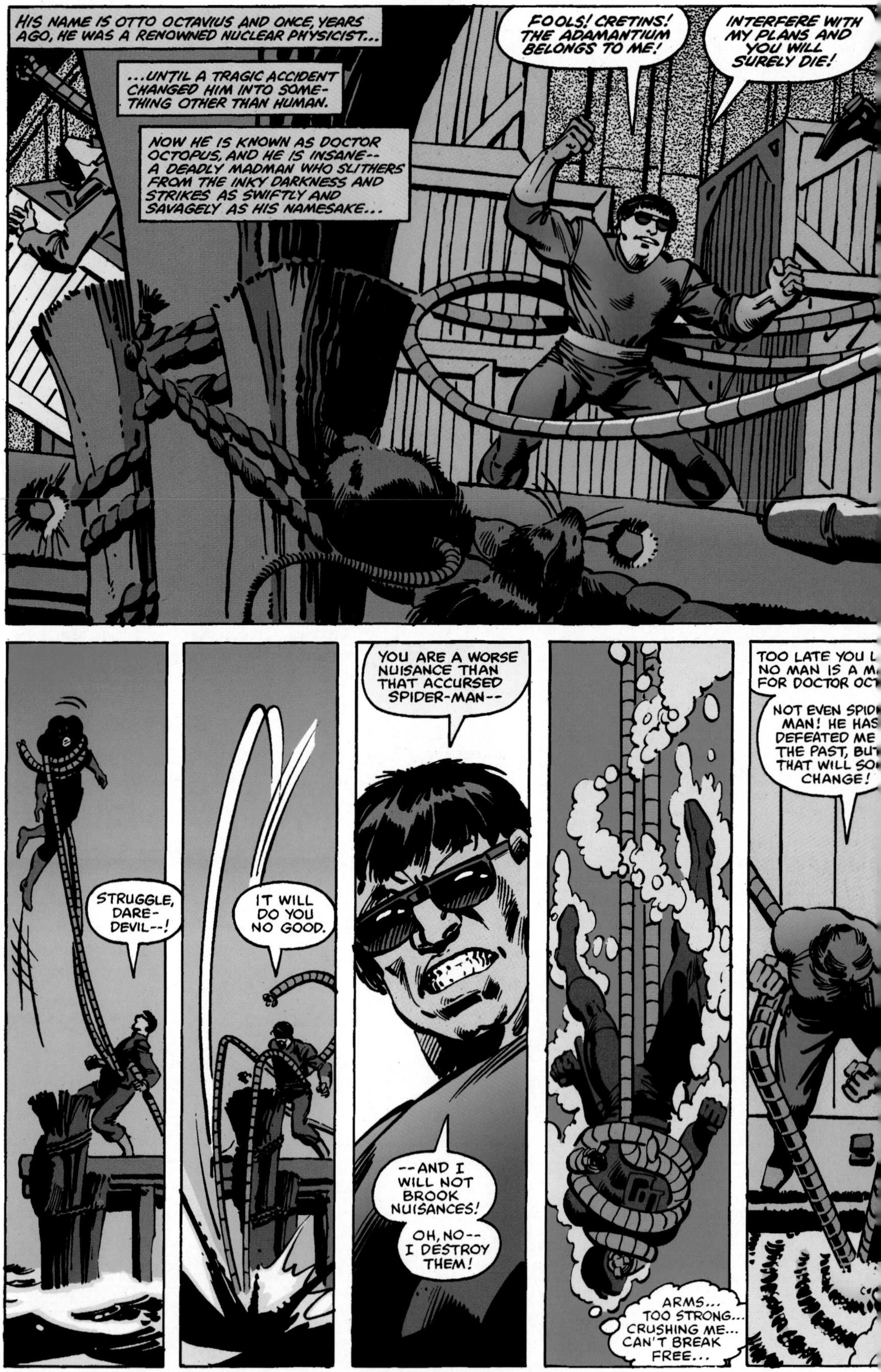

HIS NAME IS OTTO OCTAVIUS AND ONCE, YEARS AGO, HE WAS A RENOWNED NUCLEAR PHYSICIST...
...UNTIL A TRAGIC ACCIDENT CHANGED HIM INTO SOMETHING OTHER THAN HUMAN.
NOW HE IS KNOWN AS DOCTOR OCTOPUS, AND HE IS INSANE-- A DEADLY MADMAN WHO SLITHERS FROM THE INKY DARKNESS AND STRIKES AS SWIFTLY AND SAVAGELY AS HIS NAMESAKE...
FOOLS! CRETINS! THE ADAMANTIUM BELONGS TO ME!
INTERFERE WITH MY PLANS AND YOU WILL SURELY DIE!
STRUGGLE, DAREDEVIL--!
IT WILL DO YOU NO GOOD.
YOU ARE A WORSE NUISANCE THAN THAT ACCURSED SPIDER-MAN--
--AND I WILL NOT BROOK NUISANCES!
OH, NO-- I DESTROY THEM!
ARMS... TOO STRONG... CRUSHING ME... CAN'T BREAK FREE...
TOO LATE YOU L
NO MAN IS A M
FOR DOCTOR OC
NOT EVEN SPID
MAN! HE HAS
DEFEATED ME
THE PAST, BU
THAT WILL SO
CHANGE!

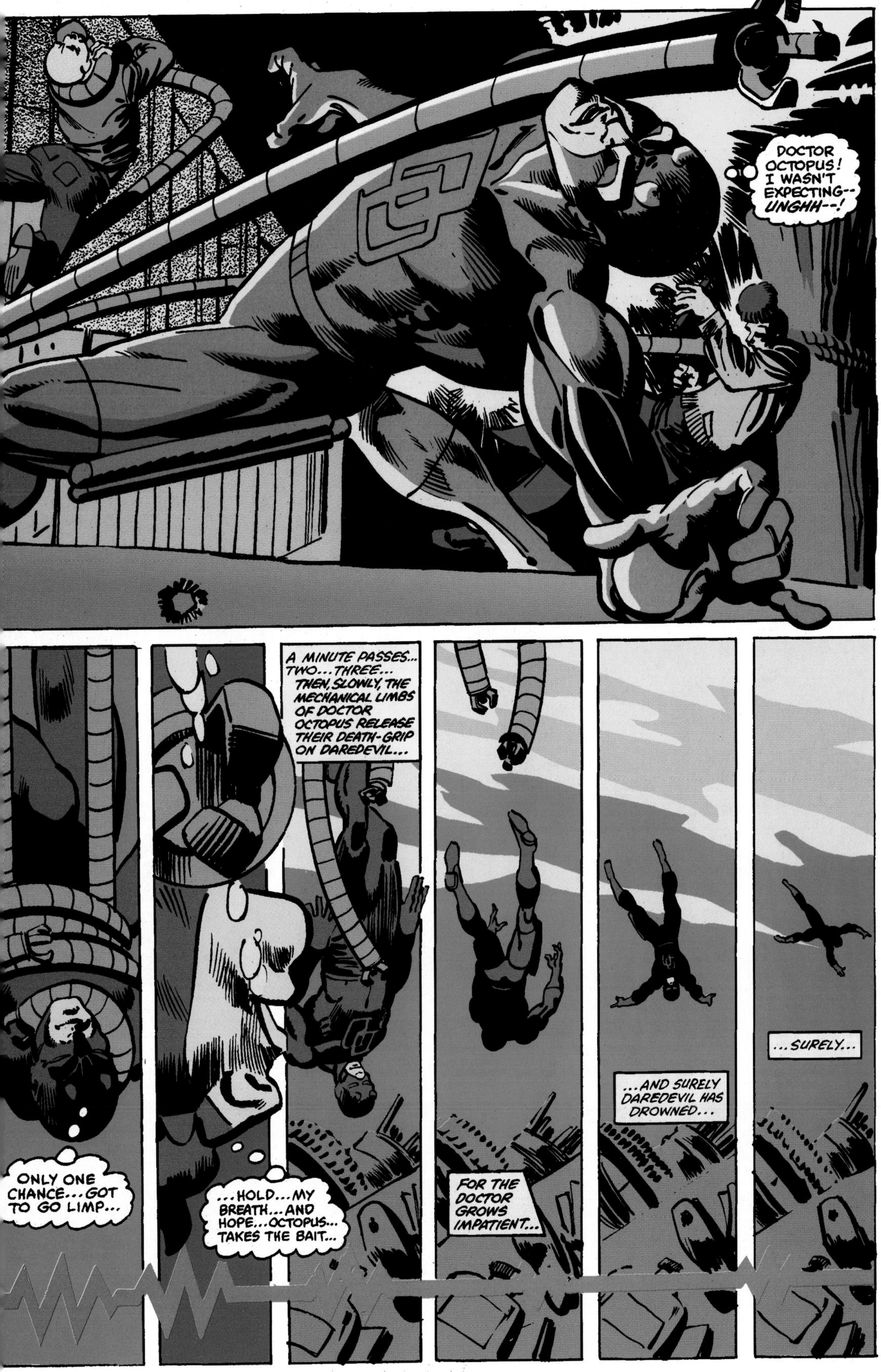
DOCTOR OCTOPUS! I WASN'T EXPECTING-- UNGHH--!
ONLY ONE CHANCE... GOT TO GO LIMP...
...HOLD... MY BREATH... AND HOPE... OCTOPUS... TAKES THE BAIT...
A MINUTE PASSES... TWO... THREE... THEN, SLOWLY, THE MECHANICAL LIMBS OF DOCTOR OCTOPUS RELEASE THEIR DEATH-GRIP ON DAREDEVIL...
FOR THE DOCTOR GROWS IMPATIENT...
...AND SURELY DAREDEVIL HAS DROWNED...
...SURELY...

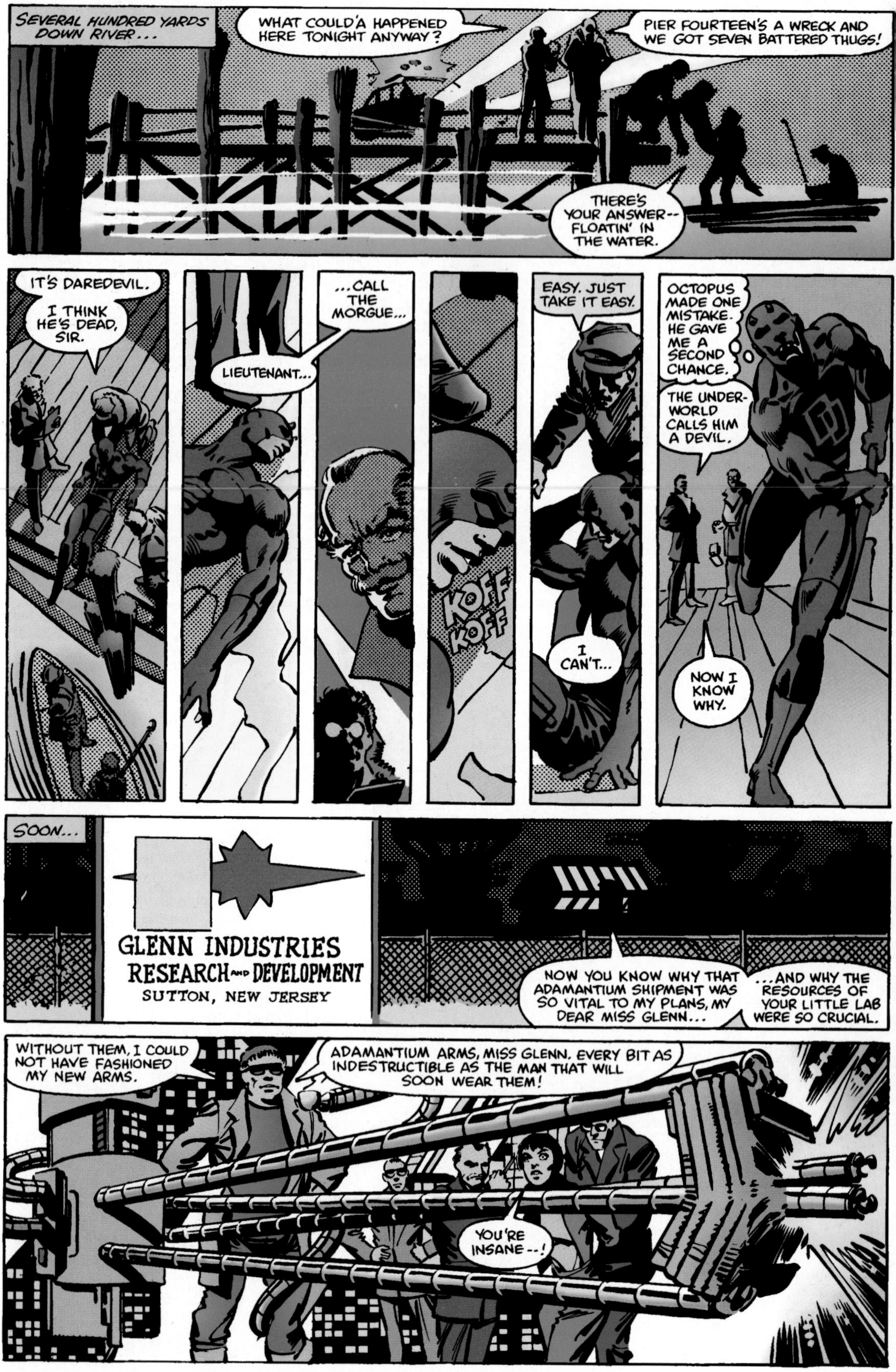
SEVERAL HUNDRED YARDS DOWN RIVER...
WHAT COULD'A HAPPENED HERE TONIGHT ANYWAY?
PIER FOURTEEN'S A WRECK AND WE GOT SEVEN BATTERED THUGS!
THERE'S YOUR ANSWER-- FLOATIN' IN THE WATER.
IT'S DAREDEVIL. I THINK HE'S DEAD, SIR.
LIEUTENANT...
...CALL THE MORGUE...
KOFF KOFF
EASY. JUST TAKE IT EASY.
I CAN'T...
OCTOPUS MADE ONE MISTAKE. HE GAVE ME A SECOND CHANCE.
THE UNDERWORLD CALLS HIM A DEVIL.
NOW I KNOW WHY.
SOON...
GLENN INDUSTRIES
RESEARCH AND DEVELOPMENT
SUTTON, NEW JERSEY
NOW YOU KNOW WHY THAT ADAMANTIUM SHIPMENT WAS SO VITAL TO MY PLANS, MY DEAR MISS GLENN...
...AND WHY THE RESOURCES OF YOUR LITTLE LAB WERE SO CRUCIAL.
WITHOUT THEM, I COULD NOT HAVE FASHIONED MY NEW ARMS.
ADAMANTIUM ARMS, MISS GLENN. EVERY BIT AS INDESTRUCTIBLE AS THE MAN THAT WILL SOON WEAR THEM!
YOU'RE INSANE--!

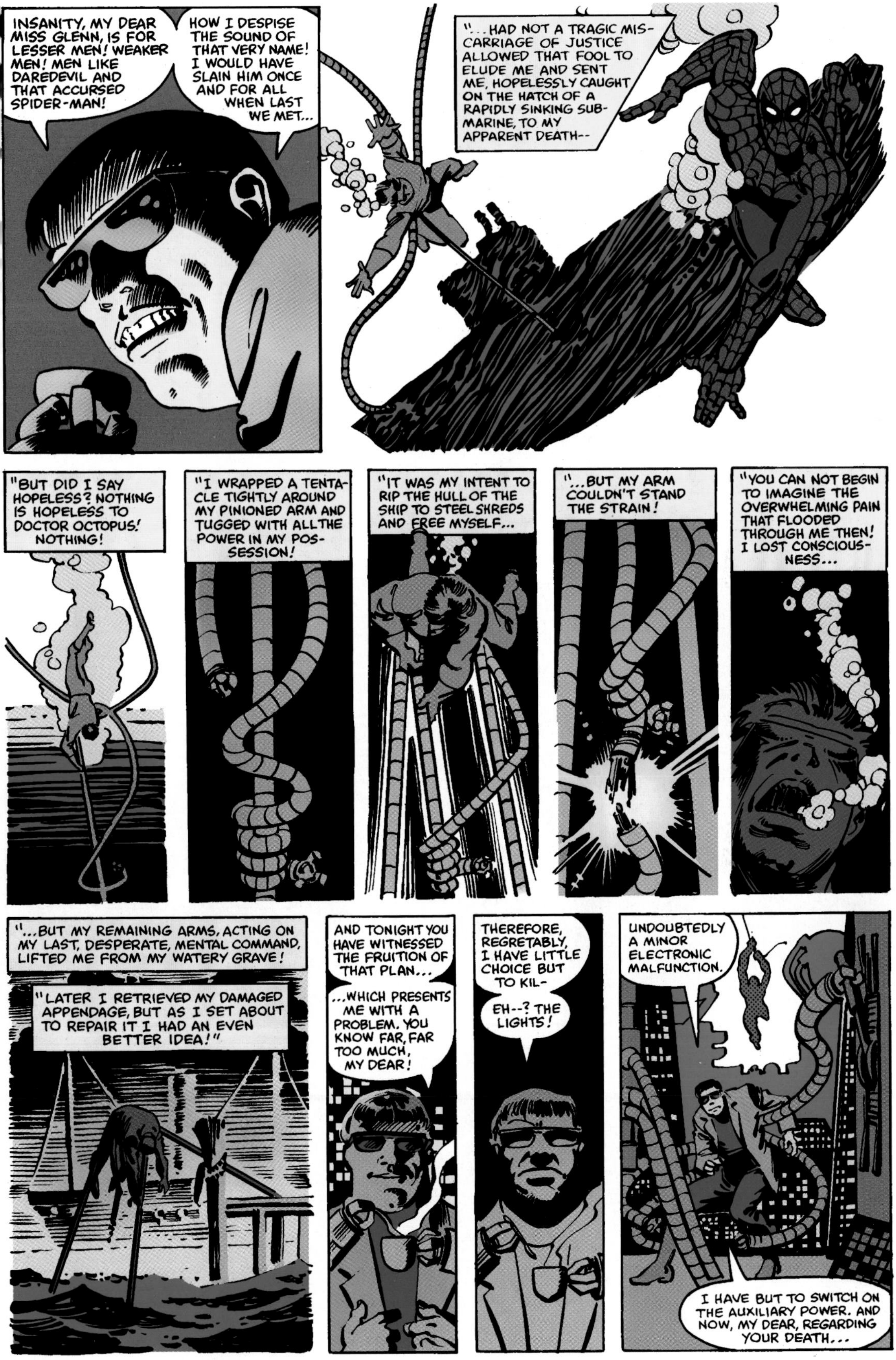
INSANITY, MY DEAR MISS GLENN, IS FOR LESSER MEN! WEAKER MEN! MEN LIKE DAREDEVIL AND THAT ACCURSED SPIDER-MAN!
HOW I DESPISE THE SOUND OF THAT VERY NAME! I WOULD HAVE SLAIN HIM ONCE AND FOR ALL WHEN LAST WE MET...
"...HAD NOT A TRAGIC MIS-CARRIAGE OF JUSTICE ALLOWED THAT FOOL TO ELUDE ME AND SENT ME, HOPELESSLY CAUGHT ON THE HATCH OF A RAPIDLY SINKING SUB-MARINE, TO MY APPARENT DEATH--
"BUT DID I SAY HOPELESS? NOTHING IS HOPELESS TO DOCTOR OCTOPUS! NOTHING!
"I WRAPPED A TENTA-CLE TIGHTLY AROUND MY PINIONED ARM AND TUGGED WITH ALL THE POWER IN MY POS-SESSION!
"IT WAS MY INTENT TO RIP THE HULL OF THE SHIP TO STEEL SHREDS AND FREE MYSELF...
"...BUT MY ARM COULDN'T STAND THE STRAIN!
"YOU CAN NOT BEGIN TO IMAGINE THE OVERWHELMING PAIN THAT FLOODED THROUGH ME THEN! I LOST CONSCIOUS-NESS...
"...BUT MY REMAINING ARMS, ACTING ON MY LAST, DESPERATE, MENTAL COMMAND, LIFTED ME FROM MY WATERY GRAVE!
"LATER I RETRIEVED MY DAMAGED APPENDAGE, BUT AS I SET ABOUT TO REPAIR IT I HAD AN EVEN BETTER IDEA!"
AND TONIGHT YOU HAVE WITNESSED THE FRUITION OF THAT PLAN...
...WHICH PRESENTS ME WITH A PROBLEM. YOU KNOW FAR, FAR TOO MUCH, MY DEAR!
THEREFORE, REGRETABLY, I HAVE LITTLE CHOICE BUT TO KIL-
EH--? THE LIGHTS!
UNDOUBTEDLY A MINOR ELECTRONIC MALFUNCTION.
I HAVE BUT TO SWITCH ON THE AUXILIARY POWER. AND NOW, MY DEAR, REGARDING YOUR DEATH...

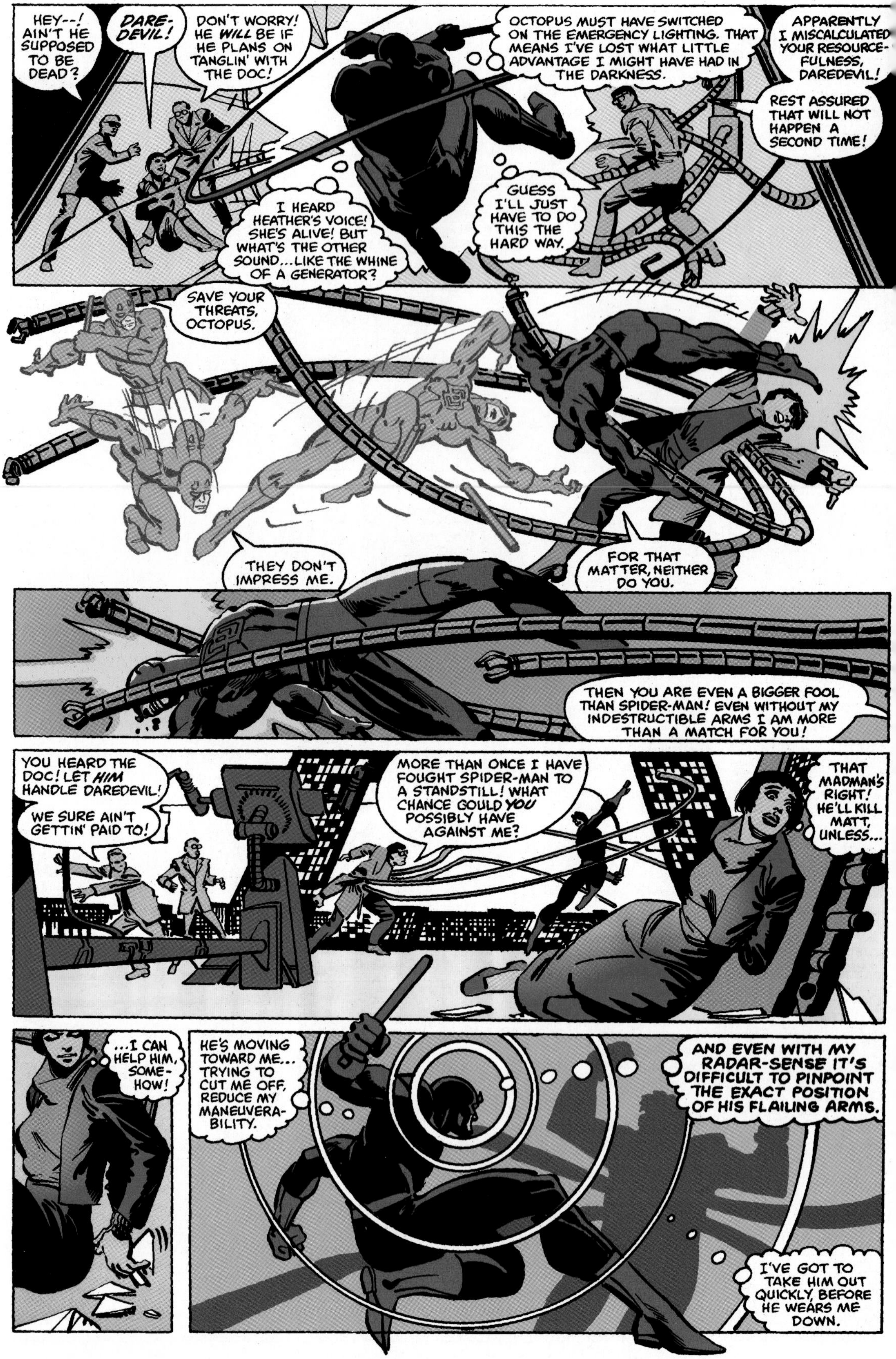
HEY--! AIN'T HE SUPPOSED TO BE DEAD?
DARE-DEVIL!
DON'T WORRY! HE WILL BE IF HE PLANS ON TANGLIN' WITH THE DOC!
OCTOPUS MUST HAVE SWITCHED ON THE EMERGENCY LIGHTING. THAT MEANS I'VE LOST WHAT LITTLE ADVANTAGE I MIGHT HAVE HAD IN THE DARKNESS.
APPARENTLY I MISCALCULATED YOUR RESOURCE-FULNESS, DAREDEVIL!
REST ASSURED THAT WILL NOT HAPPEN A SECOND TIME!
I HEARD HEATHER'S VOICE! SHE'S ALIVE! BUT WHAT'S THE OTHER SOUND...LIKE THE WHINE OF A GENERATOR?
GUESS I'LL JUST HAVE TO DO THIS THE HARD WAY.
SAVE YOUR THREATS, OCTOPUS.
THEY DON'T IMPRESS ME.
FOR THAT MATTER, NEITHER DO YOU.
THEN YOU ARE EVEN A BIGGER FOOL THAN SPIDER-MAN! EVEN WITHOUT MY INDESTRUCTIBLE ARMS I AM MORE THAN A MATCH FOR YOU!
YOU HEARD THE DOC! LET HIM HANDLE DAREDEVIL!
WE SURE AIN'T GETTIN' PAID TO!
MORE THAN ONCE I HAVE FOUGHT SPIDER-MAN TO A STANDSTILL! WHAT CHANCE COULD YOU POSSIBLY HAVE AGAINST ME?
THAT MADMAN'S RIGHT! HE'LL KILL MATT, UNLESS...
...I CAN HELP HIM, SOME-HOW!
HE'S MOVING TOWARD ME... TRYING TO CUT ME OFF, REDUCE MY MANEUVERA-BILITY.
AND EVEN WITH MY RADAR-SENSE IT'S DIFFICULT TO PINPOINT THE EXACT POSITION OF HIS FLAILING ARMS.
I'VE GOT TO TAKE HIM OUT QUICKLY, BEFORE HE WEARS ME DOWN.

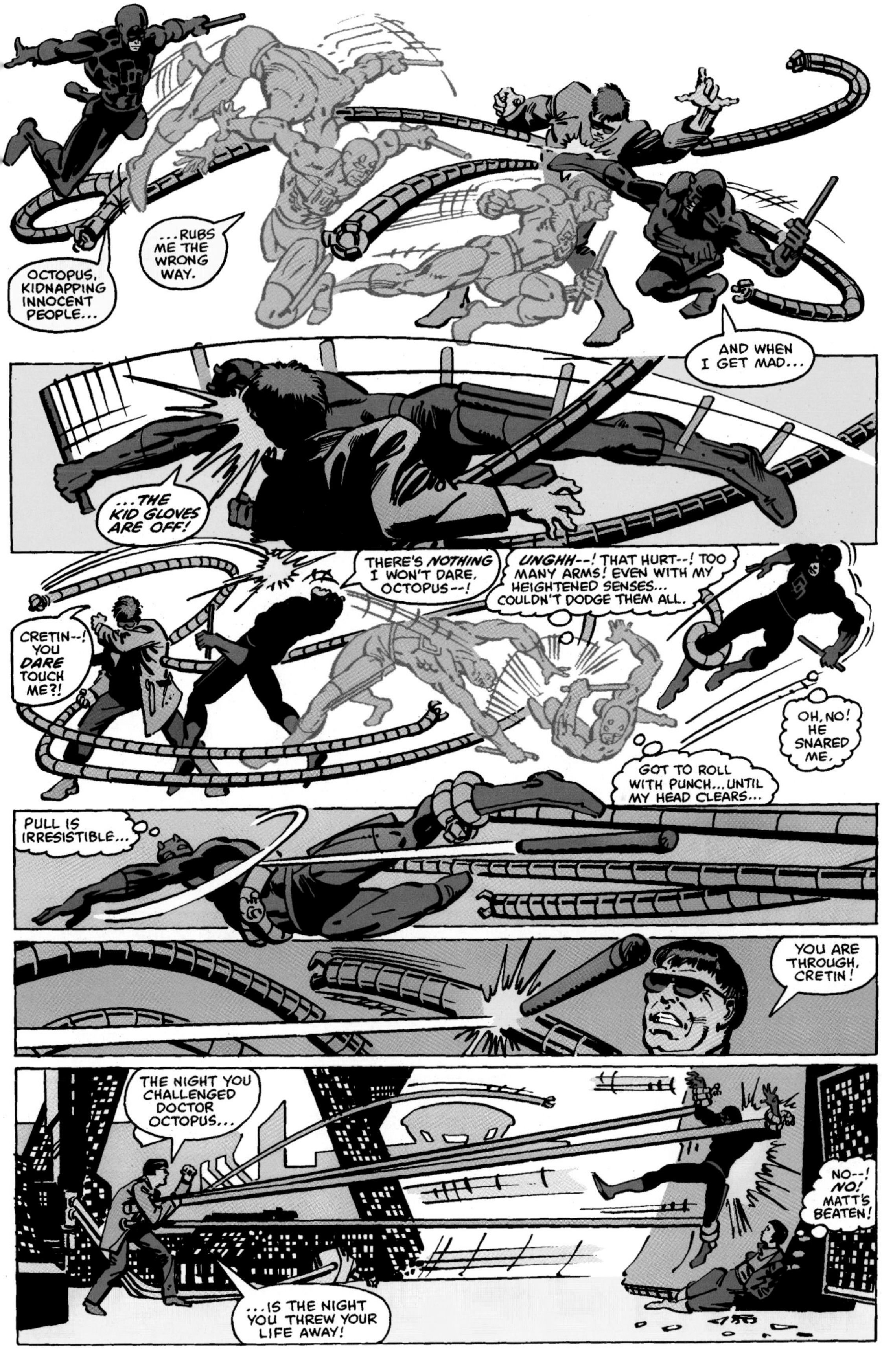
OCTOPUS, KIDNAPPING INNOCENT PEOPLE...
...RUBS ME THE WRONG WAY.
AND WHEN I GET MAD...
...THE KID GLOVES ARE OFF!
CRETIN--! YOU DARE TOUCH ME?!
THERE'S NOTHING I WON'T DARE, OCTOPUS--!
UNGHH--! THAT HURT--! TOO MANY ARMS! EVEN WITH MY HEIGHTENED SENSES... COULDN'T DODGE THEM ALL.
OH, NO! HE SNARED ME.
GOT TO ROLL WITH PUNCH...UNTIL MY HEAD CLEARS...
PULL IS IRRESISTIBLE...
YOU ARE THROUGH, CRETIN!
THE NIGHT YOU CHALLENGED DOCTOR OCTOPUS...
...IS THE NIGHT YOU THREW YOUR LIFE AWAY!
NO--! NO! MATT'S BEATEN!

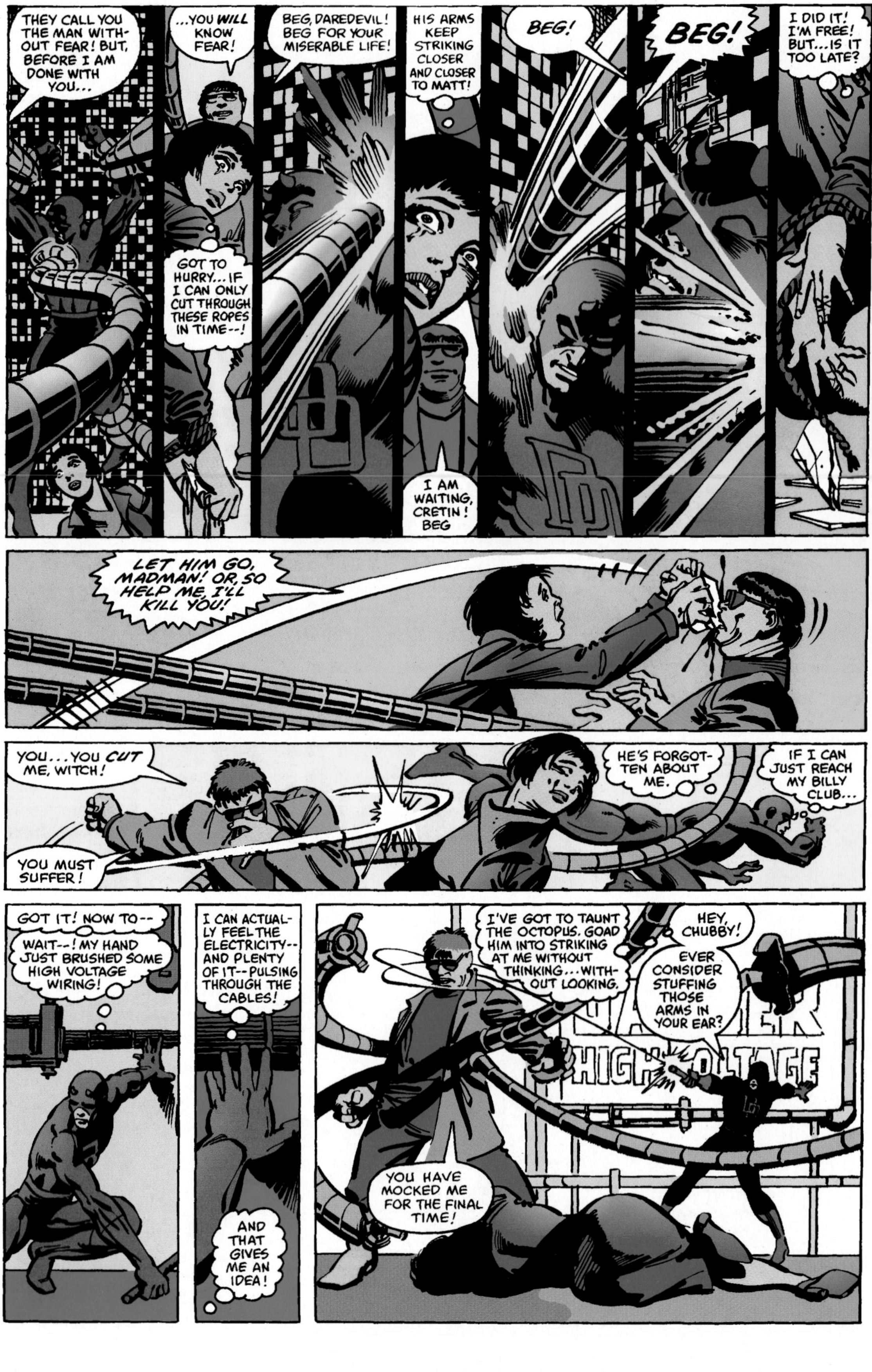
THEY CALL YOU THE MAN WITHOUT FEAR! BUT, BEFORE I AM DONE WITH YOU...
...YOU WILL KNOW FEAR!
GOT TO HURRY... IF I CAN ONLY CUT THROUGH THESE ROPES IN TIME--!
BEG, DAREDEVIL! BEG FOR YOUR MISERABLE LIFE!
HIS ARMS KEEP STRIKING CLOSER AND CLOSER TO MATT!
I AM WAITING, CRETIN! BEG
BEG!
BEG!
I DID IT! I'M FREE! BUT... IS IT TOO LATE?
LET HIM GO, MADMAN! OR, SO HELP ME, I'LL KILL YOU!
YOU... YOU CUT ME, WITCH!
YOU MUST SUFFER!
HE'S FORGOTTEN ABOUT ME.
IF I CAN JUST REACH MY BILLY CLUB...
GOT IT! NOW TO--
WAIT--! MY HAND JUST BRUSHED SOME HIGH VOLTAGE WIRING!
I CAN ACTUALLY FEEL THE ELECTRICITY-- AND PLENTY OF IT--PULSING THROUGH THE CABLES!
AND THAT GIVES ME AN IDEA!
I'VE GOT TO TAUNT THE OCTOPUS. GOAD HIM INTO STRIKING AT ME WITHOUT THINKING... WITHOUT LOOKING.
HEY, CHUBBY!
EVER CONSIDER STUFFING THOSE ARMS IN YOUR EAR?
HIGH VOLTAGE
YOU HAVE MOCKED ME FOR THE FINAL TIME!

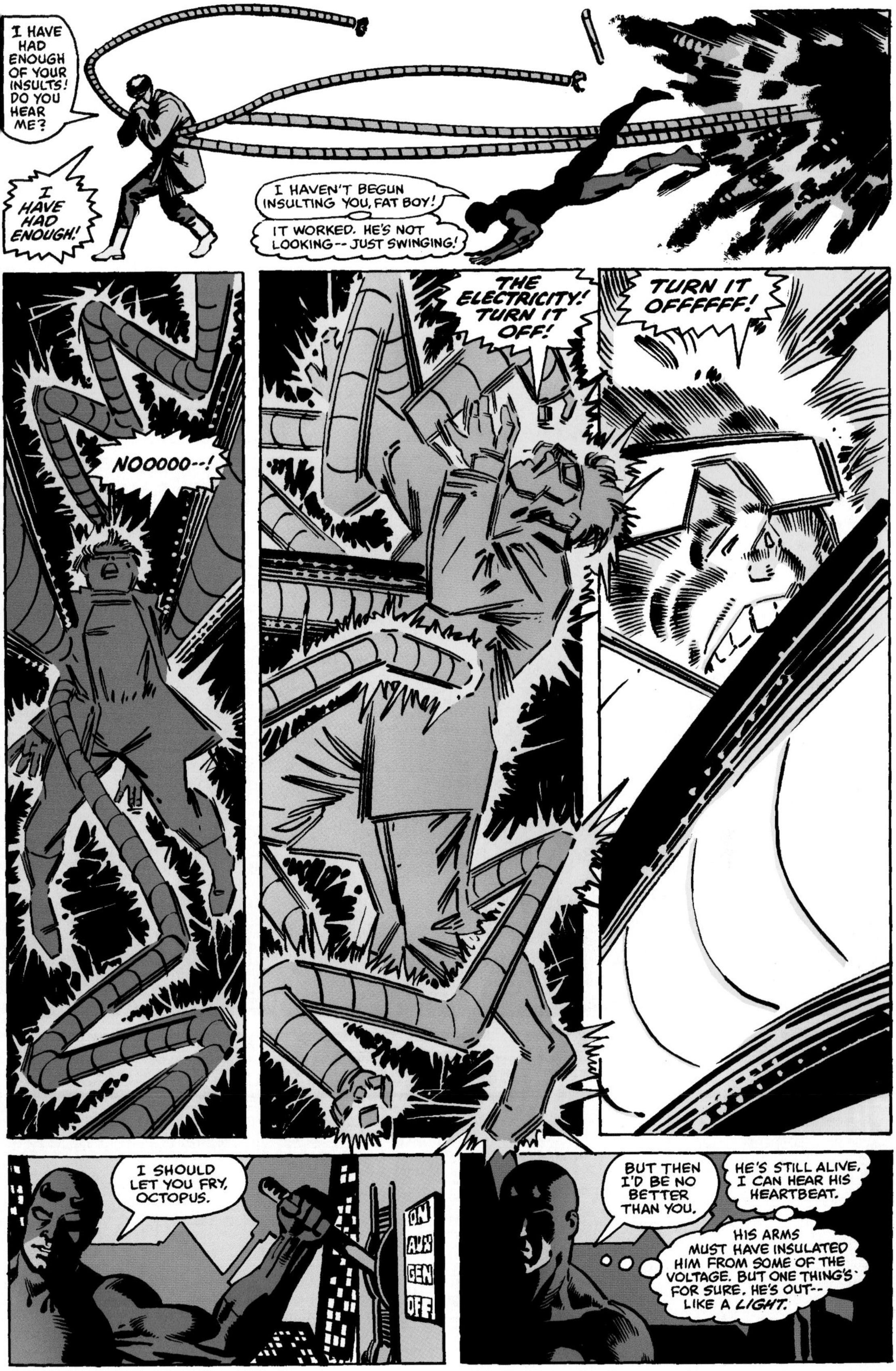

I HAVE HAD ENOUGH OF YOUR INSULTS! DO YOU HEAR ME?
I HAVE HAD ENOUGH!
I HAVEN'T BEGUN INSULTING YOU, FAT BOY!
IT WORKED. HE'S NOT LOOKING-- JUST SWINGING!
NOOOOO--!
THE ELECTRICITY! TURN IT OFF!
TURN IT OFFFFFF!
I SHOULD LET YOU FRY, OCTOPUS.
ON
AUX
GEN
OFF
BUT THEN I'D BE NO BETTER THAN YOU.
HE'S STILL ALIVE. I CAN HEAR HIS HEARTBEAT.
HIS ARMS MUST HAVE INSULATED HIM FROM SOME OF THE VOLTAGE. BUT ONE THING'S FOR SURE. HE'S OUT-- LIKE A *LIGHT*.

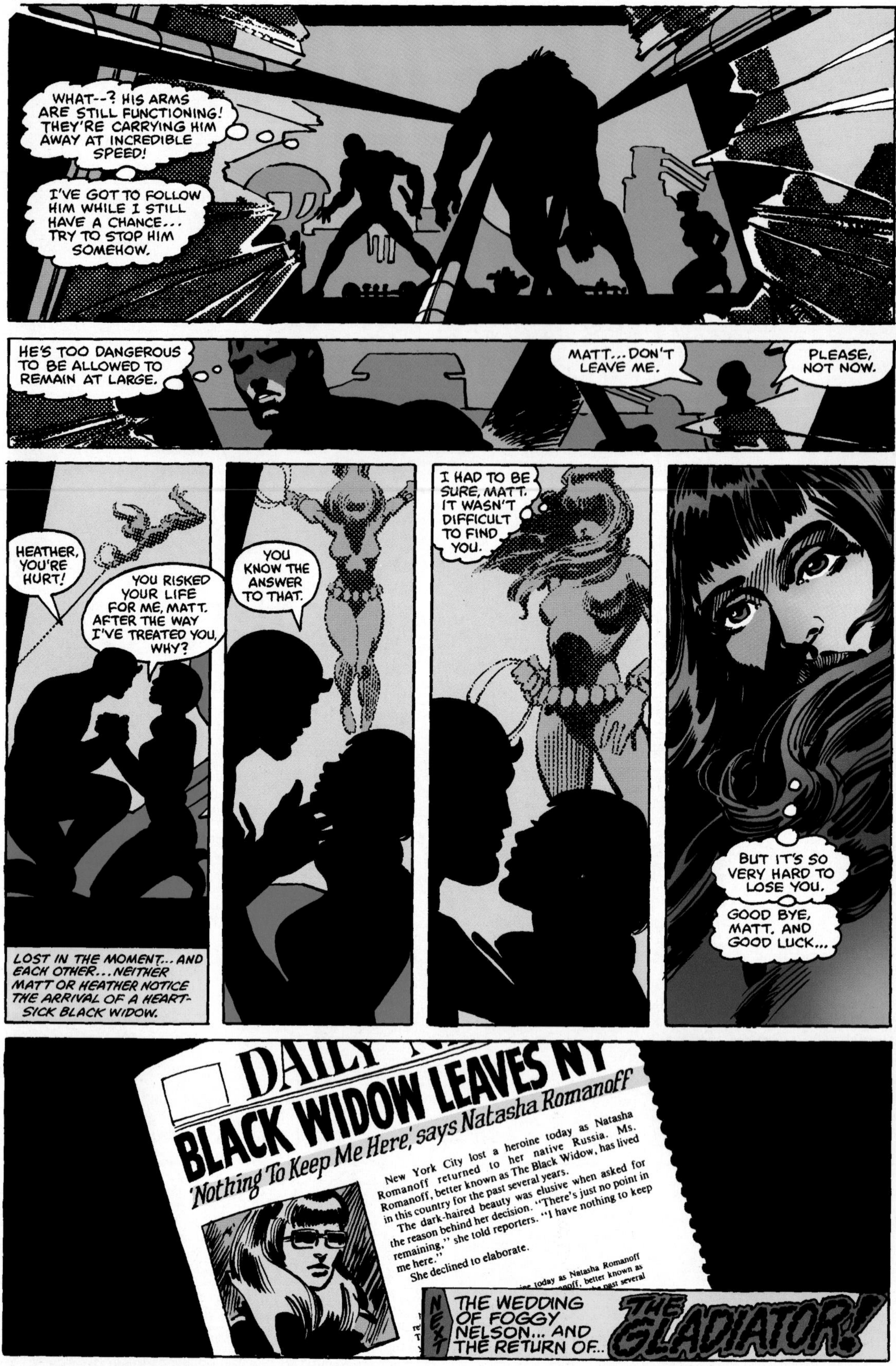
WHAT--? HIS ARMS ARE STILL FUNCTIONING! THEY'RE CARRYING HIM AWAY AT INCREDIBLE SPEED!
I'VE GOT TO FOLLOW HIM WHILE I STILL HAVE A CHANCE... TRY TO STOP HIM SOMEHOW.
HE'S TOO DANGEROUS TO BE ALLOWED TO REMAIN AT LARGE.
MATT... DON'T LEAVE ME.
PLEASE, NOT NOW.
HEATHER, YOU'RE HURT!
YOU RISKED YOUR LIFE FOR ME, MATT. AFTER THE WAY I'VE TREATED YOU, WHY?
LOST IN THE MOMENT... AND EACH OTHER... NEITHER MATT OR HEATHER NOTICE THE ARRIVAL OF A HEART-SICK BLACK WIDOW.
YOU KNOW THE ANSWER TO THAT.
I HAD TO BE SURE, MATT. IT WASN'T DIFFICULT TO FIND YOU.
BUT IT'S SO VERY HARD TO LOSE YOU.
GOOD BYE, MATT. AND GOOD LUCK...
DAILY
BLACK WIDOW LEAVES NY
'Nothing To Keep Me Here,' says Natasha Romanoff
New York City lost a heroine today as Natasha Romanoff returned to her native Russia. Ms. Romanoff, better known as The Black Widow, has lived in this country for the past several years.
The dark-haired beauty was elusive when asked for the reason behind her decision. "There's just no point in remaining," she told reporters. "I have nothing to keep me here."
She declined to elaborate.
NEXT
THE WEDDING OF FOGGY NELSON... AND THE RETURN OF... THE GLADIATOR!

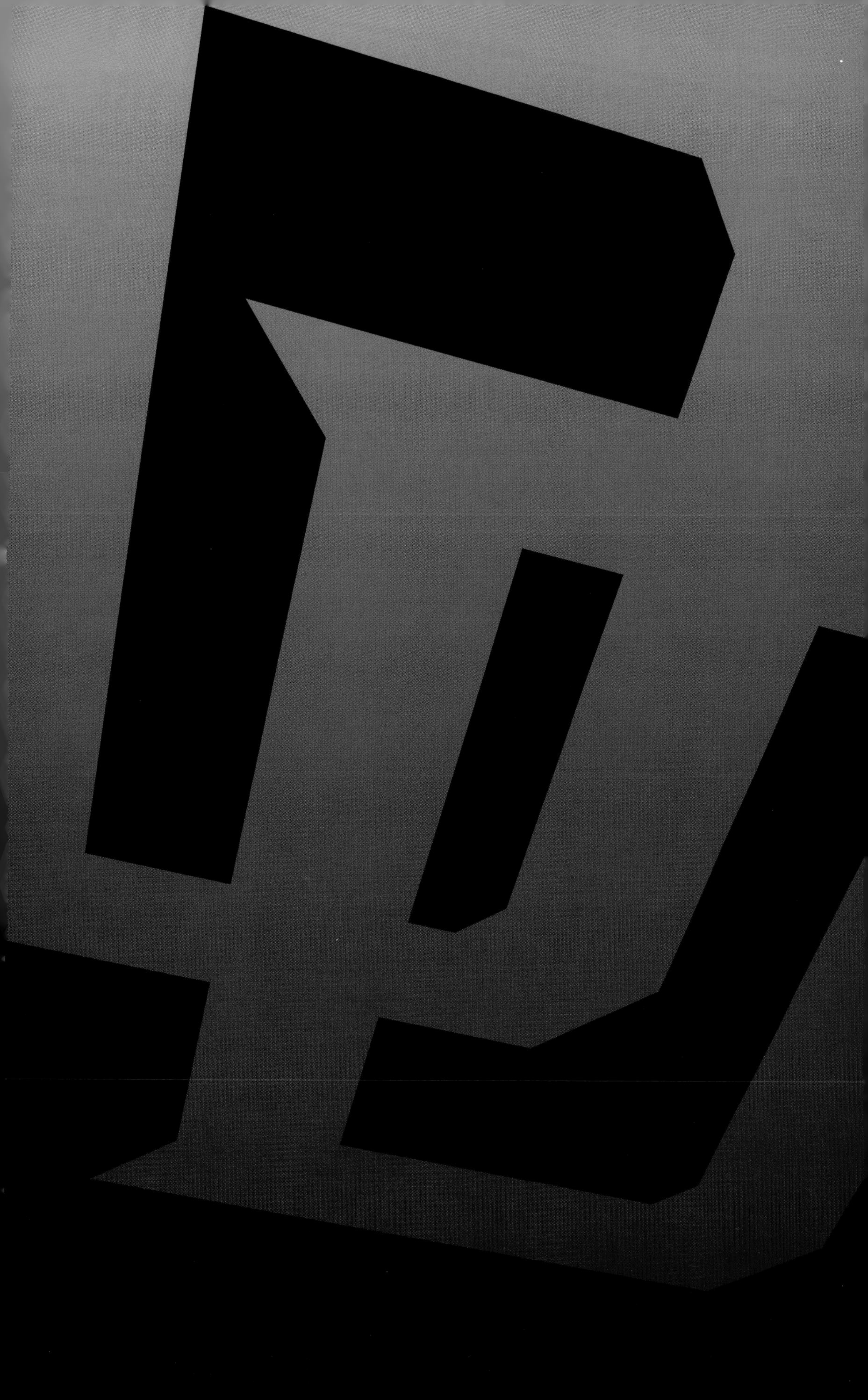

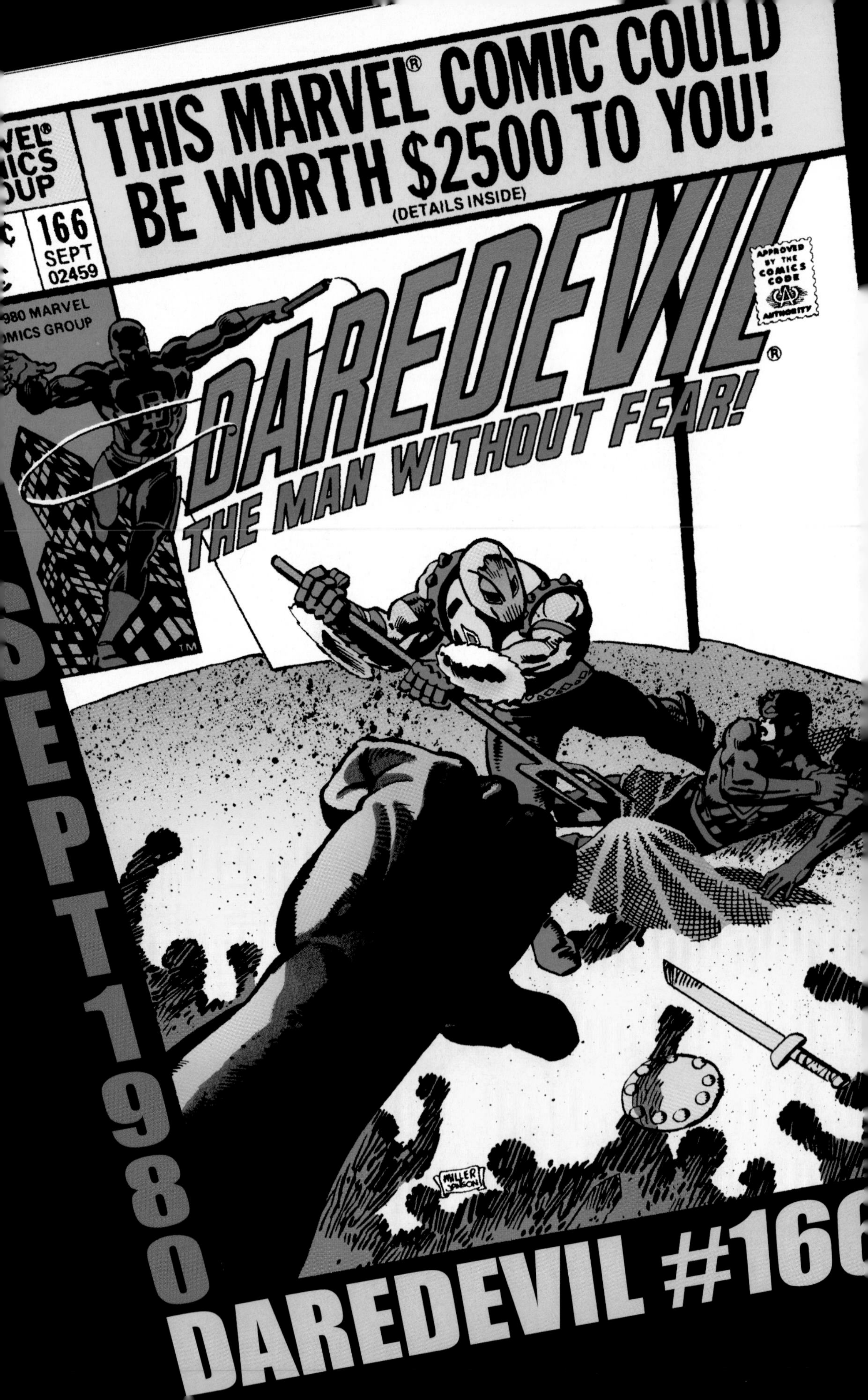
THIS MARVEL® COMIC COULD BE WORTH $2500 TO YOU!
(DETAILS INSIDE)
166 SEPT 02459
DAREDEVIL®
THE MAN WITHOUT FEAR!
APPROVED BY THE COMICS CODE AUTHORITY
MILLER JANSON
SEPT 1980
DAREDEVIL #16

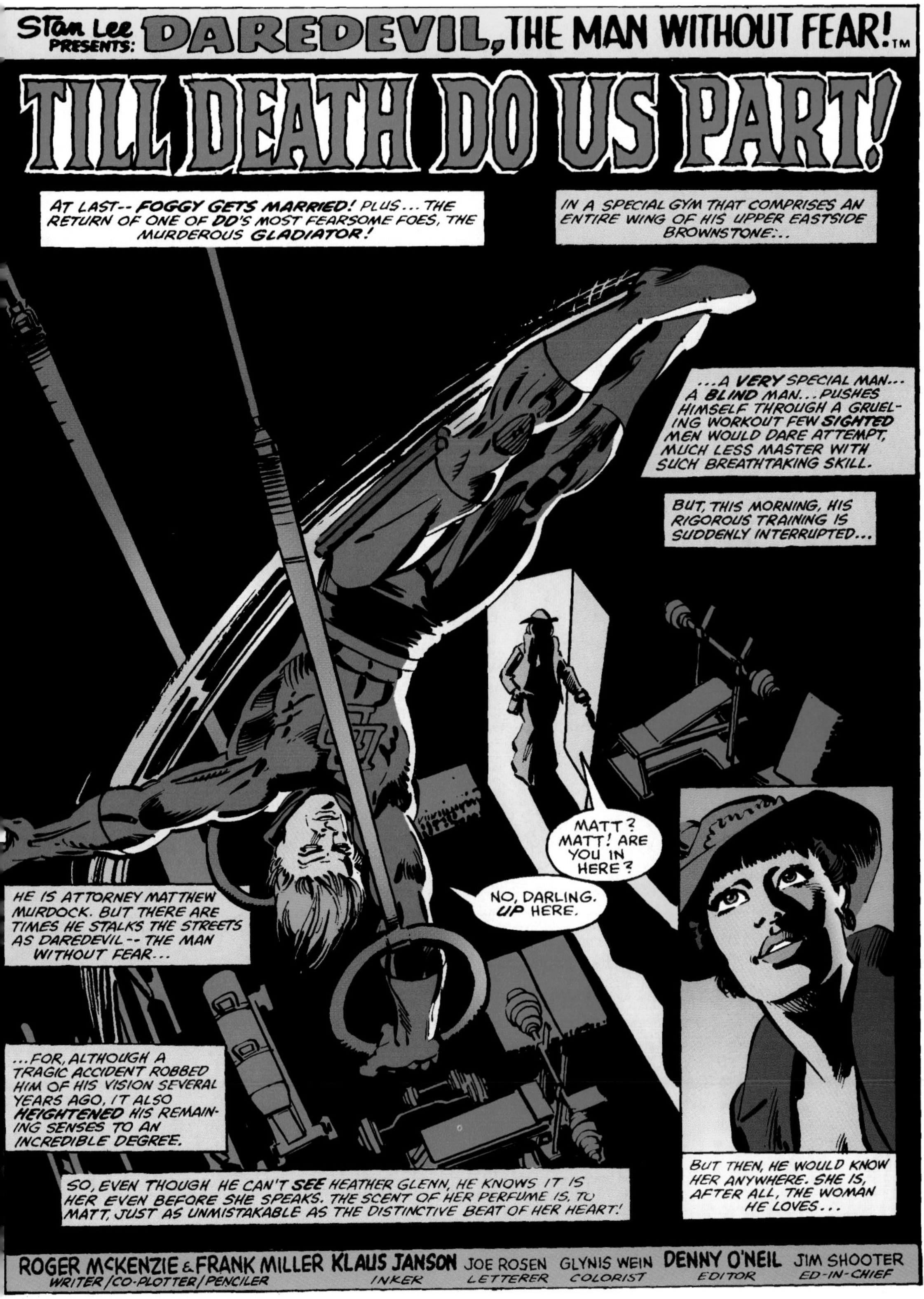
STAN LEE PRESENTS: DAREDEVIL, THE MAN WITHOUT FEAR! TM
TILL DEATH DO US PART!
AT LAST-- FOGGY GETS MARRIED! PLUS... THE RETURN OF ONE OF DD'S MOST FEARSOME FOES, THE MURDEROUS GLADIATOR!
IN A SPECIAL GYM THAT COMPRISES AN ENTIRE WING OF HIS UPPER EASTSIDE BROWNSTONE:..
...A VERY SPECIAL MAN... A BLIND MAN... PUSHES HIMSELF THROUGH A GRUELING WORKOUT FEW SIGHTED MEN WOULD DARE ATTEMPT, MUCH LESS MASTER WITH SUCH BREATHTAKING SKILL.
BUT, THIS MORNING, HIS RIGOROUS TRAINING IS SUDDENLY INTERRUPTED...
MATT? MATT! ARE YOU IN HERE?
NO, DARLING. UP HERE.
HE IS ATTORNEY MATTHEW MURDOCK. BUT THERE ARE TIMES HE STALKS THE STREETS AS DAREDEVIL-- THE MAN WITHOUT FEAR...
...FOR, ALTHOUGH A TRAGIC ACCIDENT ROBBED HIM OF HIS VISION SEVERAL YEARS AGO, IT ALSO HEIGHTENED HIS REMAINING SENSES TO AN INCREDIBLE DEGREE.
SO, EVEN THOUGH HE CAN'T SEE HEATHER GLENN, HE KNOWS IT IS HER EVEN BEFORE SHE SPEAKS. THE SCENT OF HER PERFUME IS, TO MATT, JUST AS UNMISTAKABLE AS THE DISTINCTIVE BEAT OF HER HEART!
BUT THEN, HE WOULD KNOW HER ANYWHERE. SHE IS, AFTER ALL, THE WOMAN HE LOVES...
ROGER McKENZIE & FRANK MILLER WRITER/CO-PLOTTER/PENCILER
KLAUS JANSON INKER
JOE ROSEN LETTERER
GLYNIS WEIN COLORIST
DENNY O'NEIL EDITOR
JIM SHOOTER ED-IN-CHIEF

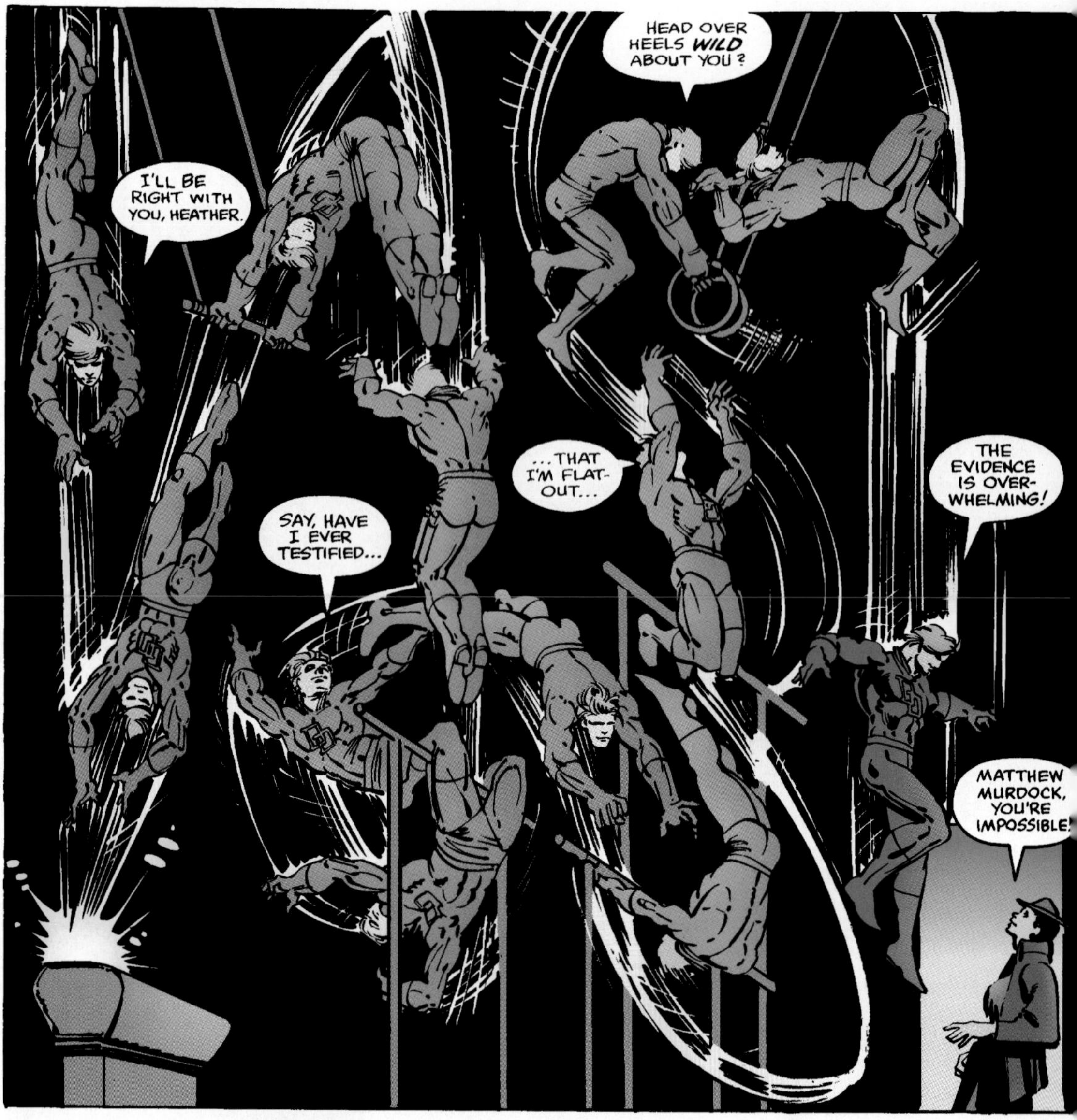
I'LL BE RIGHT WITH YOU, HEATHER.
HEAD OVER HEELS WILD ABOUT YOU?
SAY, HAVE I EVER TESTIFIED...
...THAT I'M FLAT-OUT...
THE EVIDENCE IS OVER-WHELMING!
MATTHEW MURDOCK, YOU'RE IMPOSSIBLE!

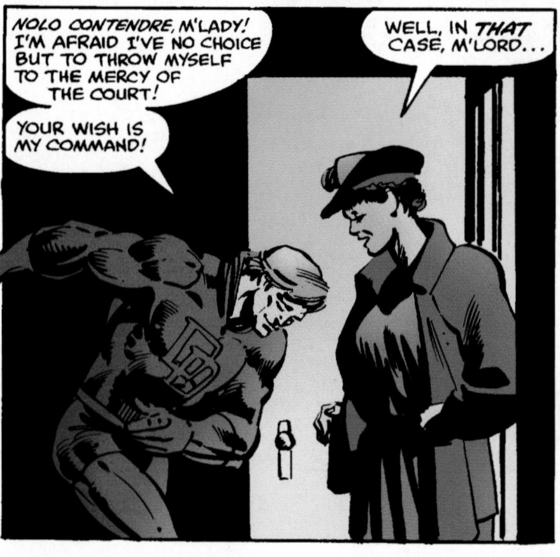
NOLO CONTENDRE, M'LADY! I'M AFRAID I'VE NO CHOICE BUT TO THROW MYSELF TO THE MERCY OF THE COURT!
YOUR WISH IS MY COMMAND!
WELL, IN THAT CASE, M'LORD...

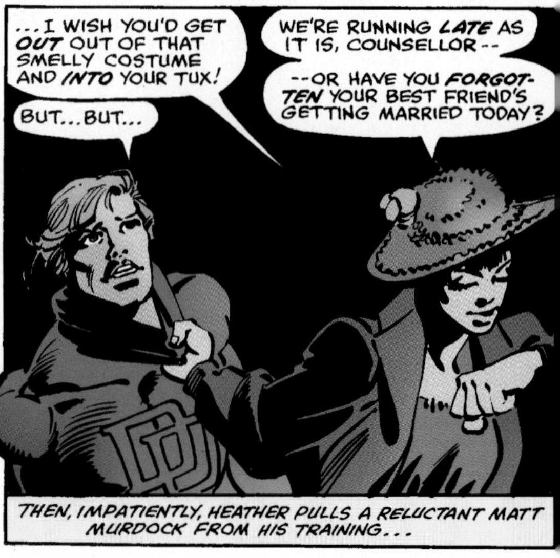
...I WISH YOU'D GET OUT OUT OF THAT SMELLY COSTUME AND INTO YOUR TUX!
BUT...BUT...
WE'RE RUNNING LATE AS IT IS, COUNSELLOR--
--OR HAVE YOU FORGOT-TEN YOUR BEST FRIEND'S GETTING MARRIED TODAY?
THEN, IMPATIENTLY, HEATHER PULLS A RELUCTANT MATT MURDOCK FROM HIS TRAINING...

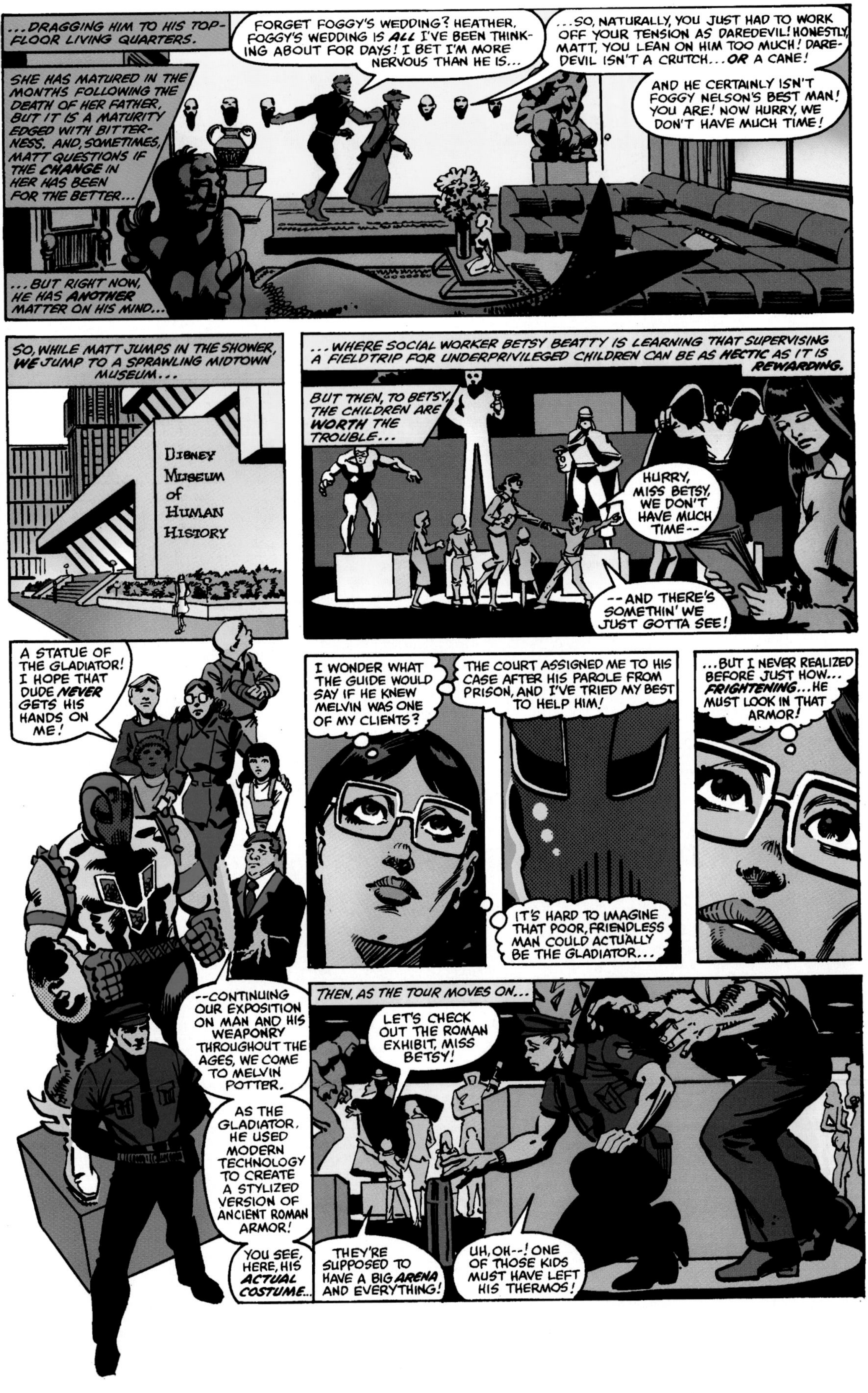
...DRAGGING HIM TO HIS TOP-FLOOR LIVING QUARTERS.
FORGET FOGGY'S WEDDING? HEATHER, FOGGY'S WEDDING IS ALL I'VE BEEN THINKING ABOUT FOR DAYS! I BET I'M MORE NERVOUS THAN HE IS...
...SO, NATURALLY, YOU JUST HAD TO WORK OFF YOUR TENSION AS DAREDEVIL! HONESTLY, MATT, YOU LEAN ON HIM TOO MUCH! DAREDEVIL ISN'T A CRUTCH...OR A CANE!
AND HE CERTAINLY ISN'T FOGGY NELSON'S BEST MAN! YOU ARE! NOW HURRY, WE DON'T HAVE MUCH TIME!
SHE HAS MATURED IN THE MONTHS FOLLOWING THE DEATH OF HER FATHER, BUT IT IS A MATURITY EDGED WITH BITTERNESS. AND, SOMETIMES, MATT QUESTIONS IF THE CHANGE IN HER HAS BEEN FOR THE BETTER...
...BUT RIGHT NOW, HE HAS ANOTHER MATTER ON HIS MIND...
SO, WHILE MATT JUMPS IN THE SHOWER, WE JUMP TO A SPRAWLING MIDTOWN MUSEUM...
DISNEY MUSEUM of HUMAN HISTORY
...WHERE SOCIAL WORKER BETSY BEATTY IS LEARNING THAT SUPERVISING A FIELDTRIP FOR UNDERPRIVILEGED CHILDREN CAN BE AS HECTIC AS IT IS REWARDING.
BUT THEN, TO BETSY, THE CHILDREN ARE WORTH THE TROUBLE...
HURRY, MISS BETSY, WE DON'T HAVE MUCH TIME--
--AND THERE'S SOMETHIN' WE JUST GOTTA SEE!
A STATUE OF THE GLADIATOR! I HOPE THAT DUDE NEVER GETS HIS HANDS ON ME!
--CONTINUING OUR EXPOSITION ON MAN AND HIS WEAPONRY THROUGHOUT THE AGES, WE COME TO MELVIN POTTER.
AS THE GLADIATOR, HE USED MODERN TECHNOLOGY TO CREATE A STYLIZED VERSION OF ANCIENT ROMAN ARMOR!
YOU SEE, HERE, HIS ACTUAL COSTUME...
I WONDER WHAT THE GUIDE WOULD SAY IF HE KNEW MELVIN WAS ONE OF MY CLIENTS?
THE COURT ASSIGNED ME TO HIS CASE AFTER HIS PAROLE FROM PRISON, AND I'VE TRIED MY BEST TO HELP HIM!
IT'S HARD TO IMAGINE THAT POOR, FRIENDLESS MAN COULD ACTUALLY BE THE GLADIATOR...
...BUT I NEVER REALIZED BEFORE JUST HOW... FRIGHTENING...HE MUST LOOK IN THAT ARMOR!
THEN, AS THE TOUR MOVES ON...
LET'S CHECK OUT THE ROMAN EXHIBIT, MISS BETSY!
THEY'RE SUPPOSED TO HAVE A BIG ARENA AND EVERYTHING!
UH, OH--! ONE OF THOSE KIDS MUST HAVE LEFT HIS THERMOS!

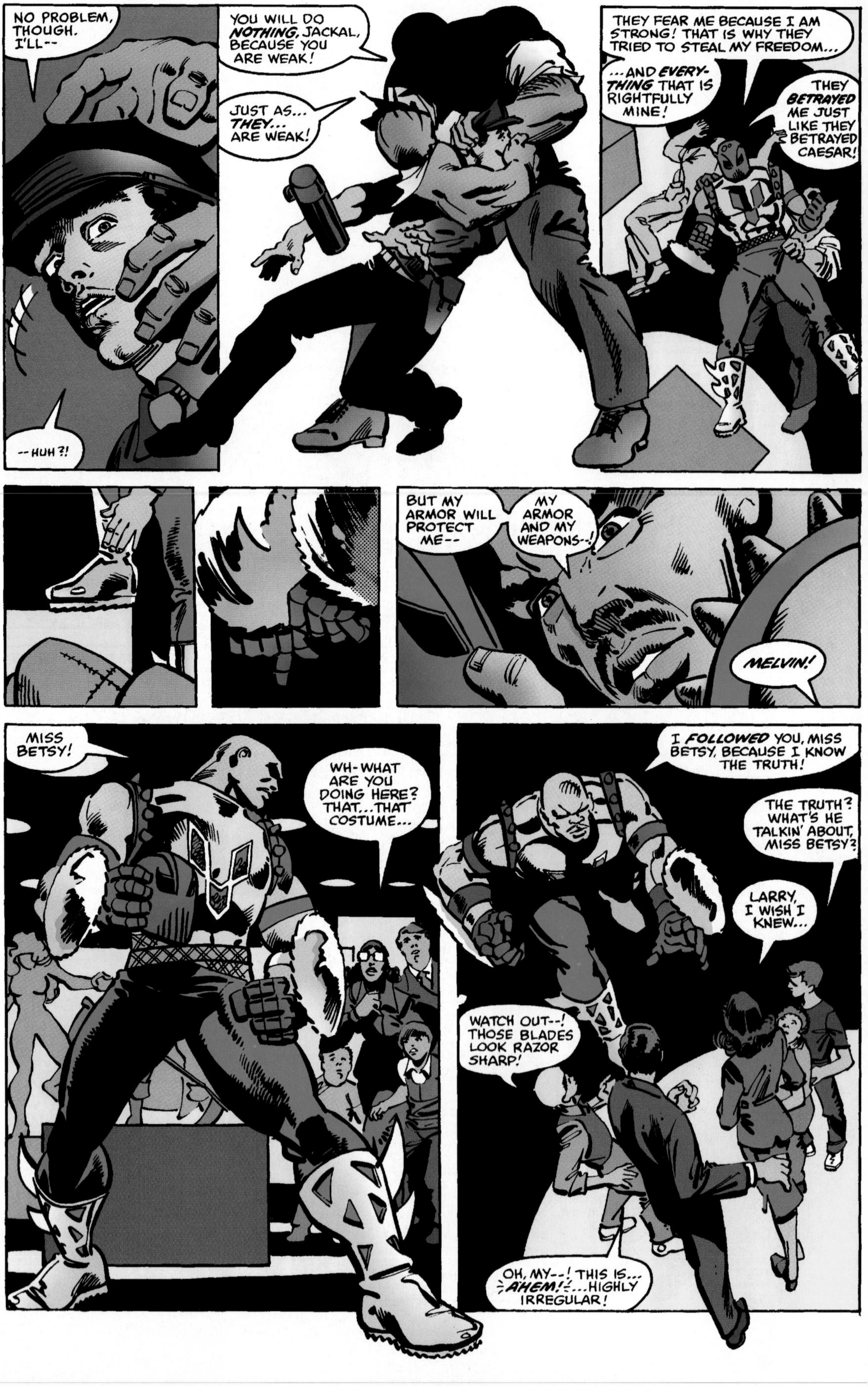

NO PROBLEM, THOUGH. I'LL--
--HUH?!
YOU WILL DO NOTHING, JACKAL, BECAUSE YOU ARE WEAK!
JUST AS... THEY... ARE WEAK!
THEY FEAR ME BECAUSE I AM STRONG! THAT IS WHY THEY TRIED TO STEAL MY FREEDOM...
...AND EVERYTHING THAT IS RIGHTFULLY MINE!
THEY BETRAYED ME JUST LIKE THEY BETRAYED CAESAR!
BUT MY ARMOR WILL PROTECT ME--
MY ARMOR AND MY WEAPONS--!
MELVIN!
MISS BETSY!
WH-WHAT ARE YOU DOING HERE? THAT...THAT COSTUME...
I FOLLOWED YOU, MISS BETSY, BECAUSE I KNOW THE TRUTH!
THE TRUTH? WHAT'S HE TALKIN' ABOUT, MISS BETSY?
LARRY, I WISH I KNEW...
WATCH OUT--! THOSE BLADES LOOK RAZOR SHARP!
OH, MY--! THIS IS... AHEM!...HIGHLY IRREGULAR!

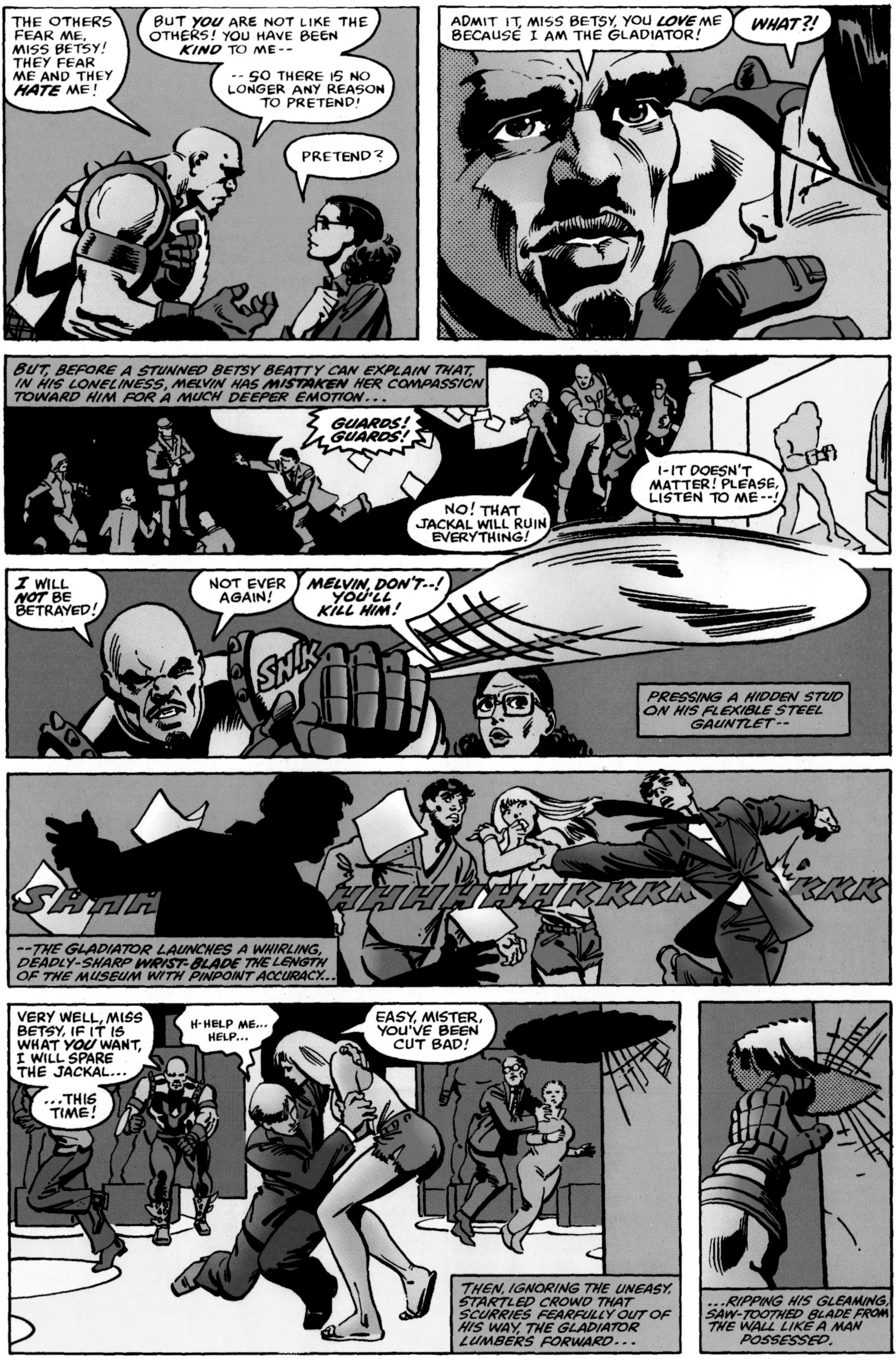
THE OTHERS FEAR ME, MISS BETSY! THEY FEAR ME AND THEY HATE ME!
BUT YOU ARE NOT LIKE THE OTHERS! YOU HAVE BEEN KIND TO ME--
-- SO THERE IS NO LONGER ANY REASON TO PRETEND!
PRETEND?
ADMIT IT, MISS BETSY, YOU LOVE ME BECAUSE I AM THE GLADIATOR!
WHAT?!
BUT, BEFORE A STUNNED BETSY BEATTY CAN EXPLAIN THAT, IN HIS LONELINESS, MELVIN HAS MISTAKEN HER COMPASSION TOWARD HIM FOR A MUCH DEEPER EMOTION...
GUARDS! GUARDS!
I-IT DOESN'T MATTER! PLEASE, LISTEN TO ME--!
NO! THAT JACKAL WILL RUIN EVERYTHING!
I WILL NOT BE BETRAYED!
NOT EVER AGAIN!
MELVIN, DON'T--! YOU'LL KILL HIM!
SNIK
PRESSING A HIDDEN STUD ON HIS FLEXIBLE STEEL GAUNTLET--
SHHHHHHHHHKKKKKKK
--THE GLADIATOR LAUNCHES A WHIRLING, DEADLY-SHARP WRIST-BLADE THE LENGTH OF THE MUSEUM WITH PINPOINT ACCURACY...
VERY WELL, MISS BETSY, IF IT IS WHAT YOU WANT, I WILL SPARE THE JACKAL...
...THIS TIME!
H-HELP ME... HELP...
EASY, MISTER, YOU'VE BEEN CUT BAD!
THEN, IGNORING THE UNEASY, STARTLED CROWD THAT SCURRIES FEARFULLY OUT OF HIS WAY, THE GLADIATOR LUMBERS FORWARD...
...RIPPING HIS GLEAMING, SAW-TOOTHED BLADE FROM THE WALL LIKE A MAN POSSESSED.

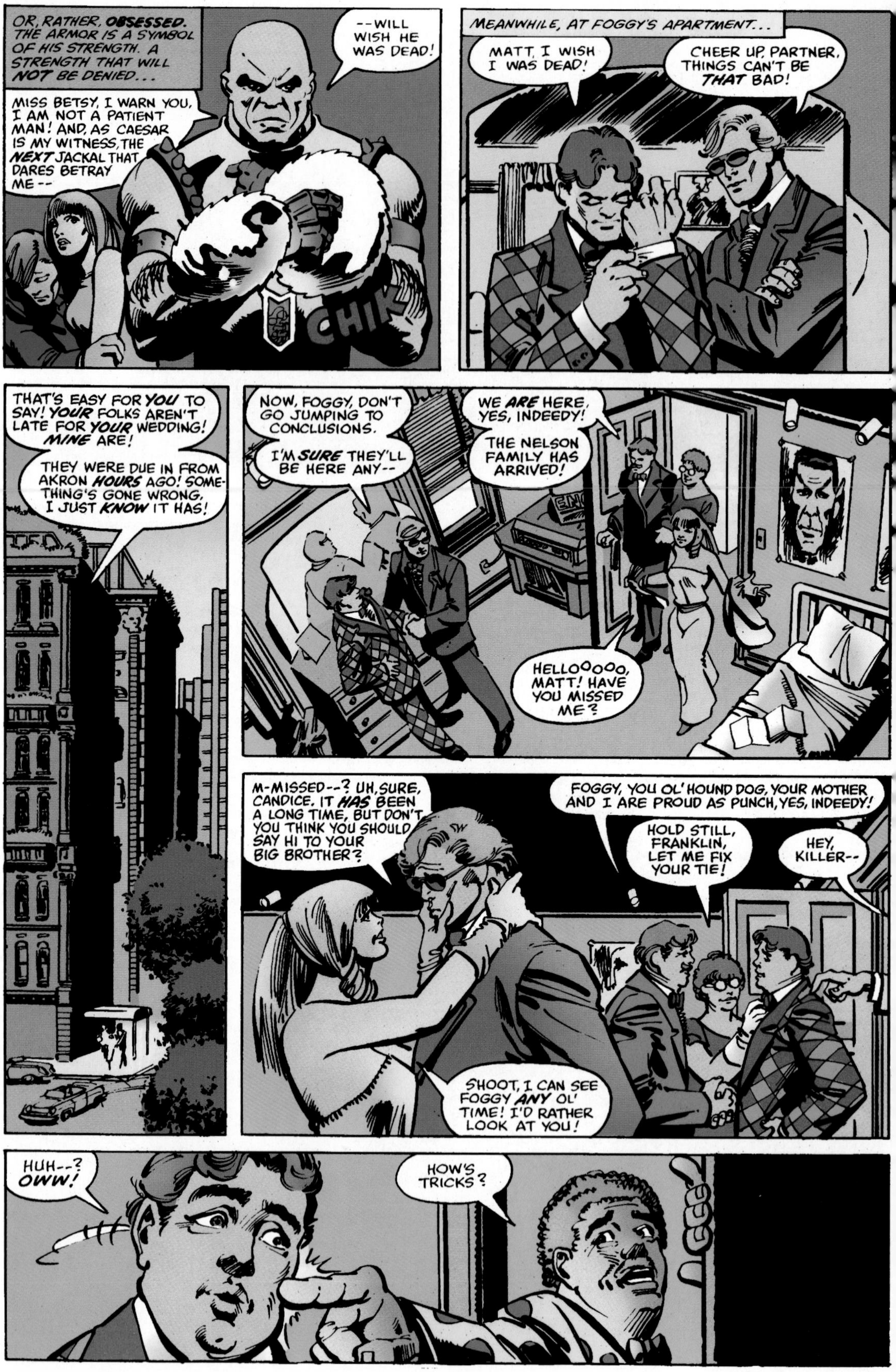
OR, RATHER, OBSESSED. THE ARMOR IS A SYMBOL OF HIS STRENGTH. A STRENGTH THAT WILL NOT BE DENIED...
--WILL WISH HE WAS DEAD!
MISS BETSY, I WARN YOU, I AM NOT A PATIENT MAN! AND, AS CAESAR IS MY WITNESS, THE NEXT JACKAL THAT DARES BETRAY ME--
CHIK
MEANWHILE, AT FOGGY'S APARTMENT...
MATT, I WISH I WAS DEAD!
CHEER UP, PARTNER, THINGS CAN'T BE THAT BAD!
THAT'S EASY FOR YOU TO SAY! YOUR FOLKS AREN'T LATE FOR YOUR WEDDING! MINE ARE!
THEY WERE DUE IN FROM AKRON HOURS AGO! SOMETHING'S GONE WRONG, I JUST KNOW IT HAS!
NOW, FOGGY, DON'T GO JUMPING TO CONCLUSIONS.
I'M SURE THEY'LL BE HERE ANY--
WE ARE HERE, YES, INDEEDY!
THE NELSON FAMILY HAS ARRIVED!
HELLOOOOO, MATT! HAVE YOU MISSED ME?
M-MISSED--? UH, SURE, CANDICE. IT HAS BEEN A LONG TIME, BUT DON'T YOU THINK YOU SHOULD SAY HI TO YOUR BIG BROTHER?
FOGGY, YOU OL' HOUND DOG, YOUR MOTHER AND I ARE PROUD AS PUNCH, YES, INDEEDY!
HOLD STILL, FRANKLIN, LET ME FIX YOUR TIE!
HEY, KILLER--
SHOOT, I CAN SEE FOGGY ANY OL' TIME! I'D RATHER LOOK AT YOU!
HUH--? OWW!
HOW'S TRICKS?

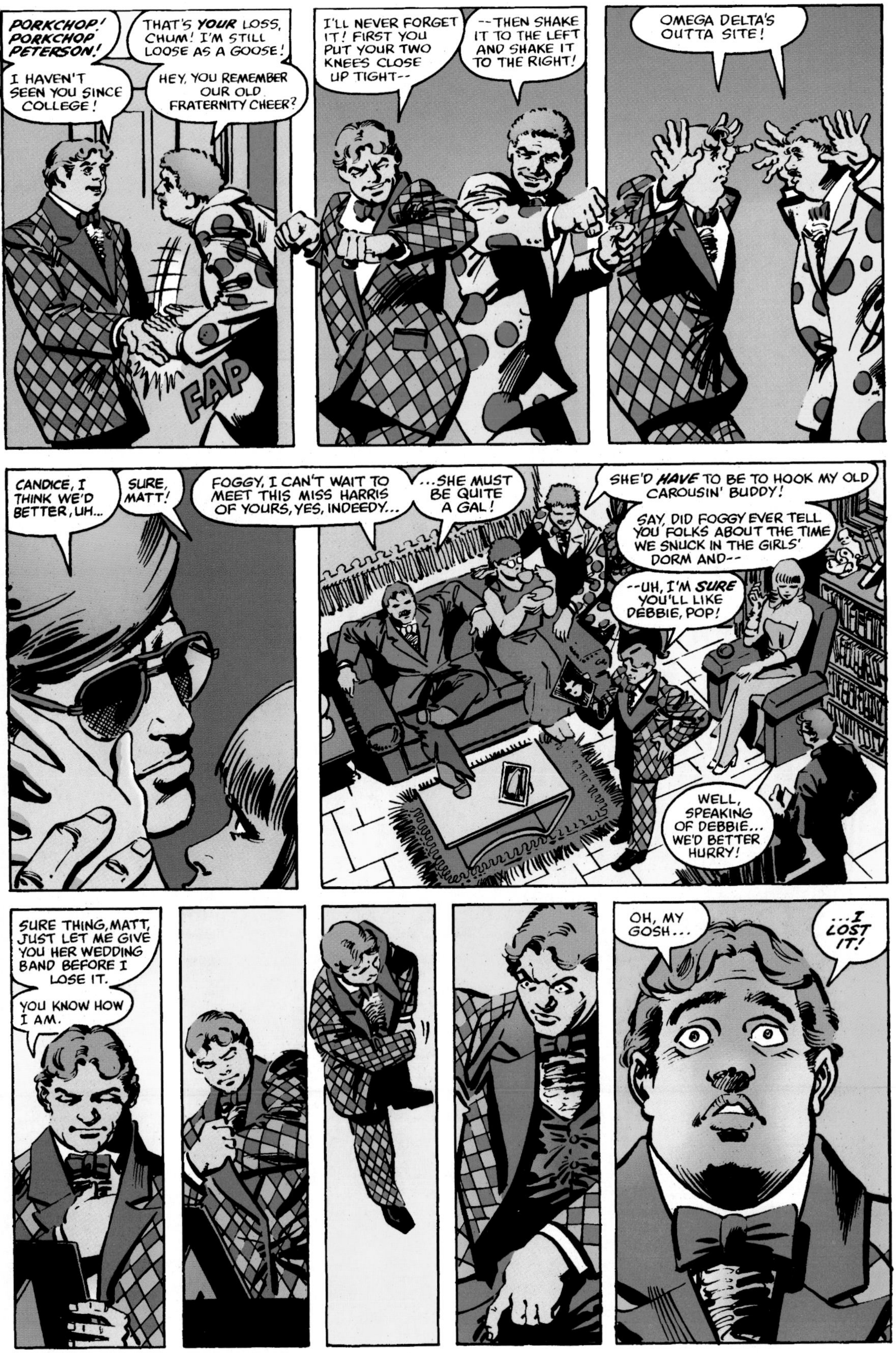
PORKCHOP! PORKCHOP PETERSON!
I HAVEN'T SEEN YOU SINCE COLLEGE!
THAT'S YOUR LOSS, CHUM! I'M STILL LOOSE AS A GOOSE!
HEY, YOU REMEMBER OUR OLD FRATERNITY CHEER?
FAP
I'LL NEVER FORGET IT! FIRST YOU PUT YOUR TWO KNEES CLOSE UP TIGHT--
--THEN SHAKE IT TO THE LEFT AND SHAKE IT TO THE RIGHT!
OMEGA DELTA'S OUTTA SITE!
CANDICE, I THINK WE'D BETTER, UH...
SURE, MATT!
FOGGY, I CAN'T WAIT TO MEET THIS MISS HARRIS OF YOURS, YES, INDEEDY...
...SHE MUST BE QUITE A GAL!
SHE'D HAVE TO BE TO HOOK MY OLD CAROUSIN' BUDDY!
SAY, DID FOGGY EVER TELL YOU FOLKS ABOUT THE TIME WE SNUCK IN THE GIRLS' DORM AND--
--UH, I'M SURE YOU'LL LIKE DEBBIE, POP!
WELL, SPEAKING OF DEBBIE... WE'D BETTER HURRY!
SURE THING, MATT, JUST LET ME GIVE YOU HER WEDDING BAND BEFORE I LOSE IT.
YOU KNOW HOW I AM.
OH, MY GOSH...
...I LOST IT!

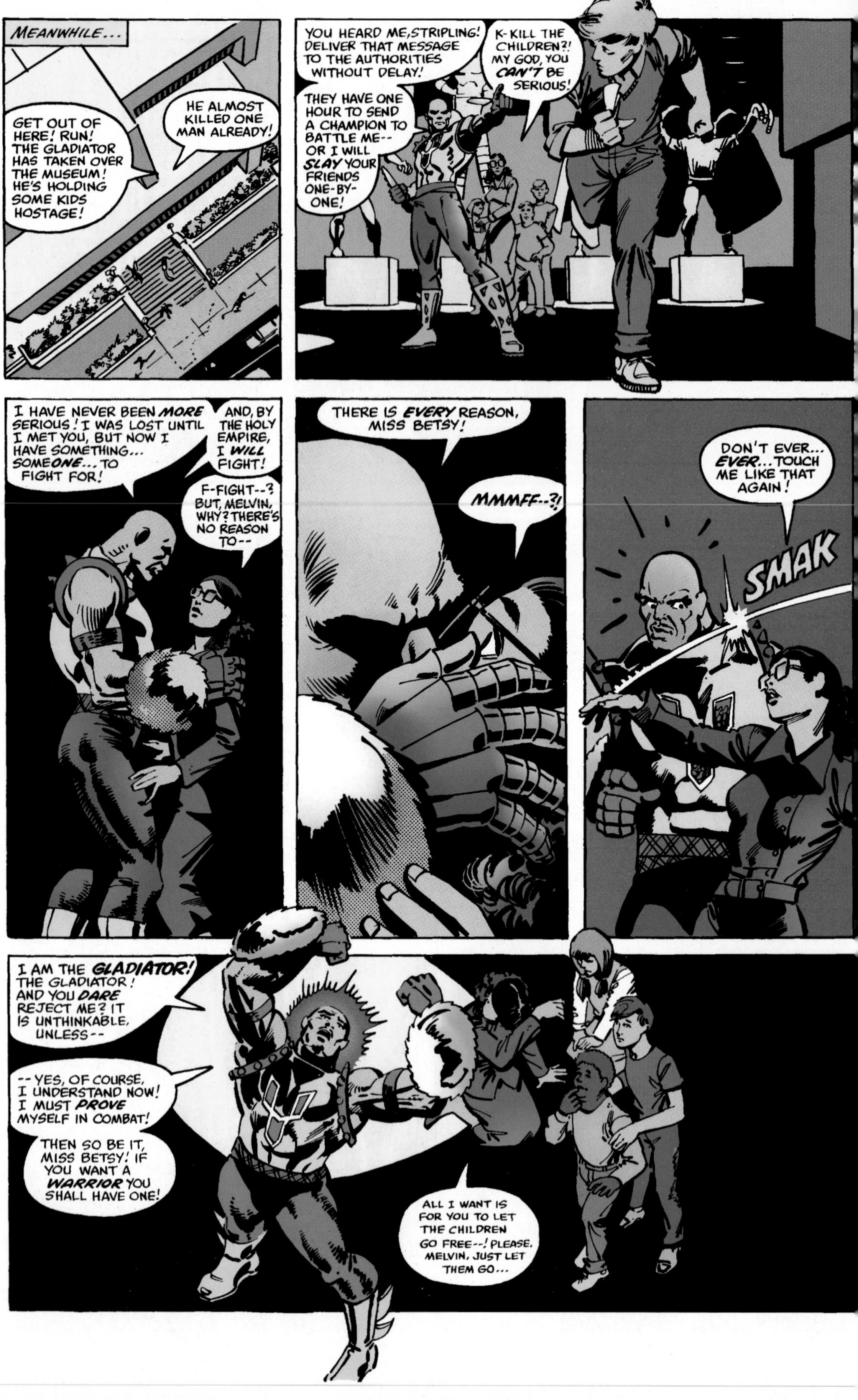
MEANWHILE...
GET OUT OF HERE! RUN! THE GLADIATOR HAS TAKEN OVER THE MUSEUM! HE'S HOLDING SOME KIDS HOSTAGE!
HE ALMOST KILLED ONE MAN ALREADY!
YOU HEARD ME, STRIPLING! DELIVER THAT MESSAGE TO THE AUTHORITIES WITHOUT DELAY!
THEY HAVE ONE HOUR TO SEND A CHAMPION TO BATTLE ME-- OR I WILL SLAY YOUR FRIENDS ONE-BY-ONE!
K-KILL THE CHILDREN?! MY GOD, YOU CAN'T BE SERIOUS!
I HAVE NEVER BEEN MORE SERIOUS! I WAS LOST UNTIL I MET YOU, BUT NOW I HAVE SOMETHING... SOMEONE... TO FIGHT FOR!
AND, BY THE HOLY EMPIRE, I WILL FIGHT!
F-FIGHT--? BUT, MELVIN, WHY? THERE'S NO REASON TO--
THERE IS EVERY REASON, MISS BETSY!
MMMFF--?!
DON'T EVER... EVER... TOUCH ME LIKE THAT AGAIN!
SMAK
I AM THE GLADIATOR! THE GLADIATOR! AND YOU DARE REJECT ME? IT IS UNTHINKABLE, UNLESS--
--YES, OF COURSE, I UNDERSTAND NOW! I MUST PROVE MYSELF IN COMBAT!
THEN SO BE IT, MISS BETSY! IF YOU WANT A WARRIOR YOU SHALL HAVE ONE!
ALL I WANT IS FOR YOU TO LET THE CHILDREN GO FREE--! PLEASE, MELVIN, JUST LET THEM GO...

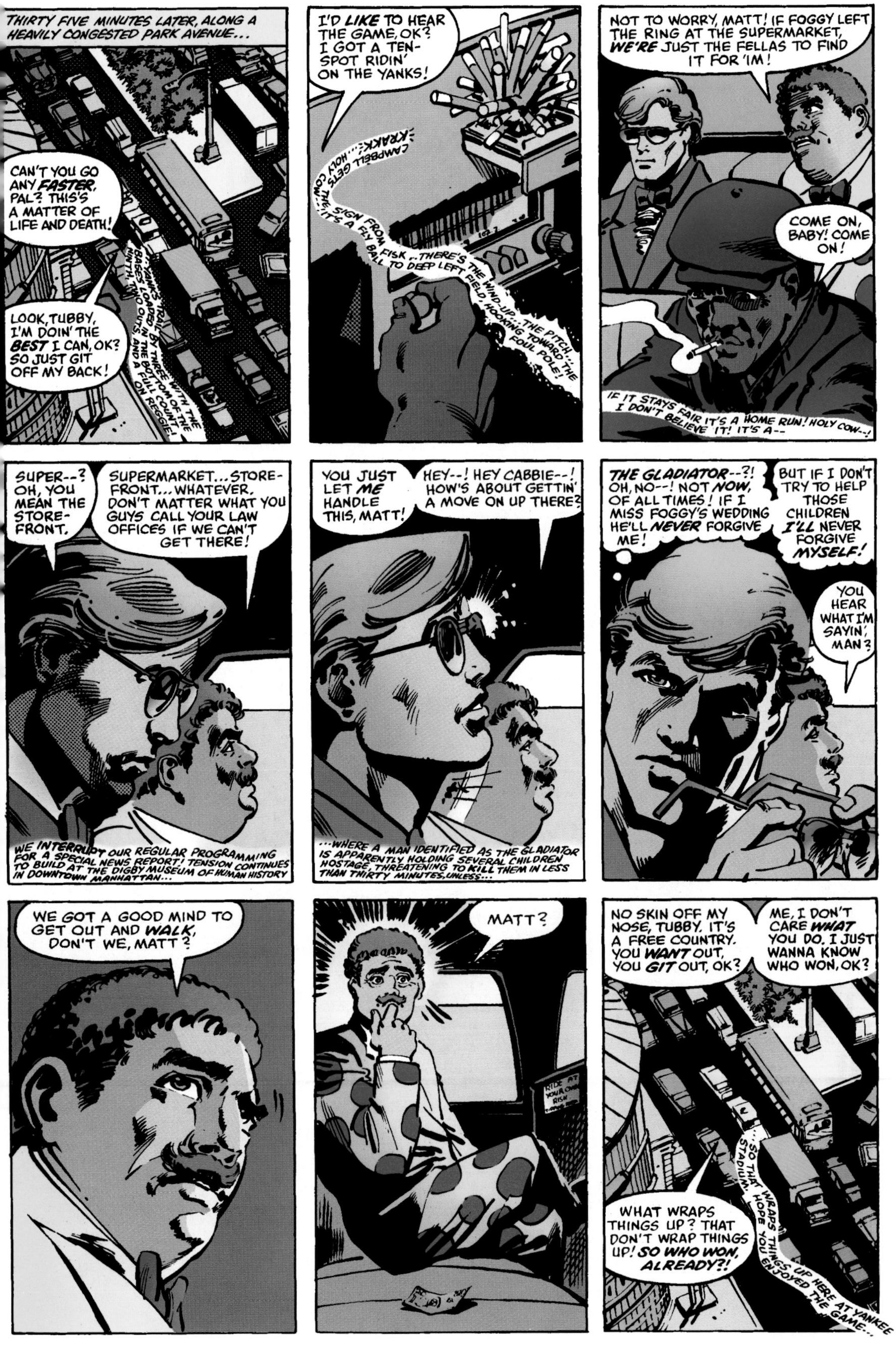
THIRTY FIVE MINUTES LATER, ALONG A HEAVILY CONGESTED PARK AVENUE...
CAN'T YOU GO ANY FASTER, PAL? THIS'S A MATTER OF LIFE AND DEATH!
LOOK, TUBBY, I'M DOIN' THE BEST I CAN, OK? SO JUST GIT OFF MY BACK!
...YANKS TRAIL BY THREE WITH THE BASES LOADED IN THE BOTTOM OF THE NINTH. TWO OUTS, AND A FULL COUNT ON REGGIE!
I'D LIKE TO HEAR THE GAME, OK? I GOT A TEN-SPOT RIDIN' ON THE YANKS!
CAMPBELL GETS THE SIGN FROM FISK... THERE'S THE WIND-UP... THE PITCH... KRAKK!... HOLY COW... IT'S A FLY BALL TO DEEP LEFT FIELD, HOOKING TOWARD THE FOUL POLE!
NOT TO WORRY, MATT! IF FOGGY LEFT THE RING AT THE SUPERMARKET, WE'RE JUST THE FELLAS TO FIND IT FOR 'IM!
COME ON, BABY! COME ON!
IF IT STAYS FAIR IT'S A HOME RUN! HOLY COW--! I DON'T BELIEVE IT! IT'S A--
SUPER--? OH, YOU MEAN THE STORE-FRONT.
SUPERMARKET... STORE-FRONT... WHATEVER. DON'T MATTER WHAT YOU GUYS CALL YOUR LAW OFFICES IF WE CAN'T GET THERE!
WE INTERRUPT OUR REGULAR PROGRAMMING FOR A SPECIAL NEWS REPORT! TENSION CONTINUES TO BUILD AT THE DIGBY MUSEUM OF HUMAN HISTORY IN DOWNTOWN MANHATTAN...
YOU JUST LET ME HANDLE THIS, MATT!
HEY--! HEY CABBIE--! HOW'S ABOUT GETTIN' A MOVE ON UP THERE?
...WHERE A MAN IDENTIFIED AS THE GLADIATOR IS APPARENTLY HOLDING SEVERAL CHILDREN HOSTAGE, THREATENING TO KILL THEM IN LESS THAN THIRTY MINUTES, UNLESS...
THE GLADIATOR--?! OH, NO--! NOT NOW, OF ALL TIMES! IF I MISS FOGGY'S WEDDING HE'LL NEVER FORGIVE ME!
BUT IF I DON'T TRY TO HELP THOSE CHILDREN I'LL NEVER FORGIVE MYSELF!
YOU HEAR WHAT I'M SAYIN', MAN?
WE GOT A GOOD MIND TO GET OUT AND WALK, DON'T WE, MATT?
MATT?
NO SKIN OFF MY NOSE, TUBBY. IT'S A FREE COUNTRY. YOU WANT OUT, YOU GIT OUT, OK?
ME, I DON'T CARE WHAT YOU DO. I JUST WANNA KNOW WHO WON, OK?
...SO THAT WRAPS THINGS UP HERE AT YANKEE STADIUM. HOPE YOU ENJOYED THE GAME...
WHAT WRAPS THINGS UP? THAT DON'T WRAP THINGS UP! SO WHO WON, ALREADY?!

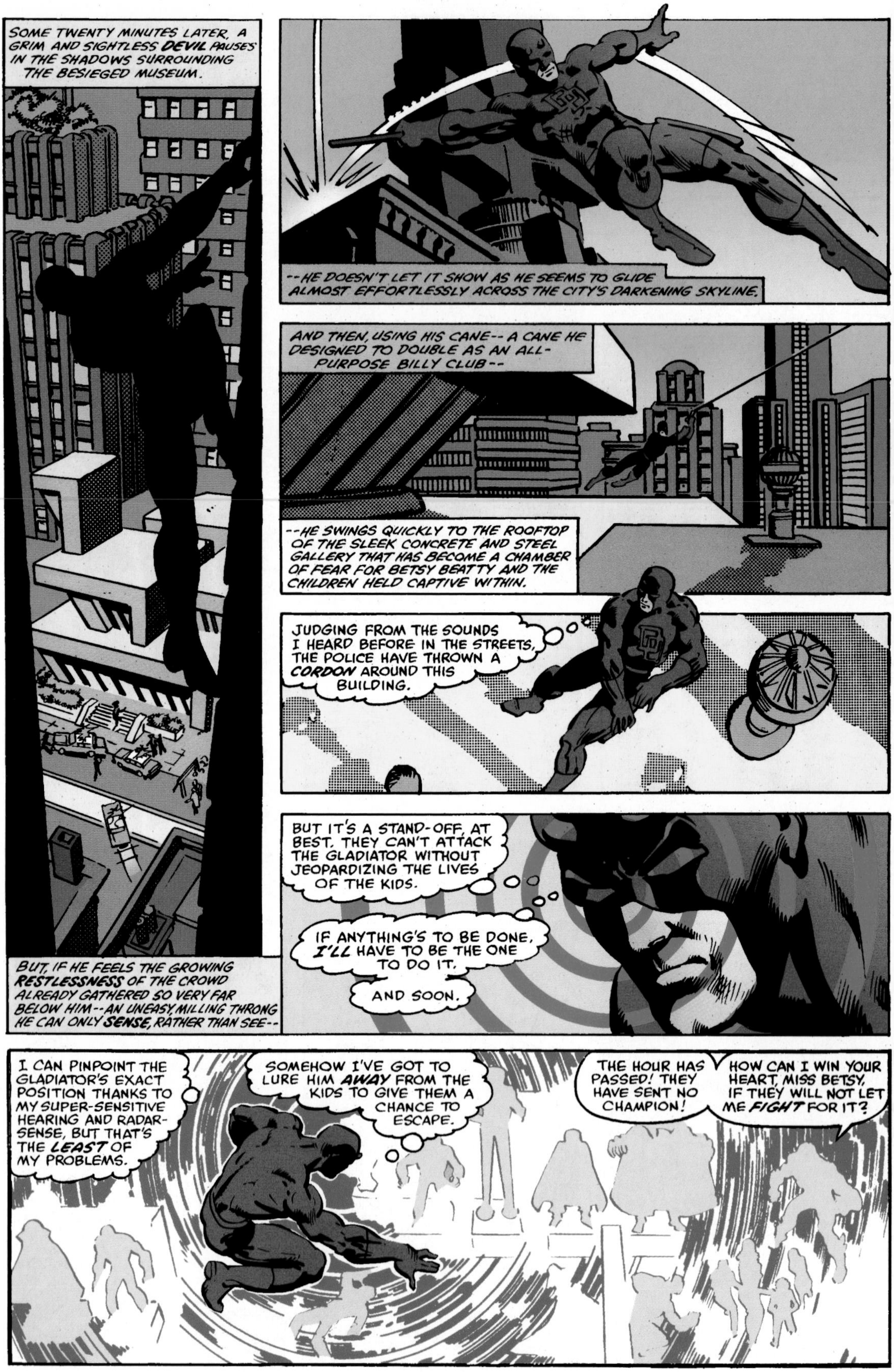
SOME TWENTY MINUTES LATER, A GRIM AND SIGHTLESS DEVIL PAUSES IN THE SHADOWS SURROUNDING THE BESIEGED MUSEUM.
BUT, IF HE FEELS THE GROWING RESTLESSNESS OF THE CROWD ALREADY GATHERED SO VERY FAR BELOW HIM--AN UNEASY, MILLING THRONG HE CAN ONLY SENSE, RATHER THAN SEE--
--HE DOESN'T LET IT SHOW AS HE SEEMS TO GLIDE ALMOST EFFORTLESSLY ACROSS THE CITY'S DARKENING SKYLINE.
AND THEN, USING HIS CANE--A CANE HE DESIGNED TO DOUBLE AS AN ALL-PURPOSE BILLY CLUB--
--HE SWINGS QUICKLY TO THE ROOFTOP OF THE SLEEK CONCRETE AND STEEL GALLERY THAT HAS BECOME A CHAMBER OF FEAR FOR BETSY BEATTY AND THE CHILDREN HELD CAPTIVE WITHIN.
JUDGING FROM THE SOUNDS I HEARD BEFORE IN THE STREETS, THE POLICE HAVE THROWN A CORDON AROUND THIS BUILDING.
BUT IT'S A STAND-OFF, AT BEST. THEY CAN'T ATTACK THE GLADIATOR WITHOUT JEOPARDIZING THE LIVES OF THE KIDS.
IF ANYTHING'S TO BE DONE, I'LL HAVE TO BE THE ONE TO DO IT.
AND SOON.
I CAN PINPOINT THE GLADIATOR'S EXACT POSITION THANKS TO MY SUPER-SENSITIVE HEARING AND RADAR-SENSE, BUT THAT'S THE LEAST OF MY PROBLEMS.
SOMEHOW I'VE GOT TO LURE HIM AWAY FROM THE KIDS TO GIVE THEM A CHANCE TO ESCAPE.
THE HOUR HAS PASSED! THEY HAVE SENT NO CHAMPION!
HOW CAN I WIN YOUR HEART, MISS BETSY, IF THEY WILL NOT LET ME FIGHT FOR IT?

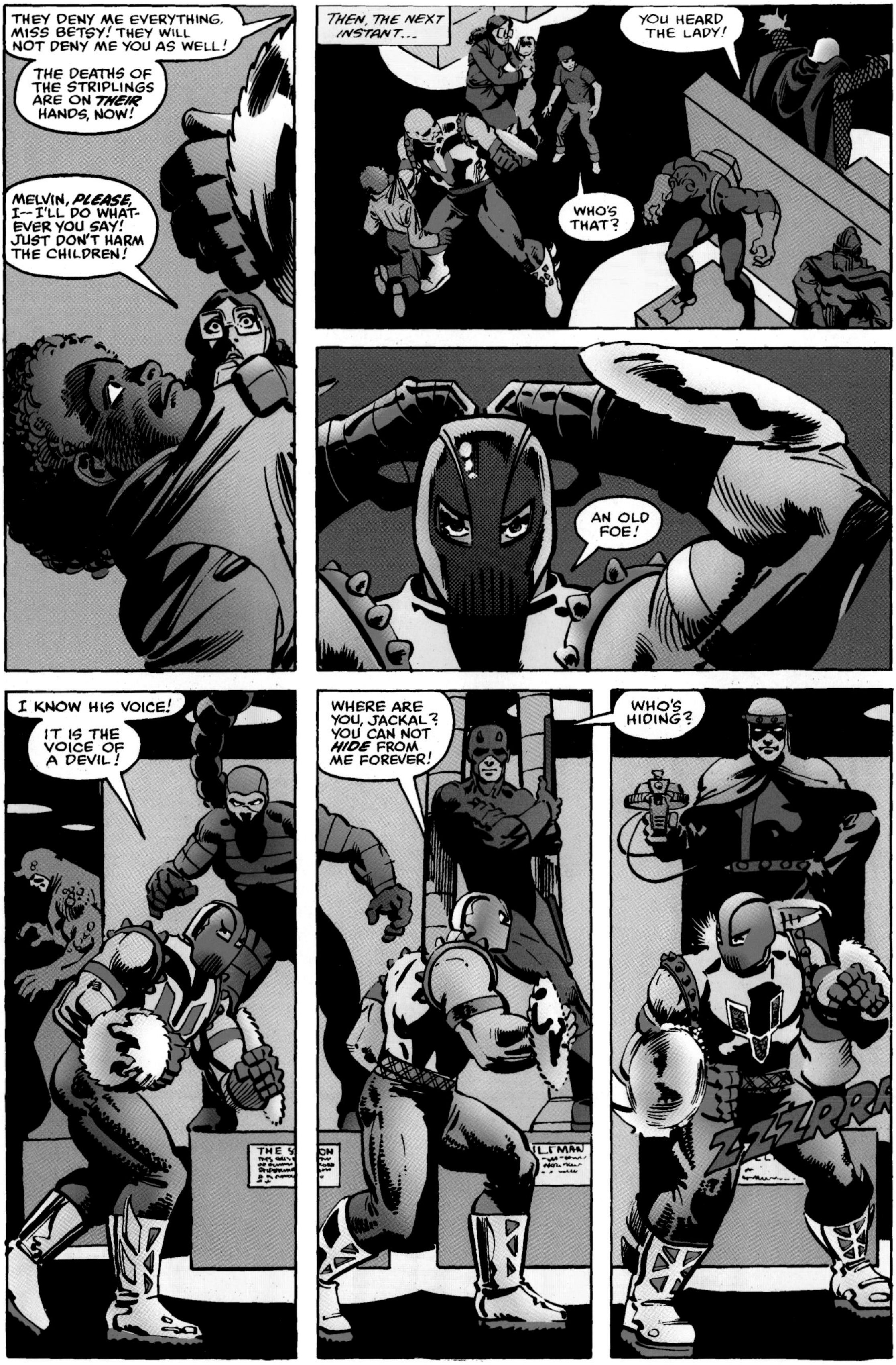
THEY DENY ME EVERYTHING, MISS BETSY! THEY WILL NOT DENY ME YOU AS WELL!
THE DEATHS OF THE STRIPLINGS ARE ON THEIR HANDS, NOW!
MELVIN, PLEASE, I-- I'LL DO WHAT-EVER YOU SAY! JUST DON'T HARM THE CHILDREN!
THEN, THE NEXT INSTANT...
YOU HEARD THE LADY!
WHO'S THAT?
AN OLD FOE!
I KNOW HIS VOICE!
IT IS THE VOICE OF A DEVIL!
WHERE ARE YOU, JACKAL? YOU CAN NOT HIDE FROM ME FOREVER!
WHO'S HIDING?
ZZZRRR

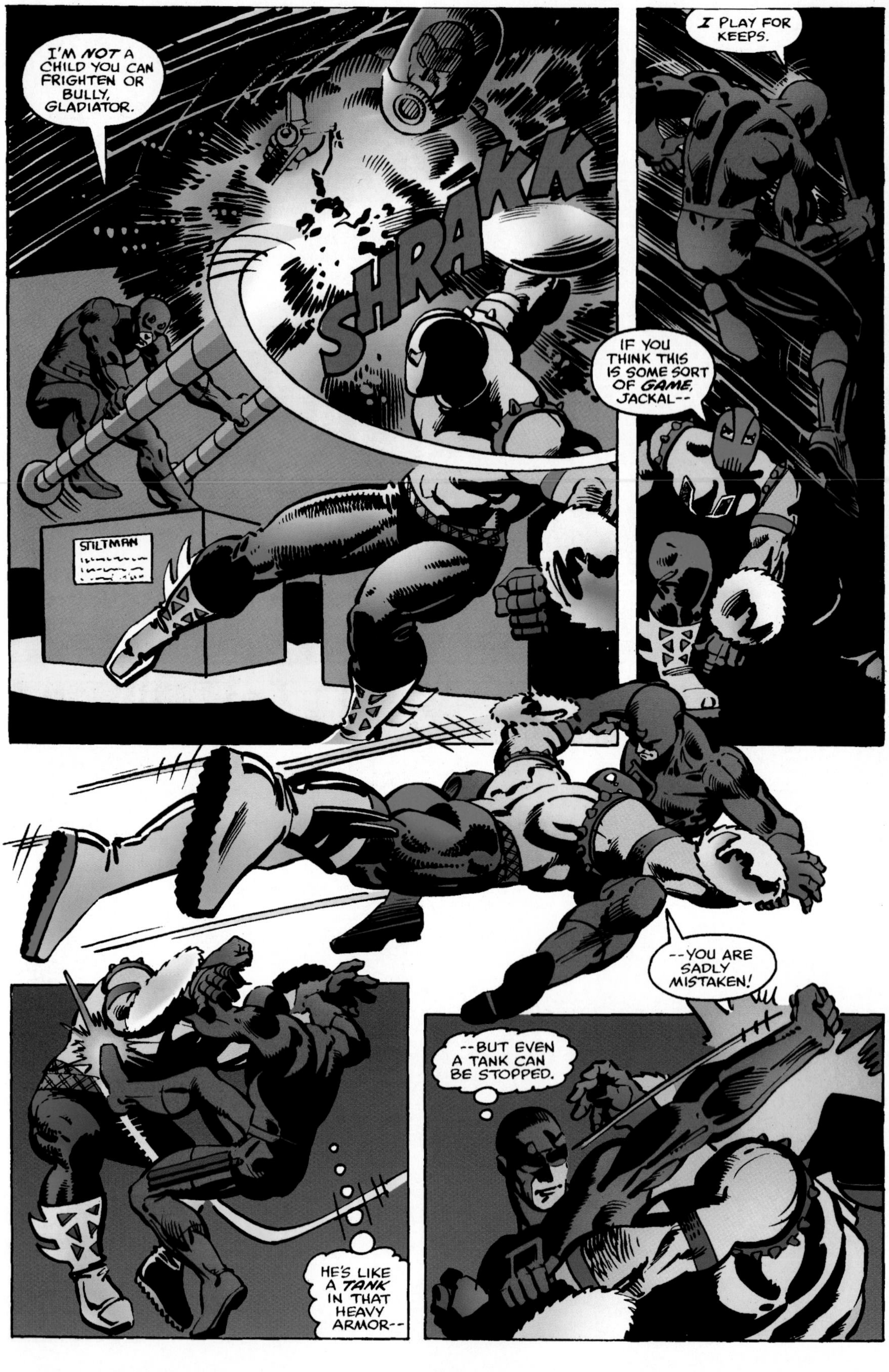

I'M NOT A CHILD YOU CAN FRIGHTEN OR BULLY, GLADIATOR.
SHRAKK
STILTMAN
I PLAY FOR KEEPS.
IF YOU THINK THIS IS SOME SORT OF GAME, JACKAL--
--YOU ARE SADLY MISTAKEN!
HE'S LIKE A TANK IN THAT HEAVY ARMOR--
--BUT EVEN A TANK CAN BE STOPPED.

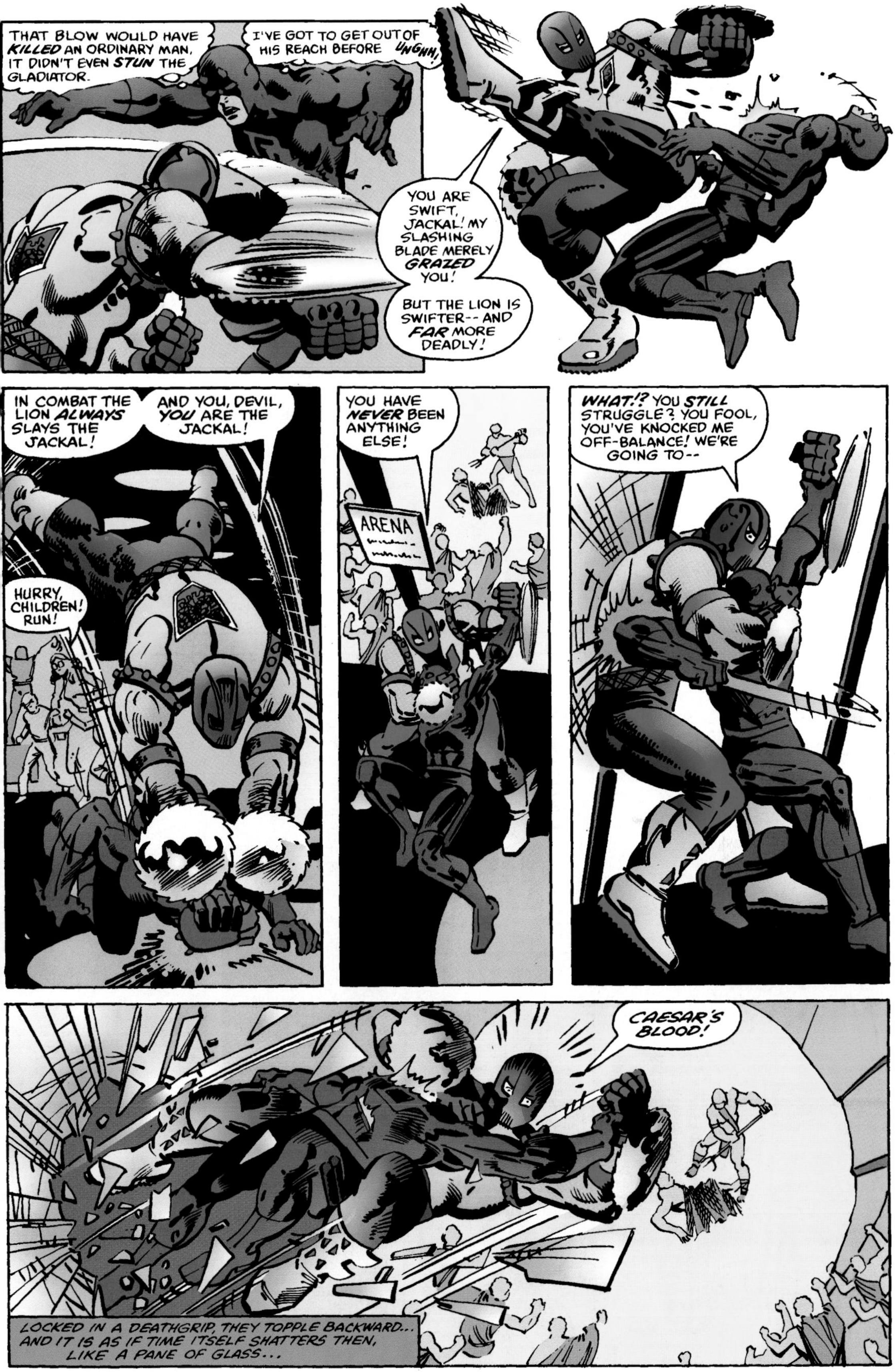

THAT BLOW WOULD HAVE KILLED AN ORDINARY MAN, IT DIDN'T EVEN STUN THE GLADIATOR.
I'VE GOT TO GET OUT OF HIS REACH BEFORE UNGHH!
YOU ARE SWIFT, JACKAL! MY SLASHING BLADE MERELY GRAZED YOU!
BUT THE LION IS SWIFTER-- AND FAR MORE DEADLY!
IN COMBAT THE LION ALWAYS SLAYS THE JACKAL!
AND YOU, DEVIL, YOU ARE THE JACKAL!
HURRY, CHILDREN! RUN!
YOU HAVE NEVER BEEN ANYTHING ELSE!
ARENA
WHAT!? YOU STILL STRUGGLE? YOU FOOL, YOU'VE KNOCKED ME OFF-BALANCE! WE'RE GOING TO--
CAESAR'S BLOOD!
LOCKED IN A DEATHGRIP, THEY TOPPLE BACKWARD... AND IT IS AS IF TIME ITSELF SHATTERS THEN, LIKE A PANE OF GLASS...

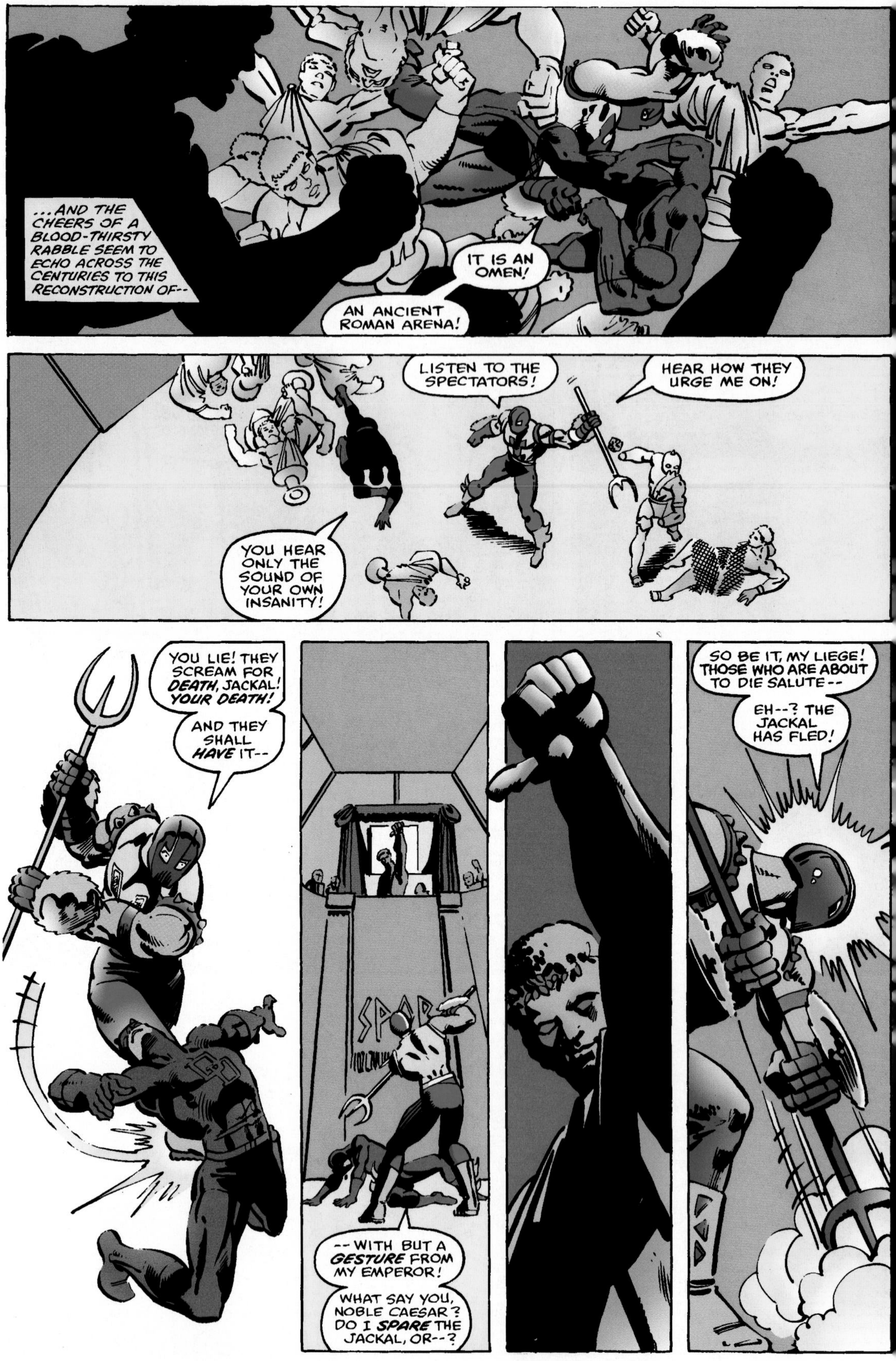
...AND THE CHEERS OF A BLOOD-THIRSTY RABBLE SEEM TO ECHO ACROSS THE CENTURIES TO THIS RECONSTRUCTION OF--
IT IS AN OMEN!
AN ANCIENT ROMAN ARENA!
LISTEN TO THE SPECTATORS!
HEAR HOW THEY URGE ME ON!
YOU HEAR ONLY THE SOUND OF YOUR OWN INSANITY!
YOU LIE! THEY SCREAM FOR DEATH, JACKAL! YOUR DEATH!
AND THEY SHALL HAVE IT--
--WITH BUT A GESTURE FROM MY EMPEROR!
WHAT SAY YOU, NOBLE CAESAR? DO I SPARE THE JACKAL, OR--?
SO BE IT, MY LIEGE! THOSE WHO ARE ABOUT TO DIE SALUTE--
EH--? THE JACKAL HAS FLED!

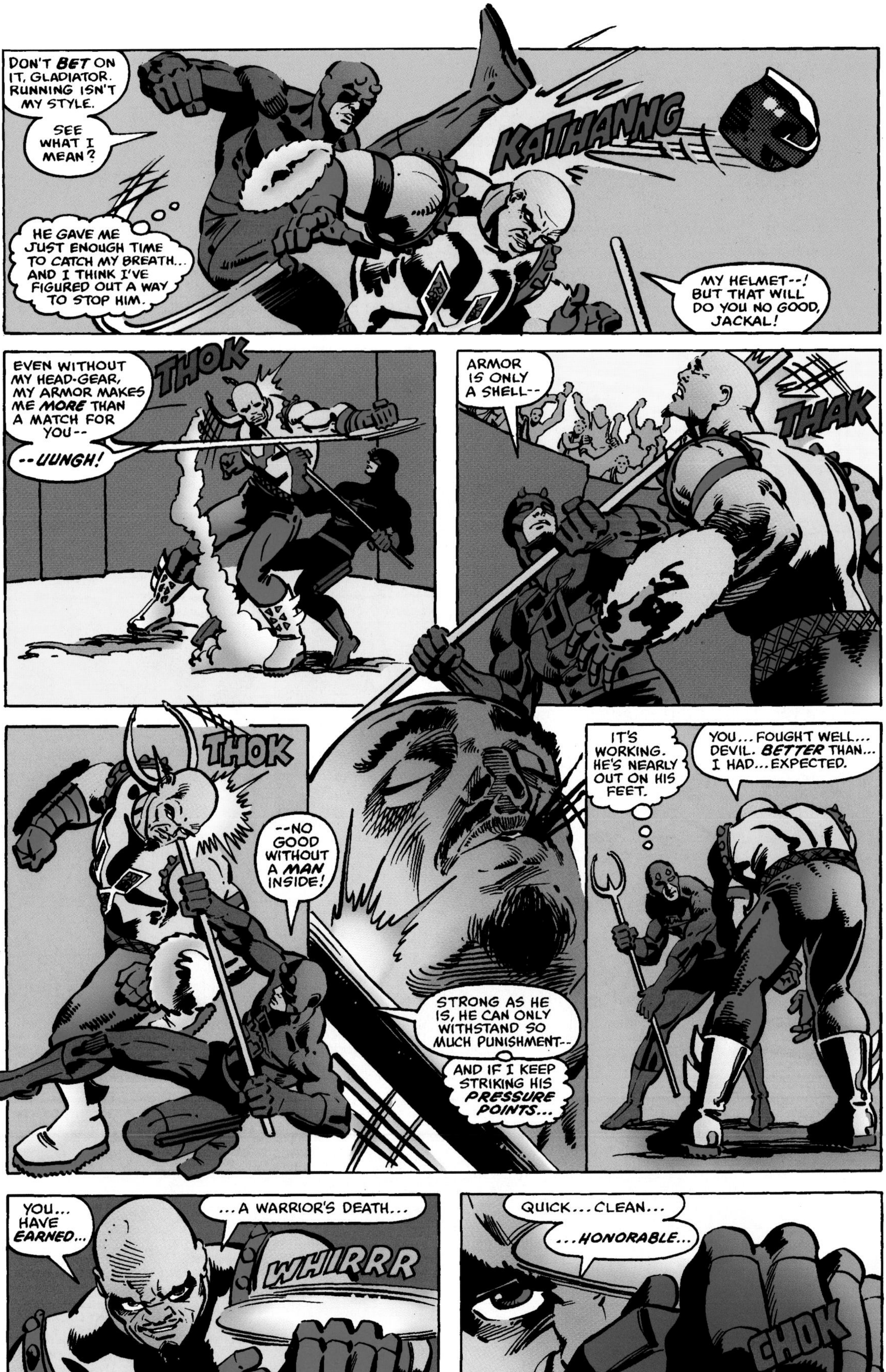

DON'T BET ON IT, GLADIATOR. RUNNING ISN'T MY STYLE.
SEE WHAT I MEAN?
KATHANNG
HE GAVE ME JUST ENOUGH TIME TO CATCH MY BREATH... AND I THINK I'VE FIGURED OUT A WAY TO STOP HIM.
MY HELMET--! BUT THAT WILL DO YOU NO GOOD, JACKAL!
EVEN WITHOUT MY HEAD-GEAR, MY ARMOR MAKES ME MORE THAN A MATCH FOR YOU--
--UUNGH!
THOK
ARMOR IS ONLY A SHELL--
THAK
THOK
--NO GOOD WITHOUT A MAN INSIDE!
STRONG AS HE IS, HE CAN ONLY WITHSTAND SO MUCH PUNISHMENT--
AND IF I KEEP STRIKING HIS PRESSURE POINTS...
IT'S WORKING. HE'S NEARLY OUT ON HIS FEET.
YOU... FOUGHT WELL... DEVIL. BETTER THAN... I HAD... EXPECTED.
YOU... HAVE EARNED...
...A WARRIOR'S DEATH...
WHIRRR
QUICK... CLEAN...
...HONORABLE...
CHOK

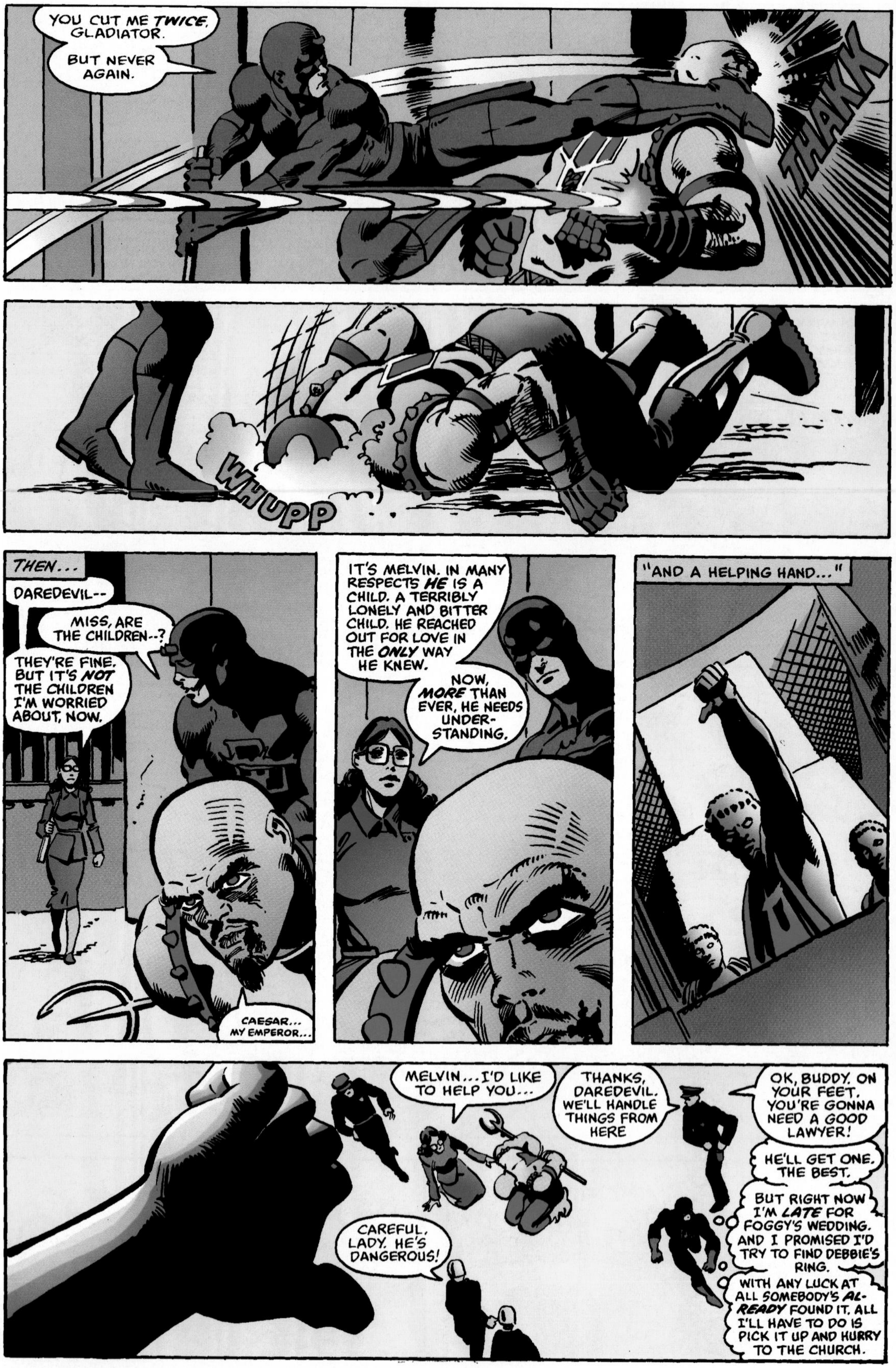
YOU CUT ME TWICE, GLADIATOR.
BUT NEVER AGAIN.
THAKK
WHUPP
THEN...
DAREDEVIL--
MISS, ARE THE CHILDREN--?
THEY'RE FINE. BUT IT'S NOT THE CHILDREN I'M WORRIED ABOUT, NOW.
CAESAR... MY EMPEROR...
IT'S MELVIN. IN MANY RESPECTS HE IS A CHILD. A TERRIBLY LONELY AND BITTER CHILD. HE REACHED OUT FOR LOVE IN THE ONLY WAY HE KNEW.
NOW, MORE THAN EVER, HE NEEDS UNDER-STANDING.
"AND A HELPING HAND..."
MELVIN... I'D LIKE TO HELP YOU...
CAREFUL, LADY. HE'S DANGEROUS!
THANKS, DAREDEVIL. WE'LL HANDLE THINGS FROM HERE
OK, BUDDY. ON YOUR FEET. YOU'RE GONNA NEED A GOOD LAWYER!
HE'LL GET ONE. THE BEST.
BUT RIGHT NOW I'M LATE FOR FOGGY'S WEDDING. AND I PROMISED I'D TRY TO FIND DEBBIE'S RING.
WITH ANY LUCK AT ALL SOMEBODY'S AL-READY FOUND IT. ALL I'LL HAVE TO DO IS PICK IT UP AND HURRY TO THE CHURCH.

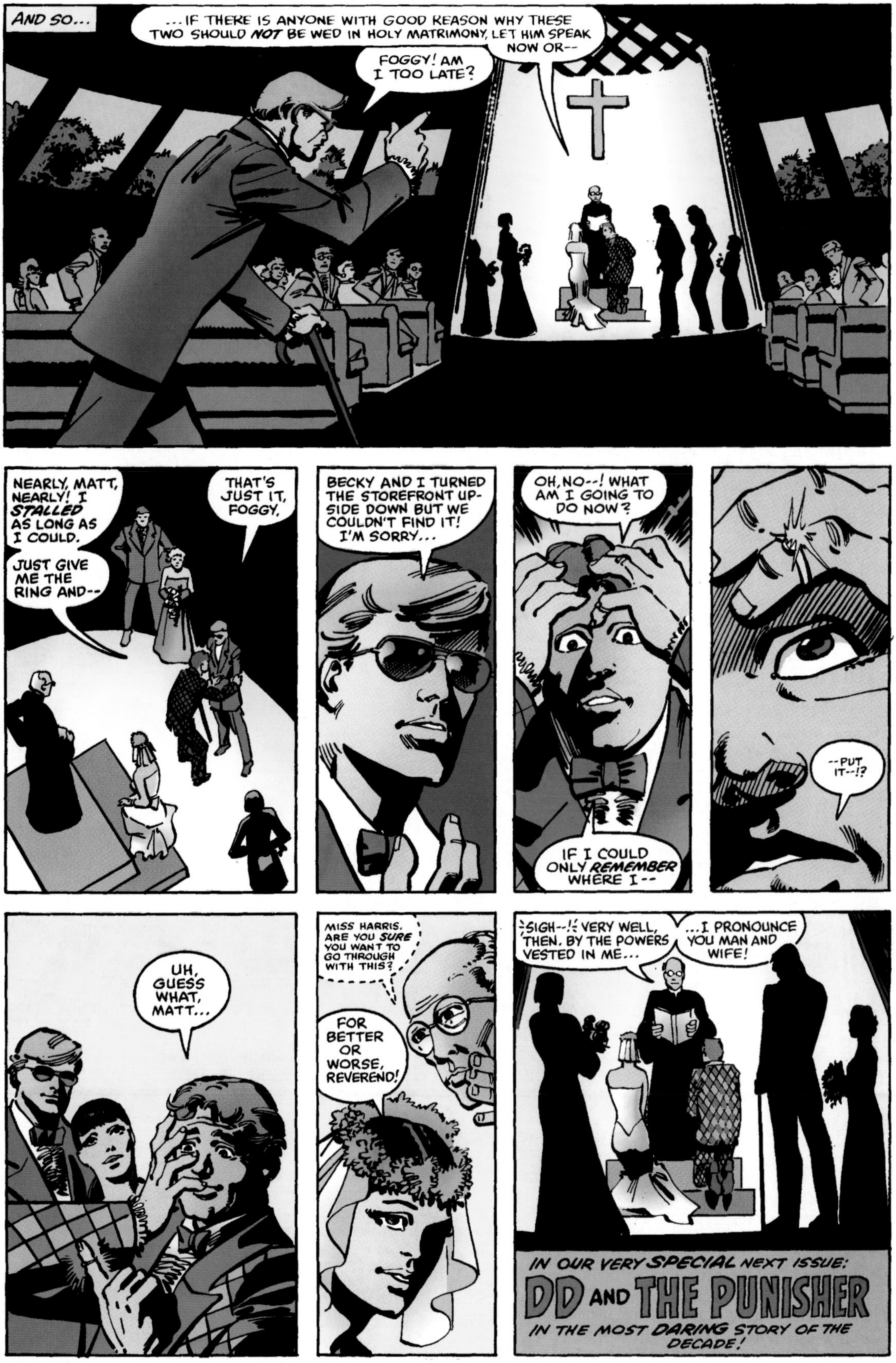
AND SO...
...IF THERE IS ANYONE WITH GOOD REASON WHY THESE TWO SHOULD NOT BE WED IN HOLY MATRIMONY, LET HIM SPEAK NOW OR--
FOGGY! AM I TOO LATE?
NEARLY, MATT, NEARLY! I STALLED AS LONG AS I COULD.
JUST GIVE ME THE RING AND--
THAT'S JUST IT, FOGGY.
BECKY AND I TURNED THE STOREFRONT UPSIDE DOWN BUT WE COULDN'T FIND IT! I'M SORRY...
OH, NO--! WHAT AM I GOING TO DO NOW?
IF I COULD ONLY REMEMBER WHERE I--
--PUT IT--!?
UH, GUESS WHAT, MATT...
MISS HARRIS, ARE YOU SURE YOU WANT TO GO THROUGH WITH THIS?
FOR BETTER OR WORSE, REVEREND!
SIGH--! VERY WELL, THEN. BY THE POWERS VESTED IN ME...
...I PRONOUNCE YOU MAN AND WIFE!
IN OUR VERY SPECIAL NEXT ISSUE:
DD AND THE PUNISHER
IN THE MOST DARING STORY OF THE DECADE!

DAREDEVIL #167

NOV 1980

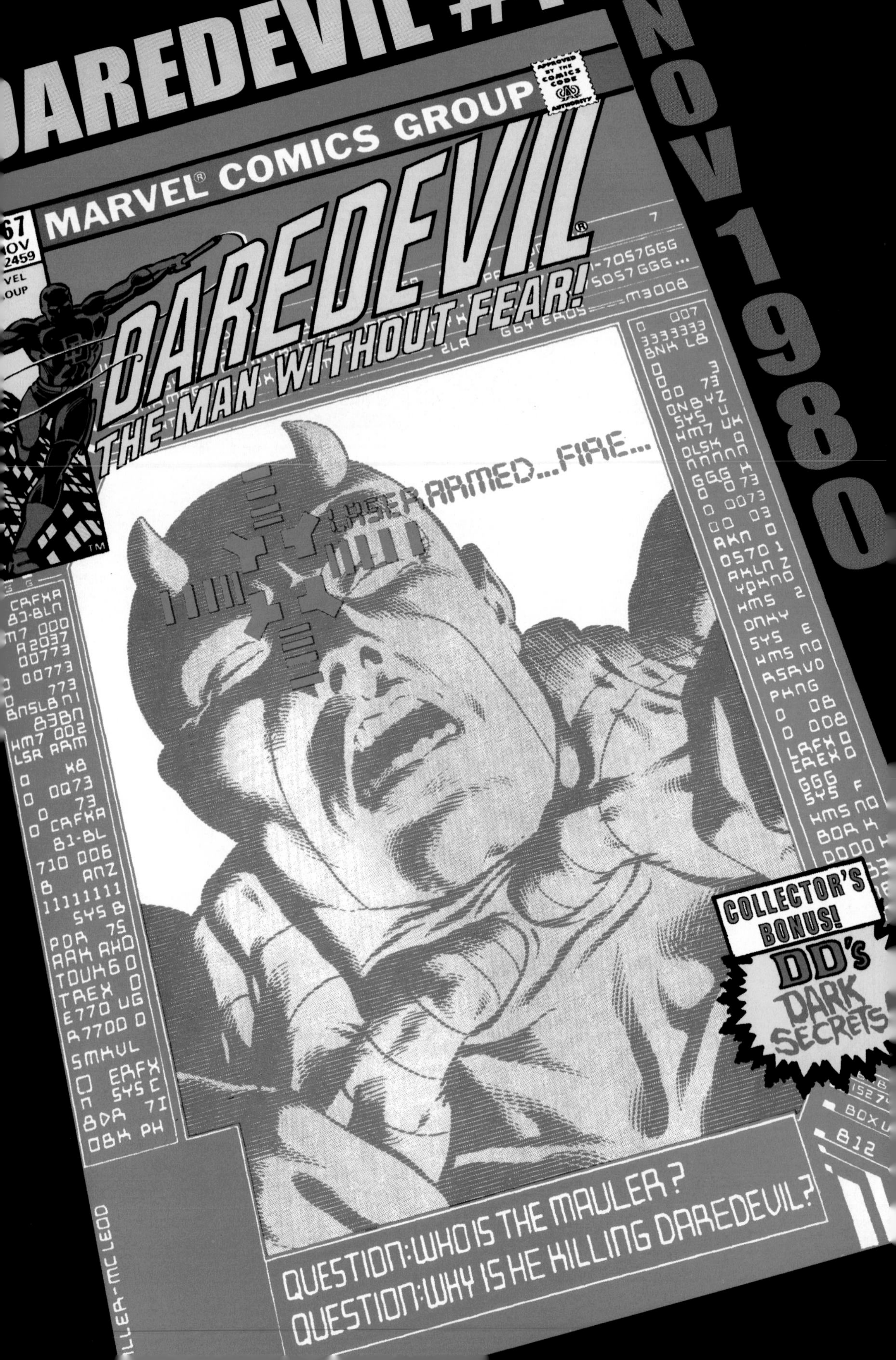

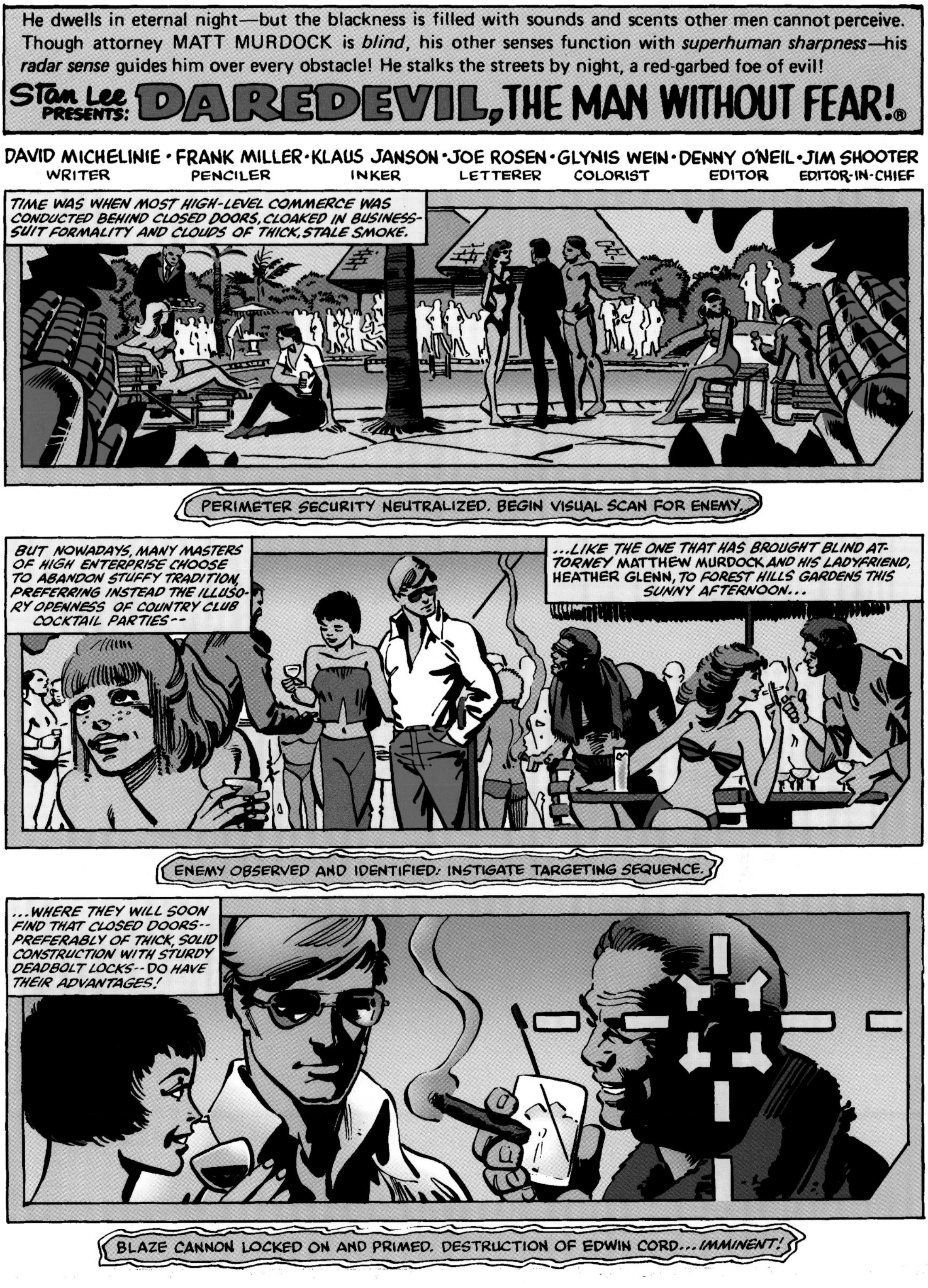
He dwells in eternal night—but the blackness is filled with sounds and scents other men cannot perceive. Though attorney MATT MURDOCK is blind, his other senses function with superhuman sharpness—his radar sense guides him over every obstacle! He stalks the streets by night, a red-garbed foe of evil!
Stan Lee PRESENTS: DAREDEVIL, THE MAN WITHOUT FEAR!®
DAVID MICHELINIE WRITER • FRANK MILLER PENCILER • KLAUS JANSON INKER • JOE ROSEN LETTERER • GLYNIS WEIN COLORIST • DENNY O'NEIL EDITOR • JIM SHOOTER EDITOR-IN-CHIEF
TIME WAS WHEN MOST HIGH-LEVEL COMMERCE WAS CONDUCTED BEHIND CLOSED DOORS, CLOAKED IN BUSINESS-SUIT FORMALITY AND CLOUDS OF THICK, STALE SMOKE.
PERIMETER SECURITY NEUTRALIZED. BEGIN VISUAL SCAN FOR ENEMY.
BUT NOWADAYS, MANY MASTERS OF HIGH ENTERPRISE CHOOSE TO ABANDON STUFFY TRADITION, PREFERRING INSTEAD THE ILLUSORY OPENNESS OF COUNTRY CLUB COCKTAIL PARTIES--
...LIKE THE ONE THAT HAS BROUGHT BLIND ATTORNEY MATTHEW MURDOCK AND HIS LADYFRIEND, HEATHER GLENN, TO FOREST HILLS GARDENS THIS SUNNY AFTERNOON...
ENEMY OBSERVED AND IDENTIFIED: INSTIGATE TARGETING SEQUENCE.
...WHERE THEY WILL SOON FIND THAT CLOSED DOORS--PREFERABLY OF THICK, SOLID CONSTRUCTION WITH STURDY DEADBOLT LOCKS--DO HAVE THEIR ADVANTAGES!
BLAZE CANNON LOCKED ON AND PRIMED. DESTRUCTION OF EDWIN CORD... IMMINENT!

THANKS AGAIN FOR INVITING US, MR. CORD.

YES, IT'S A WONDERFUL PARTY.

HEY, THE PLEASURE'S MINE, I'VE BEEN WANTING TO DISCUSS SOMETHING WITH MATT HERE FOR SOME TIME, ANYWAY.

WELL, THEN, IF YOU TWO ARE GOING TO TALK BUSINESS, I THINK I'LL JUST MIX A BIT.

BUT WE'RE NOT--!

SURE WE ARE, M'BOY.

TELL ME, HAVE YOU EVER CONSIDERED THE ADVANTAGES OF A STAFF POSITION? THE CORD CONGLOMERATE COULD USE A BRIGHT YOUNG LAWYER ON ITS TEAM.

YOU COULD NAME YOUR OWN SALARY, AND THERE'D BE PLE OF OTHER BENEFITS-- ONES FRIENDLY FOLKS AT THE I.R.S WOULDN'T HAVE TO KNOW AB IF YOU CATCH MY DRIFT.

WHAT DO YOU SAY?

HOWEVER, NEITHER MATT NOR HEATHER HAVE THAT CHANCE, AS SUDDENLY TERROR CRASHES THE PARTY IN AN EXPLOSION OF SHATTERING GLASS!

FR-R-RATCH

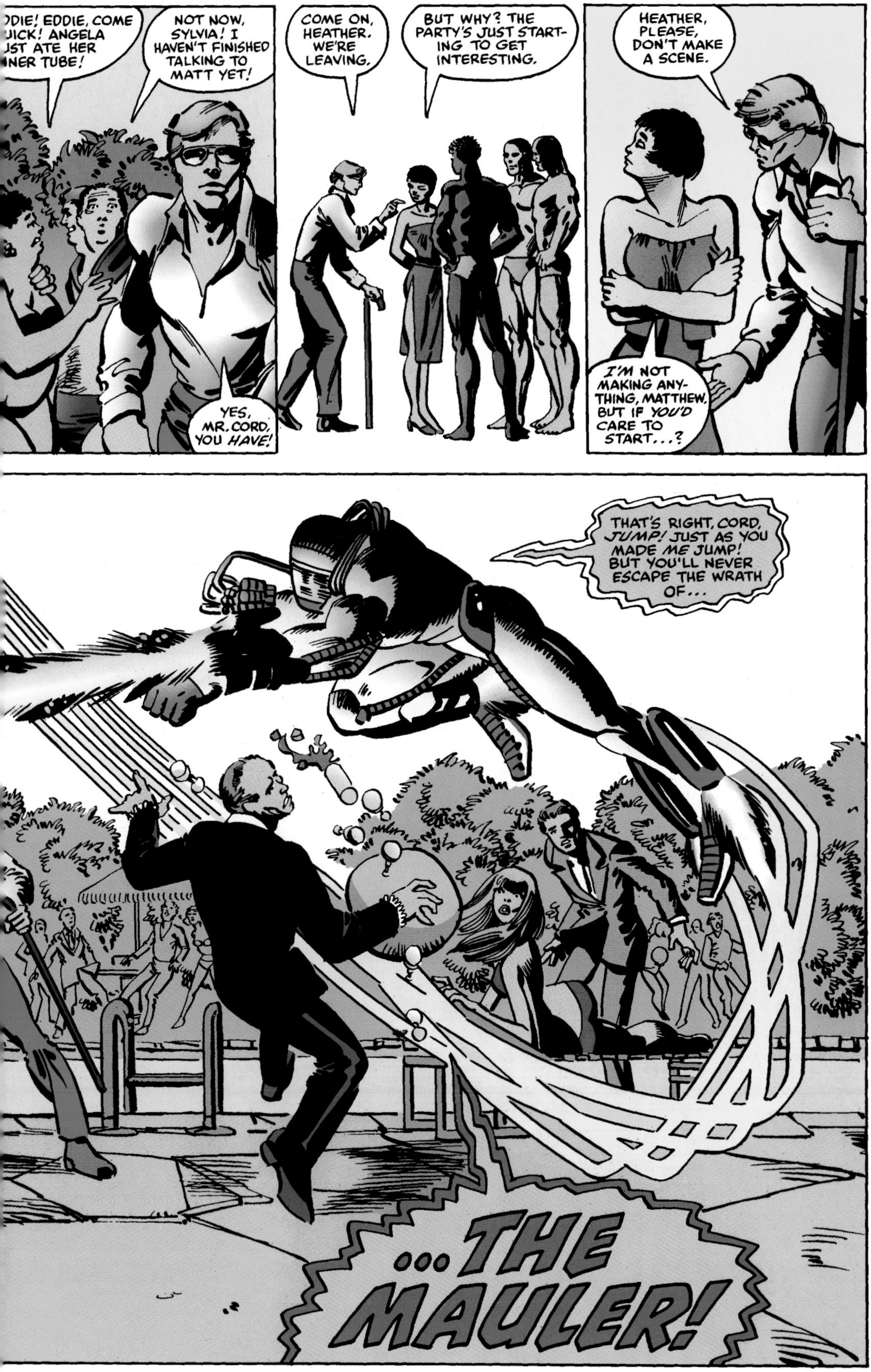
DDIE! EDDIE, COME UICK! ANGELA UST ATE HER NER TUBE!
NOT NOW, SYLVIA! I HAVEN'T FINISHED TALKING TO MATT YET!
YES, MR. CORD, YOU HAVE!
COME ON, HEATHER. WE'RE LEAVING.
BUT WHY? THE PARTY'S JUST STARTING TO GET INTERESTING.
HEATHER, PLEASE, DON'T MAKE A SCENE.
I'M NOT MAKING ANYTHING, MATTHEW, BUT IF YOU'D CARE TO START...?
THAT'S RIGHT, CORD, JUMP! JUST AS YOU MADE ME JUMP! BUT YOU'LL NEVER ESCAPE THE WRATH OF...
...THE MAULER!

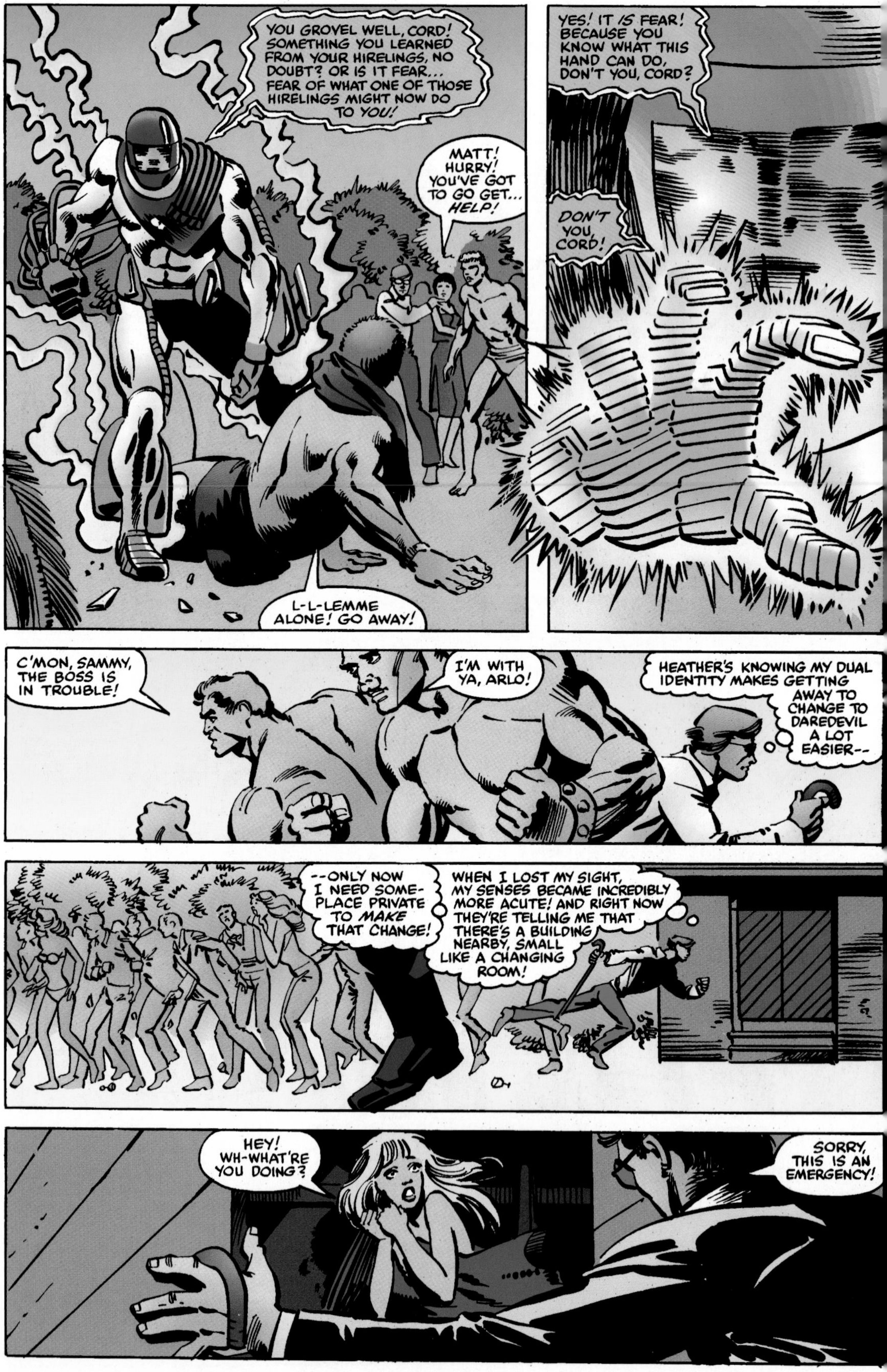
YOU GROVEL WELL, CORD! SOMETHING YOU LEARNED FROM YOUR HIRELINGS, NO DOUBT? OR IS IT FEAR... FEAR OF WHAT ONE OF THOSE HIRELINGS MIGHT NOW DO TO YOU!
MATT! HURRY! YOU'VE GOT TO GO GET... HELP!
L-L-LEMME ALONE! GO AWAY!
YES! IT IS FEAR! BECAUSE YOU KNOW WHAT THIS HAND CAN DO, DON'T YOU, CORD?
DON'T YOU CORD!
C'MON, SAMMY, THE BOSS IS IN TROUBLE!
I'M WITH YA, ARLO!
HEATHER'S KNOWING MY DUAL IDENTITY MAKES GETTING AWAY TO CHANGE TO DAREDEVIL A LOT EASIER--
--ONLY NOW I NEED SOME-PLACE PRIVATE TO MAKE THAT CHANGE!
WHEN I LOST MY SIGHT, MY SENSES BECAME INCREDIBLY MORE ACUTE! AND RIGHT NOW THEY'RE TELLING ME THAT THERE'S A BUILDING NEARBY, SMALL LIKE A CHANGING ROOM!
HEY! WH-WHAT'RE YOU DOING?
SORRY, THIS IS AN EMERGENCY!

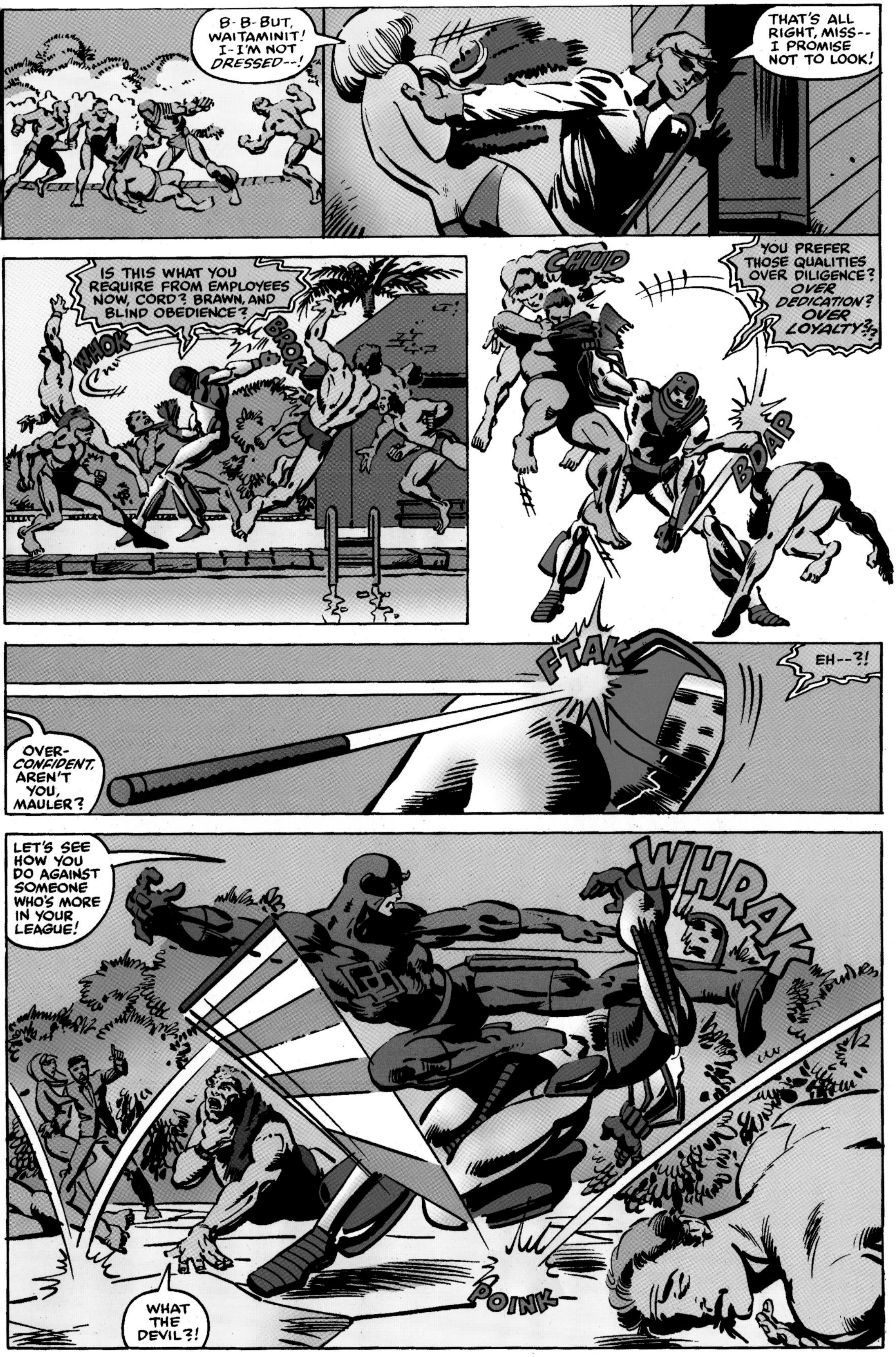
B-B-BUT, WAITAMINIT! I-I'M NOT DRESSED--!
THAT'S ALL RIGHT, MISS-- I PROMISE NOT TO LOOK!
IS THIS WHAT YOU REQUIRE FROM EMPLOYEES NOW, CORD? BRAWN, AND BLIND OBEDIENCE?
WHOK
BROK
CHUD
YOU PREFER THOSE QUALITIES OVER DILIGENCE? OVER DEDICATION? OVER LOYALTY?!?
BDAP
FTAK
EH--?!
OVER-CONFIDENT, AREN'T YOU, MAULER?
LET'S SEE HOW YOU DO AGAINST SOMEONE WHO'S MORE IN YOUR LEAGUE!
WHRAK
POINK
WHAT THE DEVIL?!

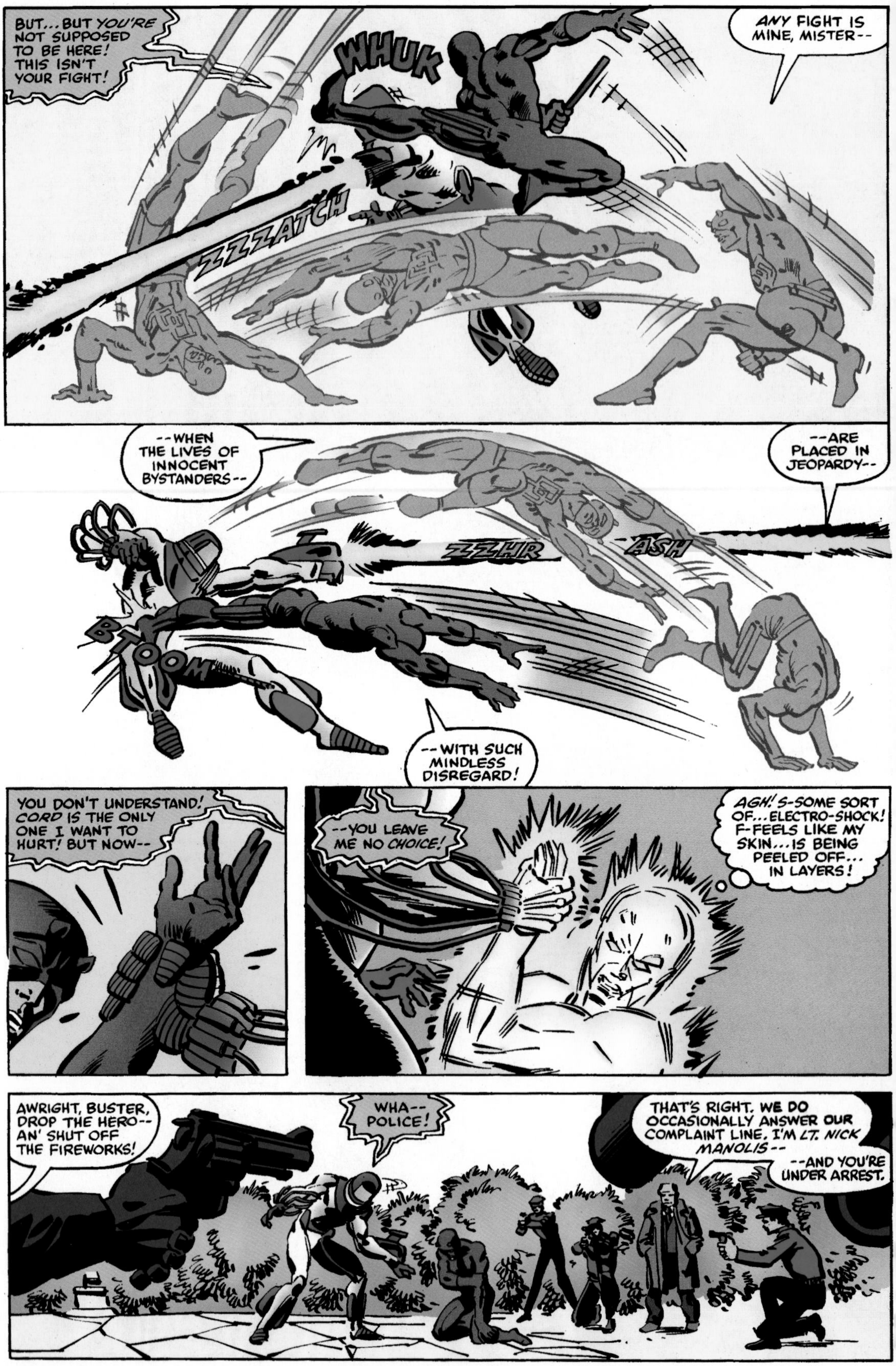
BUT... BUT YOU'RE NOT SUPPOSED TO BE HERE! THIS ISN'T YOUR FIGHT!
WHUK
ANY FIGHT IS MINE, MISTER--
ZZZATCH
--WHEN THE LIVES OF INNOCENT BYSTANDERS--
--ARE PLACED IN JEOPARDY--
ZZZHR
ASH
BTOOM
--WITH SUCH MINDLESS DISREGARD!
YOU DON'T UNDERSTAND! CORD IS THE ONLY ONE I WANT TO HURT! BUT NOW--
--YOU LEAVE ME NO CHOICE!
AGH! S-SOME SORT OF... ELECTRO-SHOCK! F-FEELS LIKE MY SKIN... IS BEING PEELED OFF... IN LAYERS!
AWRIGHT, BUSTER, DROP THE HERO-- AN' SHUT OFF THE FIREWORKS!
WHA-- POLICE!
THAT'S RIGHT. WE DO OCCASIONALLY ANSWER OUR COMPLAINT LINE. I'M LT. NICK MANOLIS--
--AND YOU'RE UNDER ARREST.

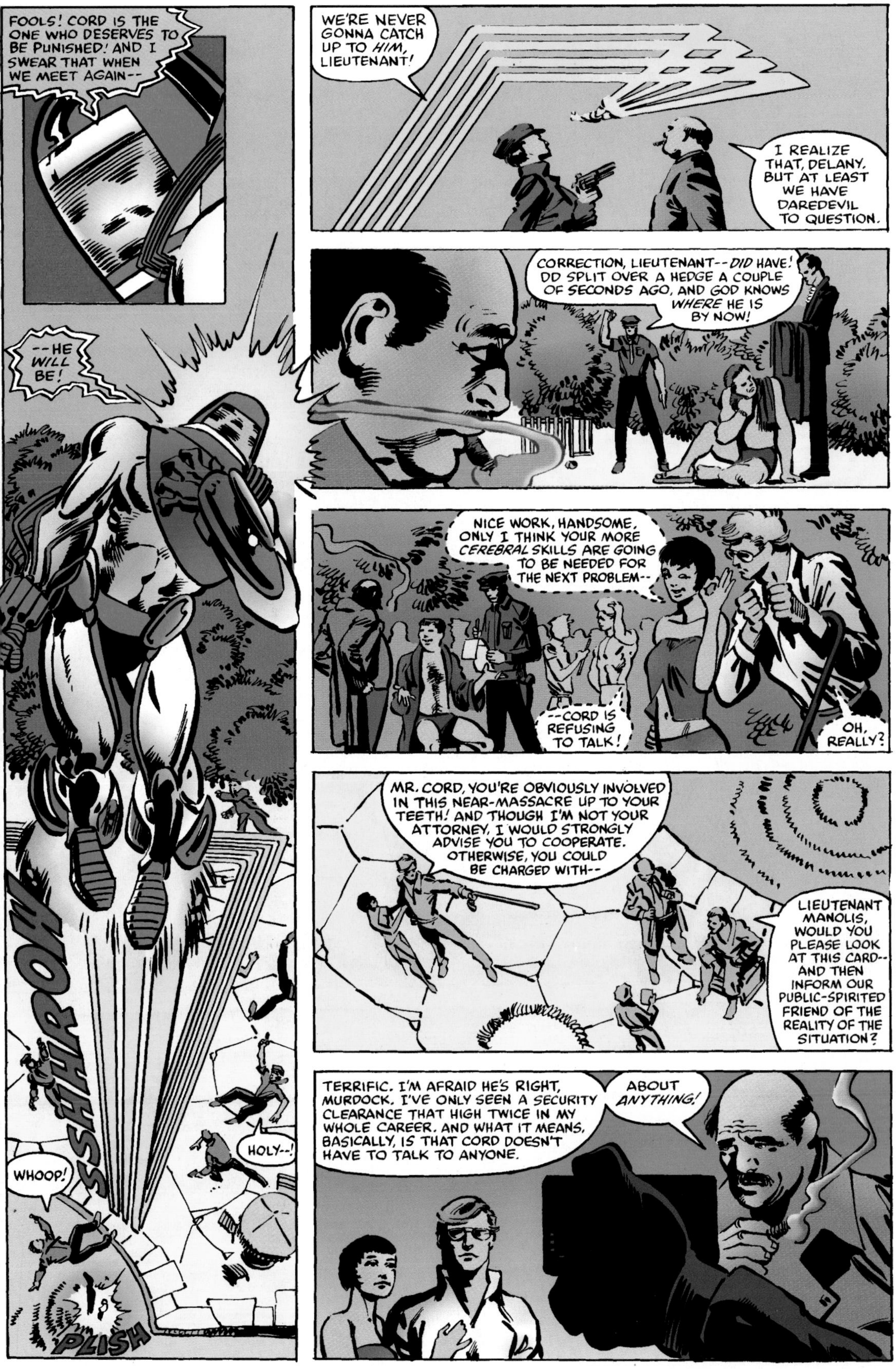
FOOLS! CORD IS THE ONE WHO DESERVES TO BE PUNISHED! AND I SWEAR THAT WHEN WE MEET AGAIN--
--HE WILL BE!
SSHHROW!
WHOOP!
HOLY--!
PLISH
WE'RE NEVER GONNA CATCH UP TO *HIM*, LIEUTENANT!
I REALIZE THAT, DELANY, BUT AT LEAST WE HAVE DAREDEVIL TO QUESTION.
CORRECTION, LIEUTENANT--*DID* HAVE! DD SPLIT OVER A HEDGE A COUPLE OF SECONDS AGO, AND GOD KNOWS *WHERE* HE IS BY NOW!
NICE WORK, HANDSOME, ONLY I THINK YOUR MORE *CEREBRAL* SKILLS ARE GOING TO BE NEEDED FOR THE NEXT PROBLEM--
--CORD IS REFUSING TO TALK!
OH, REALLY?
MR. CORD, YOU'RE OBVIOUSLY INVOLVED IN THIS NEAR-MASSACRE UP TO YOUR TEETH! AND THOUGH I'M NOT YOUR ATTORNEY, I WOULD STRONGLY ADVISE YOU TO COOPERATE. OTHERWISE, YOU COULD BE CHARGED WITH--
LIEUTENANT MANOLIS, WOULD YOU PLEASE LOOK AT THIS CARD--AND THEN INFORM OUR PUBLIC-SPIRITED FRIEND OF THE REALITY OF THE SITUATION?
TERRIFIC. I'M AFRAID HE'S RIGHT, MURDOCK. I'VE ONLY SEEN A SECURITY CLEARANCE THAT HIGH TWICE IN MY WHOLE CAREER. AND WHAT IT MEANS, BASICALLY, IS THAT CORD DOESN'T HAVE TO TALK TO ANYONE.
ABOUT *ANYTHING*!

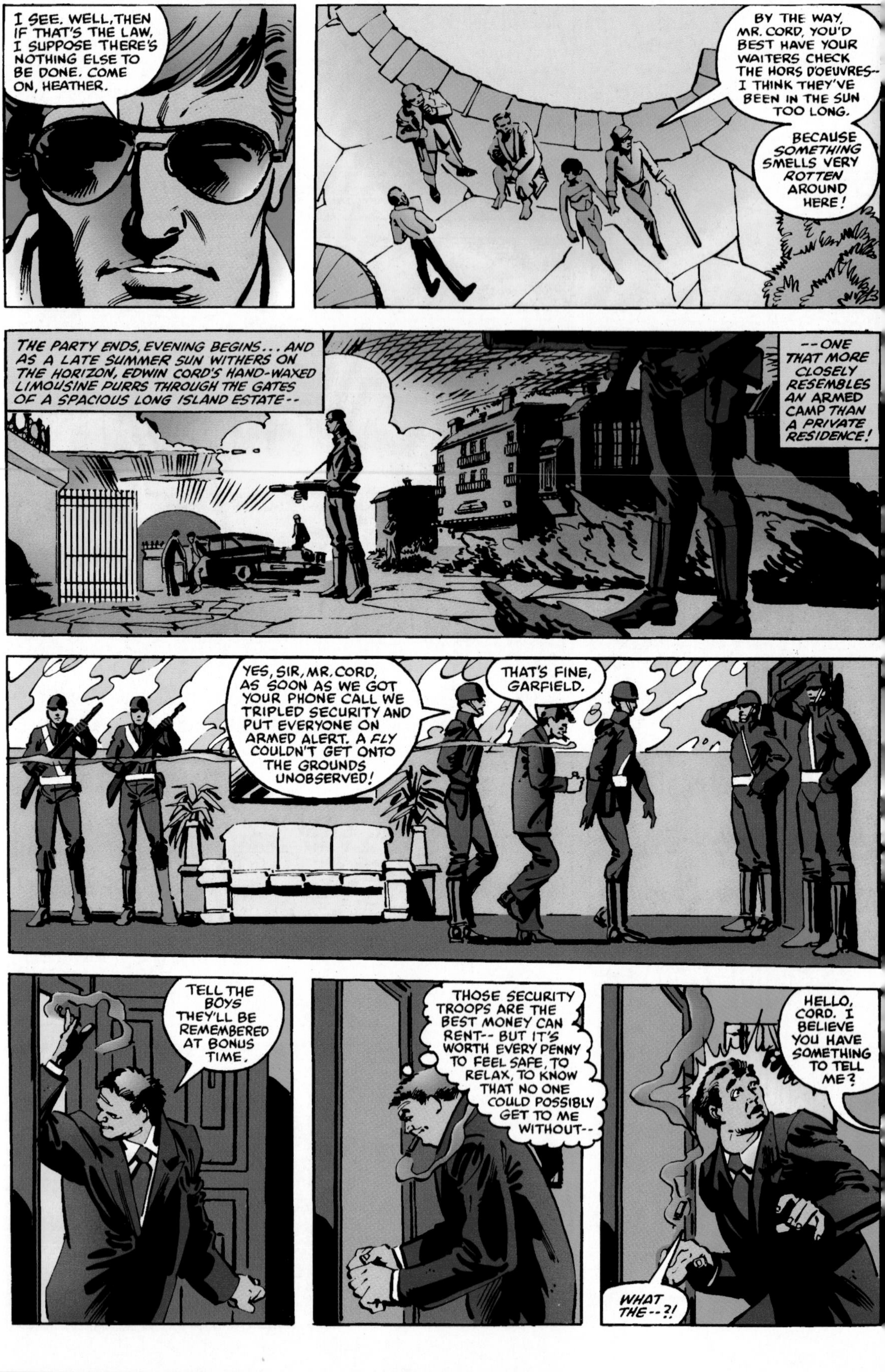

I SEE. WELL, THEN IF THAT'S THE LAW, I SUPPOSE THERE'S NOTHING ELSE TO BE DONE. COME ON, HEATHER.
BY THE WAY, MR. CORD, YOU'D BEST HAVE YOUR WAITERS CHECK THE HORS D'OEUVRES-- I THINK THEY'VE BEEN IN THE SUN TOO LONG.
BECAUSE SOMETHING SMELLS VERY ROTTEN AROUND HERE!
THE PARTY ENDS, EVENING BEGINS... AND AS A LATE SUMMER SUN WITHERS ON THE HORIZON, EDWIN CORD'S HAND-WAXED LIMOUSINE PURRS THROUGH THE GATES OF A SPACIOUS LONG ISLAND ESTATE--
--ONE THAT MORE CLOSELY RESEMBLES AN ARMED CAMP THAN A PRIVATE RESIDENCE!
YES, SIR, MR. CORD, AS SOON AS WE GOT YOUR PHONE CALL WE TRIPLED SECURITY AND PUT EVERYONE ON ARMED ALERT. A FLY COULDN'T GET ONTO THE GROUNDS UNOBSERVED!
THAT'S FINE, GARFIELD.
TELL THE BOYS THEY'LL BE REMEMBERED AT BONUS TIME.
THOSE SECURITY TROOPS ARE THE BEST MONEY CAN RENT-- BUT IT'S WORTH EVERY PENNY TO FEEL SAFE, TO RELAX, TO KNOW THAT NO ONE COULD POSSIBLY GET TO ME WITHOUT--
HELLO, CORD. I BELIEVE YOU HAVE SOMETHING TO TELL ME?
WHAT THE--?!

DAREDEVIL! B-BUT, HOW DID YOU--I-I MEAN, I DIDN'T EXPECT SUCH AN ILLUSTRIOUS VISITOR!

PLEASE, FORGIVE MY POOR MANNERS. WOULD YOU LIKE SOMETHING TO DRINK?

I'LL JUST RING FOR THE BUTLER AND--

GET YOUR FINGER OFF THAT BUTTON, CORD-- IF YOU WANT TO KEEP IT ON YOUR HAND!

BUT, WH-WHAT DO YOU WANT FROM ME? WHAT?

INFORMATION, CORD, THERE WAS SOME RATHER SEVERE UNPLEASANTNESS AT YOUR COUNTRY CLUB TODAY--

--AND YOU'RE GOING TO TELL ME WHY.

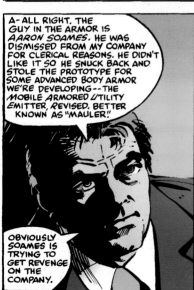

A-ALL RIGHT, THE GUY IN THE ARMOR IS AARON SOAMES. HE WAS DISMISSED FROM MY COMPANY FOR CLERICAL REASONS. HE DIDN'T LIKE IT SO HE SNUCK BACK AND STOLE THE PROTOTYPE FOR SOME ADVANCED BODY ARMOR WE'RE DEVELOPING--THE MOBILE ARMORED UTILITY EMITTER, REVISED, BETTER KNOWN AS "MAULER!"

OBVIOUSLY SOAMES IS TRYING TO GET REVENGE ON THE COMPANY.

I DON'T THINK YOU'RE TELLING ME EVERYTHING, CORD, BUT AT LEAST YOU'VE GIVEN ME SOMETHING TO THINK ABOUT. NOW I'LL GIVE YOU SOMETHING TO THINK ABOUT: IF I FIND YOU'VE LIED TO ME--

--I'LL BE BACK.

KLIK

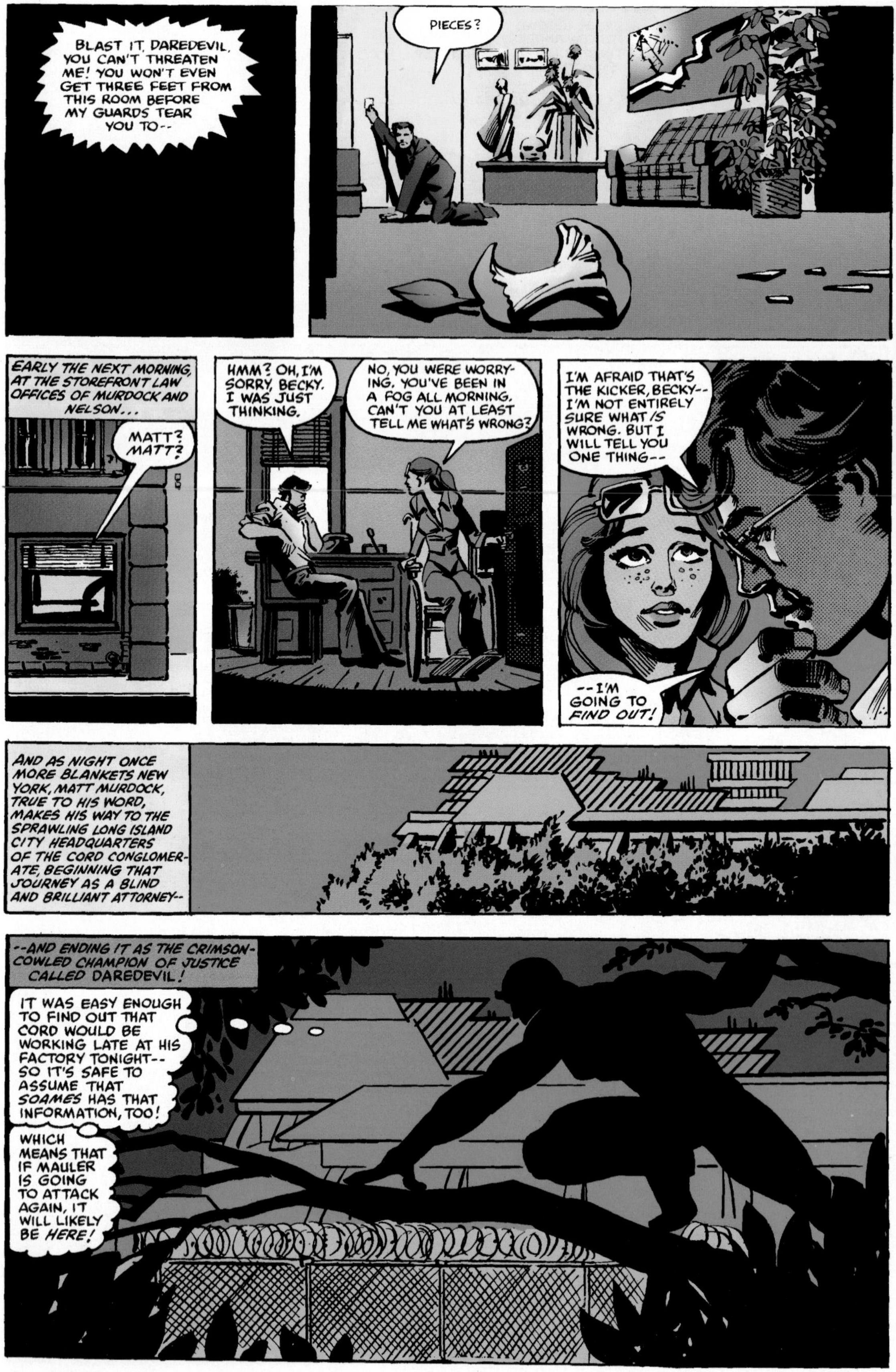
BLAST IT, DAREDEVIL, YOU CAN'T THREATEN ME! YOU WON'T EVEN GET THREE FEET FROM THIS ROOM BEFORE MY GUARDS TEAR YOU TO--
PIECES?
EARLY THE NEXT MORNING, AT THE STOREFRONT LAW OFFICES OF MURDOCK AND NELSON...
MATT? MATT?
HMM? OH, I'M SORRY, BECKY. I WAS JUST THINKING.
NO, YOU WERE WORRYING. YOU'VE BEEN IN A FOG ALL MORNING. CAN'T YOU AT LEAST TELL ME WHAT'S WRONG?
I'M AFRAID THAT'S THE KICKER, BECKY-- I'M NOT ENTIRELY SURE WHAT IS WRONG. BUT I WILL TELL YOU ONE THING--
--I'M GOING TO FIND OUT!
AND AS NIGHT ONCE MORE BLANKETS NEW YORK, MATT MURDOCK, TRUE TO HIS WORD, MAKES HIS WAY TO THE SPRAWLING LONG ISLAND CITY HEADQUARTERS OF THE CORD CONGLOMERATE, BEGINNING THAT JOURNEY AS A BLIND AND BRILLIANT ATTORNEY--
--AND ENDING IT AS THE CRIMSON-COWLED CHAMPION OF JUSTICE CALLED DAREDEVIL!
IT WAS EASY ENOUGH TO FIND OUT THAT CORD WOULD BE WORKING LATE AT HIS FACTORY TONIGHT-- SO IT'S SAFE TO ASSUME THAT SOAMES HAS THAT INFORMATION, TOO!
WHICH MEANS THAT IF MAULER IS GOING TO ATTACK AGAIN, IT WILL LIKELY BE HERE!

AND THUS THE MAN WITHOUT FEAR CROUCHES, MUSCLES AS LITHE AND LEAN AS THOSE OF SOME PREDATORY CAT, WILLING TO WAIT FOR THE PROPER PREY.

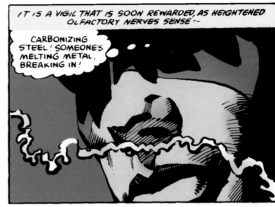

IT IS A VIGIL THAT IS SOON REWARDED, AS HEIGHTENED OLFACTORY NERVES SENSE--

CARBONIZING STEEL! SOMEONE'S MELTING METAL, BREAKING IN!

ALMOST WITHOUT CONSCIOUS THOUGHT HE UNSHEATHES THE BILLY CLUB AT HIS SIDE, PRESSING A HIDDEN STUD TO SEND A HIGH-TENSILE GRAPPLING WIRE UNREELING--

...ALLOWING HIM TO ARC THROUGH THE NIGHT LIKE A SILENT, SOARING SHADOW!

I'M PICKING UP HEARTBEATS FROM SEVERAL MEN, TOO SLOW-- UNCONSCIOUS!

AND MORE FROM INSIDE THE BUILDING! ONE EXCITED, SCARED! THE OTHER MASKED BY SOME SORT OF ENERGY FIELD! IT'S GOT TO BE--

--MAULER! LEAVE HIM ALONE!

YOU?! STAY OUT OF THIS!

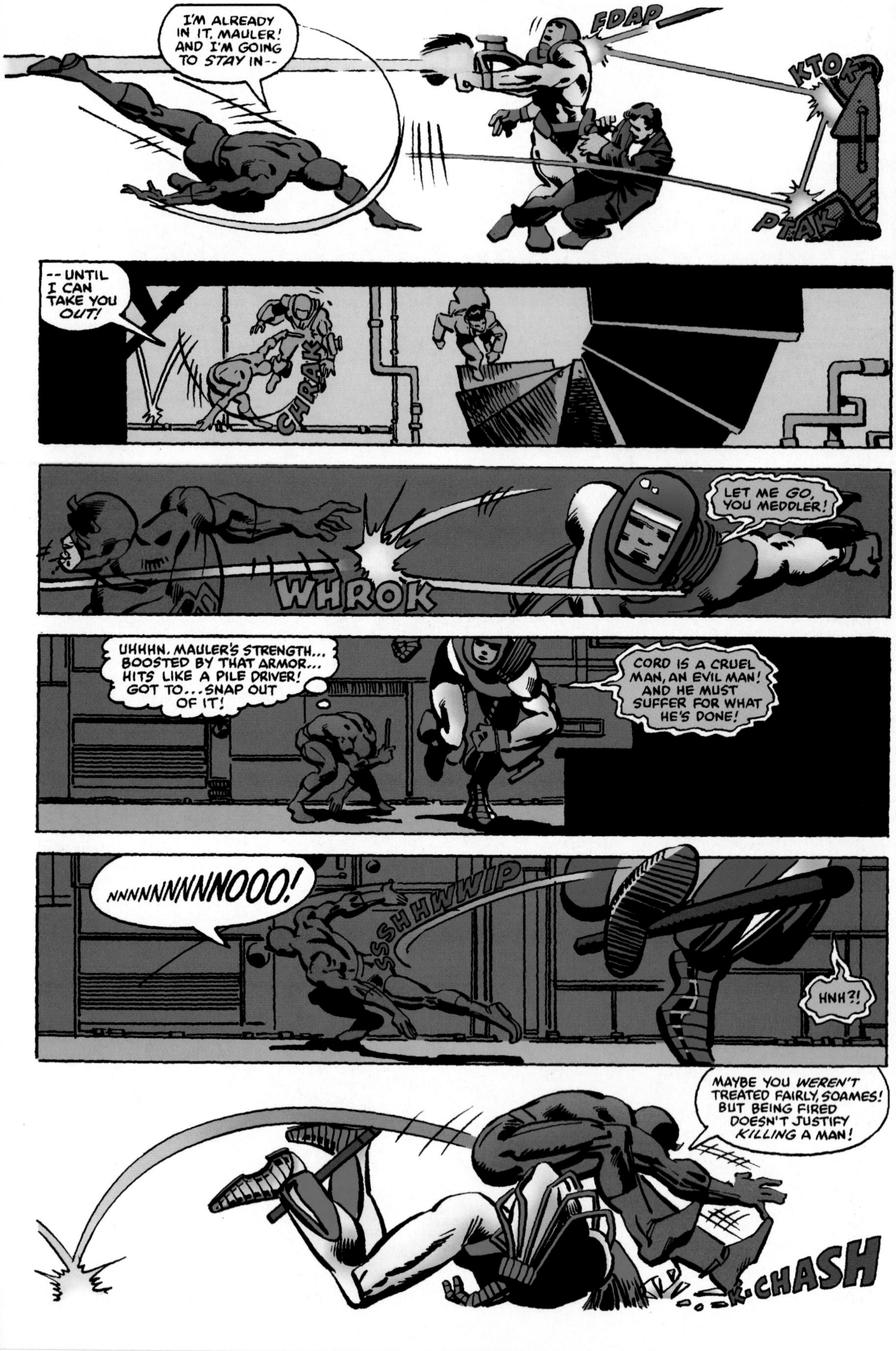

I'M ALREADY IN IT, MAULER! AND I'M GOING TO STAY IN--
FDAP
KTOK
PTAK
-- UNTIL I CAN TAKE YOU OUT!
CHRAK
LET ME GO, YOU MEDDLER!
WHROK
UHHHN. MAULER'S STRENGTH... BOOSTED BY THAT ARMOR... HITS LIKE A PILE DRIVER! GOT TO... SNAP OUT OF IT!
CORD IS A CRUEL MAN, AN EVIL MAN! AND HE MUST SUFFER FOR WHAT HE'S DONE!
NNNNNNNNNOOO!
SSSHHWWIP
HNH?!
MAYBE YOU WEREN'T TREATED FAIRLY, SOAMES! BUT BEING FIRED DOESN'T JUSTIFY KILLING A MAN!
K-CHASH

"FIRED"? IS THAT WHAT HE TOLD YOU?

"FIRED"?!

THUB

LOOK AT THIS FACE, MAN! DO I LOOK LIKE THE KIND OF PERSON WHO'D GET HIMSELF FIRED?

YOUR VOICE! WITHOUT THE MASK TO MUFFLE IT, IT SOUNDS--

--OLD? THAT'S BECAUSE I AM OLD! SIXTY-THREE YEARS OLD! THIRTY-FIVE OF THEM SPENT AS A FILE CLERK FOR EDWIN CORD--

--UNTIL HE BROUGHT IN A COMPUTER TO DO MY JOB QUICKER AND CHEAPER.

BUT THE BIG SURPRISE CAME WHEN I TRIED TO COLLECT MY PENSION. SEEMS THE YOUNG HOT-SHOT WHO PROGRAMMED THE NEW COMPUTER HIT THE WRONG KEY--AND WIPED OUT MY ENTIRE 35-YEAR WORK RECORD!

I WENT TO MR. CORD ABOUT IT, AND YOU KNOW WHAT HE DID?

HE SMILED. HE SAID, "SORRY, SOAMES--NO RECORD, NO PENSION."

AND HE SMILED.

I APPLIED FOR SOCIAL SECURITY-- BUT THE INTERVIEWER DOZED OFF WHILE I WAS TRYING TO EXPLAIN!

SO I SPENT THE LAST OF MY SAVINGS ON A FANCY LAWYER, AND SURE ENOUGH, HE GOT ME A COURT DATE--

--A YEAR FROM NEXT THURSDAY!

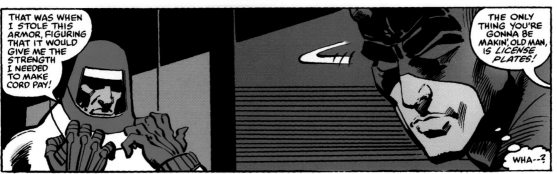

THAT WAS WHEN I STOLE THIS ARMOR, FIGURING THAT IT WOULD GIVE ME THE STRENGTH I NEEDED TO MAKE CORD PAY!

THE ONLY THING YOU'RE GONNA BE MAKIN', OLD MAN, IS LICENSE PLATES!

WHA--?

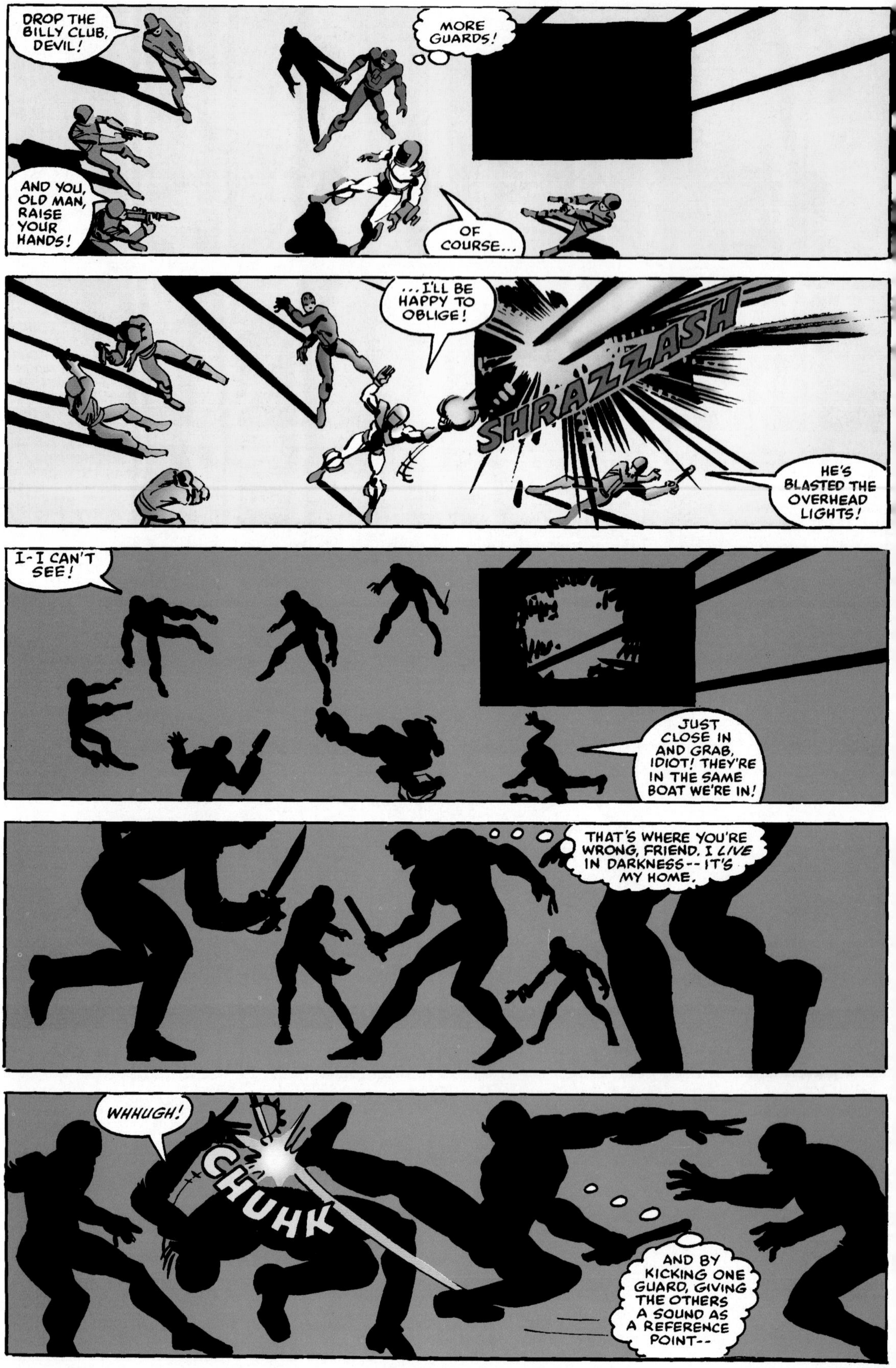
DROP THE BILLY CLUB, DEVIL!
MORE GUARDS!
AND YOU, OLD MAN, RAISE YOUR HANDS!
OF COURSE...
...I'LL BE HAPPY TO OBLIGE!
SHRAZZASH
HE'S BLASTED THE OVERHEAD LIGHTS!
I-I CAN'T SEE!
JUST CLOSE IN AND GRAB, IDIOT! THEY'RE IN THE SAME BOAT WE'RE IN!
THAT'S WHERE YOU'RE WRONG, FRIEND. I LIVE IN DARKNESS-- IT'S MY HOME.
WHHUGH!
CHUHK
AND BY KICKING ONE GUARD, GIVING THE OTHERS A SOUND AS A REFERENCE POINT--

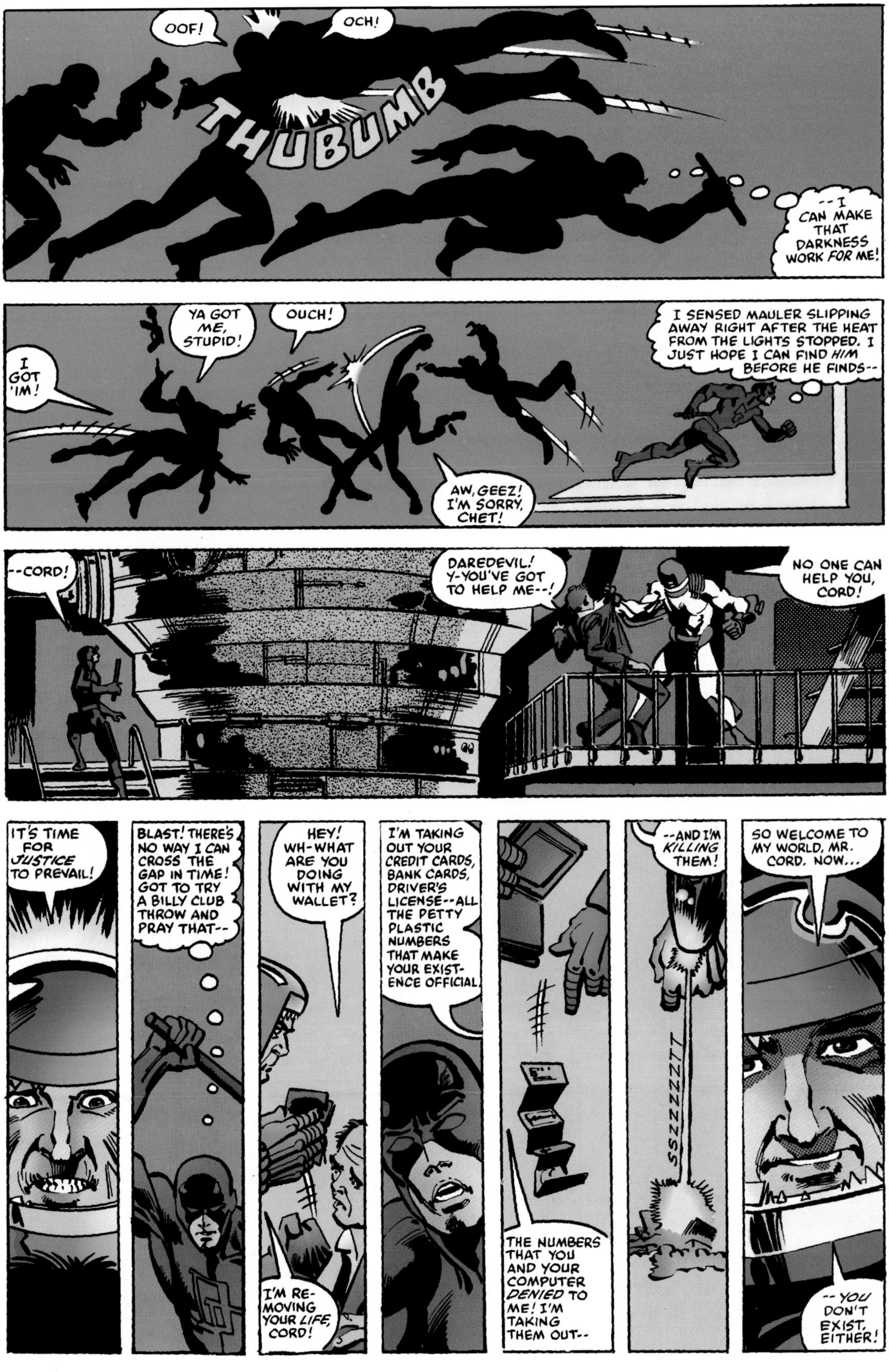
OOF!
OCH!
THUBUMB
--I CAN MAKE THAT DARKNESS WORK *FOR* ME!
I GOT 'IM!
YA GOT ME, STUPID!
OUCH!
AW, GEEZ! I'M SORRY, CHET!
I SENSED MAULER SLIPPING AWAY RIGHT AFTER THE HEAT FROM THE LIGHTS STOPPED. I JUST HOPE I CAN FIND *HIM* BEFORE HE FINDS--
--CORD!
DAREDEVIL! Y-YOU'VE GOT TO HELP ME--!
NO ONE CAN HELP YOU, CORD!
IT'S TIME FOR *JUSTICE* TO PREVAIL!
BLAST! THERE'S NO WAY I CAN CROSS THE GAP IN TIME! GOT TO TRY A BILLY CLUB THROW AND PRAY THAT--
HEY! WH-WHAT ARE YOU DOING WITH MY WALLET?
I'M RE-MOVING YOUR *LIFE*, CORD!
I'M TAKING OUT YOUR CREDIT CARDS, BANK CARDS, DRIVER'S LICENSE--ALL THE PETTY PLASTIC NUMBERS THAT MAKE YOUR EXIST-ENCE OFFICIAL.
THE NUMBERS THAT YOU AND YOUR COMPUTER *DENIED* TO ME! I'M TAKING THEM OUT--
--AND I'M *KILLING* THEM!
SSZZZZZZTT
SO WELCOME TO MY WORLD, MR. CORD. NOW...
--*YOU* DON'T EXIST, EITHER!

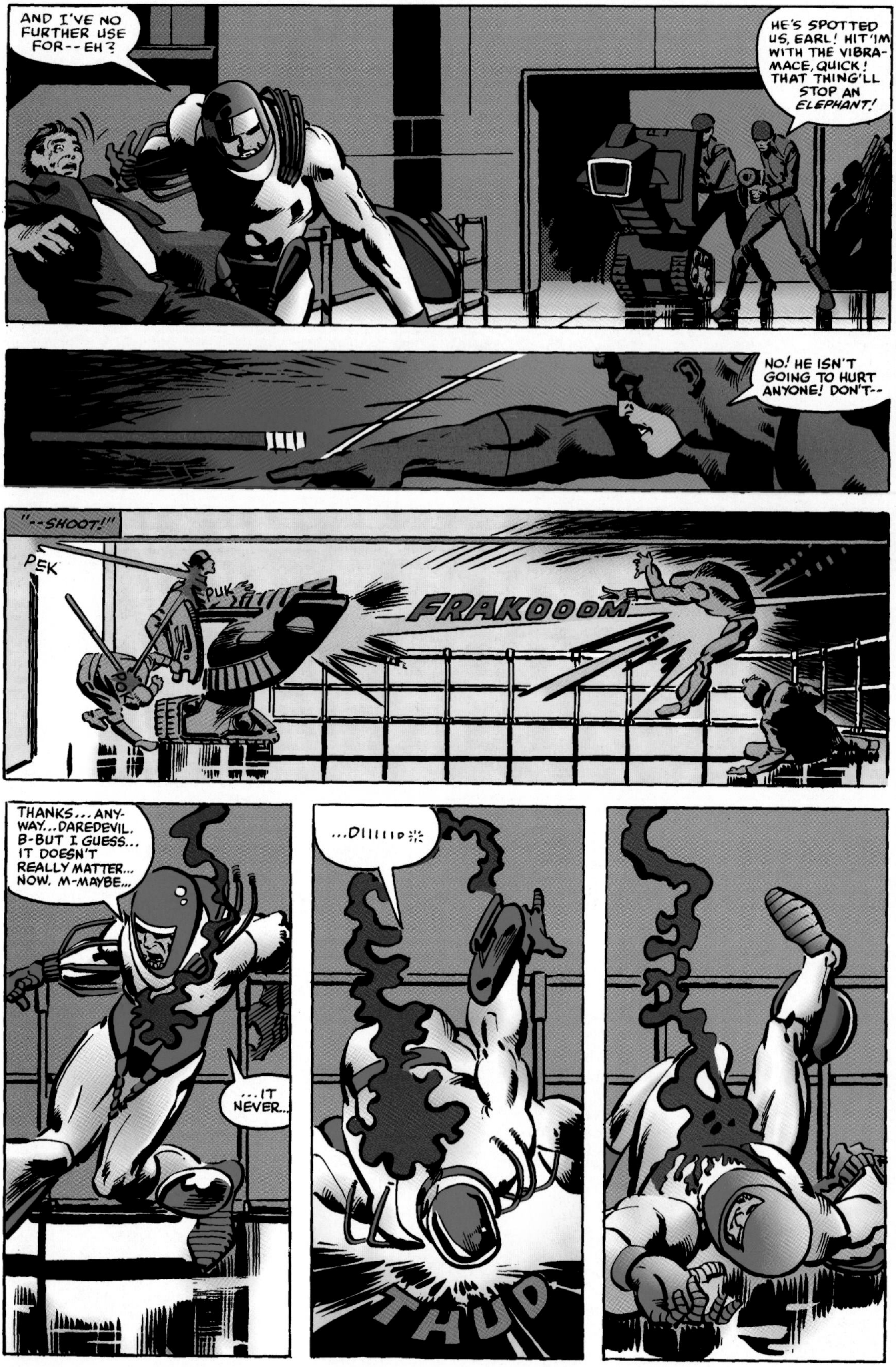

AND I'VE NO FURTHER USE FOR--EH?
HE'S SPOTTED US, EARL! HIT 'IM WITH THE VIBRA-MACE, QUICK! THAT THING'LL STOP AN ELEPHANT!
NO! HE ISN'T GOING TO HURT ANYONE! DON'T--
"--SHOOT!"
PEK
PUK
FRAKOOOM
THANKS... ANY-WAY... DAREDEVIL. B-BUT I GUESS... IT DOESN'T REALLY MATTER... NOW. M-MAYBE...
...IT NEVER...
...DIIIIID
THUD

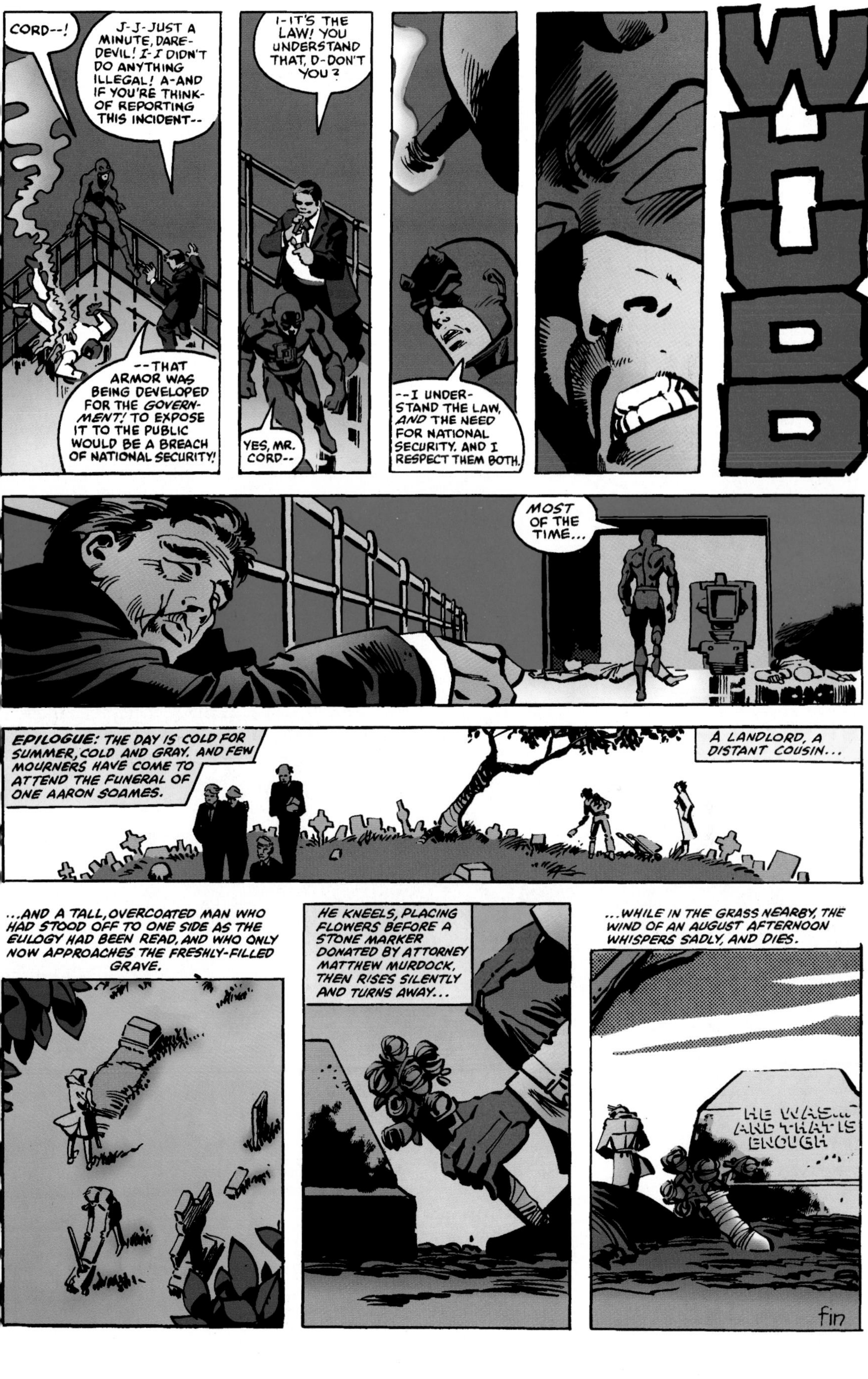
CORD--!
J-J-JUST A MINUTE, DARE-DEVIL! I-I DIDN'T DO ANYTHING ILLEGAL! A-AND IF YOU'RE THINK-OF REPORTING THIS INCIDENT--
--THAT ARMOR WAS BEING DEVELOPED FOR THE GOVERNMENT! TO EXPOSE IT TO THE PUBLIC WOULD BE A BREACH OF NATIONAL SECURITY!
I-IT'S THE LAW! YOU UNDERSTAND THAT, D-DON'T YOU?
YES, MR. CORD--
--I UNDERSTAND THE LAW, AND THE NEED FOR NATIONAL SECURITY. AND I RESPECT THEM BOTH.
WHUDD
MOST OF THE TIME...
EPILOGUE: THE DAY IS COLD FOR SUMMER, COLD AND GRAY. AND FEW MOURNERS HAVE COME TO ATTEND THE FUNERAL OF ONE AARON SOAMES.
A LANDLORD, A DISTANT COUSIN...
...AND A TALL, OVERCOATED MAN WHO HAD STOOD OFF TO ONE SIDE AS THE EULOGY HAD BEEN READ, AND WHO ONLY NOW APPROACHES THE FRESHLY-FILLED GRAVE.
HE KNEELS, PLACING FLOWERS BEFORE A STONE MARKER DONATED BY ATTORNEY MATTHEW MURDOCK, THEN RISES SILENTLY AND TURNS AWAY...
...WHILE IN THE GRASS NEARBY, THE WIND OF AN AUGUST AFTERNOON WHISPERS SADLY, AND DIES.
HE WAS... AND THAT IS ENOUGH
fin

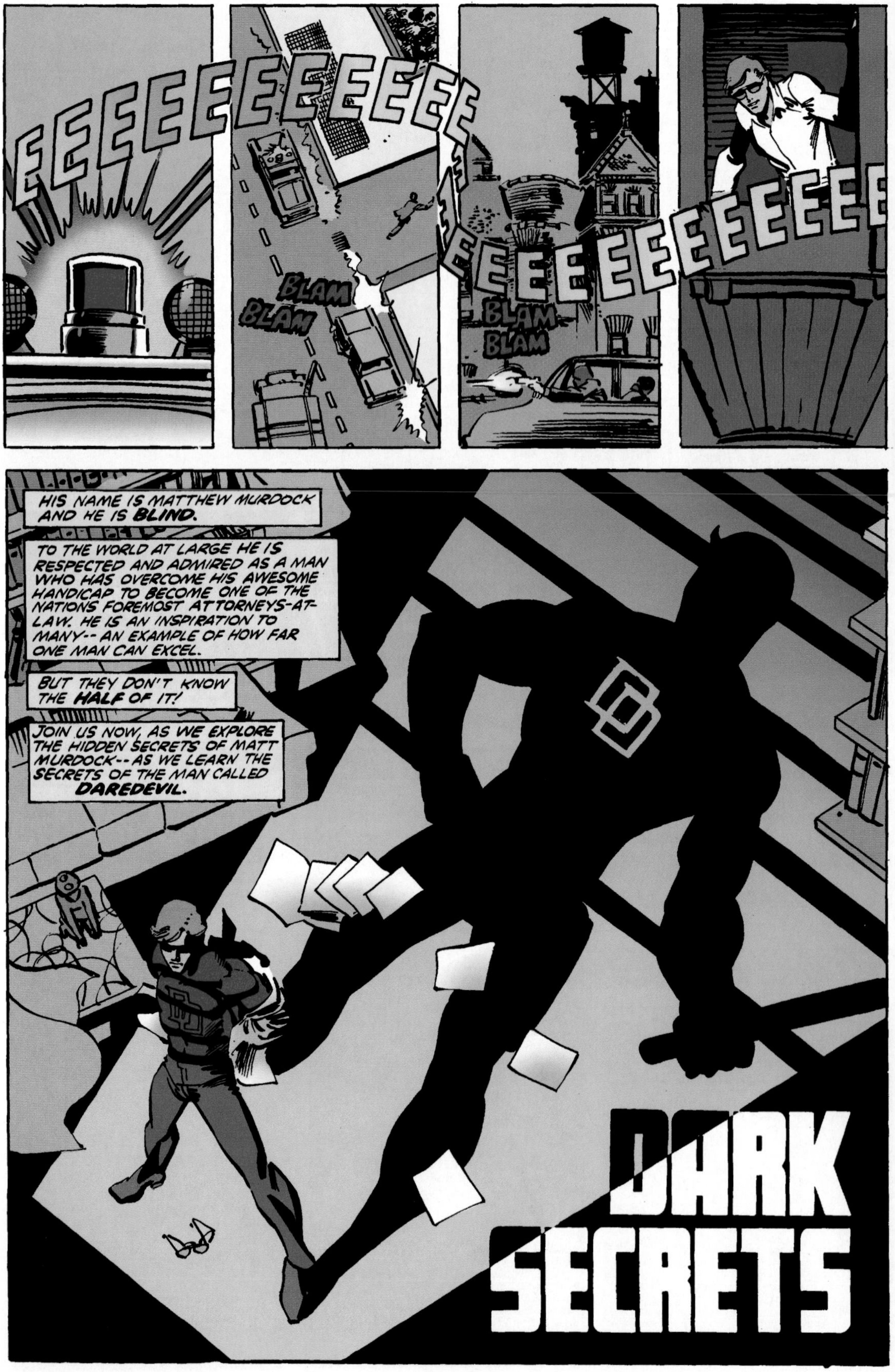
EEEEEEEEEEEE
BLAM
BLAM
EEEEEEEEEEEEEE
BLAM
BLAM
HIS NAME IS MATTHEW MURDOCK AND HE IS BLIND.
TO THE WORLD AT LARGE HE IS RESPECTED AND ADMIRED AS A MAN WHO HAS OVERCOME HIS AWESOME HANDICAP TO BECOME ONE OF THE NATIONS FOREMOST ATTORNEYS-AT-LAW. HE IS AN INSPIRATION TO MANY-- AN EXAMPLE OF HOW FAR ONE MAN CAN EXCEL.
BUT THEY DON'T KNOW THE HALF OF IT!
JOIN US NOW, AS WE EXPLORE THE HIDDEN SECRETS OF MATT MURDOCK--AS WE LEARN THE SECRETS OF THE MAN CALLED DAREDEVIL.
DARK SECRETS

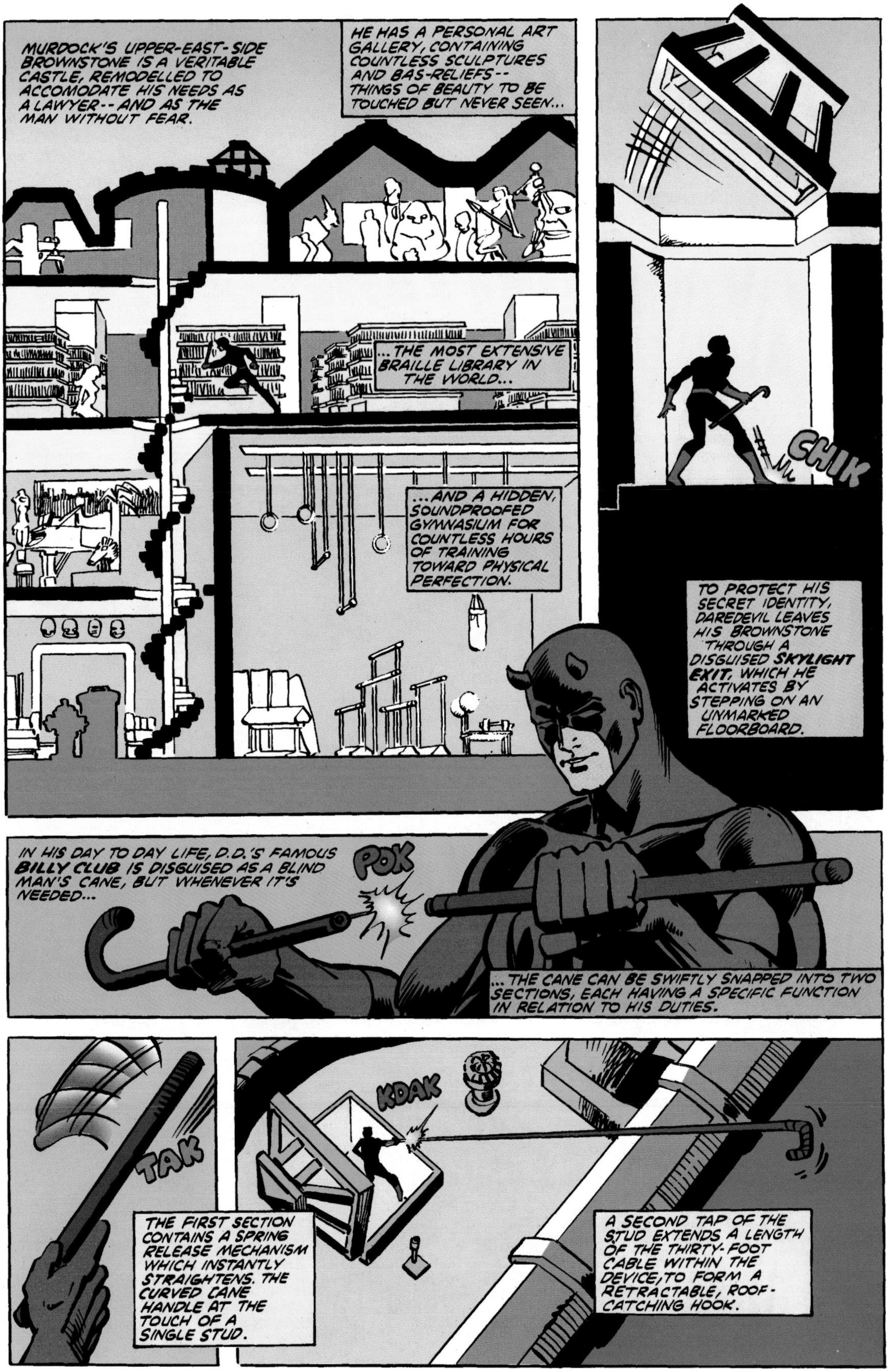
MURDOCK'S UPPER-EAST-SIDE BROWNSTONE IS A VERITABLE CASTLE, REMODELLED TO ACCOMODATE HIS NEEDS AS A LAWYER-- AND AS THE MAN WITHOUT FEAR.
HE HAS A PERSONAL ART GALLERY, CONTAINING COUNTLESS SCULPTURES AND BAS-RELIEFS-- THINGS OF BEAUTY TO BE TOUCHED BUT NEVER SEEN...
...THE MOST EXTENSIVE BRAILLE LIBRARY IN THE WORLD...
...AND A HIDDEN, SOUNDPROOFED GYMNASIUM FOR COUNTLESS HOURS OF TRAINING TOWARD PHYSICAL PERFECTION.
CHIK
TO PROTECT HIS SECRET IDENTITY, DAREDEVIL LEAVES HIS BROWNSTONE THROUGH A DISGUISED SKYLIGHT EXIT, WHICH HE ACTIVATES BY STEPPING ON AN UNMARKED FLOORBOARD.
IN HIS DAY TO DAY LIFE, D.D.'S FAMOUS BILLY CLUB IS DISGUISED AS A BLIND MAN'S CANE, BUT WHENEVER IT'S NEEDED...
POK
...THE CANE CAN BE SWIFTLY SNAPPED INTO TWO SECTIONS, EACH HAVING A SPECIFIC FUNCTION IN RELATION TO HIS DUTIES.
TAK
THE FIRST SECTION CONTAINS A SPRING RELEASE MECHANISM WHICH INSTANTLY STRAIGHTENS. THE CURVED CANE HANDLE AT THE TOUCH OF A SINGLE STUD.
KDAK
A SECOND TAP OF THE STUD EXTENDS A LENGTH OF THE THIRTY-FOOT CABLE WITHIN THE DEVICE, TO FORM A RETRACTABLE, ROOF-CATCHING HOOK.

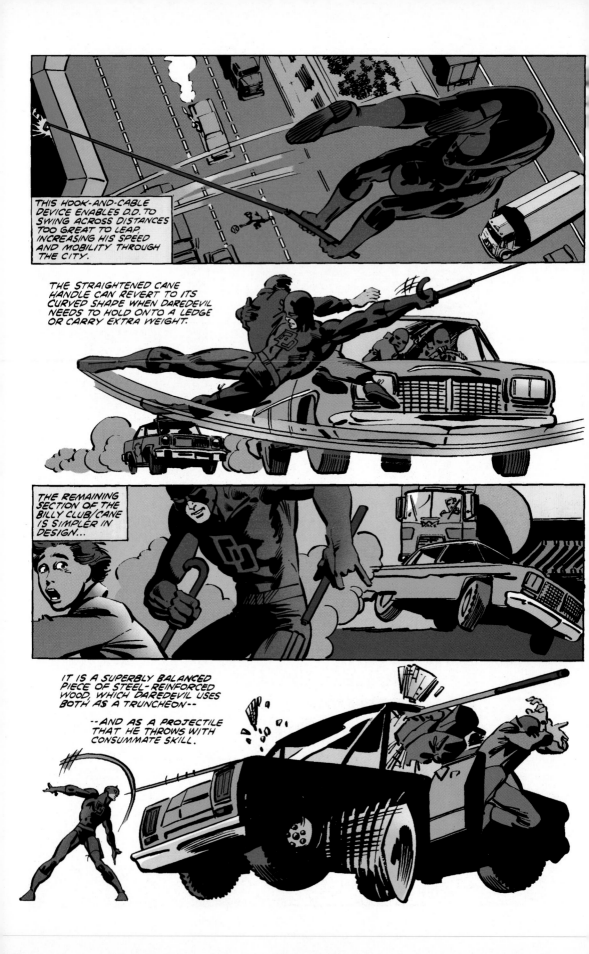

THIS HOOK-AND-CABLE DEVICE ENABLES D.D. TO SWING ACROSS DISTANCES TOO GREAT TO LEAP, INCREASING HIS SPEED AND MOBILITY THROUGH THE CITY.

THE STRAIGHTENED CANE HANDLE CAN REVERT TO ITS CURVED SHAPE WHEN DAREDEVIL NEEDS TO HOLD ONTO A LEDGE OR CARRY EXTRA WEIGHT.

THE REMAINING SECTION OF THE BILLY CLUB/CANE IS SIMPLER IN DESIGN...

IT IS A SUPERBLY BALANCED PIECE OF STEEL-REINFORCED WOOD, WHICH DAREDEVIL USES BOTH AS A TRUNCHEON--

--AND AS A PROJECTILE THAT HE THROWS WITH CONSUMMATE SKILL.

SO GREAT IS DAREDEVIL'S SKILL W[ITH] HIS BILLY CLUB THAT IT OFTEN SEE[MS] TO BE ALIVE. HE NEVER HAS TO LOO[K] TO FIND IT, BUT THEN, HE **CAN'T** LOO[K]

...HOWEVER, THE RADIO-ACTIVE CANNISTER THAT PERMANENTLY BLINDED YOUNG MATT MURDOCK LEFT HIM WITH SENSES FAR BEYOND THOSE OF NORMAL MEN.

HE CAN **TOUCH** A PRINTED PAGE AND READ IT BY FEELING THE VAGUE IMPRESSION OF THE INK...

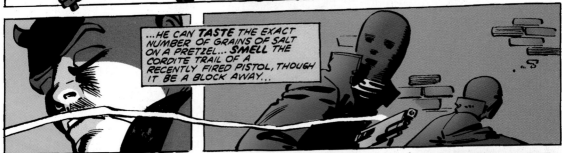

...HE CAN **TASTE** THE EXACT NUMBER OF GRAINS OF SALT ON A PRETZEL... **SMELL** THE CORDITE TRAIL OF A RECENTLY FIRED PISTOL, THOUGH IT BE A BLOCK AWAY...

...HE CAN ACTUALLY **HEAR** A MAN'S HEARTBEAT AT A DISTANCE OF ONE HUNDRED FEET.

WHEN THESE HYPER-SENSES ARE FOCUSED ON A FLEETING ENEMY, NO MATTER HOW FAST OR FAR HIS PREY MAY RUN--

--DAREDEVIL CANNOT BE ELUDED.

THE DARKNESS IS NO HIDING PLACE IT IS THERE THAT DAREDEVIL IS MOST DANGEROUS.

WHILE WE HAVE EYES THAT ARE TRICKED BY SHADOWS AND SEE NOTHING WITHOUT LIGHT--

DAREDEVIL HAS AN UNCANNY RADAR-SENSE. LIKE A BAT. HE EMITS PROBING, HIGH FREQUENCY WAVES.

WAVES WHICH BREAK AGAINST ANY SOLID OBJECT, AND BREAKING, SEND BACK SIGNALS AUDIBLE ONLY TO DAREDEVIL.

FROM THESE SIGNALS, HIS BRAIN INSTANTLY FORMS SILHOUETTE IMAGES OF EVERY-THING AROUND HIM. IN THIS MANNER, HE 'SEES' IN EVERY DIRECTION.'

BUT NONE OF HIS AMAZING HYPER-SENSES WOULD BE ENOUGH...

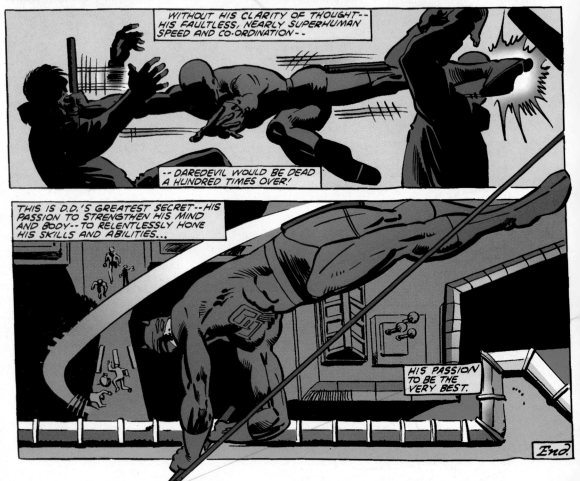

WITHOUT HIS CLARITY OF THOUGHT-- HIS FAULTLESS, NEARLY SUPERHUMAN SPEED AND CO-ORDINATION--

--DAREDEVIL WOULD BE DEAD A HUNDRED TIMES OVER!

THIS IS D.D.'S GREATEST SECRET--HIS PASSION TO STRENGTHEN HIS MIND AND BODY--TO RELENTLESSLY HONE HIS SKILLS AND ABILITIES...

HIS PASSION TO BE THE VERY BEST.

End.